RESEARCH IN PARAPSYCHOLOGY 1982

Jubilee Centenary Issue

Abstracts and Papers from the Combined
Twenty-fifth Annual Convention of the
Parapsychological Association and the
Centenary Conference of the
Society for Psychical Research

WILLIAM G. ROLL,
JOHN BELOFF,
and
RHEA A. WHITE
Editors

The Scarecrow Press, Inc.
Metuchen, N.J., & London
1983

ISBN 0-8108-1627-X
Manufactured in the United States of America
Library of Congress Catalog Card No. 66-28580
Copyright © 1983 by the Parapsychological Association

CONTENTS

Preface (John Beloff) xi
Introduction (William G. Roll) xv

1. Symposia

THEN AND NOW (Convener: Ian Stevenson) 1

    1882 and All That (Alan Gauld) 1
    Psychical Research in 1957 and 1982
      (Gertrude R. Schmeidler) 3
    The Contemporary Scene in Psychical Research
      (Adrian Parker) 6

THE CASE FOR SKEPTICISM (Convener: Christopher Scott) 11

    Why Parapsychology Demands a Skeptical
      Response (Christopher Scott) 11
    The Hume Game (Piet Hein Hoebens) 15
    Prospects for a Psi Inhibitory Experimenter
      (Susan J. Blackmore) 17
    Does the Ganzfeld Experiment Answer the Critics'
      Objections? (Ray Hyman) 21
    Response to Hyman's Critique (Charles Honorton) 23
    Thoughts on Testimony to the Paranormal
      (Donald J. West) 27

PSYCHOKINETIC METAL-BENDING (PKMB) (Convener:
    Julian Isaacs) 31

    A Twelve-Session Study of Micro-PKMB Training
      (Julian Isaacs) 31
    The Problem of Pseudo-PKMB and the Distribution of
      PKMB (Jürgen Keil) 35
    PKMB Research with Piezoelectric Sensors (John B.
      Hasted, David Robertson, and Peter Arathoon) 39
    A New Israeli Metal-bender (with Film) (Hans C.
      Berendt) 43

THE BATCHELDOR APPROACH (Convener: Julian Isaacs) 45

    Contributions to the Theory of PK Induction from
      Sitter-Group Work (Kenneth J. Batcheldor) 45

Variations on a Theme from Batcheldor
(James McClenon and Rhea A. White) 48
The Batcheldor Approach: A Critique
(Julian Isaacs) 52
Hypnosis and Psi: A Research Program Related
to the Theory of Kenneth Batcheldor (John Palmer) 55
ESP and Hypnotic Imagination: A Group Free-
Response Study (John Palmer and Ivo van der
Velden) 58

2. Papers and Research Briefs (RB)

THE McDONNELL LABORATORY TEAM 62

An ESP Drawing Experiment with Two Ostensible
Psychokinetes (Michael A. Thalbourne and
Mark G. Shafer) 62
A PK Experiment with Random and Pseudorandom
Targets (RB) (Mark G. Shafer) 64
PK Experiments with Two Special Subjects (RB) (Mark
G. Shafer, Michael K. McBeath, Michael A. Thal-
bourne, and Peter R. Phillips) 66

HISTORICAL PERSPECTIVES 69

Retrocognitive Dissonance (Brian Inglis) 69
The Mediumship of Stefan Ossowiecki (Mary Rose
Barrington) 72
Palladino at Cambridge (Manfred Cassirer) 75
A Century of Investigations--Some Lessons (Andrew
MacKenzie) 77

THEORETICAL ISSUES 81

Morphic Resonance, Memory, and Psychical Research
(Rupert Sheldrake) 81
On the Limitations of Psi--A System-theoretic Approach
(Walter von Lucadou and Klaus Kornwachs) 85
A Proposed Mechanism for the Sheep-Goat Effect and Its
Relation to Psi-Missing, Experimenter Effect, and the
Problem of Repeatability (Michael A. Thalbourne) 89

MISCELLANEOUS RESEARCH REPORTS 93

ESP and Memory: Some Limiting Conditions
(Gertrude R. Schmeidler) 93
Exploring the Fundamental Hypothesis of the Observa-
tional Theories Using a PK Test for Babies (RB)
(Dick J. Bierman) 97
Learning to Use Psychokinesis: Theoretical and
Methodological Notes (Charles T. Tart) 97

Infrared Measurements of Healer-Treated Water
   (Douglas Dean)   100
Laboratory PK: Frequency of Manifestation and
   Resemblance to Precognition (Charles T. Tart)   101
The Mobius Psi-Q Test (RB) (Stephan A. Schwartz and
   Randall J. De Mattei)   103
Recording of Sudden Paranormal Changes of Body
   Weight (RB) (John B. Hasted, David Robertson,
   and Ernesto Spinelli)   105
Some Attempts to Detect the Human Aura (RB)
   (G. Karolyi, D. Nandagopal, and H. H. Wigg)   107
Some Observations on the Phantom Leaf Effect (RB)
   (P. C. Kejariwal, A. Chattopadhya, and J. K.
   Choudhury)   110

MACRO-PK: THREE NEGATIVE REPORTS   112

   A Test of Psychokinetic Metal-bending: An Aborted
      Experiment (RB) (James Randi)   112
   An Attempted Replication of the Cox Films of PK (RB)
      (Peter R. Phillips and Michael K. McBeath)   113
   An Investigation of Macro-PK: The SORRAT (RB)
      (George P. Hansen and Richard S. Broughton)   115

SURVIVAL RESEARCH   117

   The Psi Structure Theory of Survival (William G. Roll)   117
   Some Views on Survival (T. N. E. Greville)   120
   Assumptions and Recurrent Features in Survival
      Research (RB) (Arthur S. Berger)   123
   The Forlorn Quest (George Zorab)   125
   After One Hundred Years: Time for a Change in
      Apparition Research (Karlis Osis)   128
   A Haunting-Type RSPK Case in New England (William
      G. Roll and Steven Tringale)   132

MISCELLANEOUS CONTRIBUTIONS FROM THE CONTINENT   137

   Some Recommendations for the Future Practice of
      Parapsychology (Gerd H. Hövelmann)   137
   The Rule of Improbability (RB) (Ulrich Timm)   141
   Meaningful Clairvoyant Mistakes (RB) (Hans Bender)   143
   An Evaluation of Hansel's Critique of Helmut
      Schmidt's Experiments (RB) (Kaare Claudewitz)   145
   A Dermo-Optic Perception Test (RB) (Yvonne DuPlessis)   147
   Screening for Good ESP Subjects with Object-Reading
      (RB) (Jan Kappers)   150

COMPUTERS AND REGS   152

   A Preliminary Study with a PK Game Involving
      Distraction from the Psi Task (RB) (Ephraim I.
      Schechter, Pat Barker, and Mario Varvoglis)   152

An REG Experiment with Large Data Base Capability, II (Brenda J. Dunne, Robert G. Jahn, and Roger D. Nelson) 154
Feedback and Participant-Selection Parameters in a Computer RNG Study (RB) (Charles Honorton, Patricia Barker, and Nancy Sondow) 157
Analytical Judging Procedure for Remote Perception Experiments, II (Robert G. Jahn, Brenda J. Dunne, Roger D. Nelson, Eric G. Jahn, T. Aaron Curtis, and Ian A. Cook) 159
Psi Tests with ALGERNON, a Computer Oracle (RB) (William Braud and Winona Schroeter) 163
A New Computer-Controlled Device for Testing Different PK Hypotheses (RB) (Walter von Lucadou and Johannes Mischo) 165
Outline of a Multivariate PK Experiment (RB) (Walter von Lucadou and Johannes Mischo) 168
An Inexpensive Electronic Clairvoyance Tester/Trainer for Parapsychologists (RB) (Charles T. Tart) 170
A Randomicity Test Program for Pseudo-RNG Routines on the HP-41C (RB) (Charles T. Tart) 173

MENTAL STATE VARIABLES 178

Possible Psi-Mediated Perceptual Effects of Similarity of REG Alternatives to the PK Target: A Double-Blind Study (Rex G. Stanford) 178
Psi Functioning and Assessed Cognitive Lability (William Braud, Donna Shafer, and Judith Mulgrew) 182
The Noise-Silence and Target-Encodability Variables in a Ganzfeld Word-Association ESP Task (RB) (Rex G. Stanford and Raymond F. Angelini) 185
Prolonged Visualization Practice and Psychokinesis: A Pilot Study (RB) (William Braud) 187
ESP and SP in TM and Non-TM Groups (RB) (P. V. Krishna Rao and K. Ramakrishna Rao) 189
Two Series of Volitional Studies with Competition Set (K. Ramakrishna Rao, Carl Sargent, and Marilyn J. Schlitz) 190
Resistance, Belief, and Replication (RB) (David Hess) 193

PERSONALITY VARIABLES 195

Target Affect, Anxiety, and Belief in ESP in Relation to ESP Scoring (John Ballard, Joseph C. Cohee, and Telena M. Eldridge) 195
Retest Reliability of ESP and Sheep-Goat Scores (RB) (Erlendur Haraldsson) 197
Some Further Tests of the Extraverted Sheep Versus Introverted Goats Hypothesis (RB) (Michael A. Thalbourne, John Beloff, Deborah Delanoy, and Janet Jungkuntz) 199

An Attempted Replication of Sex Differences in
Volitional Studies (K. Ramakrishna Rao and
Beverly Norwood) 200
Sheep-Goat Effect and the Illusion of Control (RB)
(Tom Troscianko and Susan J. Blackmore) 202

SPONTANEOUS CASES AND REAL LIFE PHENOMENA 204

Spontaneous Sightings of Seemingly Autonomous
Humanoid Entities (Hilary Evans) 204
Cryptomnesic and Paranormal Personation: Two
Contrasting Examples (James F. McHarg) 207
Toward a Model for Mental Healing Studies in Real
Life Settings (Gerald F. Solfvin) 210
A Review and Analysis of "Unsolved" Cases of the
Reincarnation Type (Emily Williams Cook, Satwant
Pasricha, Godwin Samararatne, U Win Maung, and
Ian Stevenson) 214

PHYSIOLOGICAL MEASURES 218

Psi Sources and Brain Events (Jeffrey Owen Katz) 218
Physiological Correlates of Psi Reception (Charles
T. Tart) 221
Transmission of Emotion by Psi under Hypnosis as
Measured by Galvanic Skin Response (RB)
(Cambridge University Society for Psychical
Research) 224

DREAMS AND ALTERED STATES 226

Déjà Vu: A Parapsychological Approach (RB)
(Vernon M. Neppe) 226
Dream States and ESP: A Distance Experiment with a
Single Subject (RB) (Betty Markwick and John Beloff) 228
The OBE as a Near-Birth Experience (RB) (Barbara
Honegger) 230
Imagery and the OBE (RB) (Susan J. Blackmore) 231
OBEs and Perceptual Distortions in Schizophrenic
Patients and Students (RB) (Susan J. Blackmore
and John Harris) 232
The Olfactory Hallucination in the Psychic (Vernon M.
Neppe) 234
A Phenomenological Approach to Experimental Para-
psychology (RB) (Ralph G. Locke and Marilyn J.
Schlitz) 238

ANTHROPOLOGICAL RESEARCH

Parapsychological Anthropology: Multi-Method Approaches
to the Study of Psi in the Field Setting (Patric V.
Giesler) 241

The Effect of Schooling on the Manifestation of Clairvoyant Abilities Among Isnag Children of Northern Philippines (Diane M. Murray)	245
Ritual Trance Consultation Practices of the Afro-Brazilian Umbanda Cult (RB) (Patric V. Giesler)	248

3. Roundtables — 251

THE FUTURE OF PSI RESEARCH (Convener: Keith Harary) — 251

The Future of Parapsychology (Rhea A. White)	251
The Marketing of Socially Relevant Research (Keith Harary)	252
Meaning and Future Research in Parapsychology (Patric V. Giesler)	254
The Past is Prologue (Stephan A. Schwartz)	256

SOCIAL AND ETHICAL ISSUES IN PSI RESEARCH (Convener: Stanley Krippner) — 258

Parapsychological Exchange as an Avenue to World Peace (Stanley Krippner)	258
Support Networks for Researchers Who Are Investigating Massive Psi Phenomena (Janet Lee Mitchell)	259
The Esalen Institute Soviet-American Exchange Program (James L. Hickman)	261

APPLICATIONS OF PSI (Convener: K. Ramakrishna Rao) — 263

On the Question of Application (K. Ramakrishna Rao)	263
Proposed Application of Associational Remote Viewing to Oil and Natural Resource Recovery (Russell Targ)	264
The Possible Application of Psi to Healing (Marilyn J. Schlitz)	266
The Matter of Redundancy (George P. Hansen)	268

THEORIES FOR RSPK (Convener: William G. Roll) — 270

Similarities Between RSPK and Psychomotor Epilepsy (William G. Roll and Elson de A. Montagno)	270
A Neurobiological Model for Psychokinesis (Elson de A. Montagno and William G. Roll)	272
Difficulties of Interpretation and Theory in Minor Hauntings (Alan Gauld)	274

4. Invited Speakers from the People's Republic of China — 275

Report on Investigations into "Exceptional Human Body Function" in the People's Republic of China (Harold E. Puthoff)	275

Study of the Extraordinary Function of the Human
Body in China (Chen Hsin and Mei Lei) 278

5. Invited Addresses 283

    Psychical Research and Parapsychology: Notes on
the Development of Two Disciplines (Ivor Grattan-
Guinness) 283
The Survival of Death (Robert H. Thouless) 304
A Tribute to Robert H. Thouless (Arthur S. Berger) 306
Parapsychology, the Wild Card in a Stacked Deck
(Abstract) (Robert A. McConnell) 316

6. Presidential Address 317

    Three Open Questions (John Beloff) 317

7. The J. B. Rhine Lecture 328

    Parapsychology: Status and Prospects (Hans J. Eysenck) 328

Errata 336

Name Index (Compiled by Emily Cook Williams) 337

Subject Index (Compiled by Emily Cook Williams) 344

PREFACE

This Centenary-Jubilee volume of Research in Parapsychology is, as its title indicates, a very special collection of proceedings since it commemorates the one hundredth anniversary of the founding of the Society for Psychical Research, which by a happy conjunction falls in the same year as the twenty-fifth anniversary of the founding of the Parapsychological Association. To mark the occasion the PA decided to join forces with the SPR so that their 25th Annual Convention could be combined with the annual international conference of the SPR. The result was an intensive week-long conference at Trinity College, Cambridge. The appositeness of this venue should be evident when one recalls that three of the most important founders of the SPR--Henry Sidgwick, Frederic Myers, and Edmund Gurney--were all Fellows of this college. Moreover, Cambridge University has kept alive the tradition of psychical research and there is an active student society which, on this occasion, provided some of the volunteers who, under the direction of our organizing committee in Cambridge, did so much to insure the smooth running of the conference. If attendance is anything to go by this combined effort proved well justified since there were just over 300 registrants this year despite the fact that a number of Americans whom we usually see at PA conventions were unfortunately deterred from coming due to the high cost of travel. There were also a record number of entries so that even after rejecting many worthy scripts and introducing parallel sessions for most of the time we were still left with an uncomfortably crowded timetable.

As befitted the occasion there were a fair number of historical papers this time, including the opening symposium, "Then and Now." It was, however, unfortunate that its distinguished convener, Ian Stevenson, who had been spending a sabbatical year in Cambridge and had served on the Program Committee, was unable to be present, having been obliged to return to Charlottesville for family reasons. Of the remaining three symposia the one convened by Christopher Scott was notable in providing a forum for those of our critics who are not yet satisfied that there are any genuine paranormal phenomena to be investigated. Although it gave rise to some fairly heated exchanges, especially on the validity of the evidence based on the "Ganzfeld technique" (Charles Honorton was allowed to take the platform immediately after Ray Hyman's paper so that he would be able to reply formally to his criticisms), it was generally agreed that the event was well worthwhile and it certainly spoke well for the growing maturity of our field that skeptics and believers should be able to engage in constructive dialogue in this way. The two other symposia were both convened by Julian Isaacs. One dealt with the ever contentious issue of PK metal-bending, the other with the much discussed "Batcheldor technique," with a paper from its originator, Kenneth Batcheldor.

The distinction between an official symposium and a session composed of papers on some common theme is bound to be a somewhat artificial one. This year, as usual, the entries tended to group themselves. A number of papers expressing a diversity of viewpoints all fell under the rubric of "survival research"; other such broad themes included psi-conducive conditions, psi-positive personalities, dreams and other altered states, computers and REGs, and other topics that have for some time formed the staple of parapsychological conferences. As always, a good many papers and briefs could not be classified under such convenient headings and had to be relegated to sessions devoted to miscellaneous reports.

The four roundtables featured many well-known members of the PA and dealt with themes that tend to recur whenever parapsychologists come together: the future of parapsychology, its potential applications and the social and ethical issues that it poses, etc. There was also one roundtable devoted to theories of RSPK. The workshops, as usual, are not reported in this volume but deserve a mention. Only two of the workshops were submitted in time to gain a place in the published program: the one convened by W. E. Cox on the SORRAT investigation and that convened by W. G. Roll on physical mediumship. As could have been anticipated, given its controversial nature, the Cox workshop proved to be the most heated session of the entire conference. However, with Stanley Krippner in the Chair, order was duly maintained. Roll's workshop consisted mainly of reports on the Brazilian physical medium Thomas Coutinho, for whom some incredible claims are made. Although the workshop was initially submitted as a symposium, the committee felt that since most of the reports had to rely on field observation rather than on controlled laboratory testing, it would be more appropriate if presented as a workshop. The two workshops convened at short notice were on psychic healing, with Daniel Benor as its convenor and L. LeShan, S. Krippner, J. Solfvin, E. Montagno, and others as participants, and on observational theory, in which E. H. Walker, Brian Josephson, Dick Bierman and others took part.

A peculiar feature of this volume, and one that has contributed to its bulk, is the number of invited addresses, which are here printed in full in accordance with our custom. At regular PA conventions these are usually limited to the J. B. Rhine address, which follows the banquet and was this year given by Hans Eysenck, and the presidential address. This time there were four additional invited addresses, including one by veteran British psychical researcher R. H. Thouless, to whom a fitting tribute was paid by Arthur Berger of the Survival Research Foundation. A scholarly review of the development and divergence of two disciplines, psychical research and parapsychology, was presented by Ivor Grattan-

Guinness of the SPR. "Parapsychology, the Wild Card in a Stacked Deck: A Look at the Near Future of Mankind," was delivered by Robert A. McConnell. We regret that it was too lengthy for inclusion in these proceedings but it will appear in a book edited and published by Dr. McConnell entitled <u>Parapsychology and Self-Deception in Science</u>. Originally we had also set aside time for invited speakers from both the Soviet Union or Eastern Europe and the People's Republic of China. Our Soviet guests were unable to come but we were fortunate in having two delegates from China, one of whom presented a paper dealing with recent research using the exceptional children about whom so much has been heard in the West. This paper, duly translated, was introduced by Hal Puthoff, who had organized this event, having recently visited the People's Republic himself.

The contributions to this volume represent, we believe, a fair sample of the sort of work that is going on today in parapsychology one hundred years after the first concerted attempt was made to place the field on a scientific basis. Which of these seeds will flourish and which will wither will be revealed, no doubt, during the coming century of research. In the meantime we want to express our gratitude to the authors who sent us their abstracts and made it possible to have as complete a record as our means would permit of this unique commemorative event. Thanks are also due to the members of the Program Committee, who performed a valuable service in reviewing an unusually large number of papers: Anita Gregory, Julian Isaacs, Martin Johnson, John Palmer, Ian Stevenson, and Donald West. Finally, we wish to express our gratitude to the Organizing Committee in Cambridge: Tony Cornell, Bernard Carr, and Carl Sargent.

                                                John Beloff
                                                Chairperson
                                                Program Committee

INTRODUCTION

The year 1982 marks not only the 100th anniversary of the Society for Psychical Research and the 25th of the Parapsychological Association but also the 11th year of Research in Parapsychology. RIP was launched in 1972 as successor to the Proceedings of the Parapsychological Association, which covered the 1964 to 1971 conventions. Before that, from 1957 through 1963, the Journal of Parapsychology provided this service.

For most of this time, I have been senior editor, a position I now relinquish, leaving RIP in the capable hands of Rhea White. The duties of the RIP editors concern the form of the volume, not its contents, these being determined by the convention program. I shall use this occasion for some words on the contents of RIP, which is to say, on the development of thinking and research in the field. There are many facets to psi research and I shall restrict myself to a small cluster that is projecting a promising image of what we are about and has given me at least a sense that the field is moving in the right direction.

The creation of the Parapsychological Association is due to J. B. Rhine, whom we remember formally by the annual banquet address named in his honor. Rhine looked to parapsychology for evidence that the materialistic conception of the world is incomplete and that human minds exist as distinct and autonomous entities. In this respect he followed the Cartesian philosophy of the founders of the Society for Psychical Research and with them he believed that the same empirical research which had eroded the spiritual foundation of human nature could restore it. Like the SPR founders, Rhine regarded psi phenomena as evidence for a nonphysical, mental component in humankind, thereby providing a scientific basis for human values that formerly religion had upheld by means of faith and creed.

Over the years, as the search for proof of the reality of psi was augmented by a search for process--the conditions on which psi may depend--the assumption that psi is a mental activity was translated into studies of the psychological conditions associated with the outcomes of psi tests. Many of the papers in RIP concern the influence on psi of cognitive factors, personality traits, and states of consciousness. This work was successful, but only up to a point. The failure except within very broad limits to replicate results indicated that the picture of psi was incomplete.

In the meantime, developments in physics suggested to some that the material world in certain respects may also be a mental one, and parapsychologists became increasingly attentive to the possibility that the missing parts of the puzzle might be found with the aid of concepts and procedures originating in modern physics. About the same time neurophysiology advanced to the point of detailing how mental or psychological conditions, including those apparently related to psi, might be the outcomes of specific functions of the nervous system. This research is giving a more solid status to psychological concepts and suggests that the brain is a possible gate to a person's psi environment (which may also be a physical one, according to recent formulations). The speculations regarding possible interfaces between physics, neurophysiology, and psi research are now leading to predictive hypotheses which over the next decades should tell us whether we finally are on the right track.

An interesting aspect of some contemporary views of the physical world is that they, to an extent, were anticipated in traditional religious conceptions, including those of Hinduism and Buddhism. These beliefs include neurophysiological procedures whereby human beings supposedly may experience and somewhat control their psi environment. Also in the pages of RIP we learn of practices in contemporary tribal and other communities concerning psi-conducive procedures which also may involve neurophysiological processes.

At the same time as these traditional or folk practices may provide ideas for research they are reminders that the real test is the extent to which this work is meaningful in terms of human needs. Over the past years it has become a tradition to include a workshop in the convention program on social and practical applications of psi. Topics covered in these and other contributions have included the use of psi for healing, archeology, and public safety. There is also increasing awareness of parapsychology as a way for the individual to explore new and closer modes of relation to his or her social and physical environment.

At central stage in the first fifty years or so of the Society for Psychical Research was the issue whether personality and consciousness outlast the lifespan of the biological organism. This research faltered when it was supposed that the evidence for survival could be accounted for by the psi abilities of the living. With the new conceptions of the physical universe, the possibility has been raised that personality may continue in the same dimensions of the world where other psi interactions may take place. In the years ahead we may find that research into the connective matrix where psi interactions presumably occur may also hold the life histories of the deceased.

There is, of course, much doubt and wavering about psi research as the volumes of RIP testify, this volume more than most. At the same time the facts, none of which may seem convincing in isolation, are falling into patterns. These patterns are not suggestive of occult scenarios, but they are consistent with what other disciplines are telling us about humankind and its world.

William G. Roll

Part 1: Symposia

THEN AND NOW*

1882 AND ALL THAT

Alan Gauld (University of Nottingham)

My task today is to speak about psychical research as it was in 1882. Most of my audience will already know the essential facts about this, the heroic age of psychical research. Under these circumstances, I shall adopt the following strategy. Taking, as it were, a vantage point in the year 1882, I shall raise and briefly discuss several historical issues, discussion of which will require us to look either forward or back from this chosen vantage point.

The first issue is this: Why did psychical research come to be about those phenomena which have since been generally agreed to constitute its subject-matter? The original aims and objects of the SPR were stated to be to investigate "without prejudice or prepossession ... those faculties of man, real or supposed," not explicable "on any generally recognized hypothesis." This definition is too wide; it would cover much of conventional psychology. On the other hand, to define psychical research as the scientific study of the alleged phenomena of ESP and PK is too narrow. In practice, however, the founders of the SPR had little difficulty in marking out the phenomena to be initially attacked. The mesmeric and Spiritualist movements had brought into prominence various supposed human faculties, or aspects of human nature, not recognized by orthodox psychology and physiology. Psychical research emerges as the investigation of these rejected phenomena. To the extent that psychical research is successful in gaining acceptance for these phenomena, it should disappear. The fact that we are now celebrating the SPR's centenary is not therefore necessarily an indication of a success story.

---
*Organized by Ian Stevenson (University of Virginia); chaired by Gertrude R. Schmeidler (City College of the City University of New York)

My second issue concerns the relative prominence of the different kinds of phenomena investigated by the SPR in its early days. The relative space allotted in the SPR's early publications to the various categories of phenomena reflects in a rough and ready way the actual frequency or inducibility of such happenings in our society. After 1890 the volumes are increasingly filled with long papers on Mrs. Piper, the cross-correspondences, etc., but the prominence given to these topics is due to their unusual interest rather than to the ready availability of such materials. Some categories of phenomena--for instance, paranormal healing, miraculous events occurring in a Catholic context, and cases of ostensible reincarnation--are perhaps under-represented. The reasons for this are obscure.

The third issue is a source almost of bewilderment to me. The SPR was run from 1882 to the time of the First World War and after, mainly by the members of a rather small group of closely associated persons who were also responsible for a considerable percentage of the material published in the Society's Proceedings and Journal. The 28 volumes of Proceedings and 16 of Journal published up to 1915 contain between them 21,000 pages, which must represent getting on for ten million words. A good deal of this work is of a very high standard and lays down the issues and the lines of argument that have dominated discussion ever since. How did this small group of people manage to achieve so much? A simple picture of them that is often painted is that they were members of a now largely defunct leisured class, possessed of ample time and money, and by education and background disposed to regard religious and philosophical issues as of the highest importance. We, their successors, do not have these advantages and must struggle along as best we can, on limited funds and in such time as we can spare from the humdrum routine of earning our bread and butter. There are some elements of truth in this picture. But the SPR's early leaders, though some were well off, were not exceedingly wealthy, and most of them had other and time-consuming occupations. If we do not fully measure up to them, it is mainly because we lack their qualities, and only to a limited extent because of advantages that they enjoyed and we do not.

The last issue I shall raise has to do with public attitudes towards the SPR and its work. In its early years it was the target of a good deal of humor and a certain amount of ill-will; but by the time of the First World War it had won for itself a grudging respect both amongst the literate public and among savants. That the SPR was by 1914 held in some degree of respect by the learned world can be seen just by looking at the many distinguished persons whose names appear in its published membership lists, and at the number of librarians of public and university libraries around the world who paid institutional subscriptions. One reason for the growing respectability of psychical research was that it harmonized with many features of the psychology and psychotherapy of the day. In the light of Darwinism, mental unity was not something God-given, but a potential that has evolved in the history of the species and must be developed during the life of the individual. The mind, as Henry Maudsley, the celebrated English psychopathologist, remarked, is a federation of functions, and like other federations may split into more or less autonomous components when the going is tough. Cases of fugues, multiple personality, etc., came to be widely regarded in terms such as these, and so did the amnesias, sensory and motor automatisms, psychosomatic effects, etc., producible by hypnosis. The possible relationships of these phenomena with the cases of trance mediumship, automatic writing, sensory hallucination, and so forth, published by the SPR are obvious, and Janet, or Bernheim, or Freud, or Milne Bramwell, or Morton Prince, or William James, or any other psychologist or psychotherapist could find the publications of the SPR of interest without necessarily having to believe in ESP or any other paranormal phenomenon.

After the First World War the psychological climate changed considerably and the older kind of psychical research did not consort well with it. Yet despite the vicissitudes and fluctuations of fortune which the subject has undergone, the enterprise of 1882 is still recognizably continuous with that of 1982. The phenomena and the issues with which we now attempt to grapple are unmistakably derived from those that were analyzed and marked out by the founders of the subject; the standards that we consciously strive to reach and the ideals that we consciously strive to follow are very much those laid down a century ago. This continuity has in part been due to an unusual continuity of personnel. But mostly it is due to the sheer impetus which the immense labors, unswerving dedication, and great abilities of the early psychical researchers gave to the nascent subject. That impetus is, perhaps, even now not completely at an end. It must be the hope of each one of us that this centenary conference may do at least a little to renew it.

PSYCHICAL RESEARCH IN 1957 AND IN 1982

Gertrude R. Schmeidler (City College of the City University of New York)

When Dr. Stevenson arranged this symposium, he set an interesting task for me: to compare "psychical research" (a term I use interchangeably with "parapsychology") in 1957 and the present. He agreed to accept an impressionistic rather than a scholarly report, and that is what you will have. It will begin with an explanation of his choosing 1957 as a comparison year.

The Parapsychological Association (PA) was founded in 1957. If you wonder why this should have happened in the 1950s rather than in an earlier or later decade, you will find your answer in the career of J. B. Rhine. Although he had been primarily an experimenter in 1934, when he published <u>Extra-Sensory Perception</u>, some twenty years later he was primarily an organizer. His efforts went into administration and fund-raising, writing and lecturing, thinking and planning. These activities led him to conceive the idea of a professional organization for those who worked actively in parapsychology.

Rhine thought then, as some of us do today, that research findings on ESP and PK were growing into "a well-organized network of lawful relationships" (JP, 1958, 147). His laboratory therefore offered, in the early summer of 1957, what we could now call a mini-course in parapsychology. He invited several outsiders for guest lectures and chose us especially, I think, because our travel expenses would not be high. At the end of the course he proposed that an association for parapsychologists be formed with charter membership for all those present. The idea was enthusiastically received by his staff and his students; his guests concurred. An organizational meeting was held forthwith and the PA was born.

We immediately began our plans for the first of the PA's annual conventions, in 1958. One difference from the present was conspicuous: we were fewer. There were only 17 papers: one of the smaller classrooms at the City College of New York sufficed for all who attended. But it seems to me that similarities were conspicuous, too. Then, as now, we were conscious of our long history but still felt ourselves to be pioneers. We were defensive about the unscientific claims that outsiders mistakenly associated with our approach. And most of all, parapsychology evoked intense interest among those of us who worked in it. Newcomers often remark on one indication of this interest: though at professional conventions in most fields the conversation between sessions is likely to be about personal chitchat, at PA meetings it is likely to be about methods, data, theories. The content of our field is important to us.

There are other similarities. Psychical research then attracted many graduate students and other bright young people who were eager to work in it. Funds were insufficient to support them so that most turned to other careers. Their openness stood in marked contrast to the closed-mindedness and either lack of interest or overt disapproval of their professors. It was hoped in the 1950s that as these young people became established in some scholarly field they would create an academic atmosphere more favorable to psychical research. The change in that direction has been so slow that we still hope the bright young research people whom parapsychology cannot support will, when they turn to another field for their livelihood, leaven the next generation of scientists, of other professionals, and of influential people in general.

Of those who actively worked in parapsychology in the 1950s, then, only a very few made it their primary profession. I doubt that the proportion has changed. Most of our active workers still have their career in some different field, perhaps another science, mathematics, philosophy, engineering, medicine, teaching, the law, and so on. The reason for this lack of change is simple--but I was astonished to hear myself blurting it out between sessions at the last PA convention. A student introduced me to her psychology professor and as soon as she had completed the introduction he confronted me by asking rather aggressively, "What does parapsychology need?" I found myself answering, "Money."

Dr. Stevenson suggested that we respond to a list of questions which he proposed. Two more of his questions, I think, deserve similar answers for 1957 and 1982. "How are we supported financially?" To some extent, by the organizations where we work, as when a university offers laboratory facilities or even a teaching stipend for psychical research. Probably to a greater extent by grants, chiefly from foundations or private individuals. And largely by our own donations of our time and sometimes our research expenses.

The second of these questions is, "How is our research received by other scientists?" Occasionally but very seldom, then or now, a scientist will examine it with enough care to give it appropriate, useful criticism or else the thoughtful appraisal which leads to integration with his or her own work. But then and now, the common reception has been only a vague, transitory interest. Scientists hear us. They give us surface tolerance in the name of academic freedom; but then comes either a slipshod dismissal ("Something must be wrong") or an uncritical, slipshod approval ("It looks as if there's something there"). It reminds me of the aphorism that consciousness acts as a filter system. Most scientists seem to so effectively filter out our methods and our findings that little or none reaches their long-term memory store.

Differences are more interesting. The incisive criticism that rankled most in 1957 was E. G. Boring's: All the careful research had yielded only an "empty correlation" between targets and responses, i.e., we had no theory for our data. There are theories now, exciting ones. There are so many sophisticated and testable models and theories that the need has reversed and is now for more research to test the theories' predictions.

Another difference: new and promising lines of research have developed since the 1950s because of technological advances. Especially noteworthy are the Random Event Generators with their automated recording and their flexibility, but the list of important new research tools is a long one. I mention only a few: the improved EEGs, which let us study evoked potential and locus of brain function; a variety of other devices to measure small physical and physiological changes; video cameras and computer games; better computers for analysis of our data.

Other major research advances show innovative thinking in the use of simpler, familiar equipment, as with the Ganzfeld technique, remote viewing, and other research on relaxation (variously induced) that have so amplified and begun to clarify the earlier hints from hypnosis. Many other areas that were not entirely neglected in the 1950s are also being investigated more vigorously and ingeniously now. Examples are psychic healing, psychic dreams, psychic archaeology, out-of-body experiences, and the near-death experiences which partially overlap with them. And with Dr. Stevenson as the convener of this symposium, it is unnecessary to remind you that research on reincarnation has a status which it lacked in 1957.

A further important but gradual change has been the consolidation of methodological advances. Many had been recognized as desirable in the 1950s, such as double blinds, hyper-careful check on randomization of targets, and the use of parametric statistics such as analysis of variance. The difference is that now they are more likely to be considered essential. We are even beginning to pay more systematic attention to the experimenter effect. Along with these I class a major advance in editorial method: increased willingness to publish null data so that we can better evaluate how productive or unproductive any approach has been.

In summary, since 1957 we have grown in numbers of parapsychologists, of research reports, even of parapsychological journals; but the growth has been slow. We have grown in academic appointments and the introduction of parapsychology courses and laboratories, but this has been slow, too. We still find our fellow scientists have little interest in integrating our findings with theirs; but in partial compensation we retain the eagerness and warmth of an in-group. We have grown in financial support, but there is probably still the same high ratio of able, even brilliant applicants who are unsupported. We have branched into new and promising directions, both in research techniques and in theory.

The parapsychologists of 1957 would, I think, blend almost imperceptibly into our group today; the field has changed but it has not been transformed. And as for the direction of change, I hope you will not think my glasses unduly rose-colored for seeing almost all the differences as healthy, encouraging, and hope-inspiring advances.

THE CONTEMPORARY SCENE IN PSYCHICAL RESEARCH

Adrian Parker (Child and Youth Psychiatry Clinic, Gothenburg, Sweden)

It is not an easy task to present an overall view of this field today while maintaining some depth of perspective. Clearly the subject matter has become diverse and specialized. There are few, even amongst professional parapsychologists, who can master, for example, the intricacies of observational theories while being fully acquainted with research on, say, secondary personality and reincarnation claims. This reflects in part the way the field is no longer exclusively the province of psychologists and amateur investigators but has attracted a substantial number of physicists. It is significant that the hyphen in the word para-psychology is now redundant as a temporary demarcation of the field's belongingness to its mother science. Instead, the implication is that parapsychology is becoming a distinct hybrid of psychophysical science.

What are the characteristic features of the field today? Taking the Parapsychological Association's membership list and a survey contained in Martin Johnson's book (Parapsykologi, 1980) as source material, some factual conclusions are as follows. The PA membership is now 280 with the vast majority of full members possessing a doctorate and an affiliation with an academic or research institution. Of these, however, I estimate that only some 60 members are active in the sense of having published an investigative study during the last five years.

Looking now at the institutions that promote psi research, it is convenient to consider North America and central Europe separately. In North America there are seven major research centers supporting approximately 15 research workers. In addition there appears to be about an equal number of universities where individual teaching staff give their research time to parapsychology. However, to my knowledge it is only the Division of Parapsychology at the University of Virginia that has any assurance of permanency. In Europe there is a different picture. Serious research is conducted at five, possibly six, universities (with two offering permanency) where a total of ten staff members are engaged in psi research. The discrepancy with the earlier estimate of 60 active PA members is accounted for mainly by student associate members who carry out parapsychology as part of their course work. In this latter respect the United Kingdom can still claim some leadership: six doctorates with dissertations in the area of experimental parapsychology have been awarded there during the last five years. A survey of the major journals also confirms this general impression that most of the current research in parapsychology is linked to universities and private research centers. Serious parapsychological research as a spare-time activity has virtually ceased, and the reason for this is probably that the specialization and resources needed are excessive.

The number of professional workers in the field, however, must by any standard of comparison be regarded as extremely limited; this is even truer for the amount of financial support available. The most reliable estimate of funding comes from Tart's survey (RIP 1978, 54-55) of American research centers. He found the median budget of nine centers to be $17,000. A comparison figure to support a single U.S. research scientist engaged in a conventional discipline was given as $75,000.

Despite these restrictions the field covered by contemporary psychical research appears to have grown larger, which in itself creates certain logistic problems with sufficient manpower to follow up all research leads. Surveying the Wolman Handbook of Parapsychology and recent RIPs also gives an impression of a further trend: the "pure" (experimental) and "applied" (spontaneous cases) seem to be more equally represented in recent years. Within these investigative areas there appears to be fairly stable continuity, for instance, in the search after psychological correlates of psi and the case studies of poltergeists and apparitions.

The survival problem also appears to have returned to a fairly central position. In addition to these, new topical areas have arisen during the 1960s and 1970s. Here I am thinking of the Ganzfeld technique, remote viewing, OBE research, reincarnation studies, metal bending, and observational effects. These have all recently come into vogue although some, such as remote viewing, can be seen as the re-emergence of old phenomena under new names. At the same time there has been some effort to limit the field. Kirlian photography, plant telepathy, and pyramid effects have, for instance, been shown to be on the whole unjustified claims, which is a healthy sign of the discriminatory power of empirical research in this field. Some areas have also witnessed a decline either in research interest or in the occurrence of phenomena. This seems to be true of physical and mental mediumship and recently even the source of high-scoring subjects seems to have dried up--or is it the re-diversion of our limited resources to other areas, such as developing psi-conducive techniques?

The research methodologies of parapsychology have originally been lifted from social psychology and psychophysiology with efforts directed towards identifying specific correlational variables (e.g., sheep/goat attitudes, extraversion, alpha rhythm). In more recent years there has been a focus on more functional relationships (e.g., the change in state hypothesis) and the application of experiential scales in process research (e.g., Betts' imagery scale). There has even been a loose alliance between parapsychology and the approach that has become known as humanistic psychology. But equally important has been the refinement of statistical procedures (e.g., Kennedy, JASPR, 1979, 1-16) to reduce artifactual findings, and of instrumentation to increase sensitivity (e.g., Dunseath et al., JASPR, 1981, 311-320).

What findings can parapsychology claim? I believe it was Encyclopaedia Britannica which in giving parapsychology an entry listed the sheep/goat effect as a finding in addition to the basic psi phenomena. Today there appears to be little that we can add to this with certainty. It is true that there do appear to be empirical links of the sheep/goat effect with extraversion which in its turn also seems to be a positive correlate of ESP. Yet all this may be no more than a syndrome of positive attitudes to the psi-testing situation rather than more stable variables. In addition to this there is, of course, some evidence that psi occurs during periods of EMG-defined relaxation, internally redirected imagery, reduced sensory input, and possibly nonanalytic right-hemispherical activity. Some authorities would further claim that we have a measure of repeatability in the Ganzfeld technique with a 50% rate of replication which can compare favorably with that of orthodox psychology. Others counter this, claiming that we have instead merely an extensive experimenter effect or, worse, a collection of methodologically flawed experiments. It is important to resolve this. Recently Nils Wiklund and I (JSPR, 1982, submitted) undertook a critical review of all Ganzfeld experiments, both published and unpublished (49 studies in total), up to the end of 1980. Using a fairly loose criterion of admission (e.g., including studies allowing possible sensory cues), but excluding studies with major flaws or insufficient detail, gave a replicability rate of 26%; however, when applying very strict criteria every study was found wanting on some aspect. It would thus seem that replicability claims are premature --at least in the sense of being able to convince the skeptic. High standards of methodological finesse can, of course, be demanded of us because of the negative definition of ESP in terms of exclusion.

A positive change has occurred in the type of theories relating to psi phenomena. They have become more precise and lead to specific predictions. Field theories of psi and concepts of ESP as a form of perception have been replaced by conformance theory and observational theory. The former stresses the teleological function of psi in altering the randomicity of simple systems to fulfill the organism's needs and the latter focuses on consciousness as a hidden variable affecting the outcome of quantum processes at a neural level. Specific predictions, evidence, and counter evidence have already been accumulated for both of these theories. The third main theoretical approach that is in current vogue is General Systems theory. Whilst not leading in itself to any specific predictions, it serves as a building block incorporating such submodels as Honorton's internal attention theory, and findings relating to personality traits and feedback reinforcement learning, which do lead to specific predictions.

Finally, I would like to devote a little time to the current status and problems of parapsychology/psychical research. It seems undeniable that some progress has been made in professionalizing the field. The PA educational program, its code of ethics, the membership in the AAAS, and the output of doctorates in the field are all evidence of this. Nevertheless, it is clear that we have made little if any progress in convincing critics, in attracting funding, or in establishing new research positions. The rise of public interest in occultism during the 1960s and 1970s has in fact been in the long run a disservice. To some extent there has been a backlash from the hostile skeptical community. An example of this is the formation of the Committee for the Scientific Investigation of Claims of the Paranormal, although I think in this case we must take some responsibility ourselves through a lack of internal criticism and collaboration with external skeptics. As far as psychologists who do give parapsychology some kind of fair hearing are concerned, most place it in some borderline category awaiting either a replicable experiment or an assimilating theory. It may be of interest to note in this respect that parapsychology made it into the Annual Review of Psychology for 1981, where Leone Tyler placed it as one of psychology's "doubtful extensions." I would also like to draw attention to a little-known finding of the late Christopher Evans. In his New Scientist survey (1973, 209), although the majority of his respondents were favorably impressed with the evidence for ESP, 53% thought that little or no progress was being made in the field. Clearly we have a vicious circle: no research funding, no progress; no progress, no research funding. I would like to make some recommendations:

(1) It is vital to maintain methodological standards. Even the two-experimenter design should be retained.

(2) It is important to maintain communication and collaboration with critics. In my opinion some excellent examples of this are to be found in the Zetetic Scholar, which provides a forum for this kind of exchange. Whilst The Skeptical Inquirer may be a different kind of species, even here (1980, 1, 63-7) Jeffrey Mishlove was successful in publishing his interview with Ray Hyman. On the other hand, I am not convinced that we can win over our critics by intellectual argument alone. The level of emotion that this field arouses seems to exceed that of other areas of scientific research, so much so that one wonders if there can be some validity to Charles Tart's speculation that the psi controversy challenges something fundamental in our nature.

(3) It is important to establish collaboration at an internal level between experimenters who are successful at eliciting psi and those who are not. I think it is unfortunate for instance that the planned joint projects between Princeton and Utrecht and between Cambridge and Utrecht did not materialize.

(4) It is important to distinguish the field in the public's mind from occultism. A revival in the use of the term "psychical research" may help in this respect.

(5) A more positive definition of the field and of psi phenomena is badly needed instead of the conventional "other than" definitions. Perhaps we need to stress the psychophysical aspect of the relation of consciousness to the brain and external world as being the real center of our subject matter.

THE CASE FOR SKEPTICISM*

WHY PARAPSYCHOLOGY DEMANDS A SKEPTICAL RESPONSE

Christopher Scott (London, England)

The evidence presented by parapsychologists has several features which are rare or unique in the scientific domain and which together account for the persistence, and perhaps the character, of the conflict which has always surrounded the subject. The best known of these features is nonrepeatability.

Though the exact sense in which psi is nonrepeatable can be disputed, there is no doubt about the following negative formulation: failure to replicate is never regarded by parapsychologists as evidence against psi. This position, while not in itself unscientific, rules out at one stroke the normal avenue of scientific falsifiability, namely experimentation, and allows falsification to be attempted only by attacking the individual experiments done by parapsychologists. Thus there is no evidence against psi, only criticism of the evidence for psi. This accounts for the confrontational character of the controversy. Moreover, it gives the evidence a historical rather than an experimental character: evidence for psi consists not of experiments but of reports of experiments. The distinction is important because reports may be inaccurate or incomplete and the critic must raise this as an issue, along with the almost inevitable implications of motivated incompetence or even fraud.

A second unusual feature of parapsychology is its essentially negative definition. The parapsychologist aims to get a result which is, in normal terms, inexplicable. He then argues: I cannot think of a normal explanation so this must be a psi effect. If the critic can think of an explanation the ensuing dialogue takes the form of an argument about the feasibility, or plausibility, of this alternative. To define a concept purely by eliminating alternatives, with no positive content whatever in the concept, seems to be unknown outside parapsychology. In other sciences when a hypothetical substance or structure is invoked to explain observed phenomena the

---
*Organized by Christopher Scott (London, England); chaired by Donald J. West (Cambridge University)

"dialogue" proceeds by a consideration of the properties of the hypothesized entity and experiments are devised to test these. But in parapsychology this never happens because psi has no properties. Indeed, I suspect that the failure of parapsychologists to come up with something that psi can not do is the main reason, rather than nonrepeatability, for the continuing skepticism of mainstream science in regard to psi. This merits further discussion.

Parapsychologists can reasonably blame nature for the nonrepeatability of psi: it is not their fault if results refuse to come at the will of the investigator. On the other hand, they have only themselves to blame for not investigating the properties of psi. I pointed out long ago one direction in which such an investigation might be pursued (PSPR, 1961, 195-225). There are many others. For example, by using unsymmetrical shapes on transparent cards it would be easy to determine, given a source of psi, whether the target is being viewed from one side or the other. One could proceed from this to more or less exact localization in space of the ESP point of view. Parapsychologists have systematically shunned any experiment of this type. There seems to be a hidden agreement that you do not investigate the modus operandi of psi. This strange attitude has received surprisingly little comment. Yet what makes psi remarkable is that it seems to do things that should be impossible; surely the priority questions ought to be, what can it do and how does it do it? But, for many years now, virtually the only feature of psi that has interested parapsychologists has been its psychological correlates. Why? It is as if they do not want to find out how it works.

A third unusual feature of the evidence for psi is the fact that only some people seem able to produce it. This so-called "experimenter effect" not only aggravates the problem of conducting parapsychological research, it threatens by implication practically the whole of science, which is based on the assumption that objective observation is possible. What becomes of the concept of a control experiment, fundamental to medicine and the behavioral sciences, if the observer determines the data?

Besides being obstacles to research, the three features I have mentioned--nonrepeatability, the absence of any properties for psi, and the correlation between results and the experimenter-- are a potent source of suspicion among skeptics, for each feature is exactly what would be expected if psi were an artifact of selection of evidence, incompetence, and fraud. And at the same time the deliberate avoidance of experiments on the properties, or limitations, of psi encourages a further suspicion that parapsychologists are, by motivation, not problem-solvers but mystery-mongers.

But to these suspicious features we must add an even more obvious reason for doubt: the fact that psi conflicts with the corpus of existing scientific knowledge. This conflict, though sometimes denied, is in fact inherent in the definition of the paranormal as well as in the explicit objectives of bodies like the SPR and the

from them more rigorous evidence than is often demanded in other sciences. Parapsychology is in a unique position and will need to make unique efforts if it is to convince mainstream science to accept its results.

THE HUME GAME

Piet Hein Hoebens (Amsterdam, The Netherlands)

The present belief in psi is based on anecdotal accounts of strange events. These accounts may be true or they may be somehow erroneous; the time barrier prevents us from investigating directly. The matter would soon be settled if we had at our disposal a Time Machine, enabling us to make repeated journeys into the past and to test our conjectures on the spot.

Assume that a Time Machine were to be constructed and sent to Ashley House, London, December 1868. Assume that the crew were to be equipped with an "infallible" recording apparatus. Assume that all parties were to agree that the case for psi would stand or fall with the authenticity of the claim that, on that date and that location, D. D. Home performed a genuine levitation. Then a "skeptic" could be defined as someone who, prior to departure, would be willing to bet that no truly paranormal occurrence is to be registered.

Time Machines do not yet exist, but the thought experiment sketched above is basically a perfect version of a game that can be played in real life. Palmer has called this game the "Hume Game." Parapsychologists have frequently criticized David Hume's celebrated argument against miracles for being "tautological" and "unfalsifiable." It can, indeed, be employed as an a priori argument for dismissing any sort of evidence for the paranormal. If psi is seen as a violation of a law of Nature and if laws of Nature, by definition, cannot be violated, then the Humean observer would always have to prefer the false testimony hypothesis to the psi hypothesis. Palmer and others have complained that the skeptic cannot possibly lose the Hume Game.

However, their objections do not apply if the Humean argument is somewhat amended. Hume himself suggested a "potential falsifier" by referring to testimony whose falsehood would be more miraculous than the miracle itself. Elaborating on this idea I suggest that the proponent of some "miraculous" claim can make his case provided that he strengthen his "testimony" in such a way that to deny it would entail a rejection of a more fundamental principle of science than is violated by the claimed phenomenon.

Here the proponent has a fair chance to win the game. All

he has to do is to transform his anecdote into some sort of "hypothesis" which successfully predicts future, repeatably and intersubjectively testable observations which rival "hypotheses" cannot adequately account for. Then the skeptic will be compelled either to accept the claim or to sacrifice the very principles (repeatability, intersubjectivity, predictive power) on which his belief in the "laws of Nature" is ultimately based. However, as long as the proponent is unable to meet this requirement, the skeptic may cite a priori reasons for remaining skeptical.

In my version of the Hume Game, the skeptic bets that the parapsychologists will never succeed in taking this hurdle. If psi exists, the unbeliever is likely to lose his money some day. In order to be able to play this game, the skeptic does not have to examine the existing, historical evidence. He merely has to predict that the evidence for psi will never transcend the anecdotal. However, as long as no one pretends that the matter of psi can be settled on this level, a critical examination of the relevant anecdotes can be very useful. This game--an informal, "no-winners-no-losers" version of the Hume Game--will reveal the relative strengths and weaknesses of the proponents' and skeptics' positions. The results of attempts to debunk or vindicate "classical cases" will tell us something about parapsychology's chances of winning the wager.

On a fairly modest level, my own investigations of the evidence surrounding the celebrated Dutch clairvoyant Gerard Croiset may serve as a practical illustration. When, in 1978, I first published some newspaper articles critical of occult claims I was immediately attacked by Dutch "believers" who challenged me to come to terms with what they assumed to be the most striking evidence for psi: the "rigorously scientific work of Professor Tenhaeff" with "the Caruso among the psychics--Gerard Croiset."

While I thought the suggestion implicit in this challenge (failure on the part of the critic to debunk the claims amounts to a vindication of the paranormal) to be fallacious, I took up the gauntlet as part of the "informal" version of the Hume Game. I first examined Tenhaeff's several reports of a transatlantic ESP experiment with Croiset--hailed as a prize case both by Tenhaeff and by another Dutch university professor of parapsychology. The more miraculous features of the case turned out to be the result of gross misreporting on the part of Tenhaeff.

A third Dutch parapsychologist then suggested that the discrepancies which I had discovered might constitute an isolated lapse. He preferred to give Tenhaeff the benefit of the doubt unless it could be demonstrated that the Professor's accounts of other prize cases contained similar inaccuracies and distortions. A critical examination of the evidence surrounding some of the classical "police cases" revealed just that. In one instance I even found that Tenhaeff's main evidence consisted of a nonexistent police protocol.

After my reports had appeared, the German parapsychologist Professor Hans Bender made an attempt to compensate for the damage by publishing a reappraisal of one of his favorite "chair experiments" with Croiset. This experiment, performed in 1953 in Pirmasens, had been supervised by Bender himself. It is claimed that the sensitive scored amazing hits in his attempts to "see" a person who would later, by chance, occupy a certain seat in a Pirmasens auditorium and the equally unknown owner of an "inductor" object to be randomly selected.

Bender's reappraisal may be seen as another challenge, for I was formally invited to comment on his enthusiastic conclusions. Analysis of the evidence revealed serious flaws in the experimental design, and also certain inadequacies in the reporting of the data. My chief objection, however, is that Bender had fallen victim to the fallacy of "subjective validation" by projecting his (often far-fetched) interpretations on stimulus configurations that would have allowed many different "matches." In order to test my conjecture I repeated the entire experiment, using Croiset's original 1953 Pirmasens reading but pretending that the statements were meant to apply to target persons in 1981 Amsterdam. The results were at least as striking as the ones reported by Bender.

These findings do not prove anything about ESP, but they certainly corroborate skeptical suspicions.

PROSPECTS FOR A PSI-INHIBITORY EXPERIMENTER

Susan J. Blackmore (Brain and Perception Laboratory, University of Bristol)

I carried out my first parapsychological experiment with high hopes of success and enthusiastic ambition to test a "memory theory of ESP." The negative results of several years of ESP research were at first a shock. Only later did I come to expect nothing else. If the experimenter's beliefs or expectations play a role, then the later experiments never stood a chance.

The reason I mention this, and the point I wish to make, is that my skepticism, like that of many others, did not stem from any theoretical prejudice, nor from a "common sense" rejection of the possibility of psi, but from negative results. At one level at least this is how scientists should proceed. If their results are not what were predicted then they should change their expectations and hypotheses and try again.

Now, there are several possible reactions for a parapsychologist in this position.

1) He or she can remain confident of the existence of psi, attributing negative results to the subjects, conditions, or experimenter effects and alter his or her methods accordingly.

2) He or she can move to other areas of parapsychology, arguing that laboratory psi is too elusive, or even non-existent, but that the "real thing" happens in spontaneous cases.

3) He or she can become skeptical of the existence of any form of psi and seek to explore that hypothesis.

4) He or she can investigate phenomena traditionally a part of psychical research or parapsychology, but working on the hypothesis that they do not involve psi.

5) He or she can lose interest altogether and leave the field.

I believe that all these reactions are reasonable and to be encouraged except for the last. However, the last is all too often what happens because, I would suggest, of an intolerance of skepticism among many parapsychologists. I would like to argue that what we need is more, not less, skepticism within parapsychology. We need a subject prepared to ask the awkward question, Does psi exist? and then tolerate every shade of opinion on the issue and include work starting from every viewpoint.

To some extent I have followed all the paths except the last. I spent four years changing my experimental conditions, using Ganzfeld, child subjects, and volunteers with psychic claims. The results were all close to chance expectation. With diminishing hope for laboratory psi I moved next to testing Tarot cards, investigating poltergeists and, in most depth, studying out-of-body experiences (OBEs). Again the results revealed no evidence of psi. Not surprisingly I began to ask myself the big question, Does psi exist?

But how can it be answered? One inevitably faces the negative definition of psi. The skeptic's hypothesis, that psi does not exist, can neither be confirmed nor falsified. The history of our subject reveals this all too well. One hundred years and numerous "successful" experiments have not established the existence of psi beyond reasonable doubt, but nor has psi been dismissed. However often fraud, inadequate experimental design, or faulty statistics are suspected, or even proved, there will always be more experiments.

That is why I do not believe we shall find the answer by continuing this way. Rather, I believe the answer may become increasingly obvious as research and theory develop on both sides. In Lakatos' terms one approach will provide a progressive research program and the other a degenerating one. Many parapsychologists argue for process-oriented research, assuming that psi exists and proceeding to try to find out how and why. Perhaps we can do the same thing from a skeptical viewpoint. That is, assume that psi does not exist and investigate how and why people report apparently psychic phenomena. The same people could work on both, with a knowledge of both. With these two types of research at hand we should have a more open-minded parapsychology than we have at present, and one that would benefit by whatever answers our research provided.

I would like briefly to mention some of the research I have been doing along these lines. Starting from the fact that people report apparent telepathy, clairvoyance, ghosts, astounding coin cidences and so on, one can ask what normal psychological processes could account for this. Among those suggested is the inaccuracy of people's judgments of the probabilities of everyday events and coincidences. One need not be stupid to make misjudgments and most people do. Some events are labelled as psychic because of their perceived unlikeliness, but this may be only loosely related to their objective probability. For example, the ease with which an outcome can be imagined affects its perceived probability.

This leads to the hypothesis that if misjudgments of likeliness are at the root of some psychic belief then goats should show superior judgment to sheep. Troscianko and I carried out studies with students and schoolchildren comparing sheep and goats. Computer games involved judging whether series of events were randomly chosen or not, the gambler's fallacy, and other probability-related tests. The design aimed to distinguish generalized shifts in criterion from the tendency to errors. On the whole the goats scored higher than the sheep as predicted, although the effects were not large. Further work is planned.

Similarly, people may choose to label an event as "psychic" because they have no other explanation and cannot tolerate having none. We might therefore expect sheep to have lower tolerance for ambiguity or cognitive dissonance than goats, and a greater need to make sense out of chaos, or see cause where none exists.

In situations resembling skilled tasks there can be an "illusion of control"; people see themselves as controlling objectively chance outcomes. Troscianko and I are carrying out experiments to test whether sheep are more prone to this than goats.

It is known that negative relationships have relatively little effect on beliefs as compared with positive ones. The effect of a chance pairing of two events is not appropriately cancelled out by many non-pairings, and in judging correlations people tend to ignore the crucial negative relationships. Human beings just do not think of contingency tables.

In coin-tossing experiments it has been shown that when subjects are told they had decreasing success they see themselves as better at the task, remember greater success, and predict more for the future than those told they had random results or inclining success. It seems that the early trials gave them a hypothesis of ability which was unaltered by later failure. The relevance of this for psi is salutory. If some chance event gives someone the idea that he is psychic, that notion will be hard to shift by subsequent failure. The same thing may even happen in psi experiments where initial success (due to chance, experimental error or whatever) may produce an illusion of success which is relatively little affected by later chance results.

Memory is also important. It has often been pointed out that people remember coincidences and forget the thousands of events which do not coincide. Memory may also play tricks with the way purportedly psychic events are retold. We are carrying out a study in which "psychic" stories are retold many times to determine whether the retelling influences the closeness of the coincidence, or the perceived psychic content.

The aim is to understand why people experience and report "psychic" events and why belief in the paranormal is so widespread. Just how much will prove to be explicable without recourse to the psi hypothesis is, of course, what we have to find out. But whatever the answer, there is value in this alternative approach.

The fourth path is partner to the third. As an example, I have carried out research into OBEs beginning from the hypothesis that nothing paranormal is involved and the experience is psychological. OBEs have traditionally been part of parapsychology and I believe they should continue to be so regardless of whether any psi is involved. Here again, the two paths should go hand in hand. But sadly, it seems more likely at present that such topics will be dropped from parapsychology should they prove not to involve psi. Or more dangerous still there will be a split between parapsychologists investigating OBEs, near-death experiences, and apparitions from one point of view and psychologists from another. If this happens I believe the loser will be parapsychology.

Finally, what about the last path--leaving the field altogether? This has been the ultimate fate of many apparently psi-inhibitory experimenters and I firmly believe it should not be. Rather, I would like to see more skeptical parapsychologists--people who, for one reason or another, doubt the existence of psi but have the knowledge and enthusiasm to pursue that doubt. Not only is there a case for skepticism, but a case for greater skepticism within parapsychology.

DOES THE GANZFELD EXPERIMENT ANSWER THE CRITICS' OBJECTIONS?

Ray Hyman (University of Oregon)

What happens when a responsible critic accepts the parapsychologists' challenge to examine carefully the best evidence for the reality of psi? For this purpose I chose the research on the Ganzfeld/psi phenomenon. Many parapsychologists believe that this paradigm holds the most promise of producing the elusive replicable experiment. Current estimates in the literature place the success rate of this experiment in the neighborhood of 50 to 58%.

Charles Honorton supplied me with copies of reports of Ganzfeld/psi experiments which described all the known studies conducted from 1974 through 1981. This database consisted of a total of 42 separate experiments described in 34 publications. Honorton classifies 23 of these experiments as significantly demonstrating psi at the .05 level, an overall rate of success of 55%.

My first step was to revise this estimate down to 45%, mainly by designating two studies which found psi-missing as unsuccessful (which is consistent with criteria established by Sargent and others) and by adding five negative studies that Honorton did not include for reasons that I do not think are justified. The next step was to further revise the estimate of achieved success by taking into account unknown or unreported studies. In a survey of PA members, Susan Blackmore uncovered 19 completed and previously unreported Ganzfeld/psi experiments. Of these, seven were described by the investigators as "successful." This would lead to an estimate of 37% successes for unpublished studies.

But such an estimate is probably too optimistic. Blackmore had to rely upon the respondents' self-evaluation of the study as successful. In almost all of the published studies classified as "failures" by Honorton, the authors clearly felt they had successfully demonstrated psi. This suggests that many of the seven reported successes would very likely be classified as failures by other parapsychologists. If we conservatively estimate that at least two of the seven unpublished "successes" fall into this category, we would have a revised estimate of 26% success rate for unreported studies.

It also seems reasonable to suppose that many more unreported studies exist beyond the 19 uncovered by Blackmore's survey. Blackmore restricted her population to PA members. It seems reasonable to assume that many parapsychologists who are not PA members as well as students may have tried to conduct a Ganzfeld/psi study (I know of one or two in this category). Furthermore, Blackmore obtained responses from only 47% of her sample. It does not seem unreasonable, then, to suppose that there may exist as many unreported experiments as there are reported ones.

If this is so, the best overall estimate of actual rate of success would be the simple average of the 45% for the reported and the 26% for the unreported experiments. This would produce a new revised estimate of actual successes of 36%.

Arguments can be made for revising this estimate even further downwards. Indirect evidence suggests that a bias may exist for not reporting failures. An almost significant tendency (p=.06, two-tailed) exists in the present database for experiments with the smaller number of replications to have a higher rate of success. This is surprising because we should expect a strong tendency in just the reverse direction--the power of a test increases with the square-root of the number of replications. The most plausible explanation that occurs to me for this surprising relation is that experimenters who get nonsignificant results with small samples fail to report their findings on the assumption that their experiment was insensitive. On the other hand, an experimenter who gets significant results with a small sample will not hesitate to publish it.

Just how much to further adjust the estimate downwards is not clear. We can conservatively assume that the actual rate of success is around 33% (and given an assumed body of 80 Ganzfeld/psi experiments this would provide 95% confidence limits of 23 and 44%).

But even a success rate of 33% is impressive and significant if we can assume that the chance rate is 5%. An examination of the database, however, indicates that this is far from a safe assumption. At least 60% of the experimenters conducted several different tests of significance on their data. In the others it is not always clear how many tests were considered. Indeed, only two experimenters explicitly mentioned that they selected one index and test of significance in advance of obtaining the data. All of this indicates that the actual probability of getting a significant result in this body of experiments was much higher than the advertised .05. Considering the number of tests that appear to have been done, the true chance rate could easily be closer to .25.

In response to an earlier draft of this paper, Charles Honorton adjusted the levels of significance for multiple tests. He still found 38% were significant by a two-tailed test (45% if a one-tailed criterion is used). However, we disagree greatly in terms of how many tests were possible and how severe the adjustments should be. Furthermore, such post hoc adjustments cannot correct for another factor that inflates the significance levels.

Even if each individual experimenter scrupulously employed a single significance test in such a manner as to guarantee a true chance level of .05 for his or her experiment, this same chance rate would hold for the total set of experiments only if the same test and same index of success was employed in all the experiments. But this was blatantly not the case. The index of success, and the manner of testing for it, varied greatly from experiment to experiment. To accept different indices as successful replications of one another implies the use of a disjunctive criterion of success: a successful outcome involves significance at the .05 level on index A or B or index C or index D, etc. Such a disjunctive criterion inflates the overall significance level.

So far my argument has been based on statistical considerations. The result has been a narrowing of the gap between the actual success rate and the true chance level. If my adjustments have been reasonable, the gap has just about vanished. But even if one wishes to quarrel with the exact level of the adjustments, the gap is still much smaller than has previously been supposed.

In addition to statistical weaknesses, the Ganzfeld/psi experiments have been plagued by a number of methodological flaws. Most of these are known to parapsychologists, having been discussed in the literature. One defense of these flaws has been to assert that they cannot account for the significant results because the proportion of successes is approximately the same for flawed and unflawed studies.

But close examination reveals that this defense does not hold. In the database of 42 studies, the three most common flaws were multiple tests of significance (64%), possibilities of sensory leakage (60%), and inadequate randomization (45%). The average number of these three defects for the successful studies (using Honorton's criterion for success) was 2.04. The average for the unsuccessful experiments was 1.37. This difference is statistically significant at the .01 level (t= 2.85, 40 degrees of freedom). Thus there is a strong tendency for the rate of success to increase with the number of obvious defects.

Critical examination of the Ganzfeld/psi results, then, strongly indicates that the current optimistic statements about its success rate are premature. Critics will not be convinced that the repeatable experiment in psi has been achieved until the same success rate is obtained with studies that are obviously not flawed. If the next wave of Ganzfeld/psi experiments meet this requirement, then the time will have come for me and my fellow critics to join you in joint efforts to find out what this means for us and science.

RESPONSE TO HYMAN'S CRITIQUE OF PSI GANZFELD STUDIES

Charles Honorton (Psychophysical Research Laboratories)

Dr. Hyman's critique of psi Ganzfeld studies is a welcome contribution to the evaluation and development of this area of research. At issue is how we should interpret the moderate level of interlaboratory replicability which accounts for the growth of interest in this paradigm. The basic claim is a replication claim. As such, it will stand or fall on the basis of further research. Dr. Hyman and I agree on that. We have thus far failed to agree on the status of the present Ganzfeld database, but we have both accepted an invitation from the Journal of Parapsychology to present our respective cases with complete documentation in a forthcoming issue of that journal. What follows is an outline of my response to Dr. Hyman's major points.

Before proceeding, however, I must express puzzlement over the statement in Dr. Hyman's abstract, that his first step in revising the estimate of Ganzfeld success included adding five negative studies which he says I excluded for reasons he regards as unjustified. There is no reference to these studies in Dr. Hyman's full paper where he cites 42 studies. Those present at the Cambridge symposium may recall that I surveyed 47 studies. Five additional unsuccessful studies were added by me following receipt of an unpublished paper by Adrian Parker and Nils Wiklund. My database summaries of these studies were distributed to a number of people in Cambridge, including Ray Hyman. I have subsequently added one further study by Blackmore, whose unpublished report I received in Cambridge. This brings the total to 48 studies.

Estimating Ganzfeld Success Rate. There is no way of knowing with absolute certainty how many unreported studies may exist in any research domain. With regard to psi Ganzfeld research, the available evidence fails to support the hypothesis that the reported Ganzfeld success rate reflects a selective reporting bias: a substantial number of Ganzfeld studies (roughly half of those reported) have reported overall nonsignificant psi results and Blackmore's attempt to survey unreported studies provides no support for the notion that there are large numbers of unreported failures. Given the existing Ganzfeld database, it would be necessary to posit an additional 221 unreported studies (all with $p > .05$) to raise the probability of the known successes to $p > .05$. That is nearly five times the size of the existing database. Extrapolating from the existing studies, which average 37.1 trials per study, this would amount to more than 8,000 unknown Ganzfeld trials. Assuming an hour per session, including preliminaries and judging (mean Ganzfeld duration = 29.1 min.), and 40-hour work weeks, this translates into approximately four laboratory years!

Dr. Hyman is mistaken when he says that almost all of the authors of studies I classified as nonsignificant claimed success for their studies. Although it is true that a number of studies with overall nonsignificant results have included significant secondary analyses based on relationships between psi performance and psychological variables, previously published estimates of psi Ganzfeld replicability have been based on overall ESP performance, not upon secondary analyses of this type.

Dr. Hyman suggests that there may be a tendency for unsuccessful small studies to go unreported and he reports an "almost

significant" tendency for successful results in experiments with
small numbers of trials. Dr. Hyman's abstract reports p = .06,
two-tailed, for this analysis. (The value cited in his full paper is
p = .07.) I can find no relationship between the significance or
nonsignificance of a study and the number of trials. The mean number of trials are 37.58 (significant studies) and 36.83 (nonsignificant
studies). The correlation (point biserial) between number of trials
and classification of significance is very close to zero (r = .012,
46 df).

On the issue of multiple analysis, Dr. Hyman makes an extremely important point. Though this topic has been discussed before in the literature, nowhere, to my knowledge, has the potential
danger of failing to correct for multiple tests been dramatized as
forcefully as in Dr. Hyman's worst case scenario. I agree that
some correction for multiple tests is necessary and that all or most
of us have been guilty of reporting multiple tests without applying
appropriate adjustments for the number of tests used. I trust we
will discontinue this practice.

When the studies in the existing Ganzfeld database are adjusted for multiple analysis using the Bonferroni inequality, 19 of
the 23 originally classified significant studies survive the adjustment
of a one-tailed criterion and 16 survive two-tailed. The adjustment
leads to a revised estimate of success of between 33%-40% with the
chance rate guaranteed to be no higher than 5%. (The Bonferroni
adjustment will be fully documented in my forthcoming paper in JP.)

Dr. Hyman argues that these adjustments cannot be made after the fact. The alternative he offers, however, is numerical
speculation. Dr. Hyman believes that combining studies with different dependent variable measures creates a "disjunctive criterion"
that somehow inflates the overall significance level. I do not follow
this. Be that as it may, there is another solution with respect to
the Ganzfeld work: Select one measure and use it as a uniform index to estimate the overall significance level. Fifteen of the originally classified significant studies employed direct hits (ranks of 1
assigned to the actual target) as an index of success. Ten of these
15 studies are significant using one-tailed Bonferroni criteria, nine
are significant by two-tailed criteria. Assume that all nonsignificant
studies included a direct hit measure (they did not). This gives a
worst case direct hit success rate between 23% and 25% with chance
expectation guaranteed by the Bonferroni protection to be no higher
than 5%. The binomial probability of 10 successes in 40 trials with
p(success) = .05, gives p < .00005.

Flaws. Dr. Hyman reports a statistically significant relationship between number of potential flaws in a study and its classification of significance. After seeing this claim in an earlier draft of
his paper, I performed my own analysis. In order to eliminate subjectivity in the ratings, my rating criteria were defined in terms of
specific procedural descriptors (or their absence) in the research
reports. The following analysis is based on the 47 studies that were

available to me at the time of the Cambridge symposium. Three ratings were assigned to each study.

The CUE rating assessed adequacy of control against potential handling cues in the judging period. CUE ratings of 2 were assigned to studies reporting use of duplicate target sets, outside judges or Maimonides target coding (n=25). CUE ratings of 1 were assigned to studies employing subject judging with a single target set handled by a sender or experimenter (n=20). CUE ratings of 0 were assigned to studies involving direct contact between the subject and a person knowing the target prior to subject blind judging (n = 2, both nonsignificant). Using the Bonferroni classification of significance, the mean CUE ratings are 1.53 (significant studies) and 1.46 (nonsignificant studies). A Mann-Whitney U test indicates no statistical relationship between study outcome and level of cue control (Z' = -.141).

The RND rating assessed target randomization method. RND ratings of 2 were assigned to studies documenting use of random number tables or random generators for target selection (n = 25). RND ratings of 1 were assigned to studies involving shuffling techniques (n = 7). A RND rating of 0 was assigned for any other method of target selection or if the method of target selection was not described in the report (n = 15). The mean RND ratings are 1.42 (significant studies) and 1.07 (nonsignificant studies). A Mann-Whitney U test indicates no statistical relationship between study outcome and method of target selection (Z' = -.921).

Since Dr. Hyman claims there is "a strong tendency for the rate of success to increase with the number of obvious defects," an overall rating was composed by summing each study's CUE and RND ratings. The means are 2.95 (significant studies) and 2.54 (nonsignificant studies). Once again the difference is nonsignificant (Z' = -1.1). Fifteen studies received composite ratings of 4 (i.e., CUE and RND ratings of 2). Of these, seven are significant and eight are nonsignificant.

Methodological Improvement. Using the CUE, RND, and composite indices described above, I have also examined changes in psi Ganzfeld methodology across the two four-year periods in which Ganzfeld studies have been reported: 1974-77 and 1978-81. I am pleased to report that there has been significant improvement between these two periods for significant studies (t = 4.34. 17 df. p < .001) as well as nonsignificant studies (t = 2.57. 26 df. p < .015). Even in the earlier period, however, there is no relationship between methodological indices and study outcome (t = .65. 22 df).

The analyses summarized above will be documented on a study-by-study basis in my JP paper.

THOUGHTS ON TESTIMONY TO THE PARANORMAL

Donald J. West (Cambridge University)

To a very large extent parapsychology has to rely upon human testimony. Evidence for spontaneous psychic experiences is necessarily anecdotal and requires trust in the accuracy and credibility of the individuals who report them. Laboratory experiments are in a slightly different category in so far as they are usually team enterprises with the results recorded in ways that do not depend upon the accuracy of any one observer. Even so, because similar results cannot be guaranteed when other workers try to reproduce them, the evidence remains dependent upon the testimony of the original experimenters.

Testimony to paranormal events is affected by the pervasive need to believe in the supernatural. Mysteries suggestive of interventions from another world, or of the existence of transcendental faculties in man, arouse hope of an existence beyond human limitations, beyond the sad decay and extinction that seem the inescapable fate of all living things. To many people, observations that heighten a mystery are more congenial and more acceptable than those which point to some prosaic, disillusioning explanation.

This natural bias insures the popularity of writings that enhance the attractiveness of testimony to marvels by selecting out details that might direct attention to normal interpretations. In this way versions of events considerably more mysterious than the original story gradually gain acceptance. A good example is the legend of the Bermuda Triangle, a stretch of ocean where numerous boats and aircraft are said to have vanished in mysterious circumstances. Lawrence Kusche (Bermuda Triangle Mystery Solved, 1975), a pertinacious librarian at Arizona State University, tracked down the original sources of many of these stories and found that, for most of the incidents, a logical explanation was forthcoming once sufficient information was collected and fictional accretions discounted.

A similar tendency to vulgarization and exaggeration of original reports is to be found in popular writing on psychical research topics. The case of Borley Rectory and the famous "Adventure" at Versailles, are two outstanding examples. For a sane assessment of the latter case, one need go no further than the politely dismissive anonymous reviews in SPR publications (JSPR, 1931, 139-140; PSPR, 1911, 353-360).

Although sadly neglected by academic psychologists, psychical research literature contains some of the best authenticated and most spectacular examples of distorted perception and reporting. The best recorded example of distorted reporting of séances is the classic study of Hodgson and Davey (PSPR, 1887, 381-495). Carefully stated slate-writing tricks and phantom materializations were performed before audiences who were invited to submit detailed written accounts of what they had seen. They were not told whether the effects were supposed to be produced paranormally, but many concluded that they were and sent in reports of what they considered totally inexplicable marvels.

Hallucinatory perceptions may also occur spontaneously and in the full light of day. In the famous Census of Hallucinations, conducted by the SPR in the last century, a sample of 17,000 persons were questioned and one in ten claimed to have had at least one definite, waking hallucination, most often a vision of a realistic human figure (Sidgwick, H., et al., PSPR, 1894, 25-422). Over half a century later a similar inquiry was put to a Mass Observation panel and 14% of the respondents claimed to have had a hallucination, again most often a vision of a realistic human figure. Unlike the crisis apparitions of special interest to psychical investigators, the majority of these experiences do not coincide with or appear to represent any external event (West, D. J., JSPR, 1948, 187-196). A comparable incidence of apparitional experiences (17% of the two thirds of the sample who sent in a reply) was obtained in a more recent survey by postal questionnaire carried out in Charlottesville, Virginia (Palmer, J., JASPR, 1979, 221-251).

Spontaneous hallucinations are probably more prevalent when some emotional need for them exists. In a survey published in the British Medical Journal, 81% of the widowed people residing in a defined area of Wales were interviewed and 14% of the interviewed sample claimed to have "seen" the dead spouse (Rees, D., 1971, 37-41).

The main weakness of the hallucination theory of testimony to the paranormal is that, in contrast to the distortions of perception provoked by staged performances in the séance room or elsewhere, most spontaneous hallucinations of the healthy, although momentarily convincing, are brief, out of context with the surroundings, and soon recognized as unreal. This rule does not apply, however, to persons who are subject to periods of mental dissociation, when fantasy memories or perceptions may take over and displace reality for protracted periods. Again, it is the literature of psychical research, dealing with such topics as automatic writing, mediumistic trance, "out-of-the-body" experiences, reincarnation cases, and multiple personality, where the best examples can be found. When startling simulations of deceased personalities are produced, or artistic creations of varying merit appear (such as the writings of Patience Worth or the piano compositions of Rosemary Brown) it is sometimes difficult to credit the medium with processing a personal store of mental images sufficient to sustain such dramatic constructions. However, as Ian Wilson (Mind Out of Time, 1981) aptly commented in the conclusion to his recent review of cases of purported reincarnation: "We are each of us tenants of a vast universe within ourselves, a dynamic, ever restless kaleidoscope of images, ideas, dreams, emotions, the complexity and extent of which we have scarcely as yet begun to grasp." This conclusion comes as no surprise to those familiar with the older literature on creative automatism (Myers, F. W. H., Human Personality and Its Survival of Bodily Death, 1903; Muhl, A., Automatic Writing, 2nd ed., 1963).

Wilson cites other, more conclusive instances in which the mundane, personal origin of seemingly paranormal utterances have been traced. For example, the psychiatrist Reima Kampman (Acta Universitatis Ouluensis, Series D. Medica No. 6, Psychiat. No. 3, 1973, 7-116) induced his hypnotic subject, a Finnish schoolgirl, to "remember" various former lives, including one in which she was an innkeeper's daughter named Dorothy who lived in East Anglia in the thirteenth century. She recalled in impressive detail happenings in England at the time and sang a "Summer Song" in archaic English which specialists declared authentic to the period. Hypnotized again and asked to remember when, during her present life, she had first heard the "Summer Song," she remembered having once browsed through a book by Benjamin Britten and Imogen Holst and noticed the song.

In multiple personality phenomena an individual may be genuinely unaware of the thoughts and tricks of his alter ego, even though at some deep level he has created that alter ego to express some facet of his own character. One can conceive, in exceptional cases, that frauds might be perpetrated during phases of mental dissociation, leaving the dominant personality with a genuine conviction of innocence. The idea becomes a degree less far-fetched than at first it appears when one considers the elaborate, unconscious cheating involved in the production of fake paralyses and other imitations of the symptoms of organic disease by hysterical patients.

Suggestions of this kind have been made in the case of S. G. Soal by people loath to believe that a scientist would consciously cheat. It is beyond dispute that in both his Shackleton and Stewart experiments Soal claimed to be using undoctored, randomized targets when in fact he was not (Markwick, B., PSPR, 1978, 250-81; Nicol, J. F., IJP, 1959, 47-63) and it is virtually certain that he produced at least some of his results by alteration or manipulation of the target series. Yet psychical research was Soal's great preoccupation for most of his life and he appeared to be an almost obsessive devotee of careful standards. Even in advanced old age, when his mind could no longer cope with mathematical arguments, he went on struggling to refute detailed criticisms of his results. His former collaborator, Mrs. K. M. Goldney, who knew him well, found it almost impossible to believe that he would betray the work so close to his heart. But Soal was a medium who produced automatic writing and was the creator of scripts purportedly inspired by Oscar Wilde and by a nineteenth-century poetess, Margaret Veley (Salter, W. H., & "Mr. V.," PSPR, 1929, 281-374).

It is not suggested that dissociation is necessarily the explanation of the Soal enigma, but it is a possibility. Plain dishonesty is the usual explanation of faked results.

Fraudulent reporting by scientists, though difficult to prove, is by no means unknown. Some examples have become publicly famous, such as Blondlot's "N-rays" (Rostand, J., Error and Deception in Science, 1960), Kammerer's midwife toad (Koestler, A., The Case of the Midwife Toad, 1971), and the Piltdown skull (Weiner, J. S., The Piltdown Forgery, 1955). In the more obscure field of the biochemistry of cancerous cells, some recent results obtained by a brilliant young research worker at Cornell are said to have been achieved by illicit introduction of an alien compound into the test materials (New Scientist, 1981, 781-782). Following his death in 1971, some of the later publications by the famous psychologist Sir Cyril Burt were publicly exposed as blatantly dishonest (Hearnshaw, L. S., Cyril Burt Psychologist, 1979).

The world of parapsychology is a small circle of individuals with unorthodox interests and varied background. A formal qualification for entry has yet to be devised. Within that small community fame comes swiftly once some positive findings are claimed. Moreover, unlike the natural sciences, where the failure of other workers to replicate one's findings would lead to immediate loss of reputation, such failure in parapsychology merely leads to a reinforcement of the common belief that results are as much a function of the experimenter as of the experiment. In this situation, the promulgation of bogus findings is a much greater danger than in better established disciplines.

One final point. Testimony to spontaneous occurrences or to experimental findings would be more convincing if the claims being made had not shifted in a suspicious manner with the passage of time. Before the requisite techniques of statistical evaluation were developed and applied, psychic effects in telepathy experiments and in mediumistic utterances were reportedly of such enormous magnitude that tests of significance were superfluous. No sooner did such tests come into use, however, than the phenomena changed in character, dwindling, in the majority of cases, almost to insignificance. Similarly, in relation to alleged metal-bending in daylight, a phenomenon so gross that one might think immediate and conclusive verification would be simple, no sooner were sensitive methods of detection with strain gauges introduced than subjects reportedly produced much smaller effects, sometimes indistinguishable from random noise due to electrical interferences acting upon the measuring equipment. This kind of retreat from the dramatic and obvious to the subtle and largely concealed is, to say the least, a curious and unfortunate inconsistency to the evidence.

PSYCHOKINETIC METAL-BENDING (PKMB)*

A TWELVE-SESSION STUDY OF MICRO-PKMB TRAINING

Julian Isaacs (University of Aston, Birmingham, England)

The Choice of Micro-PKMB as PK Training Task. Case study and anecdotal literature suggest that once discovered, psychokinetic metal-bending (PKMB) ability can improve with practice and may be a learnable PK ability. Random event generator (REG)-based PK detection systems would seem to offer less than optimal performance as PK training devices because they present beginning trainees with a confusingly high level of hits which are due to chance rather than PK, given the low percentile rates of success generally achieved. Trainees may thereby be prevented from identifying their internal states that correlate with PK hitting, which would prevent learning.

The micro-PKMB detection system used for this study provides an extremely stable output in the absence of PK and consequently does not present subjects with false positive feedback. It provides a readily discriminable response to very low levels of micro-PKMB and indicates the instantaneous magnitude of micro-PKMB effects as they occur. That these detection-system characteristics should make micro-PKMB a more suitable form of PK for training purposes than REG effects led to its adoption in this study.

Security Against Fraud. Although the macroscopic form of PKMB in which visible bending occurs is difficult to obtain when subjects are prevented from touching the metal sample, the micro-PKMB effect is readily obtained under "no touch" conditions when subjects are not allowed to touch the PKMB target. All training sessions were conducted under observation by the experimenter (J.I.). No PKMB signals were accepted as valid unless they occurred while the experimenter could observe a clear gap between subject and PKMB target.

Subject Selection. Five female subjects participated (S.D.,

---

*Organized by Julian Isaacs (University of Aston, Birmingham, England); chaired by Charles Honorton (Psychophysical Research Laboratories)

M. H., P. W., H. H., M. B.), their ages ranging from 28 to 65. All subjects had shown some ostensible PKMB ability prior to training although this varied widely. All except S. D. had participated previously in spiritualist psi training groups for varying periods. M. H., P. W., and M. B. were found at the experimenter's mass screenings for PKMB agents (Psychoenergetic Systems, 1979, 37-69), while H. H. was reported by her husband, who attended a screening. S. D. was reported by friends as having once experienced a spontaneous PKMB event, although she reported no further PKMB or other spontaneous psi events.

Apparatus. Three channels were utilized, two of which were used to detect possible sources of artifact while the third detected micro-PKMB effects. The three channels' electrical outputs were recorded by chart recorder (JJ type 553) at a chart speed of 1mm/sec. The micro-PKMB sensor consisted of an electrostatically screened 2-cm. strip of ceramic piezoelectric multimorph element. This was fixed to the lower end of a 250-gram lead plumb bob and placed within a coaxially-mounted, clear plastic tube sealed to the base of the bob and open at the lower end. The bob was compliantly suspended from a wooden frame which was mounted on a small table isolated from environmental sources of vibration and at which the subject sat in the "near" condition.

Screened leads took the electrical output from the sensor to the amplifier/signal processor unit and chart recorder which were placed on a separate table. The sensor's output was amplified using a gain of 22, full wave rectified, and held at its peak value by peak-hold circuitry, which was reset to zero volts by a 5-millisecond clock pulse every .75 seconds. The output was chart-recorded at 10 millivolts (mV) full scale deflection (FSD). Noise in the PKMB channel as measured by chart recorder (all other output figures will be as measured by chart recorder) was well below .4 mV peak to peak amplitude. No signal in the PKMB channel was accepted as candidate PKMB unless it was of 2 mV or greater amplitude.

The major source of artifactual signals in the PKMB channel is airborne sound or mechanically transmitted vibration. A high output crystal microphone was mounted in direct contact with the sensor stand and monitored environmental sound and vibration using an amplifier gain of 20 and similar rectifier and peak holding circuitry to the PKMB channel. If sound transients of greater than 6 mV occurred in the sound monitoring channel, simultaneously occurring signals in the PKMB channel were invalidated. The sound channel chart record operated at 100 mV FSD sensitivity.

A third channel monitored the output of the electrical mains to exclude mains interference as a source of artifactual signals in the PKMB channel. The mains channel chart recording was made at 1 volt FSD sensitivity and any transient greater than 60 mV invalidated simultaneously occurring signals in the PKMB channel.

Feedback of their PKMB effects to subjects took the form of a continuous audio tone which increased in pitch with increases in the voltage output of the PKMB channel.

Training Session Procedure. Twelve weekly sessions of 45 minutes' duration were held with each subject at her home. Sessions employed three conditions: "near" trials in which the subject attempted to produce effects while seated at the table on which the PKMB sensor was placed; "rest" periods in which the subject sat in a chair some two meters from the sensor and rested; and "distant" trials in which the subject remained in her rest chair and attempted to cause effects at a distance.

Each session comprised six near trials of total duration of 10 minutes, four distant trials occupying 6 minutes, and seven rest periods occupying 29 minutes. The longest trial period was 2 minutes; the shortest, 1 minute. Rest periods lengthened during the session and trial periods shortened.

Silence was maintained in all trial periods but subject and experimenter freely conversed in rest periods while the timing cassette played music. All timing and other instructions were given to subject and experimenter by means of an audio cassette played during each training session.

Results. Signals of 2 mV or greater occurring in the PKMB channel were accepted as PK if there were no simultaneous invalidating signals present in the sound and mains monitoring channels and no annotation on the chart record invalidating the signal for any other reason.

The effects detected were of fast rise time and short duration. They can validly be treated as discrete pulselike events and the score for each session was obtained by summing the voltage values of all valid pulses obtained in the session. This procedure collapses the data across the three conditions and analysis by condition will not be presented. Questionnaire data will not be presented here either.

Subject S.D. failed to score in any session. Subject M.H. scored 3.2 mV in session 1; no scores in sessions 2, 3, 4, and 5; 4.7 mV in session 6; 7.4 mV in session 7; 0 in sessions 8, 9, 10, and 11; and 11.4 mV in 12.

Subject M.H. had a strongly psi-inhibitory experience in session 7 when she appeared to psychometrically "read" the experimenter's depressed state.

Subject P.W. scored 2.4 mV in session 1; no scores in sessions 2, 3, 4, 5, and 6; 4.4 mV in session 7; 0 in 8; 5.0 mV in 9; 5.4 mV in 10; 0 in 11; and 32.8 mV in 12.

Subject H.H. scored nothing in the first six sessions, except

for session 3 (2.0 mV). In session 7 she scored 18.0 mV, although
technical difficulties prevented her full score of more than four times
this figure from being counted formally. In session 8 she scored
17.0 mV; in sessions 9, 10, and 11 she scored 0; and in session
12 she scored 2.2 mV. H.H. reported considerable irritation with
the timing cassette, which she claimed interfered with her establishment of a psi state, the trial periods being too short. She scored
nothing in four subsequent timed sessions, but achieved dramatic
scores (36.4 mV and 140.0 mV) in two later self-paced sessions,
the latter score being the highest of any subject in any session,
timed or self-paced.

Subject M.B. achieved a score of 2.4 in session 1; 0
in sessions 2 and 3; 2.4 mV in session 4; 0 in 5; 14.6 in
session 6; 41.3 in session 7; 6.8 in 8; 17.5 in 9; 31.5 in 10;
86.4 in 11; and 139.6 in 12. Overall, this subject's performance
shows a clear incline.

Discussion. The experimenter was nondirective and subjects
were encouraged to develop their own PK-facilitating strategies even
if the experimenter felt that they would be ineffective. Subjects'
strategies differed widely. Self reports revealed that S.D. utilized
an effortful form of concentration, M.H. used a visualization technique, P.W. adopted a prayerful orientation and sought to enlist the
spirit of her deceased son, while H.H. first concentrated and later
adopted a less effortful orientation. M.B. reported a complete with-
drawal of attention from the environment and a passive, confident,
and effortless concentration state which was resistant to frustration.

Several self-paced sessions were held with all subjects after
they had completed the twelve formal sessions. In discussion all
subjects felt that the timing cassette had been inhibitory and that its
trial periods and session length were too short. When self paced,
subjects tended to adopt effort periods of ten minutes. Subjects
M.B., P.W., and H.H. all achieved higher scores in self-paced
sessions than during any of their cassette-timed sessions. It would
appear that self pacing although in some respects methodologically
unsatisfactory may allow subjects time to develop psi states and
may also add an important and relevant component to their motivation.

The fact that the three subjects found by mass screening had
not previously noted their PKMB ability prior to screening is encouraging since screenings have suggested that some 5% of the population tested shows some level of PKMB ability. This indicates
that there may be a substantial population of PKMB trainees potentially available.

It is interesting to note that in this first study, which was
tentative in a number of respects, one of the five subjects showed
a striking incline in performance, an uncommon occurrence in
parapsychological research, and three of the other four showed increases in output, even if inconsistently maintained.

Future PKMB training studies are planned in which subjects will be loaned micro-PKMB instrumentation for home practice and in which self pacing will be employed. The development of effective PK facilitating attentional strategies may also aid in promoting more consistent inclines in subjects' performances which would establish micro-PKMB as a definitely improvable PK ability.

THE PROBLEM OF PSEUDO-PKMB AND THE DISTRIBUTION OF PKMB

Jürgen Keil (University of Tasmania)

In all areas of parapsychological research problems exist. But there are indications that parapsychologists as well as critics are relatively more concerned with problems in macro-PK research than in other areas of our field. Particularly on the basis of the 1981 PA convention there is some justification for this view. Although it is difficult to compare problems in different areas I suggest that we have the same chance of overcoming problems in macro-PK research as in any other problem area; the following discussion suggests that we might tend to overrate the difficulties associated with macro-PK research.

Why, then, are we more concerned about macro-PK? Here are seven suggestions that subsequently will be discussed in more detail: (1) Fear of macro-PK, perhaps at a level below awareness. (2) Pseudo-PK based on trickery or other factors. (3) Recorded demonstrations of faked macro-PK. (4) Poor investigations. (5) Sensationalism surrounding macro-PK. (6) Less promising research strategies associated with macro-PK. (7) Expectations that particular research areas in parapsychology can already be regarded as more successful than macro-PK research.

No matter how interested we are as experimenters in observing macro-PK, the actual experience is probably not an altogether desirable one, even at the conscious level. We are not really in favor of living in a world where our physical environment can misbehave in a decidedly odd manner. It seems reasonable, therefore, to agree with Batcheldor (JSPR, 1966, 499-536; Psychoenergetic Systems, 1979, 77-93) that fears at a level below awareness may be quite common even among parapsychologists. We should keep this possibility in mind when we become particularly critical of macro-PK.

Pseudo-PK may be based on misperceptions of normal events that are either deliberately set up to appear like real PK events or occur under conditions where mistakes are made without any deliberate trickery. It is difficult to judge whether the risk of trickery is higher in macro-PK compared to other areas of research. It is not surprising, though, that critics put enormous emphasis on this possibility because in many macro-PK cases--particularly when cine or video recording exists--trickery remains the only basis on which the phenomena can be rejected. As parapsychologists we may also be alarmed because in connection with macro-PK, trickery has not infrequently been reported or suggested and is nearly always claimed by our critics. This may be partly due to the risks we take when entertainers or publicity-seeking individuals are investigated, and generally speaking, we are well advised to stay away from them. Occasionally we may almost be forced into a situation (from what might be called a psychohygiene point of view) to investigate claims that have already entered into public debates. Frequent exposures of manipulations in PK investigations--even when such discoveries are made by parapsychologists--are not the sort of news that is likely to encourage increased research activities. Nevertheless there are also indications that faults in investigations of this kind are relatively easily detected. In experiments that require a statistical evaluation, on the other hand, we must expect that significant results will occasionally occur by chance but there is little hope that we can ever detect such errors with any real confidence.

At the 1981 PA convention I had the impression that some parapsychologists were further swayed against macro-PK on account of video recordings which showed that public audiences can be easily fooled into accepting manipulations as real PK. These manipulations were revealed by an entertainer who probably derives most of his publicity from debunking parapsychology and other fields which seem to disturb him. Yet what was revealed in 1981 was not different from what was revealed in 1974 (Psychology Today, July, 74ff.) and was decidedly crude. To control such manipulation does not require a higher order of sophistication in our precautionary procedures compared to other research areas of parapsychology.

At the 1981 PA convention misgivings about macro-PK were probably also due to reports by parapsychologists that suggested inadequate controls. A clear distinction should be made between results that are presented as tentative and with clear references to control problems as against those that are presented with confidence in spite of inadequacies. We should certainly be concerned about the latter ones, particularly if discussions of certain possible control problems are rejected out of hand. The matter becomes less clear, though, when it is suggested that only tightly controlled PK investigations should be reported at all. Any restrictions with respect to controls should be clearly stated but some investigations which remain inconclusive because of such limitations should nevertheless be reported as they may convey useful information for further work. What can be regarded as useful information is difficult to define and I am simply pleading that potentially interesting reports should not be rejected or ignored because they may look foolish to some critics of parapsychology. In contrast to public statements it seems likely (see "Star Baby," Fate, 1981 [Oct.] 1-32) that some critics are not interested in rational discussion and an open scientific inquiry but are mainly concerned with rejecting and debunking the fields with which they do not agree. In some circumstances it may well be prudent to be concerned about the image of the field but if parapsychologists tend to become more and more influenced by such concerns, the fanatical critics will have achieved partial success in suppressing discussions about some aspects of the field.

Negative attitudes may also be due to assumptions by some parapsychologists that macro-PK research caters to sensational publicity. It has to be recognized that any macro-PK results, even if presented in cautious, sober terms, are likely to create more excitement among the public and representatives from the media than, for instance, statistically evaluated card tests. It would be a pity if justifiable concern about public relations is obscured by expressing general misgivings about macro-PK.

It is sometimes suggested that small effects are likely to provide a better basis for progress in parapsychology. Some justification for this view can be derived from fears that experimenters and participants alike may feel when they are confronted with macro-PK events. Batcheldor has reasonable suggestions as to how these fears may be reduced and this will be discussed separately at this convention. However, it is also time to question the term "macro-PK," which I have used only in connection with the 1981 PA convention. I would strongly suggest abandoning this term altogether. Any distinction between micro and macro is arbitrary and any micro effect could be incorporated in an appropriate system in such a way that macro consequences could be observed. In 1976 (PSPR, 197-235) we introduced a term which I regard as more appropriate if distinctions between classes of PK events are to be made. We distinguished between directly observable PK events and statistically inferred PK events. In the latter category a particular single event can never be clearly based on PK. Directly observable PK events do not need to be large in magnitude and Isaacs' and Hasted's papers include examples of rather small-scale, directly observable PK. Perhaps one reason why the term "directly observable PK" has not become well established is that it is a rather awkward one and it may be of help to introduce an acronym such as DOPK or PKDO. It would not be unreasonable, though, to think of direct PK (directly observable being understood) and to use just one additional letter in the acronym, that is, DPK, and this version I shall use from now on.

Returning briefly to the question of research strategies, there may well be advantages in investigating small-scale events in DPK. It is nevertheless also of some importance for the development of theories in our field to research the upper limits of the physical aspects of DPK.

Finally there is also the question of how far success in other areas of parapsychological research has already clearly indicated in what direction the field should move and what kind of approaches should now be abandoned. I must confess that I do not share the confidence of those who make such positive claims, even though I hope they are correct in their assessment. With only a handful of parapsychologists working full time we have far less long-term research in particular areas than seems desirable. Nevertheless, keeping in mind the peculiar relationship that individual experimenters seem to establish with the questions they investigate, I would at present be reluctant to discourage research in any particular area of our field.

Perhaps I would be less positive about PKMB as a particular section of DPK if I did not have some confidence that the Batcheldor approach and the screening methods employed by Isaacs might not enable us to generate these phenomena more frequently than has generally been possible in the past. This raises the question of the distribution of PKMB. Recent surveys in Europe suggest that PKMB ability is more widely distributed than may be expected on the basis of directly observable PK and poltergeist cases (RIP 1974, 69-71; EJP, 1979, 21 35; ZP, 1975, 219-240; ZP, 1976, 1-20). However, PKMB requires a set of psychological conditions which do not frequently occur spontaneously. Even after PKMB phenomena have occurred they cannot be readily repeated without such conditions (EJP, 1979, 21-35).

What might be called psi ability is widely and probably continuously distributed (EJP, 1980, 177-183; ZP, 1982, 83-93). With respect to PKMB my evaluation is mainly based on a field study which I conducted in Germany and Switzerland in 1978. Since not one of the persons contacted was able to demonstrate DPK, I could only estimate any possible previous PK on a post hoc basis. Such an evaluation necessarily includes subjective elements. Nevertheless, my suggestion that probably more than 5% of the sample had experienced genuine PK is in reasonable agreement with Isaacs' findings and with expectations based on the Batcheldor induction theory. It would be justified to question whether any of the cases in my sample were genuine at all and no answer in conclusive terms is possible. A number of details which emerged from the field study (EJP, 1979, 21-35) nevertheless support my fairly positive estimation (the exact percentage is of no great concern as long as it remains of some substance).

In spite of attempts by some public entertainers and others to debunk all PKMB cases, I believe we have good evidence that DPK is even more widely distributed in the general population than parapsychologists are generally inclined to accept, but there is also good evidence that particular psychological conditions have to exist or have to be created to insure that the phenomena will occur. The concepts developed by Batcheldor, the screening methods developed by Isaacs, and the instrumentation developed by Hasted seem to provide practical opportunities to make DPK phenomena available for investigations.

PKMB RESEARCH WITH PIEZOELECTRIC SENSORS

John B. Hasted,† David Robertson, and Peter Arathoon (Birkbeck College, University of London)

In our experience (JSPR, 1976, 365-383; JSPR, 1977, 583-607; JSPR, 1979, 9-20; JSPR, 1980, 379-398; JSPR, 1981, 75-86; ZP, 1979, 173) by far the most suitable experimental methods of investigating paranormal metal-bending are those in which the detection of psychokinetic effects at a metal target is achieved without the target being touched by the subject to whom it is exposed. Such an exposure requires careful observation of the subject during the entire experimental session. We describe experiments we have carried out during the past year on the detection of paranormal metal-bending signals in the presence of metal-bending subjects Stephen North, Heloise Gr., and Willie G.

The simplest physical quantity whose paranormal variation can be observed is strain, or physical deformation of the otherwise stable metal target; this can be either temporary (dynamic or elastic) or permanent (beyond a yield point). Visual observation of strain is insensitive, but transducers are available by means of which even micro-strains, proportional changes of dimension $\Delta \ell / \ell \simeq 10^{-6}$, can be detected as electrical signals, or voltages. The simplest of these is the resistive strain gauge, with which much paranormal metal-bending information has been obtained.

Another transducer suitable for such observations is piezoelectric material, particularly piezoelectric ceramics such as lead zirconate titanate (PZT). These have much greater sensitivity than the resistive strain gauge, strains as small as $\Delta \ell / \ell \simeq 10^{-10}$ being readily detectable. The background noise from a resistive strain gauge, with its attendant bridge, amplifier, and chart recorder, is electrical in origin, but with a piezoelectric sensor, amplifier, and chart recorder the acoustic sensitivity is so high that the background noise can be dominated by acoustic contributions.

In piezoelectric material the inherent electric charges are separated when mechanical stress is applied to produce a strain. The material is a good insulator, but has metal electrodes covering two opposing faces, and when first prepared commercially a high voltage is temporarily applied between these electrodes so that the material becomes "poled." On the subsequent application of stress perpendicular to these electrodes, a difference of electric charge is produced between the electrodes, this difference being proportional to the stress.

Unfortunately, its high resistance makes it almost useless for detection of paranormal metal-bending signals without modifica-

---

† - Dagger denotes speaker throughout this book.

tion. Even with some electrical screening an electrometer amplifier input terminal is enormously sensitive to stray electric charge, arising from triboelectric effects, atmospheric ions, and even paranormal (otherwise inexplicable) electrical effects (JSPR, 1981, 75-86). Experience suggests that exposed targets connected to high impedance electrometer amplifiers do not with certitude remain electrically stable.

We therefore virtually short-circuit the piezoelectric, whose capacitance is C, by connecting it across a low resistance (R = 3.5 kΩ). In this way the charge leaks away very rapidly, so that an amplifier and slow response chart recorder only records a very small fraction of it; most of the sensitivity is lost but there is ample to spare. The time constance for the leakage is RC, 3.5 kΩ x 500 pF = 1.75 μs. Owing to the slow response (0.1 s) chart recorder, we therefore lose a factor of about a hundred thousand in sensitivity. Moreover, since the voltage across R is recorded by the amplifier, it is the current through R that determines the signal; the current is proportional to the first differential of the stress with respect to time, that is, to the rate of flow of charge. It follows that a rapid elastic dynamic strain, such as a sharp tap on the specimen with a pencil, is recorded not as a single "peak," which would be the case for a resistive strain gauge, but as a peak in one direction immediately followed by a peak in the other direction.

With this arrangement of piezoelectric the sensitivity is not to be defined in terms of signal per unit stress, but rather in terms of signal per unit rate of variation of stress. Shocks produced by falling weights show sufficiently fast variation for them to be recorded more sensitively than they are with a resistive strain gauge. Falling weight calibration of our own system is as follows: 5 g falling through 10 mm onto the end of the piezoelectric produces an 8 mV chart recorded signal.

The signal across the 3.5 kΩ resistor is amplified by TD 1034A operational amplifier of gain 100, before chart recording. With this arrangement, the manufacturer's static calibrations cannot be used, although it can be shown that our experiments are consistent with them. For their piezoelectric strain gauge BSG/1-1 (length 9.5 mm, width 1.6 mm, thickness 0.3 mm) Messrs. Vernitron give a figure of 2.2×10^5 V / strain and capacitance 500 pF. For the ceramic PZT5A the appropriate piezoelectric constant is given as 2×10^{-2} V/m for unit stress 1 N/m^2.

The piezoelectric is mounted on or in the metal specimen, together with its electrical connections, using epoxy-resin. It is then further insulated with epoxy-resin and electrically screened with layers of conducting paint, which connects to the metal itself and to the screening sheath of the electrical leads; variation of the capacitance of the latter produces signals, so that they must be carefully hung and not touched, and kept as short as possible. For comparison of piezoelectric with a resistive strain gauge, the latter is mounted on the back face of the metal, opposite the piezoelectric.

Another experimental method has been to expose to the subject a larger block of piezoelectric ceramic (50 mm x 7 mm x 7 mm) without attaching it to a metal specimen. Electrical screening is still important, and this is conveniently done with a solid plastic coat covered with conducting paint.

The environment of the experimental sessions with Stephen North and with Willie G. has been an isolated basement physics laboratory in Birkbeck College. Both subjects had previous experience of visiting the laboratory for experimental sessions. The sessions with Heloise Gr. were carried out in the living room of the family house in a West Country town, since these were the first experiments in which the subject had participated. All sessions were held in the afternoon.

Within the basement physics laboratory an electrically screened room of dimensions 2.25 m x 1.6 m x 2.2 m high was constructed of 0.7 mm aluminium sheet. Care was taken to make good electrical contact between the individual metal sheets and especially to the metal sheet which formed the floor. A door 0.9 m x 2 m high was constructed of expanded aluminium with diamond-shaped apertures of axes 30 mm and 15 mm. Tests were made of the attenuation of commercial radio signals with door open and door closed. Since the screened room was in a basement laboratory and the door faced solid ground, the attenuation was only slightly affected by closing the door. This enabled us to conduct the exposure of the specimens to the subject while he was seated inside the room and observed through the expanded aluminium door, either open or closed. The mounting of the specimens was by elastic suspension from a stand which was sufficiently rigid and heavy for no signal to be produced if the stand was touched or jogged.

The protocol of the experiments has been as follows: (1) The equipment is allowed to run in the absence of the subject for a period of about 30 minutes. An experimenter must be present for part of this time and must enter the screened room and sit in the subject's chair. No signals must be recorded during any of this period. Any drifting exhibited in the chart record is adjusted by the chart recorder zeroing control. (2) The equipment must contain a "dummy channel" (JSPR, 1979, 9-20). This is an unscreened input resistance exposed within the screened room and connected to a separate amplifier channel and chart recorder channel. All amplifiers are battery-operated, but it is possible, at least outside the screened room, for electrical mains pulses to reach the circuitry despite screening. Such a pulse would show up on both dummy and sensor channels, so that such an appearance cannot be mistaken for a paranormal pulse. Inside the screened room, however, we have never observed pulses on the dummy channel. (3) With the equipment in a stable condition, and no pulses previously observed, the subject is earthed and introduced into a metal chair in the screened room. The instructions previously given to the subjects are to see if they can interact with the target or targets they see in front of them, thus producing signals on the chart recorders; they are told that they must not touch the target or electrical leads, and that they should report an inadvertent touch; no other instructions about what they do with their bodies are given. No violent movements have taken place, but a few inadvertent touches have been reported.

It is of course important that the experimenters observe the subject, and especially his or her hands and feet, during the time the subject is within reach of the specimens and leads.

It is the responsibility of the senior experimenter to terminate the session when he or she thinks that further work would not be profitable. Clearly the facts that influence such a decision are tiredness, success rate in producing signals, boredom, condition of the equipment, including possible permanent bends on the specimen, electrical failure, or termination of chart paper roll.

Two series of experiments have been carried out. One series, on seven dates in 1981, was conducted with both resistive strain gauges and with piezoelectric sensors in order to compare their relative effectiveness. A total of 194 signals was recorded, of which only 53 appeared on strain gauge specimens. The piezoelectric sensor is at least as effective as the resistive strain gauge.

In the second series of experiments, Stephen North was, in the opinion of the experimenters, already producing sufficient signals to encourage the belief that he would succeed with a timing control experiment. Stephen was then asked to say, "One, two, three, go," and attempt to produce a signal on the word "go"; he could do this however frequently or infrequently he liked, and could choose the times when he did it.

Signals occurring more than about four seconds prior to "go" are of course open to the objection that Stephen might hear the pen move, and immediately start to say, "One, two, three, go," so as to claim a certain measure of success. There have, however, been no such signals, other than signals designated "spontaneous," and after these Stephen did not attempt to count.

The results of three 1981 sessions, on October 30 and November 13 and 19, were as follows:

Failures to obtain any signal: 20, 1, and 15, respectively.

Spontaneous signals, occurring without any cue: 6, 2, and 7, respectively.

Early signals: 9, 22, and 9, respectively, averaging 1.1 seconds, 1.1 seconds, and 1.4 seconds early, respectively.

Late signals: 11, 7, and 6, respectively, averaging 1.8 seconds, 8.2 seconds, and 6.2 seconds late, respectively.

A NEW ISRAELI METAL-BENDER (WITH FILM)

H. C. Berendt (Jerusalem)

The purpose of this filmed presentation is to provide documentation of paranormal metal-bending by a young male Israeli, Rony M., aged 23 years. In the presence of a varying number of observers (two to six), including F. S. Rothschild, Professor Emeritus (Psychiatry) at the Hebrew University of Jerusalem-Hadassah Medical School; Dr. J. Schossberger, former director of the Givat Sha'ul Mental Hospital, Jerusalem, as well as other M.D.s and M.A.s; the writer witnessed the bending of spoons, forks, Yale keys; metal rods of different materials, lengths, and strengths; as well as coins and aluminum tubes, and, more recently, plastic spoons. All the items were supplied--without exception--by the experimenter and/or the observers, never by the subject.

Super 8mm Cinefilm was used when there was a chance of filming a single process within the three minutes' running time, without interruption. Since Rony M. did indeed manage to start and end the metal-bending process well within that time--indeed, sometimes within 20 to 50 seconds--we were able to film a number of complete processes without any interruption.

Some remarks about the film production would appear to be in order: (1) The film was not made under laboratory conditions, and slow-motion photography was not possible. The film was shot in a private flat. The main point was to ensure that the continuous observation of the subject should not be disturbed by disrupting the home-like atmosphere that seemed to facilitate the events that we witnessed. (2) Changing the position of the camera during the filming was kept to a minimum, priority being given to uninterrupted filming. (3) The ideal would have been the use of noiseless videotapes, synchronized from various angles. (4) Although I hope to be able to achieve this kind of documentation at a later date, I wish at the same time to express my doubts about the easiness with which that goal can be realized. The more one refines the details intended to make verification more assured and foolproof, the more thoroughly the process itself is observed, the less chance there may conceivably be for paranormal metal-bending--actually, an act of creation, like that of an artist--to occur. It may well turn out that "tightening up the conditions" may entail a failure to get a PK result at all. "Aha! When you have tight conditions you don't obtain any results because the whole thing is fraudulent!"--harboring such a view is as stupid and shortsighted as putting T. S. Eliot in a surgical operating theater, telling him that he has 17 minutes to write a poem, then exclaiming while looking at the (probably) empty page in his hand, "Aha! He is not a poet at all!"

No film can ever furnish proof, but for those who are well acquainted with parapsychology and the difficulty of documenting its different phenomena, the present film will nevertheless provide more information than I can provide for those witnessing this really "unbelievable" PK process for the first time.

By way of a résumé, I would like to mention the following remarks as regards the results obtained in our experiments on metal-bending: (1) Paranormal metal-bending is a fact, a reality. It is executed without physical force, without the application of heat, and without fraud or sleight of hand. (2) Changes of form and structure do occur when gifted persons have the will or intention (and give expression thereto) to bring about such changes. (3) There are documented cases in which no bodily contact of any kind exists between the subject and the object whose form is made to undergo change. (4) There are cases in which the bending process continues after the subject stops "treating" the object. (5) Any theory based on viewing metal-bending as a purely physical phenomenon will certainly prove to be too limited in scope. (6) It would be equally wrong to regard such a PK event as metal-bending as a purely psychological phenomenon. (7) It seems necessary to look upon metal-bending as a process involving psychophysical relations. (8) In my opinion, the Biosemiotic model developed by Prof. F. S. Rothschild, the Jerusalem psychiatrist, constitutes the nearest approach yet to an all-embracing theory, inter alia including paranormal metal-bending processes, entertaining as it does the possibility of influence on inanimate so-called dead matter (e. g., metallic molecules) being exerted by human brain activity in an on-going evolutionary development. (9) If proof of genuine precognition in parapsychology has required the necessity of facing new aspects of the problem of mind and time, proof of the genuineness of psychokinetic metal-bending requires a new orientation in connection with the question of mind and matter.

THE BATCHELDOR APPROACH*

CONTRIBUTIONS TO THE THEORY OF PK INDUCTION FROM SITTER-GROUP WORK**

Kenneth J. Batcheldor (Exeter, England)

A sitter group is a small, semi-informal group that attempts to develop paranormal physical phenomena by meeting repeatedly under conditions that resemble those of a Victorian spiritualistic séance--but (typically) without spiritistic assumptions and without a medium. The phenomena, such as rapping noises and levitation of tables, in so far as they may be paranormal, are interpreted in terms of the PK abilities of the sitters. I have reviewed the results of several such groups elsewhere (Psychoenergetic Systems, 1979, 77-93).

Two main assumptions underlie this approach: (1) that the ability to produce macroscopic PK is widely if not universally distributed, albeit in latent form, and (2) that séance-like conditions, in certain respects, are highly psi-conducive. It follows that by meeting under the appropriate conditions many ordinary people should be able to develop macro-PK, and sitter groups should provide a valuable source of strong PK for study.

Unfortunately, validation presents a serious problem. In the presence of tight controls the phenomena show a tendency to weaken or vanish. This is highly suspicious, of course, but it does not necessarily mean that no such phenomena exist, for it may be the case that tight controls (especially with novice subjects) interfere with the psychological conditions necessary for the strong manifestation of psi. If we assume the latter, then in order to encourage the phenomena to occur it would seem best--at least temporarily--to deliberately adopt loose conditions. Study of the ostensible phenomena may then reveal clues as to why they are sensitive to controls, and thus lead eventually to ways of validating them under strict conditions.

---

*Organized by Julian Isaacs (University of Aston, Birmingham, England); chaired by Rhea A. White (Parapsychology Sources of Information Center)
**Delivered by Julian Isaacs

On this basis a number of hypotheses concerning macro-PK have emerged. Many of these are generalizable to other areas of psi research, so it should be possible to test them without necessarily running a sitter group. Work in this direction has already begun (e.g., Isaacs, Palmer, Hess, Giesler, and others). The remainder of the paper surveys these hypotheses together with some of their ramifications. (In this abstract this material is much abridged.)

Physical Factors. The effect of physical factors seems to be indirect, and to depend solely on how they affect the psychological state of the sitters. Very heavy targets, for instance, are probably more difficult to influence only because they are perceived as presenting more difficulty.

Light. The adverse effect of light on such phenomena as levitation is probably not due to any physical property of light as such, but to analytical or other disturbing thoughts provoked by clear observation of the paranormality. Darkness reduces this tendency, and probably helps in other ways, too; for instance, it assists the operation of artifacts (see below).

Belief. Belief at the very instant when a PK event is expected is much more important than the long-term belief that existed beforehand. This "instant" belief should be "pure," or totally free from doubt, in order for PK to occur. This is difficult to achieve voluntarily and seems to happen most often involuntarily--in response to external suggestion from an artifact. However, verbal suggestion or autosuggestion can sometimes work. Tests and controls almost inevitably introduce an element of doubt, so success in their presence is much more difficult. Strictly speaking, belief is relevant only to consciously attempted PK.

Artifacts. These are normal events that tend to be mistaken for paranormal events. Since they have the same impact as genuine successes they powerfully stimulate belief, which in turn seems to release genuine phenomena. In a typical sitting many artifacts occur spontaneously, the most frequent being movements of the table produced by unconscious muscular action. Introducing artifacts deliberately (which amounts to deception) is therefore normally unnecessary, though this also works--trickery is probably psi-conducive. The effect of artifacts is so important that if they are very thoroughly prevented or exposed, development may be extremely slow or may not take place at all. This is another reason for sensitivity to controls.

Labile target systems as discussed by Braud (JASPR, 1980, 297-318) are probably easier to influence by PK than inert systems because their movements often act like artifacts. A table set in motion by unconscious muscular action is clearly a labile target.

Emotional Resistance. People can be upset by witnessing macro-PK events ("witness inhibition") or by possessing the power to produce them ("ownership resistance"). They then tend to behave in various defensive ways, such as making negative remarks and trying to explain everything away, which of course interferes with development. Reduction of resistance comes about through gradual desensitization during the course of many sittings, but it can also be relieved by avoiding clear observation (e.g., by sitting in dim light or darkness) and by encouraging plenty of noise, laughter, and chatter of a trivial kind.

Clear validation of paranormality under watertight conditions would obviously raise resistance to a maximum. In anticipation of this, rising resistance tends to disrupt the PK process and so prevent the validation from happening. Even if validation occurs by chance, it tends to arouse retrospective resistance which makes it difficult to repeat. This suggests that watertight demonstrations, even if possible, will not quickly win over the critics of psi.

When PK occurs without awareness, resistance is avoided completely, but since the events make no impact they have no reinforcing value.

Feedback. Immediate sensory feedback is conceived to be important in order to stimulate and reinforce belief. This differs from the usual concept of feedback as supplying corrective information. In the present view, we do not have to learn how to perform PK, but only how to get into the right state of mind to release it. Unfortunately, as belief builds up, so does resistance, so some juggling of the conditions is necessary in order to achieve the one without the other. These statements apply only to consciously attempted PK. In unconscious PK, sensory feedback (other than to inform someone of the outcome) is probably unnecessary.

Voluntary Control. Results in a sitter group are mostly intermittent and freakish, with sitters having little control over what happens. This can be attributed to their difficulty in controlling their thoughts (doubts, resistances, etc.) and their consequent dependence on accidental external suggestions from artifacts. A limited and indirect control is possible in that verbal requests or suggestions are sometimes complied with, and, with practice, it is possible for a good spokesman to secure complete "obedience" from the table (e.g., it will levitate on command, but otherwise remain still). But such control is still indirect rather than truly voluntary. Special experiments in which the sitters attempted to make their minds blank and to observe in a passive manner resulted in prolonged levitations and apparently direct control over the target's movements by thought. This was very difficult to perform, but seemed to represent true voluntary control.

"Divided" and "Blended" States. In a normal state of consciousness there is a division between the conscious and unconscious domains. Let us call this the "divided" state. The conscious cannot influence unconscious processes by direct effort, but can do so indirectly by issuing firmly believed-in suggestions. This is sometimes successful and sometimes not, and corresponds to the usual erratic, indirect control over PK. But if the conscious mind is extremely passive it seems able to influence the unconscious smoothly and directly. I call this the "blended" state, for it is as if the conscious partially blends with the unconscious. It seems similar to states aimed at in yoga and Zen, and apparently allows voluntary control of PK (and perhaps other psi abilities as well).

Conditions that are favorable to PK in one of these states are not necessarily so in the other; e.g., distraction can be favorable in the divided state but is usually adverse in the blended state.

Suggestion. Most PK is attempted in the divided state, and many features of the doctrine of suggestion (as described in older books) seem to apply to this process very well. For successful suggestion, an idea of the desired goal must be planted in the subconscious without being hindered in the slightest degree by such oppositional thoughts as doubts and fears. Hence the necessity for exceptionally pure belief and freedom from resistance. The recent parapsychological finding that egocentric effort is bad for PK was anticipated in the "Law of Reversed Effort." The recent view that PK is goal-oriented rather than means-oriented is allowed for in that suggestion is a goal-oriented process. That is, once the idea of the goal has been planted, the subconscious takes care of the means by which it will be "realized." Hypnosis should be eminently psi-conducive, but resistance, as well as belief, in both experimenter and subjects should be taken into account.

Further replication of sitter-group results is required, but not all experimenters will feel able to adopt the necessary approach. Moreover, groups are difficult to hold together. But many of the theoretical ideas are independent of the method and could be tried in other fields.

VARIATIONS ON A THEME FROM BATCHELDOR: A VARIETY OF THEORIES REGARDING THE INDUCTION OF PK

James McClenon (University of Maryland, Asian Division) and Rhea A. White (Parapsychology Sources of Information Center)

This paper compares various themes developed from Batcheldor's theories of sitter-group PK and those of the Society for Research on Rapport and Telekinesis (SORRAT). This comparison suggests that assumptions in both models may affect the phenomena that the sitter groups experience (even to the extent of thwarting or increasing the effects). It also raises a dilemma for science: the possibility that the less scientific theories may be more successful in terms of inducing PK than those that are more carefully constructed and parsimonious. A theory's aesthetic quality, or its

The Batcheldor Approach

innate appeal to the sitters, may be more instrumental in producing phenomena than its scientific validity.

Batcheldor's theory contains three major elements: (1) the artifact means of induction, (2) the role of suggestion in producing PK, and (3) the nature of resistance to PK. Batcheldor's theories regarding PK in sitter groups were derived from his study of the factors that appeared to be important in the induction and shaping of the sorts of phenomena he obtained. He hypothesizes that the "release of macro-PK phenomena (and maybe of psi in general) is dependent on a certain state of mind characterized by exceptional belief and expectation, and that in practice this state is usually attained for the first time in only one way; that is, by the impact of normal events fortuitously mistaken for paranormal events" ("Macro-PK in group sittings," unpubl., p. 44). An underlying assumption is that physical phenomena are actually a form of human behavior, one that is quite sensitive to outside intrusion.

Batcheldor has described means by which individuals tend to thwart the production of PK. There is an in-built reluctance to identify oneself directly as the source of paranormality (ownership resistance) and a deep-seated emotional reaction that occurs when individuals observe an event that is unequivocally paranormal (witness inhibition). Batcheldor proposes that loosely controlled conditions and the admittance of artifactual phenomena may reduce this conflict by allowing the individual a normal explanation for paranormal events.

Another sitter group currently reporting ostensible macro-PK is the SORRAT group in Rolla, Missouri, originated in 1961 by the late poet and critic John G. Neihardt. In order to discover the beliefs of the SORRAT group in regard to PK induction, McClenon mailed a questionnaire to 38 members, 21 of whom responded. Although the members who responded revealed many opinions concerning the ostensible phenomena they had witnessed, they were unanimous in regarding its nature as authentically paranormal. The responses of the "core" group of SORRAT members were also fairly uniform regarding the roles of suggestion, rapport, need for total belief, and the source of the phenomena. Their belief systems are described in a recent book by J. T. Richards entitled <u>SORRAT</u> (1982).

There are a number of differences regarding sitter-group PK between the ideas of the SORRAT members and those of Batcheldor. Batcheldor holds that the PK produced in his group is most likely attributable to the sitters themselves, whereas the SORRAT members attribute paranormal effects to deceased entities who are able to break through a barrier from the "other side" at those times when the group achieves sufficient rapport. The Batcheldor group sits mainly in darkness; the SORRAT group sits in only semi-dark conditions. Rather than the total belief, faith, and expectations advocated by Batcheldor, Neihardt encouraged open-minded skepticism and scientific investigation. The SORRAT members base much of their theorizing on the statements of the ostensible entities themselves and use them as guides as to how to generate phenomena. Suggestion is central to Batcheldor's theory but secondary with the SORRATs. Artifact induction, a cornerstone of the Batcheldor approach, is not an aspect of SORRAT theory. Whereas Batcheldor explains lack of phenomena by means of witness inhibition and ownership resistance, the SORRAT entities speak of "psi trauma," a form of cognitive dissonance that skeptics experience when exposed to psi. They say they deliberately may tone down the phenomena in such cases, so as not to harm the psyches of the skeptics!

There are differences, also, in the effect participation has on the sitters themselves, and on their belief systems in regard to psi. Batcheldor (personal communication to McClenon, 1981) states that "only a very small percentage of the individuals were lucky enough to have any definite 'psi experiences' in these groups.... By far, the majority of my 'sitters,' therefore, have gone away unclear as to whether they have had any psi experiences or not. It is improbable, therefore, that they have experienced any change in their 'system of beliefs' regarding psi." On the other hand, all 21 SORRAT respondents to McClenon's questionnaire were quite definite in declaring that they had had psi experiences. Many wrote that their beliefs had been changed and that until their group experience, they had harbored skepticism or held no opinion at all.

Observation of the success of these two theoretical orientations reveals that the SORRAT group has achieved a far greater variety of ostensible phenomena, paid greater attention to the "message" of the phenomena (i.e., taken it seriously), changed the belief systems of more people, and produced experiences for more people than did the Batcheldor group. An irony exists in that various fraudlike effects have occurred during investigations of SORRAT phenomena. Brookes-Smith (in an unpublished paper entitled "Paranormality--Unusual Human Behavior," 1981, p. 10) speculated that the investigators may themselves be responsible (through their subconscious suggestions) for making mediums produce what seem to be spurious phenomena. This idea would be consistent with Batcheldor's theory. The possibility also exists that the so-called entities producing the SORRAT phenomena might produce ambiguous fraudlike effects in order to reduce the psi trauma of investigating skeptics as well as to reduce their level of scrutiny. Our inability to determine the ontological status of the phenomena produced by either the Batcheldor or SORRAT groups makes hypothesis-testing difficult. Nor, until the question of the survival of human personality after death is settled, can we evaluate the differences between the two orientations except insofar as they obtain results not explicable by any hypothesis save that of psi.

A third theory, proposed by McClenon, is possible. It attempts to combine both the ideas of Batcheldor and those of the Sorrats. This orientation would consider the ostensible psi as evidence of a paranormal form of consciousness with the following attributes: (1) It can take on some of the qualities of the sitters and will tend to do so. (2) Its ability to perform psi tasks is reduced by witness inhibition and ownership resistance. If it seeks to overcome these resistances, it may create ambiguous fraudlike effects (especially if held under scrutiny for extended periods of time). This reduces the psi-trauma of skeptics who conclude nothing is happening, thus allowing the phenomena to continue in the presence of believers. (3) If the orientation of the group allows for it, it can manifest attributes of deceased persons. These entities can be said to be "surviving" to the degree that these attributes are peculiar to specific individuals. (Although they do not survive "exactly" as when in the body, yet they cannot be said to be "totally dead.") In his poem "April Trilogy," John Neihardt declares "I am a part of my God as a raindrop is part of the sea." If there are aspects of human consciousness that transcend space and time (as the evidence regarding ESP seems to indicate) then it should not be surprising that these aspects can become apparent in the forms of consciousness that are produced through paranormal means.

This third theory or theme suggests that these forms of consciousness may be induced by numerous means such as suggestion, deep rapport, extreme crisis, dreams, meditation, deep relaxation, and so forth. The possibility that both the induction process and the type of phenomena produced depend, to a degree, on the form of consciousness being sought should not be dismissed. If the induction process is dependent simply upon suggestion, as Batcheldor theorizes, then the possibility exists that only those forms of consciousness and those types of phenomena will be produced that are in line with that hypothesis. (In fairness to Batcheldor it should be pointed out that he has said that the phenomena in his group behaved as if they were produced by an entity, and sometimes it was easiest to treat it as such, but in theorizing he prefers to assume they were a product of the subconscious minds of his sitters.) It could be that other, more mystical means of induction, such as positing deceased entities or beings from outer space or religious figures such as saints or deified beings might lead to less limited forms of consciousness and be associated with more specialized types of phenomena. (It should also be pointed out that another link here with Batcheldor is that a theory that attributes its phenomena to some kind of "entity" has a built-in scapegoat, which of course would reduce ownership resistance.)

All these variations on a theme from Batcheldor contain components that lack measurability. Their value lies in their ability to motivate individuals to follow the "hints" or rules of procedure specified by their guidelines. To the degree that these assumptions produce ostensible psi, the means of induction can be said to have heuristic value. It may be that one theme cannot be said to be better or more scientifically valid than another. A theme or theory may "work" better for a group because it is more appealing, aesthetically, than others. Themes may be more akin to music than to scientific theories in the so-called hard sciences. They successfully induce PK when sung harmoniously and with vigor.

The paradox that confronts parapsychology is illustrated by these variations. Batcheldor himself is very aware that the seeming fact that his group, for example, requires darkness to achieve results is more likely due to psychological factors than to its being an ontological necessity. Others may require a more restricted and confining vehicle of expression in order to function. What we may have here in the sitter-PK situation is a case of what Ehrenwald long ago called "doctrinal compliance," a variation of the experimenter effect. In the following definition of doctrinal compliance offered by Ehrenwald, the word "sitter" has been substituted for "patient" and "experimenter" for "therapist" in order to highlight the relevance of this concept to the present situation. Doctrinal compliance is "compliance by the sitter with the experimenter's unconscious wishes and expectations regarding the validity of his theories, and their apparent confirmation by the sitter's productions. Doctrinal compliance is thus closely related to the familiar concept of suggestion, but differs from it by its essentially unconscious or unintentional nature" (Journal of the History of the Behavioral Sciences, 1966, 51-57).

We would like to close with a plea for open-mindedness toward both the phenomena we are investigating and the nature of the dynamic that is producing them. What seems to call out the phenomena is a construct that appeals personally to the participants. The philosophical implications of this possibility are beyond the scope of this paper yet the relationship between religious, aesthetic, and ethical values and the objective scientific ethos cannot be ignored forever--at least, not by us.

THE BATCHELDOR APPROACH: A CRITIQUE

Julian Isaacs (University of Aston, Birmingham, England)

Research into macro-PK has suffered from a chronic shortage of human sources for these effects. Given this shortage of gifted PK agents a fruitful strategy may be the development of PK training regimens which might in the long term provide a more plentiful supply of PK agents. Interest in this possibility has recently increased: I have already reported a study of micro-psychokinetic metal-bending training (see p. 31), Tart has discussed REG-based PK training (see p. 170), and Palmer has outlined an extensive project researching PK training combined with hypnotic facilitation (see p. 55).

However, Batcheldor's sitter-group technique (SGT) antedates these approaches (JSPR, 1966, 339-56) and differs from them in being based on a group rather than individuals. The technique derives from Batcheldor's theory of PK induction (see p. 45). It represents a dissection, analysis, and resynthesis in humanist form of proce-

The Batcheldor Approach

dures originating in spiritualist physical phenomena development circles. Batcheldor emphasizes the human, rather than discarnate, source of PK in such sittings and sees the PK induction process as dependent on psychological factors engendered by the group setting rather than upon the presence of recognizably mediumistic sitters.

Parapsychologists have been slow to adopt sitter-group technique. More interest is shown towards the theory which is separable from the sitter-group context and is generalizable to provide experimentally testable hypotheses. At present the SGT suffers from several major problems when viewed as a context for the study of psychological factors in PK compared to laboratory settings. Many of these disadvantages arise from the methodologically undeveloped state in which SGT at present exists, which in turn deters experimentalists from running groups. In previously reported work (Psychoenergetic Systems, 1979, 77-93) security has depended upon the testimony of the sitters, as sittings are usually held in the dark. However, it is now possible to utilize Infra Red sensitive videotape recording to obtain visual records of sittings. In addition, secure PK tasks could be developed, perhaps using remotely located REGs or other PK sensitive electronic systems. Security against fraud need not therefore remain at its present low level. Previous sitter groups have been marked by an absence of controlled means of manipulating psychological variables in sittings and have also suffered from a lack of rigorous data-collection techniques. These features, together with poor security against fraud, have slowed the acceptance of SGT. It remains for enterprising parapsychologists to develop SGT methodology to the point where it becomes an attractive prospect. This task will be made more difficult by the many purely practical difficulties inherent in SGT. Principal amongst these is the long sequence of sittings necessary before ostensible PK begins to occur. Nor can any guarantee be given that any particular group will achieve success. Although this is an inevitable risk in all parapsychological experimentation, the undeveloped state of SGT implies that without PK events to report and in the absence of controlled psychological conditions and data collection unsuccessful sittings produce no data output except the experiences of their participants, which are of limited use and reliability.

Another obstacle preventing the wider dissemination of SGT is the paucity of published material describing either the theory or SGT itself. What little has been published may well create confusion, because the accounts by Brookes-Smith seriously distort both theory and SGT (JSPR, 1973, 69-89) and Batcheldor's accounts have been misleadingly couched in terms of belief as the pivotal concept, rather than suggestion. Since this has frequently led to misinterpretation of his theory it may be worth briefly restating his central hypothesis.

Batcheldor hypothesizes that the PK agent must have, at some subconscious level of his or her mind, an idea of the goal state which his or her PK is to achieve. PK can be executed either in the "blended" state where normally subconscious levels of the psyche are joined with conscious levels to allow voluntary control to be exercised, or (much more commonly) in the "divided" state, where the goal state is communicated to the subconscious by some process of suggestion. A wide variety of different forms of suggestion can be effective, but Batcheldor's paradigmatic example has tended to be where a sitter suddenly experiences an overwhelming and involuntarily induced belief that some PK event is happening at that moment. Frequently this belief will have been induced by the sitter misconstruing some normal motion of the PK target object as being paranormal. This intense belief, if unopposed by counter beliefs or doubts, may then act as a suggestion triggering the sitter's subconscious to generate PK. This example is confusing because it focuses attention on the temporary state of total belief as being necessary for PK to occur, whereas in reality the "total belief" scenario is only one among a wide variety of induction-by-suggestion situations that Batcheldor's theory predicates. Explicit suggestions may be generated by statements made by group members and the situationally created beliefs and expectations of the sitters. Implicit suggestions can be created in sittings by the actions of the PK target object (usually a table) or by the sitters' behavior. Many of the suggestions accepted by the sitters will not be noticed by them and will therefore not figure in their account of the sitting and will certainly not involve introspectively accessible belief states.

Belief becomes of crucial significance in its negative aspect as disbelief. Doubt is more important than positive belief because it disposes sitters both to interpret PK target movements as being of normal origin, which creates countersuggestions to PK-creating suggestions, and also tends to lead to analytical thinking which is psi inhibitory. Maintaining belief in the imminent likelihood of PK activity is PK-conducive because in this state fewer countersuggestions tend to arise within the sitters and normal movements are more readily construed as being paranormal. Conscious expectation or belief that specific PK events will occur is not strictly necessary on Batcheldor's account because some of the unnoticed implicitly created suggestions may evoke PK quite independently of the conscious belief states of the sitters.

Batcheldor's central hypothesis regarding the place of suggestion in PK induction and the critical role that this confers upon the situationally created structure of implicit beliefs and suggestions within the social setting in which the PK events occur may be an important and fruitful insight which deserves being explored in formal experimentation.

His recognition of the widespread emotional resistance to overt displays of PK and their observation ("witness inhibition") leads to his explanation of the omnipresent elusiveness of psi which has been neglected by other theorists. Batcheldor has long emphasized the importance of passive, nonstriving attitudes in PK induction. He has proposed the induction-by-artifact model to explain the first onset of PK phenomena in sitter groups. This is an important construct of relevance to recent theorizing regarding labile versus inertial PK target systems (Braud, W. G., RIP 1979, 128-131). Labile systems tend to generate apparent signs of PK success which may lead subjects to construe themselves as successful before they truly are, so causing induction by artifact. Part of the success encountered in the use of randomly behaving PK target systems such as dice and REGs may be due to this effect. In the field of psychokinetic metal-bending informal observation strongly indicates the operation of the "shyness" factor and the displacement of PK from intended targets onto unintended ones. The contagion effects noted may be mediated by suggestion.

In my own mass screen procedure (Psychoenergetics, 1981, 37-64) for finding metal-benders, much of the approach derives from Batcheldor and full use is made of suggestion. The group to be screened is given a lecture, the covert purpose of which is to convince the audience of the reality of metal-bending, even if temporarily. If any spontaneous bending events take place during delivery of the lecture this news is presented so as to suggest that the effects will spread further in the group, which sometimes happens. The sitter group's recourse to regressive behavior is duplicated when the audience is encouraged to abandon its reserve and enjoy itself in an amusing way by trying to paranormally bend cutlery. The role of humor to defuse the tension of an encounter with PK and its use to relax, to prevent overstriving, and to block analytical thinking are identical in the sitter group and mass screening situations. So, too, is the use of PK task grading--a corollary of Batcheldor's analysis of the role of belief in PK. If a screenee perceives his or her cutlery as too difficult to bend, he or she is offered a replacement. This may seem a minor point, but Batcheldor's theory clearly predicts that removing this feature would reduce the yield of paranormal metal-bending agents found. Many other features of metal-bending show phenomena that appear to be consistent with predictions derived from the theory. Formal verification of these factors is planned.

If identified narrowly with a particular variety of macro-PK, Batcheldor's theory might unjustly be condemned with the phenomena from which it was derived. The theory is separable from sitter-group technique and although the future of SGT may remain unclear, the now increasing volume of material in print dealing with the theory should encourage parapsychologists to put hypotheses derived from it to experimental test. This seems likely to be a most fruitful exercise.

HYPNOSIS AND PSI: A RESEARCH PROGRAM RELATED TO THE THEORY OF KENNETH BATCHELDOR

John Palmer (University of Utrecht)

The origin of the research program I am about to describe

is my interest in the possible role of hypnosis in improving performance on psi tasks. Previous research has revealed what by parapsychological standards is a quite consistent tendency for hypnosis to improve the rate of scoring on ESP tests as compared to scoring in "waking" control conditions (e.g., JASPR, 1969, 214-252).

There are at least two classes of psi theories that can be proposed to account for this apparent relationship. The first is that hypnosis is successful because it produces a psi-conducive altered state of consciousness characterized by relaxation and focused attention. The second is that hypnosis is successful because it includes implicit or explicit suggestions that the subject is both capable and motivated to demonstrate psi in the task. Some support exists for both hypotheses, including indirect support from research not involving hypnosis (e.g., Ganzfeld research, "sheep-goat" research). The hypotheses are not mutually exclusive and both factors could be playing a role in hypnosis-psi experiments.

Our research program focuses on the second of these hypotheses, which stresses the "suggestion" aspect of hypnosis. The only theory in parapsychology that squarely addresses the suggestion factor is that of Kenneth Batcheldor. Of particular relevance is his concept of "total belief," an idealized temporary cognitive state in which the subject totally accepts the reality of psi and all discursive thoughts and doubts are effectively blocked. The principal objective of our project is to use hypnosis to help subjects achieve the closest possible approximation to this state and through it to achieve voluntary control of psi.

Although the basic ideas underlying our research closely follow those of Batcheldor, our method of implementing those ideas differ from his in some important respects. Batcheldor's approach in his work with sitter groups can be characterized as environment-centered (EC) in that the burden is placed on the environment to create the total belief. This emphasis is reflected in the stress placed on the role of "artifacts," physical stimuli of apparently normal origin that mimic psi effects. Our approach, on the other hand, is primarily person-centered (PC) in that the total belief is generated internally by the subject in response to hypnotic suggestions. Although the PC approach may be the more difficult road to total belief, it has the advantage of allowing for greater experimental control and the possibility of producing reliable psi in the presence of neutral or even skeptical observers. Such observers would seem incompatible with the context needed to effectively implement an EC approach.

Implementation of the PC approach requires subjects with an exceptional capacity to experience and identify with cognitions in response to hypnotic suggestions. I have labelled this trait "hypnotic imagination." We began our screening process by testing 150 volunteers, most of whom were students from the University of Utrecht. Most of these subjects completed three scales designed to measure different aspects of hypnotic imagination: the Tellegen Absorption Scale, the Creative Imagination Scale, and a ten-point rating scale of hypnotic depth completed following a 20-minute, live hypnotic induction by our project hypnotist, Dr. Ivo van der Velden. The latter two scales were completed in small group sessions of 8 to 16 persons. Scores on these instruments were standardized and averaged to produce a "hypnotic index." Thirty-two subjects with index (Z) scores of +.60 or greater were invited to participate in the second phase of the project, of whom 27 chose to do so.

Each of these subjects will complete from three to five sessions of individualized hypnotic training with Dr. van der Velden. Subjects who by the end of this training can achieve "dissociation," by which we mean the capacity to fully identify with the hypnotic suggestions and block out competing thoughts, will be graduated to the third phase of the project. Dr. van der Velden will prepare for each of these subjects an individualized hypnotic induction tape with suggestions for identifying with a "reality" supportive of total belief in psi.

In the third phase of the project, these subjects will be asked to participate in various psi tasks while under hypnosis. Although decisions as to what psi tasks to use will be governed in the final analysis by what seems most suitable for each subject, my inclination is to use primarily micro-PK. All ESP tests (but especially free-response tests) confound psi with subjects' (or judges') abilities to interpret their imagery. Thus PK tests provide a purer measure of psi for our purposes. Compared to macro-PK, micro-PK has the advantages of flexibility and ease of control. Although belief-supporting feedback from macro-PK tasks (e.g., a moving table) is in general more objectively dramatic than such feedback from micro-PK tasks, the important thing is how dramatic the feedback appears to subjects within their cognitive frames of reference. These are precisely what we seek to define by means of hypnosis.

We have developed a prototype PK game that fulfills the needs of the project. Our equipment is an APPLE II microcomputer connected to a color video monitor located in another room. The computer houses an electronic noise-based random event generator (REG) board developed by Dick Bierman. For each run, the computer writes the Dutch word LIEFDE (love) on the screen in a color of the subject's choosing. The speed with which the word is written is influenced by the REG. Subjects are given the hypnotic suggestion to identify with the idea that they are writing the word with their minds and to try to write the word as fast as possible. Thus, regardless of how fast or slow the word writes, the feedback is still consistent with the belief that the subject is functioning psychically.

Although environmental artifacts are not intended to play a major role in our research, we have made provision for introducing them at appropriate points to reinforce the induced state of belief. For example, our computer program can be modified to rapidly write a small chunk of the word whenever a predefined sequence of random digits is produced by the REG. The subject would see this as a momentary but striking success. Borrowing an idea from the shamanic traditions, we may give our subjects "power objects" (e. g., crystals) to hold during the game. Although our theory does not provide for altered states directly facilitating psi, it does provide for their having an indirect effect by reducing the capacity to engage in discursive, critical thinking. Thus, for example, we may have subjects listen to pink noise (a component of the Ganzfeld procedure) during the game. Finally, throughout the project a clinical approach will be used for identifying and overcoming possible resistances to psychic functioning.

In summary, our plan is to stick religiously to our basic theoretical rationale but to modify the implementation of that rationale as we go along to best fit the needs of individual subjects. Our ultimate (and admittedly quite ambitious) goal is to develop a standardized set of techniques for developing reliable psi in suitably suggestible persons.

ESP AND HYPNOTIC IMAGINATION: A GROUP FREE-RESPONSE STUDY

John Palmer (University of Utrecht) and Ivo van der Velden (Leiden, The Netherlands)

The principal purpose of this study was to screen volunteers for participation in future research on the basis of a trait we have labelled "hypnotic imagination." We define this trait as the capacity to experience and identify with cognitions in response to hypnotic suggestion.

The study also gave us the opportunity to explore hypnotic imagination in relation to scores in a free-response ESP test conducted in a group setting. Previous research with subjects tested individually has revealed some tendency for subjects highly susceptible to hypnosis to score more positively on FR-ESP tests preceded by hypnotic suggestions (e. g., JASPR, 1972, 86-102), but the number of such studies is small. Other research has suggested that different factors might influence the direction of the relationship between ESP scores and various altered states measures (e. g., JASPR, 1977, 121-145). Based on these data, we predicted that there would be a significant positive correlation between hypnotic imagination and ESP if the overall mean ESP score was above MCE and a significant negative correlation if it was below MCE.

We also tested a secondary hypothesis based on the observational theories. If psi occurs at the time of feedback or "observation" of the results, and if hypnosis is psi-facilitatory, then it would seem to follow that subjects who visually inspect their target pictures after the test while hypnotized should manifest more psi than those who observe them only in the "waking" state. Specifically, we predicted that among subjects who reported an above-average maximum level of hypnosis in response to a hypnotic induction, those who observed their targets while under the influence of this induction would score more positively on the ESP test than those who did not if the overall ESP mean (for all subjects) was positive. If the mean was negative, the relationship would be the reverse.

The subjects were 150 Dutch volunteers, mostly college students, of whom 85 were male and 65 were female. They were tested in 12 group sessions of 8 to 15 subjects each. Subjects were seated at tables in comfortable, cushioned, straight-back chairs with armrests. In some sessions the classrooms we had to use were not shielded from traffic noise, but we have no indications that this factor affected the results. We succeeded in maintaining an informal, relaxed atmosphere throughout.

The target pool consisted of 60 magazine photographs mounted on cardboard and reflecting mostly outdoor scenes. They were divided into 15 sets of four pictures each. Two persons not otherwise involved with the experiment (Brian Millar and Jerry Solfvin) each arbitrarily picked out one of 12 opaque envelopes containing a page of random numbers from the RAND tables. Each of these selectors prepared targets for 6 of the 12 sessions, randomly determined. Starting at the top left of the page, he determined for each session a sequence of 15 target numbers (1-4), the first number corresponding to Set 1, the second to Set 2, etc. A second randomization procedure based on shuffling a deck of cards determined which target was to be assigned to which subject number in a given session. Each target picture was then covered with a piece of black construction paper and sealed inside a manila envelope. On the front of each envelope had been pasted two sheets of paper (the bottom one a carbon) with a session and subject number written in the upper left corner. These envelopes were given in numerical order to J.P. before each session. The list of targets was given to Dr. Martin Johnson until the experiment had been completed.

The great majority of subjects filled out the Tellegen Absorption Scale (TAS) at home prior to the sessions. The sessions began with administration by tape recording of the Creative Imagination Scale (CIS), using a task-motivational instructional set. This was followed by a half-hour introductory talk on hypnosis by I.V. After this, a target envelope was placed on the desk in front of each subject. If there were fewer than 15 subjects in a session, the higher numbered envelopes were not used. Then commenced a 20-minute live hypnotic induction by I.V. using a standardized set of suggestions reflecting a non-authoritarian Eriksonian approach. Deepening suggestions were based on the metaphor of a road along which the subjects could reach up to ten points, each point representing a deeper level of hypnosis. The induction concluded with suggestions for obtaining imagery of the target. This was followed by a five-minute silent ESP reception period and suggestions for wakening.

Subjects were given as much time as needed to write or draw their impressions on the blank sheets of paper pasted on the envelopes. They then were asked to record their maximum level (1-10) of hypnotic depth (HD1) in the lower right corner, rip off the top sheet, and hand it in. Subjects then completed an eight-item "sheep-goat" scale adapted from Palmer (RIP 1972, 37-39).

The next step was for the subjects to remove the target pictures from the envelopes. In half the sessions, subjects were immediately rehypnotized with a brief five-minute induction and told to open their eyes and examine the picture carefully, looking for similarities to their imagery. In the other half of the sessions, subjects were asked to carry out this analysis prior to rehypnotization. Following suggestions for wakening, subjects were again asked to record hypnotic depth ratings (HD2) on the target envelopes and hand them in. Half of the sessions assigned to each selector were randomly chosen for each level of this manipulation (2 x 2 design), with the selectors blind to their designation.

After the last session, photocopies of all response sheets were made, such that names, HD1 ratings, and any other identifying information were absent. These were rearranged in 15 packets according to target sets and mailed to two outside judges, along with blank rating sheets and a detailed set of judging instructions similar to those used in previous studies by J. P. (e.g., JASPR, 1979, 333-348). The judges also were given in succession a set of prints made from the target pictures (not the pictures handled by the subjects). The judges' task was to blind-rate the degree of correspondence between each response sheet and the four pictures in the appropriate set on a 0-20 scale. Response sheets were rated set by set, the two judges doing them in reverse order.

The ratings sent back by one judge showed insufficient variability for scoring, as did those of another judge who was explicitly instructed to distribute his ratings more widely. Finally, a second judge was found who completed the task properly. Our final two judges, a clinical psychologist and a social psychology graduate student, both completed their tasks conscientiously.

Because for both judges the variability of ratings differed from set to set, the ESP Z-scores for each judge were computed by subtracting the mean of the four ratings for each response sheet from the rating given to the target and dividing by the standard deviation of all the ratings given by the judge to pictures in that set. The Z-scores of the two judges were then averaged to obtain the subject's ESP score.

Scores on the three measures of hypnotic imagination (i.e., TAS, CIS, and HD1) were converted to Z-scores and averaged to produce a hypnotic index (HI). The component scales intercorrelated as follows: TAS-CIS = +.46; TAS-HD1 = +.39; CIS-HD1 = +.46. All were $p < .001$ (two-tailed), using Pearson r.

The ESP scores assigned by our two judges correlated +.57, which in our experience is rather good for this task. However, the distribution of these scores was leptokurtic with a moderately extreme positive skew. The mean was -.08, which did not differ significantly from chance (i.e., 0) by single-mean t-test.

Because of the nonnormative distribution of the ESP scores, nonparametric tests were used whenever possible. The Spearman correlation between ESP scores and HI was +.08, which is nonsignificant and in the opposite direction from that predicted.

The "observer" manipulation was not properly implemented in session six, so data from that session were not included in the test of this hypothesis. Among subjects whose ratings on HD2 exceeded the mean of 3.25, the mean ESP score of those who observed their target pictures under hypnosis was +.07. The mean of the other high-HD2 subjects was -.00. The difference was not significant by U-test and in the opposite direction from prediction.

Before the ESP test was judged, the "sheep-goat" scale had been reduced to four subscales reflecting Palmer's four criteria and cut-off points established. Because most subjects were "sheep," the "goat" samples tended to be small. None of the four "sheep-goat" differences were significant by U-tests, with the goats scoring slightly higher on the crucial Criterion 1.

In summary, we found no evidence of psi in these data. Because of the assumed pressure of the screening situation and the distracting atmosphere inherent in group testing, we neither expected nor predicted overall significant scoring. However, we did expect that high hypnotic imagination subjects would be better able to overcome these distractions than low hypnotic imagination subjects, and that partly for this reason they would score better on the ESP test. This prediction was not borne out.

Part 2: Papers and Research Briefs

THE McDONNELL LABORATORY TEAM*

AN ESP DRAWING EXPERIMENT WITH TWO OSTENSIBLE PSY-
CHOKINETES (RB)**

Michael A. Thalbourne† and Mark G. Shafer (McDonnell Laboratory
for Psychical Research)

   The two subjects in the present investigation will be designated as M. E. and S. S. Phillips and Shafer (RIP 1981, 144-146) have reported observations of phenomena exhibited by these two subjects that are at least suggestive of, even if not conclusive evidence for, such psychokinetic gifts as paranormal metal-bending, among others.*** These ostensible "psychokinetes," as we shall call them, have also claimed numerous spontaneous ESP experiences, and indeed exploratory testing conducted by M. S. suggested that these claims might be experimentally verifiable. M. E. and S. S. are both male, and at the time of this ESP test (February 19-21, 1982), were 20 and 21 years of age respectively. As measured by objective pencil-and-paper tests, both may be classified as being "extraverted sheep."

   The essential features of the present GESP test were that a group of agents (the authors, accompanied by a variable number of visitors) would concentrate upon a randomly-selected line-drawing, while simultaneously one or other of the ostensible psychokinetes, seated in a distant room, would attempt to draw a facsimile of the

---

*Chaired by Peter R. Phillips (McDonnell Laboratory for Psychical Research)
**Titles of research briefs are followed by (RB).
***M. E. and S. S. have recently revealed that the events described in a report by Phillips and Shafer (RIP 1981, 144-146) were brought about by fraudulent means. However, a statement to the effect that no such fraud was perpetrated in the 1982 studies (described in this paper and in that on pages 66-68) has, as of March 18, 1983, been signed and returned by M. E. to the McDonnell Laboratory for Psychical Research and another is expected from S. S.

target. Additionally, a video-camera was set up in the percipient's room, trained on the subject's hands as he drew his response-drawing, so that live feedback could be provided to the group of agents by means of a video monitor. The task of the agents can thus as readily be conceptualized as being one of PK as one of ESP.

There were 36 trials in total, 18 per psychokinete, each trial being conducted under one of four different "sending" conditions. When S.S. was percipient, the agents received live video feedback on all 18 trials, but on nine of the trials S.S.'s fellow-psychokinete M.E. was in the group of agents, while on the other nine M.E. was not present at all; it was hypothesized that ESP scores would be higher when the psychokinete was thus joining in the "sending" than when he was absent from the agent's room. When M.E. was percipient, S.S. did not participate at all in the sending: on nine of the trials the agents received live video feedback, while on the other nine the monitor was switched off, thus depriving the agents of the opportunity to observe the percipient's hands responding. It was hypothesized that the provision of concomitant feedback to the agents would be associated with higher ESP scores than in the non-monitoring condition. The order of these sending conditions was determined randomly, and the percipient, though aware of the general nature of the sending manipulations, was blind as to which condition was being employed on any given trial. Feedback was provided to the percipient after each trial, and targets were used without replacement. The percipient was permitted as much time as he wanted for each trial.

Very elaborate precautions were taken to prevent sensory leakage occurring: the agents' and percipient's rooms were separated by a distance of about 10 meters, a hallway, and three heavy closed doors; the target was chosen only when the percipient was safely seated in his room; an observer continually watched the percipient throughout the entire trial to make sure he never left his room, and took charge of the response-drawing before it was compared with its target; "ready" cards were passed between agents' room and the percipient's observer by a person stationed in the hallway who was unaware of the target or the response and who made sure that nobody left their respective rooms.

The 36 targets used had each been selected at random from 36 sets each containing five targets. Thus, four targets in each set remained unused, for controls. The procedure thus permitted an open-deck judging regime. The five targets in each of the 36 sets were preferentially ranked against each response-drawing by three independent judges. The rank-scores were summed for each target and, as recommended by Markwick, these sums were themselves ranked to yield a "super-judge" rank score. It was planned to use sum-of-ranks as the dependent measure, but owing to low interjudge concordance this turned out to be highly conservative; the analysis was therefore supplemented by a hit/miss dichotomy, eliminating scores exactly at chance (super-judge rank of 3.0). Significantly above-chance scores overall were expected.

Results. For the 36 trials, MCE sum-of-ranks was 108, and obtained S of R was 96 (p = .089, one-tailed). However, 22 of the 36 trials were hits, and only 10 misses (p = .025, one-tailed). There was some evidence that, as expected, the overall scores were significantly above chance.

When M. E. was percipient, his scores in the "live feedback" condition were higher than in the non-monitoring condition (S of R = 24.5 and 27 respectively; M.C.E. = 27), but the differences were not significant, and neither did either sum-of-ranks differ from chance. The results for M.E.'s hit-analysis were similar.

When S.S. was percipient, his scores in the "psychokinete agent present" condition were significantly above chance (S of R = 19, p = .038, one-tailed; 7 hits and 1 miss, p = .035, one-tailed), but not significantly greater than when the psychokinete agent was absent (S of R = 25.5, n. s.). His combined scores for these two conditions were also significantly above chance for the hits-measure: 13 hits and 4 misses, p = .025, one-tailed.

Thus, the highest scores were obtained when S.S. was percipient, and when the agents had live video feedback and were assisted in the sending by M. E. Though it might seem suspicious that the most significant scores were obtained under just that condition which might have permitted collusion by the two psychokinetes (e.g., using an undetected radio transmitter), we feel that hypotheses of normal communication are very unlikely: even the best of the hits are not consistent with verbal cueing, but rather exhibit consistent resemblances of form without any semantic relation.

A PK EXPERIMENT WITH RANDOM AND PSEUDORANDOM TARGETS (RB)

Mark G. Shafer (McDonnell Laboratory for Psychical Research)

In this study, preselected subjects were tested with a PK target generator supplied by Helmut Schmidt to see if extrachance scoring would be obtained with randomly-generated and/or pseudorandomly-generated targets.

The PK test machine presents the subject with a circular display of 16 lamps. Initially the topmost lamp is illuminated, and once a run is begun, lamps are illuminated one at a time successively clockwise around the circle. After a randomly determined interval, the clockwise "movement" of the illuminated lamp is halted and it remains fixed in position for a second randomly determined interval. After that the apparent movement resumes, again for a randomly determined time. A run is terminated automatically after 16 move/stop pairs of random intervals, scores for the summed move and stop intervals being displayed. The machine has a second display mode, similar to the first, in which the illuminated lamp rotates counterclockwise around the circle instead of remaining stopped for every other interval. Two speeds of operation are possible, representing an approximately twofold difference in the rate of apparent movement of the light. The device also has an optional earphone attachment that presents a tone to the subject during clockwise intervals, and no tone during stopped or counterclockwise intervals.

The experimenter can choose between two sources of randomness for determination of the random intervals for a run. The first, or random mode, is based on radioactive decay, the length of each interval being determined by the length of time between successive decays of a radioactive substance as registered by a Geiger tube. The other is a pseudorandom mode, in which the length of each interval is determined according to a sequence of quasirandom numbers that are completely determined mathematically by a seed number, which is chosen internally via the radioactive random source at the beginning of a run. The positions of prespecified numbers in the quasirandom sequence determine random interval lengths.

Generally, the subject tries to keep the light moving clockwise as long as possible, and to shorten the duration of stopped or counterclockwise movement.

Experimental subjects were preselected on the basis of practice runs with the machine over one or several screening sessions consisting of about 10 runs each. During the practice runs they tried several mental strategies: for example, imagining the light moving clockwise continuously, as around a theater marquis; or attempting to keep in mind achieving the goal of a positive score, while maintaining thoughts that made them feel good and carefree emotionally. Persons who had their own strategies were encouraged to use these if they felt confident in using them. During sessions I noted the person's most successful-seeming mental strategy, their preferred mode of display from the machine, and the rate of attempting and number of runs that seemed optimal for a session. Subjects whom I felt reasonably confident about on the basis of screening sessions were asked to participate in experimental sessions.

A total of 20 subjects participated in experimental sessions. Both session length and number of sessions per subject were variable and determined by me on the basis of my continued confidence in the likely success of that subject. I also served as a subject in the experiment, completing runs when I felt confident. Once a subject had begun participation in experimental test sessions, no practice runs were allowed.

The total number of runs for the experiment were prespecified as 400 runs. It was further prespecified that 200 runs each were to be conducted in the random and pseudorandom conditions; and I predetermined that I would contribute exactly 50 runs in each condition as subject. I decided to use only one randomness condition for each experimental session, and to alternate randomness conditions for subsequent sessions with the same subject. In this way most subjects completed approximately the same number of runs in each of the randomness modes. They were unaware of which mode was being used when. I selected the display mode of the machine on every run for each subject to maximize their likely success in my own estimation.

Results. For the 200 runs in the random mode, the total score for target direction intervals was 44,585, for nontarget intervals, 46,735, suggesting a weak psi-missing effect ($Z = -1.81$, $p < .07$, two-tailed). For the 200 pseudorandom runs, the target interval total score was 50,756, for nontarget intervals, 51,041, a nonsignificant difference in the missing direction. The combined scores for both randomness conditions do not give a significant deviation from chance. Planned control tests before, during, and after the experiment yielded nonsignificant differences between target and nontarget intervals, for 1,000 runs in each randomness condition. The variance of random-mode, experimental run-scores was not significantly different from that of random-mode control runs, but for experimental, pseudorandom-mode runs, the variance was markedly smaller relative to pseudorandom-mode control runs ($Z = -2.82$, $p = .005$, two-tailed). Since subjects were told that by chance the average lengths of target and nontarget intervals would be about even, this significantly smaller variance might be considered a psi-missing effect. Thus, some evidence was obtained in the experiment for apparent PK-missing in both the random and pseudorandom target generation modes.

PK EXPERIMENTS WITH TWO SPECIAL SUBJECTS (RB)

Mark G. Shafer,[†] Michael K. McBeath, Michael A. Thalbourne, and Peter R. Phillips (McDonnell Laboratory for Psychical Research)

We carried out two experiments with two ostensible metal-benders with whom we have worked before (Phillips and Shafer, RIP 1981, 144-146).[*]

The first experiment involved attempts to influence a mildly saline watering solution that was later used to grow rye grass, after a design by Grad. Four sealed 500 ml. bottles of sterile 0.9% saline were enclosed in opaque, labeled bags. One was randomly designated by coinflip for each of the two subjects, M. E. and S. S., the other two to be used as controls. For the PK treatment, the

---

*See footnote (***) on page 62.

two experimental bag-enclosed bottles were removed from their locked storage container by M.S., and enclosed in another opaque, labeled bag. The subjects were asked to hold their respective double-bagged bottle, while imagining "psychic energy" flowing into the saline, and imagining enhanced growth of plants later to be watered with the saline. Each subject held his bottle, under continuous observation, for a total of 30 minutes in three separate sessions over a two-day period.

For the plant-growth phase of the experiment, the four identically appearing bottles were coded and sent to the Mind Science Foundation in San Antonio where William Braud performed all the work in connection with this part of the experiment. A total of 80 peat pots were planted with five rye grass seeds each, and placed so that they would receive equal amounts of sunlight. Using a random number table, 20 pots were assigned to each of the saline bottles. On Days 1 and 2 of the experiment, each pot was watered once with 10 ml. from its own bottle of saline. On each remaining day of the experiment, each pot was watered with 10 ml. of non-saline, deionized water. It had been decided beforehand to take measurements every other day after sprouts became visible, until the 15th day of the experiment.

Sprouts appeared on Day 5, and were measured at the same time of day on Days 5, 7, 9, 11, 13, and 15. For each pot, three measurements were taken: (1) the number of plants sprouting, (2) the average height in mm. of the plants, and (3) the total height of the plants.

On all three measures, the growth of the plants watered with PK-treated saline was consistently less than that of plants watered with control saline. This difference reached significance on Day 15 for the mean height measure ($t = 2.28$, 78 df, $p = .02$, two-tailed), and for the total height measure ($t = 1.95$, 78 df, $p = .05$, two-tailed), the data having been pooled, as decided in advance, for both subjects. Thus a significant psi-missing effect was observed in this experiment.

The second of our experiments was designed to test for PK influence on blowout times of electrical fuses. A device was constructed that applies a steadily increasing voltage across two fuses that are easily visible, but which are under a transparent cover that shields them from contact and static electric effects. Once fuses are securely in place, an RNG in the microcomputer interfaced with the device selects one of the fuses as target. The distance between the two fuses may be varied, and this was also randomly chosen by the RNG for each trial, using three possible distance conditions. Once the trial has been run, the computer records the blowout time for each fuse.

It was hypothesized that, relative to its control fuse, the target fuse would blow more quickly; we also looked at a possible effect of the distance between target and control fuse.

All fuses used were pretested to eliminate broken and weak fuses, and, to control for substitution, were marked with an unusual color of paint, stored in a locked area during nonexperimental periods, and kept in the hand of the experimenter during test sessions. The computer was also kept in a locked room when unattended.

For PK trials, M.E. and S.S. worked individually, on independent visits to the lab. They completed varying numbers of trials per session, having been encouraged to make attempts only when they felt motivated. A video camera allowed us to video-record attempts. For each trial, the experimenter placed the fuses in position, and removed and retained them once blown, so that the subjects were never permitted contact with fuses.

The subjects completed a predesignated 240 trials, 80 in each distance condition. For the 240 pooled trials, mean blowout time for target fuses was 12.56 seconds, for control fuses 12.90 seconds ($t = 1.16$, 239 df, $p = .12$, one-tailed). Thus the major hypothesis was not confirmed. There was no effect of inter-fuse distance. For the 180 trials contributed by M.E., mean for target fuses was 12.36 seconds, for control fuses 12.94 seconds ($t = 1.68$, 179 df, $p = .048$, one-tailed). No effect of inter-fuse distance was found. For the 60 trials contributed by S.S., mean for target fuses was 13.15 seconds, for control fuses 12.77 seconds ($t = -.70$, 59 df, $p = .24$, one-tailed). In the case of S.S., there did seem to be a significant effect of distance, due to psi-missing at the middle-distance fuse. Thus, there is some evidence that different sorts of effects were exhibited by each subject.

HISTORICAL PERSPECTIVES*

RETROCOGNITIVE DISSONANCE

Brian Inglis (London, England)

At a centenary conference some soul-searching is called for. Where, in the past, have psychical researchers been found wanting? What can they learn from past mistakes?

There are three disorders to which they appear to have been particularly prone: "protocolitis"--contempt for evidence that cannot be replicated in controlled trials; "skepticemia"--a readiness to accept, say, the "exposure" of a medium without pausing to assess the trustworthiness of the exposer; and "retrocognitive dissonance"-- a variant of Festinger's cognitive dissonance, illustrated in Richet's recollection of his reactions to the early trials of Eusapia Palladino: "At the moment when these facts take place they seem to us certain, and we are willing to proclaim them openly. But when we feel the irresistible influence of our environment, when our friends all laugh at our credulity--then we are almost disarmed, and begin to doubt. May I not have been deceived...? And we end by letting ourselves be persuaded that we have been the victims of a trick."

Retrocognitive dissonance is infectious; doubt spreads rapidly through our societies. It is also destructive of mental balance, as can be seen in the case of Podmore. His growing antipathy to physical mediumship, and to psychokinetic phenomena in general, compelled him to rewrite history, much as Russian historians did after the Stalin purges.

Count Perovsky-Petrovo-Solovovo took a similar course, notably in his commentaries on the mediumship of D. D. Home. Initially sympathetic and quite well-balanced, they became more hostile as Perovsky grew more skeptical, until eventually he was accepting evidence which earlier he had himself shown to be unreliable.

But perhaps the most striking, and the most damaging, of all displays of retrocognitive dissonance has been the reaction of some

---
*Chaired by Renée Haynes (Society for Psychical Research)

members of our societies to the disclosure made following Perovsky's death in 1954 by Rudolf Lambert. A quarter of a century earlier, Lambert claimed, he had been shown evidence that had convinced him that the medium "Eva C" (Marthe Beraud) was a fraud. Eva had been tested by Richet, by Madame Bisson (with whom she lived), by Schrenck-Notzing, and by Geley. Over a period of close to twenty years, and under more rigorous conditions than any medium had ever been tested, she had produced physical phenomena that none of her investigators--not even Houdini, who attended one of her sittings--could attribute to deception. Following Geley's death in an air crash, however, Osty found some photographs among his effects that appeared to reveal that some of her "materializations" were all too material--they had been attached to her head by threads or wires. Showing them to Lambert, Osty explained that Richet and Schrenck had opposed publication; he had sworn Lambert to secrecy, for fear the scandal might reach the ears of that "dangerous negativist" Count Perovsky.

The impact of Lambert's disclosure has been considerable. Not merely has Eva been discredited, along with Madame Bisson, whom Lambert assumed must have been an accomplice, but the reputations of her investigators, Schrenck and Geley in particular, have also been lowered. On the evidence, either they must also have collaborated in the frauds, or they were blind to the most blatant, and indeed clumsy, deception.

Yet there is an innocent explanation. Had Lambert himself not been afflicted with retrocognitive dissonance--he had been a believer in physical phenomena, but had come to the conclusion that they were all faked--he would have realized as much. As Lambert admitted, Schrenck had published in his book on materializations in 1914 "very similar, very suspicious pictures," commenting frankly on how suspicious they looked. Lambert even conceded that "in the main, no stronger suspicion attaches to Madame Bisson after Osty's discovery than at the time of Schrenck's publications." And this, surely, suggests a different reason for Geley's failure to publish the "suspicious" pictures: that they would be pounced on as evidence for fraud--just as Schrenck's had been.

Some of Schrenck's photographs of Eva's phenomena do indeed look mightily suspicious. But this, as he and many witnesses attested, was chiefly the consequence of a curious feature of her materializations: that often they came out two-dimensional--flat. Faces, arms, and bodies looked like cut-outs. As Oesterreich, who examined them critically, put it, nobody who looked at them without further explanation "could think they are anything else than drawings on paper or material."

And there were even more serious grounds for suspicion. In one photograph the letters "M I R O" appeared on what looked like paper emerging from the top of Eva's head. A writer in a Paris occultist magazine, suspecting that this was a photograph of part of the mast-head from the journal <u>Le Miroir</u>, checked through back numbers and found that some of Eva's materialized portraits appeared to be crudely touched-up versions of pictures which had appeared in the journal. The "exposure" was gleefully picked up by Le Matin and other newspapers; and that, it seemed, was that.

But no. Schrenck was able to obtain expert testimony that although the materialized mast-head letters and portraits were related to Le Miroir, they were not touched up versions of the originals, but almost parodies of them, as if some joker had been at work on them. In any case, as all who attended the sittings agreed, not merely were the precautions so stringent that the portraits or other objects could not have been smuggled in, but the forms did not simply appear, and then disappear. The ectoplasm emerged in a thin stream, from different parts of the body, and then developed into forms, sometimes changing from one form to another. What appeared in photographs as "still life" was to onlookers very much alive, but rarely still, and never the same for long. The ectoplasm, Schrenck argued, was in some mysterious way being molded by her mental processes--"ideoplasty"; and what she had seen in Le Miroir had contributed to the performance.

To anybody who accepts at least the possibility that Eva's type of physical mediumship can be genuine, it is hard not to be impressed by the evidence for it. If she were a cheat, why did she not exploit her talent for fame and fortune, rather than put up with the discomforts and humiliations--the rectal and vaginal examinations, and the emetics (to guard against regurgitation), the suspicion, the endless hostile publicity? Although there were frequent allegations of cheating, and speculation on how she cheated, she was never detected in fraud at a séance. There is surely a good case for her rehabilitation, along with Madame Bisson.

But it is not just a matter of setting the record straight. If it is accepted that her materializations were genuine, the accounts of her tests have important implications for the study of psychokinetic phenomena today. To take just one aspect of the research: the use of photography. It is still not uncommon to hear stories of mediums "exposed" by the fact that photographs showed their ectoplasm to be some everyday material. But this is precisely what the Schrenck and Geley photographs continually showed. Not merely did the materialized portraits on paper look as if they were on real paper; there were creases and wrinkles just like those on real paper.

A further possibility has also to be considered on the evidence of one of Eva's tests in London in 1920. The sitters saw a materialized portrait, "a rough drawing, as if crudely sketched in chalk"; but to their astonishment, when the photograph taken at the time was developed, it showed a much more finished, artistic production. It was as if the medium (or her joker "control") had been able to alter it, much as the Le Miroir portraits had been altered, but directly on the photographic plate.

Now that psychokinesis once again holds the center of the parapsychological stage, there is an obvious need to study again the evidence for "ideoplasty" and its effects. By downgrading Eva and her investigators, retrocognitive dissonance has done us a disservice; and this is only one of all too many instances where its malign influence can still be seen at work.

THE MEDIUMSHIP OF STEFAN OSSOWIECKI

Mary Rose Barrington (Society for Psychical Research)

Between 1921 and 1936 ten issues of the Revue Métapsychique carried reports detailing test sessions with the remarkable medium Stefan Ossowiecki, a Polish chemical engineer of high culture and social standing. Most of the reports were by Dr. Gustave Geley, Director of the Institut Métapsychique International, and several were by Prof. Charles Richet. The purpose of this paper is to discuss whether Ossowiecki's gift is best understood as telepathy, as clairvoyance, or in other terms.

In his most characteristic performance Ossowiecki would stay in one room under observation while another person went into another room and wrote material on a card (words, drawings, symbols, or any combination); the donor of the material would return to the room and present the enveloped specimen to Ossowiecki, who would almost invariably reproduce the target material almost exactly and with little hesitation. Though many tests were carried out informally, others were performed under carefully controlled conditions, where neither the presenter of the material nor Ossowiecki himself was acquainted with the donor and had no knowledge of the material. Formal and informal tests were equally successful, and are therefore considered to form one series.

One relative failure occurred when Geley secreted two carp scales in a box for use as target material, and spent the day fishing with Ossowiecki while the medium tried to perceive the contents of the box. Ossowiecki accurately described the material as small, thin, white, round, transparent and mica-like objects, but despite the presence of Geley urging him on, and the presence of the fish, he never succeeded in identifying the objects as carp scales.

Many of the tests were designed to demonstrate clairvoyance by excluding the possibility of telepathy. Thus, on one occasion Richet obtained three apparently identical envelopes from Anna de Noailles, each containing material unknown to him. He selected one at random, and Ossowiecki correctly named a quotation from Rostand's Chantecler; Richet passed the other two envelopes to Geley, who selected one at random. Ossowiecki said: "She speaks in this letter about a great genius of our time. It is Richet. She likes him very much. She says that his genius is as great as his heart. She signs with her first name and her family name and underlines the signature. This took place at 5 or 6 p.m." The target material was: "Prof. Richet is as impressive in the sublime qualities of his heart as in his scientific genius. <u>Anna de Noialles.</u>"

It is clear that Ossowiecki must have been demonstrating paranormal cognition (called by Richet "lucidity") and it seems that his lucidity cannot be ascribed to telepathy unless some bold assumptions are made. The mind of Mme. de Noailles could be "searched" for the message, but could not know which of the three envelopes was under trial. To complete a telepathic chain of information one would have to postulate that when she passed the three envelopes to Richet she also passed to him (telepathically) knowledge of the three messages, and minute descriptions of normally imperceptible differences in the envelopes by which each message could be identified; Richet passed the same information on to Geley by the same means. This comes close to postulating a universal power to absorb and convey limitless information, including all peripheral perceptions. This is a large assumption, and it may be simpler to assume initially that Richet and Geley succeeded in the intention to exclude the operation of telepathy.

This preliminary view is encouraged by many indicators of clairvoyance, including several cases where the meaning of words escaped Ossowiecki entirely. On one occasion he was given a short English sentence to interpret. He appeared to "read it off" letter by letter, describing "consider" as "a word of eight letters starting with CONS" and "wonderful" as "a long word which is like Vendredi." He misinterpreted the word "semble" as "humble" because the handwriting suggested this wrong word, described "NON" as a three digit number with nought as the middle figure, and misread "TOI" as "TO 1." A remarkable case of apparent X-ray vision occurred when he correctly transcribed the number "102," but said (correctly) that the "2" was difficult to see (the ink had smudged).

However, despite this suggestive evidence in favor of clairvoyance, it is clear from other considerations that X-ray-like vision is not the only faculty operating, and it may not be operating at all. In the well-known experiment in which the words "SWAN INK" were the target material (together with an ink bottle) Ossowiecki transcribed the letters one by one over several days. He transcribed "SWAN" more easily and accurately (in block letters) than "INK," and yet the target word SWAN had been folded over on itself, while INK had deliberately been left unfolded and therefore easier to "see." Further, on two occasions the target material had been folded over and over, and once had been screwed into a ball.

Even a more extended concept of clairvoyance cannot account for another feature of Ossowiecki's mediumship, i.e., his capacity for describing the person who produced the target material. This extended well beyond mere physical description. Of one donor he said not only that she was "a woman, aged 30-35, tall, dark, distinguished, intelligent," but also that she had been divorced and was now married to a doctor, information that cannot be readily ascribed to "simple" clairvoyant observation even when combined with psychometry.

In one of the most curious and revealing experiments Geley wrote a complex sentence using invisible ink, a device recognized by Ossowiecki quite early on in a long-drawn out experiment. At one stage Ossowiecki gave many details surrounding the preparation of the material. "You were interrupted while you were preparing the experiment; I see you leave your office, then come back.... I see the movements you made to write this ... but I can't manage to see what is written.... You copied it, after a moment's hesitation, from a book within your hand's reach." After making these observations, Ossowiecki was able to give a good description of the material, though he could not reproduce the wording until Geley committed it to visible writing. On one hand this may appear to be yet another indicator of clairvoyance; on the other hand the explanation could be that once an agent has made a written record the material enters an accessible level of his mind from which it could be telepathically extracted in substantially the same form as the written record. Ossowiecki usually found it difficult to decipher printed or typewritten material where the same effort had not been put into the writing.

One of Ossowiecki's most characteristic devices when searching around for the target material was to describe the scene of the place and the time it was prepared, giving mostly accurate accounts of persons, actions, and environment. Some examples have already been noted. On one occasion, when the target material was in a box and wrapped in cotton wool, Ossowiecki referred to the white substance, and said that he saw a lady (Prof. Szmurlo's wife) buying it at the Marzsalkowska Street pharmacy. When he was given an undeveloped photographic plate as target (a task he found difficult) he gave a good description of the photographer, of another person who had come into the room and left again, of the studio, and of the time of day when the photographs were taken. It seemed as if he were replaying a videotape of the event in question, running it backwards and forwards until he was able to observe the target material at its inception. Bearing in mind the importance to Ossowiecki of holding or touching the envelope, box, or other container, this might be regarded as a form of retrocognitive psychometry, requiring neither mindreading nor a capacity to "see" through outer coverings. Rather than conceiving of this process as a rolling back of time it may be more realistic to return to the discarded notion of telepathy, and regard Ossowiecki's excursions into the past as a reading of a common mind, a task at which he was assisted by contact with the persons who originally contributed the target material to the general pool.

Summary

(1) Telepathy alone cannot explain the perception of random-

ly selected material unless it is also assumed to operate between the donor of the material and the presenter at hyperaesthetic level.

(2) There are strong indications against mental apprehension and in favor of visual perception, though further considerations argue against direct clairvoyant scanning.

(3) Direct scanning does not in any event account for correct descriptions of people, places, and actions.

(4) Reading of mind imagery is indicated, but this alone will not suffice to explain all the results any more than direct scanning; even taken together these faculties have to be supplemented by psychometry.

(5) A more economical explanation can be offered in terms of retrocognitive psychometry or time-tracing, which would enable all knowledge to be obtained by external observation.

(6) The concept of a common mind is consistent with the evidence, and may be preferred to the objective tracing of objects back in time.

Whether or not a close analysis of this outstanding medium would throw light on mediumship generally, an extended study of Ossowiecki is surely overdue, and one that would also take note of an earlier phase in his life when he operated as a powerful physical medium.

PALLADINO AT CAMBRIDGE

Manfred Cassirer (Society for Psychical Research)

In his Very Peculiar People (1950), Dr. E. J. Dingwall regrets that no "full and detailed report" of the Cambridge sittings with Palladino has been published (p. 189). In view of the sheer quantity of her phenomena as well as the vast bulk of recorded material about her, Palladino has been described as the "greatest" psychic ever.

Moreover, many of her investigators were competent and critical scholars, including those who would later become Nobel Prize winners. By 1895, the year of the sittings in question, she was already world-famous. The problem is not so much why she was not tested as it is one of why, having done so, the sitters virtually suppressed the results of their inquiry by publishing a misleading shortened version.

It has always been known that Palladino would occasionally

help out the phenomena, and various plausible explanations have been advanced (e.g., Carrington, The American Seances with Eusapia Palladino, 1954, 7 ff.). Some psychical researchers, notably the Sidgwicks, were not greatly enamored of "physical" (as opposed to "mental") phenomena and, moreover, regarded Palladino as a vulgar, socially inferior person. Whereas Myers, Lodge, and Richet had been converted through personal experience, Hodgson in America, who had none, was persuaded to the contrary, loudly proclaiming that all could be explained in terms of substitution of hands in the dark: "spirit touches" were by freed hands; tables and chairs rose "paranormally" with the help of mundane, all-too-human limbs.

This simplistic (though not entirely unfounded) theory failed to account for some very extraordinary incidents to be mentioned later. Again, the light was often ample for good or even close inspection. Myers was the leading expert on controlling mediums, having had much experience, and prepared and circulated a short guide on the subject. Many of Palladino's feats could by no means be accounted for by simple faulty holding. The way in which Myers and others were eventually brainwashed into accepting, against their better judgments, such an unsatisfactory hypothesis as a vade mecum forms one of the most puzzling chapters in the history of our subject.

But accepted it was, and the SPR decided that it would have no more truck with the Neapolitan "imposter." Fortunately, European scholars continued their investigations undeterred and with positive results.

As for the sittings at Cambridge, they were on the whole meticulously protocolled. For practical purposes, they may be divided into "pre-Australian" and "Australian." The former antedate the arrival of Dr. Richard Hodgson (a native of Melbourne) and were originally acclaimed by Myers and his colleagues as more or less successful or even promising, and in any case usually devoid of detected fraud. All this changed dramatically when Hodgson virtually took over at "half-time" (in half a dozen séances out of a total of 19 "official" ones). Myers wrote to his friend Lodge in near despair that after Hodgson's initial reaction (Séance 13 had "impressed" him "rather favorably") all was found to be "fraudulent."

What had brought about so drastic a change of attitude? Incredibly, Hodgson had been encouraged to relinquish effective control of the medium--"allowing any tricks" (as Myers put it)--to see how things were done by dishonest means. Lo and behold, with one hand free, they could be produced quite normally!

Throughout the emphasis had been on "touches" on sitters, as opposed to the bulging-out of curtains, strange lights, table-levitations (some of which had impressed even Hodgson), PK movements of assorted objects, raps, cold breezes, materializations of odd shapes, and phantom limbs protruding from the medium's body. Touches, at any rate, were specially marked in the margin of reports, indicating that everyone was happy with them; and these were frequent. The Society's fleeting account finally echoes Hodgson's views. But it is known for a fact that Myers at least was not entirely at ease with this negative conclusion which he, nevertheless, loyally (to his colleagues, if not to the medium) defended in public.

Later, Palladino's ultimate vindication at Naples established her once and for all as the undoubted "Queen of the Cabinet."

A CENTURY OF INVESTIGATIONS--SOME LESSONS

Andrew MacKenzie (Society for Psychical Research)

After a long study of the Journal and Proceedings of the SPR and frequent reference to the archives in order to write my book, Hauntings and Apparitions (1982), one of the Society's centenary series, it seemed to me that certain lessons for future researchers emerged. One is that it is not possible to come to a conclusion about a case without a careful reading of all the relevant literature relating to it. One of the arguments used against the Cheltenham Case, which dealt with the haunting of a house between 1882 and 1889 by the figure of a tall woman in black, was that the first publication was by a "Miss R. C. Morton" in 1892 (PSPR, 311-332), three years after the haunting had ostensibly ceased; in fact, Mrs. Sidgwick refers to the case in 1885 (PSPR, 69-150) while the haunting was still in progress, although she did not use the pseudonym "Morton." If this had been realized earlier we would have been spared some of the ill-formed comment along the lines that the figure seen by the family and some of the servants was that of a living person and not an apparition, a possibility discussed and dismissed by Mrs. Sidgwick.

Another lesson is that great patience is needed by an investigator before he commits his findings to print because once a case is published it is possible for critics to maintain that a later experience was the result of expectation created by what had been read. No better example of this admirable quality of patience exists than Professor F. J. M. Stratton's investigation of the haunting of Abbey House, Cambridge, which he studied for 40 years without committing himself to print for fear that he might contaminate the evidence of future witnesses. It was only after his death that Dr. Alan Gauld (JSPR, 1972, 464-480) felt that the time had come to publish the case because by then stories about the house had appeared several times in the local press. I was glad that I had followed Stratton's example by not committing myself to print prematurely when I had a letter from a lady describing her experiences in a certain house in Cheltenham--not the original haunted house--

which suggested that the figure of a woman in black seen by her as
a child in 1933 resembled that seen by the "Morton" (Despard) family fifty years earlier. There were also certain other happenings
in the house which suggested a haunting. When a partnership of
doctors moved into the house in 1967 some of them, and certain
members of the staff, though that the house was haunted. As
nothing had been published about this particular house suggesting
that it might be haunted, and I had not discussed it, nor had my
informant, it seemed to me that expectation of what might happen
in the house was not an objection that could be raised by critics.
This case is described in my Hauntings and Apparitions (1982).

When a haunting or poltergeist case is reported there should
be no delay in investigating it if the phenomena are still occurring.
An example of this is provided by the case of Grandfather Bull (Balfour and Piddington, JSPR, 1932, 297-304), which involved the repeated appearances to his family of the apparition of a man who had
died eight months earlier of "sooty" cancer. When the case was reported the second Lord Balfour sent a list of eight questions to be
answered by the family instead of going to the cottage at Ramsbury,
Wiltshire, or sending somebody else. The late Sir Ernest Bennett,
M.P., a member of the Society's Council, said in his Apparitions
and Haunted Houses (1939) that the Society's slowness in starting
the investigation deprived it of the opportunity for obtaining evidence
of "quite exceptional value" (p. 73). Eventually Lord Balfour went
with his friend Mr. J. G. Piddington. As it happened, the phenomena ceased about that time, so no great harm was done by their
late arrival, but they were not to know that when the information
was first given.

The main point I wish to make in this paper is that once a
case has been published in the Journal or Proceedings it should not
be regarded as the equivalent of Holy Writ, the last word having
been spoken, but should constantly be re-examined and fresh evidence sought. Take, for instance, the Versailles Case, which concerns a visit by Miss Moberly and Miss Jourdain to the park of the
Petit Trianon, Versailles, on August 10, 1901, during which they
saw figures in costumes of the past and features of the park which
were not there in 1901 but, it transpired later, could have been
found in 1770-71. The late Dame Joan Evans, who owned the copyright of An Adventure (Moberly and Jourdain, 5th ed., 1955), a
book on their experiences written by the two ladies, decided that
they could have seen the living figures of Count Robert de Montesquiou, a resident of Versailles, and his friends in costume and
mistaken them for ghosts, although there was no evidence that they
were in the park on the day concerned. Dr. Evans, as she was
then, declined to discuss alternative explanations with me and invited me to "kindly consider the matter closed." This I declined
to do. I continued my investigations and was able to prove not
only that the Count was not living in Versailles at the time of the
"adventure," but also that he had moved back to Paris some years
earlier. Miss Moberly and Miss Jourdain spent ten years in muddled research trying to prove that their experience related to 1789,

the last time Marie Antoinette was in the park of the Petit Trianon. This was based on the assumption that the phantom figure of a woman who was sketching was that of the tragic Queen, although they had no real reason for making such an assumption. But make it they did and it led them sadly astray. It is essential that investigators should start with a completely open mind and see where the trail leads them.

Let us now turn to the Cheltenham Case. The identity of the family concerned and the location of the haunting were revealed for the first time by the late B. Abdy Collins in 1948, long after the haunting of the house now known as St. Anne's had ceased, and in The Cheltenham Ghost (1948) he tells a very strange story of how after the "Morton" (Despard) family had left the house it was turned into a boys' school and was so persistently haunted that it had to be closed. I have been unable to confirm this was so and suggest that if someone from the SPR had dropped in from time to time at the house we might today know whether the school was haunted or not. Mr. Collins' book contains an account, taken from the Society's archives, of how an unnamed man had, as a small boy fifty years earlier, seen the figure of a tall woman in black at the haunted house, and, with other children, joined hands in a circle round the figure through which "she" just walked and disappeared. This man's name was George Gooding. He was a successful solicitor and as such would know the value of testimony. More firsthand evidence of what happened in Cheltenham in the 1880s could have been obtained if the SPR had followed up clues in the spring 1958 issue of Light, the journal of the College of Psychic Studies, in which it was stated that a Mrs. Maisey, then alive and living in Cheltenham, had seen the ghost, as had a man then living in the United States, who said that he had seen the ghost when a boy in Cheltenham. This, of course, was secondhand evidence, but it could have been made firsthand if someone from the SPR had realized the significance of this article and carried out the necessary interviews. Once a person is dead, vital evidence is lost forever. The lesson: collect evidence while it is still available.

The final point I wish to make is to draw attention to a remark of a former president of the SPR, Professor D. J. West, who said, "It would be a help if investigators always had a sound practical knowledge of psychology, so as to recognise when an explanation in terms of abnormal mental processes will cover some seemingly mysterious experience" (Psychical Research Today, 1954, 34). A number of times during the past twenty years I have come across cases involving a family which has reported strange experiences, causing me to think that something that might be called "psychic infection" was involved. I was glad to see an account by D. Scott Rogo of a recent investigation of a poltergeist outbreak in Los Angeles headed, "The Poltergeist and Family Dynamics" (JSPR, 1982, 233-237). In this case detailed psychological examinations were made of all the family members directly involved. In his Psychical Research Today (1954) Professor West discussed the case of "The Woman in Brown," investigated by Edward Osborn (JSPR, 1949,

123-153), who devoted 200 hours to it. Investigations revealed that the story told by a Miss Benson (a pseudonym), who saw the figure of a woman in brown in the office where she worked 13 times between November 1948 and May 1949, was a fantasy. When I was carrying out my inquiries into the Cheltenham Case I was put to a great deal of trouble in trying to confirm a story by a teenage girl that her grandmother, recently dead, had seen an apparition which could have been that of the tall woman in black, before being driven to the conclusion that the child's story was a fantasy. We hear a great deal about being on our guard against fraud but not nearly as much about also being on guard against fantasy.

THEORETICAL ISSUES*

MORPHIC RESONANCE, MEMORY, AND PSYCHICAL RESEARCH

Rupert Sheldrake (International Crops Research Institute for Semi-arid Tropics, Hyderabad, India)

Most people take it for granted that memories are somehow stored inside the brain. The idea that experiences leave traces or imprints in brain tissue has a long ancestry. Aristotle expressed this idea in terms of the analogy of the impressions left by seals in wax. From time to time the analogies have been updated, the latest being provided by the optical technique of holography.

In spite of the fact that there is very little evidence for the existence of memory traces, and in spite of the philosophical difficulties raised by any mechanistic theory of memory, the trace theory is rarely questioned. The main reason seems to be the lack of a plausible alternative. If memories are not stored inside the brain, then how do they persist?

The Hypothesis of Formative Causation. I have recently put forward a hypothesis which enables the problem of memory to be seen in a new light, although its starting point is at first sight rather remote, namely the coming-into-being of form in animals and plants (A New Science of Life, 1981).

The mechanistic approach to biology, in spite of its successes at the molecular level, has failed to shed much light on the way in which embryos develop from relatively simple egg cells into organisms containing tissues and organs of great structural complexity. During this process, more complex structures come into being from less complex ones. What are the causes of the forms they take? Biologists wedded to the reductionist or mechanistic approach assume that these must somehow be entirely explicable in terms of complex physio-chemical interactions between the parts. But others (including myself) are convinced that this mechanistic approach is too limited. There is, to say the least, an open pos-

---

*Chaired by Martin Johnson (Parapsychology Laboratory, University of Utrecht)

sibility that the phenomena of life depend on laws or factors as yet unrecognized by the physical sciences. The problem is to say what sort of things these factors are and how they work.

The most influential alternative to the mechanistic paradigm is provided by the holistic or organismic philosophy. Biologists working within this framework of thought have developed a new kind of field concept to help account for the development and maintenance of form and order in living organisms. These fields, called morphogenetic fields (from the Greek, morphe = "form" and genesis = "coming-into-being"), can be thought of by analogy with magnetic fields, which have a shape, even though they are invisible. (In the case of a magnet, this shape can be revealed by the patterns taken up by iron filings scattered around it.) Morphogenetic fields through their own structure mold developing cells, tissues, and organisms. Thus, for example, in a human embryo a developing ear is molded by an ear-shaped morphogenetic field, and a developing leg by a leg-shaped field.

But what are these fields, and where do they come from? For over fifty years, their nature and even their existence have remained obscure. However, I believe that these fields are just as real as the electromagnetic and gravitational fields of physics, but that they are a new kind of field with very remarkable properties. Like the known fields of physics, they connect together similar things across space, with seemingly nothing in between, but in addition they connect things together across time.

The idea is that the morphogenetic fields that shape a growing animal or plant are derived from the forms of previous organisms of the same species. The embryo, as it were, "tunes in" to the forms of past members of the species. The process by which this happens is called morphic resonance. Similarly, the fields that organize the activities of an animal's nervous system are derived from past animals of the same kind; in their instinctive behavior, animals draw on a sort of species "memory bank" or "pooled memory."

Experimental Tests. This new hypothesis, called the hypothesis of formative causation, leads to a range of surprising predictions that provide ways of testing it experimentally. It is in the chemical realm that the most unambiguous tests should be possible. The hypothesis of formative causation applies not only to living organisms but also to chemical systems, such as crystals. It predicts that the patterns in which molecules arrange themselves when they crystallize should be influenced by the patterns taken up in previous crystals of the same substance. This influence should act directly through both space and time with the result that substances should crystallize more readily all over the world the more often they have been crystallized before.

New chemicals synthesized for the first time are indeed usually difficult to crystallize, and do in fact tend to form crystals more readily as time goes on. The conventional explanation is that tiny fragments of previous crystals get carried from laboratory to laboratory on the clothing or beards of migrant scientists, and "infect" solutions of the substance in question. When no such carrier can be identified, crystal "seeds" are assumed to have travelled around the world as microscopic dust particles in the air. But according to the hypothesis of formative causation, crystallization should occur more readily the oftener the compound has already been crystallized, even if migrant scientists are kept well away and dust particles are filtered out of the air. This prediction could fairly easily be tested experimentally.

Another kind of experimental test is possible in the realm of animal behavior. If a number of animals, say rats, learn a new trick which rats have never performed before, then other rats of the same breed all over the world should be able to learn the same trick more easily, even in the absence of any known kind of connection or communication. The larger the number of rats that learn it, the easier it should become for subsequent rats everywhere else.

Remarkably enough, there is already evidence from a long series of experiments carried out with rats in America, Scotland, and Australia that this effect actually occurs. The rate of learning a particular task increased in successive batches of rats, whether or not they were descended from rats that had learned the task, and the increased rate of learning was found in the different laboratories separated by thousands of miles.

Tuning in to the Past. According to this hypothesis, organisms tune in to similar organisms in the past, and the more similar they are, the more specific is the tuning. This principle has important consequences for the understanding of memory. For the most specific morphic resonance acting upon an organism in the present will be that from its own past states. Thus its memories need not be stored as traces or impressions within its nervous system, but rather may be given directly from its own past states by morphic resonance.

In order to see more clearly the difference between the morphic resonance and the trace theories of memory, consider the analogy of a transistor radio. The music coming out of the loudspeaker depends on the energy supplied by the battery, on the components of the set and the way they are wired together, and on the transmissions to which the set is tuned. Slight damage to the set may lead to distortions in the sound, while more severe damage leads to a loss of the ability to receive the transmissions altogether. But, of course, these facts do not mean that the music is actually produced or stored within the set. And no more does the fact that brain damage can result in loss of memory prove that the lost memories were stored inside the brain: the damage might simply prevent the brain from tuning in to its own past states.

Now imagine that different parts of the circuitry of a normally functioning radio set are stimulated electrically by applying a low voltage current. Under some circumstances, this might affect the tuning and cause the radio to receive transmissions from a different station from that to which it was originally tuned. But this does not prove that the music coming from the new station is stored inside the part of the set that is stimulated, or indeed in any other part of the set. Likewise, the well-known experiments in which memories were evoked by the electrical stimulation of the temporal lobes of the brain do not prove that this nervous tissue contains memory traces.

The loss of memory through brain damage and the evocation of memories by electrical stimulation of the brain constitute the primary evidence taken to support the trace theory of memory. But they lose their persuasive power as soon as this alternative interpretation is considered. And not only does the trace theory have no persuasive evidence in its favor, but it also faces grave difficulties in accounting for the fact that attempts to localize memory traces or "engrams" within the brain have been remarkably unsuccessful. K. S. Lashley (Symposia of the Society of Experimental Biology, 1950, 454-482) summed up the results of hundreds of experiments carried out on trained animals as follows: "It is not possible to demonstrate the isolated localization of a memory trace anywhere within the nervous system. Limited regions may be essential for learning or retention of a particular activity, but within such regions the parts are functionally equivalent." A similar phenomenon has been demonstrated in an invertebrate, the octopus. Observations on the survival of learned habits after the destruction of various parts of the vertical lobe of the brain have led to the seemingly paradoxical conclusion that "memory is both everywhere and nowhere in particular."

These findings are extremely puzzling from a mechanistic point of view. In an attempt to account for them it has been suggested that memory traces are somehow distributed within the brain in a manner analogous to the storage of information in the form of optical interference patterns in a hologram. But this remains no more than a vague speculation.

The hypothesis of formative causation provides an alternative interpretation according to which memories are not stored inside the brain at all but given from its past states by morphic resonance.

Implications for Psychical Research. This unfamiliar way of thinking about the nature of memory enables a number of well-known problems to be seen in a new light. First, if we tune in to our own past states, rather than retrieve memories from traces within our brains, then there is no reason in principle why we should not on occasion be able to tune in to other people's memories. If this happens with very recent past states, then the result would be indistinguishable from telepathy. We might also tune in to other people's memories in our dreams and hypnagogic imagery.

Secondly, it might be possible to draw upon the memories of people now dead, as in the "memories of past lives" reported in ostensible reincarnation cases, and in mediumistic communications.

Thirdly, morphic resonance with large numbers of people in the past might result in a pooled or collective memory which could provide the basis for what C. G. Jung called the collective unconscious.

Clearly, the question of the nature of memory is of central importance for psychical research. For if memories are indeed stored inside the brain, then they must inevitably decay together with the nerve cells after death. This is the main reason why most believers in the mechanistic theory are so convinced that personal conscious survival is impossible, and why from their point of view the evidence for survival from mediumistic communications and from cases of the reincarnation type makes no sense at all.

I do not pretend that the hypothesis of formative causation provides all the answers, nor does it remove the problems concerning the relationship of the psychical to the physical. But I do think that it can help us to begin thinking about these problems in a new way.

ON THE LIMITATIONS OF PSI--A SYSTEM-THEORETIC APPROACH

Walter von Lucadou† (University of Freiburg) and Klaus Kornwaf (Fraunhofer Institut für Arbeitswirtschaft und Organisation, Stuttgart)

In spite of the impression that psi might be omnipotent, rather rigid limitations must exist in order to explain the elusiveness and rareness of psi events. It is suggested that these limitations are based on the "meaning" of the situation in which psi occurs. Recent discussion has shown, however, that there are serious problems in defining a measure for meaning. It is not possible to describe meaningful information in terms of Shannon-type information.

The purpose of this paper is to propose a new concept of information called "pragmatic information" and to describe its properties. The new model can improve the usual quantum mechanical models called "observational theories" by introducing additional postulates concerning pragmatic information.

The observational theories (B. Millar, EJP, 1978, 303-332) have had a great impact on both theoretical discussion and experimental approaches in parapsychology, but they also entail many problems. The main one is called the divergence problem and is directly connected with our subject: the limitations of psi in space-time. Following the observational theories it is supposed that psi is independent of space and time (and hence causality), and thus the influence of a future observer can only be handled by additional post hoc assumptions. It is obvious, therefore, that the limitations must be due to the "information transfer" (whatever that means). Another lack of the observational theories is that they do not explain explicitly the rareness and the elusiveness of psi. These problems are regarded as psychological conditions.

The main reason for these disadvantages seems to be that these theories use a non-classical model only in relation to the physical level, i.e. the quantum mechanical level. The explicit system-theoretical model is a purely classical one which starts from information theory in Shannon's sense. Both Walker's information transfer $W \cdot \Delta t$ and Schmidt's psi source θ are Shannon-type information sources. Therefore it is necessary to introduce a new concept of information which can describe the "meaning" of a situation. We propose the concept of "pragmatic information," which deals with the meaning of information insofar as it describes the action that meaning has in a certain context. It describes information that has been understood. It is clear that meaning depends on the context, but the context is not measurable directly. The only way to get a measure of meaning is to look at the action that is caused by the information. This is a purely pragmatic concept and can be operationalized. One might object that the concept of pragmatic information is simply a kind of classical behavioristic concept, but this is not true; pragmatic information cannot be understood as a kind of stimulus which is given under special boundary conditions and which is quantifiable in terms of Shannon's information measure. Furthermore, the concept of pragmatic information exhibits both teleological and causal features. Thus, it can account for the goal-oriented character of psi. The action is not necessarily a simple reaction. It can alter the receiving system as a whole without direct reactions. Thus, it can alter the potentialities of the system. The concept is holistic insofar as it is only definable in the context of the system as a whole. Since the action of pragmatic information has been potential it cannot be destroyed without destroying the whole system or important parts of it. The Shannon-type information in general is therefore no measure of pragmatic information.

To specify the properties of pragmatic information E. von Weizsäcker (Offene System I. Stuttgart: Klett, 1974, 83-113) has introduced two concepts as components of pragmatic information. He calls them novelty and confirmation. Pragmatic information must contain both novelty and confirmation to a certain extent. It is a kind of product of these two components. Obviously novelty and confirmation are complementary concepts. This complementary structure shows clearly that pragmatic information is a non-classical concept which entails a structure that is similar to the concept of action in quantum physics. This is based on more general system-theoretical features.

Let us reconsider Walker's theory. The only reason he starts with hidden variables is that he has to identify them with the mind (or consciousness). Hidden variables are classical concepts. They are necessary within Walker's theory because his concept of information is classical, too. Thus, if he wants to unite mind and physics he has to do this with a classical interface. We try to suggest, however, that this interface is not classical at all because pragmatic information is no classical observable. Therefore there is no need for introducing hidden variables. The information $W \cdot \Delta t$ which is introduced by Walker cannot be measured. Nevertheless, Walker's model need not be rejected as a whole. It may be regarded as a kind of first approximation which only describes the physical aspects of psi. It does not contain psychological features. To introduce them we start with a few plausible postulates of the properties of pragmatic information.

Postulate 1: The information which is transferred within the context of Walker's model is not Shannon-type information but pragmatic information. Therefore, his basic equation

$$\Delta I = W \cdot \Delta t = -\log_2 P(\Psi_o \to \Psi_i)$$

must be reformulated:

$$\Delta I_{op} = P_{op}(\Psi_o \to \Psi_i)$$

ΔI_{op} is pragmatic information which however is not a classical observable but an operator which is not yet specified. Therefore the expression $-\log_2 P$ must be replaced by the operator P_{op} which specifies the transition $\Psi_o \to \Psi_i$.

Postulate 2: Pragmatic information is a function of what we call semantic difference. This postulate entails that the change in complexity of the system is a measure of the pragmatic information that is processed in the system.

Postulate 3: Pragmatic information is a quantized quantity like action in physics where C = complexity, f and g are still unknown; and i = least action of pragmatic information:

$$\Delta I_p = i \cdot f(\Delta S, C) \, ; \quad \Delta S = g(\partial C/\partial t)$$

There exists some psychological evidence which supports such an assumption. For instance, we all know that the meaning of a joke cannot be divided into smaller parts. We call this the "heureca principle." In psychology it is known as the "gestalt-switch."

From these three postulates it is possible to deduce an extremely important conclusion. It is a kind of uncertainty principle for pragmatic information and states that the deterministic description of natural complex systems and its behavior are complementary concepts which are limited by the least action of pragmatic information (i). If we define autonomy of a system as a measure of its degree of undeterminism, the uncertainty relation can be expressed in the following way: $A \cdot R \geqslant i$

"A" means autonomy of the system; if the autonomy of a

system is very low its deterministic time invariant description is very good. High autonomy of a system means that there are many parts in the system which are not known precisely or which only can be regarded as black boxes. "R" means the reliability of the system; if the reliability of the system is high one can really predict the time protocol of the output of the system. Systems with high autonomy mainly deliver novelty, on the other hand systems with a high reliability deliver almost confirmation. The product of autonomy and reliability has therefore the same dimensions as pragmatic information which is indicated by "i" (the quantum of pragmatic information). This uncertainty principle states that if a certain pragmatic information of a system is transferred or received and the autonomy of a system is very low it turns out that the reliability must be very high and vice versa.

Even if this model is still very crude it permits many structural statements that can improve the observational theories. The divergence problem, for instance, arises because it is not clear when a measurement is finished and the influence of a future observer can be excluded. In quantum physics the measurement is complete when a particle or a single quantum has entered the measurement apparatus and is localized there. If it is true that pragmatic information is quantized, this must hold for the detection of pragmatic information, too. The information that an observer gets from an experiment, however, must be understood if such an experiment is to make any sense. The first observer who gets this pragmatic information finishes the measurement. In a parapsychological experiment this can be done by the experimenter or the subject; it depends on the experimental conditions. Any future observer, however, cannot influence these results. Note that a solution of the measurement problem does not invalidate quantum nonlocality, which is important for the functioning of Walker's model.

The next problem we want to consider is the elusiveness of psi. The uncertainty relation for pragmatic information shows that a precise description of a situation requires a certain determination of the system. Therefore, it must lose parts of its autonomy and the reliability of the system's behavior will be enhanced. This, however, means that the system cannot show any extraordinary behavior; that is, in a situation where the observer has complete control of the system a PK effect or RSPK phenomena must decline. It is known in parapsychology that the most exciting effects usually occur in unclear situations with reduced control. One has to be careful with this argument, however, because it could be misunderstood as a kind of immunizing strategy.

Concerning experiments let us assume that an experimenter has invented a new experimental technique for psi experiments. When he or she starts with the experiment the results are unknown. Let us assume further that he or she will get some positive results. These results will contain a great amount of novelty since this is the first time the experiment is performed. But it is still unreplicated and therefore there is almost no confirmation. Thus, the pragmatic information that is transferred by the experiment must be rather small. If the same experimenter or another one repeats the experiment he or she will enhance confirmation, of course. But since ΔJ_p is limited the novelty must decline. This means that the results will be less dramatic if one supposed that ΔJ_p was the maximum pragmatic information that could be gained by this experimental method. We recognize that this is an explanation for the inter- and intra-experimenter decline effect. The same argument can be applied to a single experiment to explain the normal decline effect. Often the post hoc evaluation of a telepathy experiment may show precognition or PK. This is a kind of displacement effect. Within our model it can be easily understood. If an experimenter, for example, wants to get a good and reliable result he or she may arrange the experimental conditions in such a way that if one would get a positive result one would gain more pragmatic information than the subject could pump into the system. But if this pumping really occurs it may indicate another state of the system which does really fit with the amount ΔJ_p. Since the results were not expected, confirmation will be very low, while novelty gains a certain amount.

A PROPOSED MECHANISM FOR THE SHEEP-GOAT EFFECT AND ITS RELATION TO PSI-MISSING, EXPERIMENTER EFFECT, AND THE PROBLEM OF REPEATABILITY

Michael A. Thalbourne (McDonnell Laboratory for Psychical Research)

At the 1981 SPR Conference, I presented data from three free-response GESP experiments that seemed to provide evidence for the occurrence of a sheep-goat effect (SGE). What I found was a number of significantly positive correlations between ESP score and the subjects' scores on an 11-item Sheep-Goat Scale, but only when the agent and percipient in a given pair did not have a mutually close emotional relationship with each other. A second novel aspect of the findings was that the ESP score obtained by a given pair tended to be as highly correlated with the Sheep-Goat Scale-score of the agent ($r = +.52$, $N = 53$, $p = .00006$, two-tailed) as with that of the percipient ($r = +.41$, $N = 53$, $p = .002$, two-tailed). Further analysis (partial correlation and t-tests) revealed that not only were these significances independent of the degree of correlation between the sheep-goat status of agent and percipient, but also that they were due to psi-hitting on the part of the sheep together with psi-missing on the part of the goats. This paper explores a possible mechanism for these SGEs (especially the curious Active-Agent Effect), and attempts to relate it to a number of other problematical psi effects.

I begin by explicating what I believe to be necessary to bring about psi-missing in a free-response situation. I suggest that mere "blockage" of the correct target information (as is sometimes postulated for forced-choice situations) cannot be the cause of free-response psi-missing: even if the correct target (say "Tree") was blocked from consciousness, and the percipient was left to guess from all the remaining non-Tree possibilities, he could presumably still score above chance: for he could as easily respond with "Leaf" or perhaps even "Umbrella, " and despite the fact that these responses come from the set of all "non-Tree" responses, they would still be ranked fairly high in similarity to the Tree-target. For blockage to occur in such a way as to lead to significant negative scoring, the whole network of Tree-like responses would have to be suppressed, which is to say all conventional associations to "Tree" (such as "Flower") and at the same time all graphic responses that showed some formal or structural similarity to the shape of the Tree (such as Umbrella). Thus, to achieve a significantly negative rank-score, rather than simply a chance one, the response must not simply be a non-Tree, but rather something utterly un-Tree-like--diametrically opposite to a Tree both in form and in concept (e.g., Window). It would seem much more plausible, therefore, to derive an analogy between free-response psi-missing and what psychoanalysts call "reaction formation, " in which the response on the behavioral level conveys information that is in fact diametrically opposite to what is known "deep down. " Free-response psi-missing may be an instance of psi being used to go out of its way actively to avoid giving any appearance of success.

Turning now to the question of what is the modus operandi of the SGE, I would like to follow on from John Palmer's plausible suggestion that the SGE results from the subjects' "need for vindication. " My interpretation is based on Festinger's theory of Cognitive Dissonance (dissonance being the cognitive discomfort produced by awareness of two inconsistent cognitions): I hypothesize that psi frequently operates in such a way as to reduce cognitive dissonance --by causing the world to appear to the subject to be consistent with his own beliefs as to how it should be and/or consonant with his desires as to how he wants the world to be. In Kuhnian terms, the hypothesis is that psi often operates so as to promote events that give the appearance of being consistent with a person's own "paradigm, " or view of the world, and especially to eliminate events which are anomalous with that same paradigm.

In the case of sheep, it is obvious that the attainment of above-chance scores is consistent with their beliefs about how the world works. But achieving above-chance scores would arouse dissonance in goats, who believe and probably want such a thing not to be possible. But what leads goats to psi-miss rather than simply to score at chance ? I suggest that this is due to the fact that naive persons statistically do not recognize that significant negative scoring is as much evidence for psi as is significant positive scoring; this lack of understanding leads to the belief that the true zero-point (i.e., "no ESP") is, in forced-choice tests, "no correct guesses at all, " and in free-response tests, "utterly no perceptible similarity at all between target and response. " It then follows quite naturally that naive goats should tend to be motivated towards obtaining the lowest score possible, so that "chance" may vindicate their belief that psi does not occur.

This model leads to a number of testable predictions, the most important of which is that "statistically naive" and "statistically sophisticated" goats (perhaps one and the same subjects, in a before/after design) should differ in their level of psi-scoring: the naive group should tend towards significant negative scoring, whereas the sophisticated group should score significantly closer to chance (with perhaps even significantly low variance). Such a result would suggest that the induction of dissonance about psi into statistically sophisticated persons can lead those persons to use their psi so as to produce scores which superficially indicate chance results!

If such an experiment ever confirmed these predictions, then it would probably have momentous implications for parapsychology. The evidence already provided by my own sheep-goat experiments suggests that under certain social conditions a distant person (the agent) can influence the outcome of an event (namely, the drawing of a response by the percipient) in accordance with his sheep-goat attitude. Could it be the case that experimenters can, on occasion, unwittingly act the part of agent and thereby influence the outcome of their own research? Could decline effects be causally related to changes in the sheep-goat motivation of the experimenter, as the initial desire for "significant results, " once fulfilled, begins to give way to ambivalence (Could it be a Type I error? Is there a flaw in the methodology somewhere? Can the effect be replicated?); or could it even give way to uneasiness or threat, as the prospect of further significant results turns into a specter? (What sort of dynamite are we playing with? Are we immune from the evil thoughts of others? How private are our innermost thoughts?) Furthermore, could not this teleological effect be exerted by other researchers in the same profession, or even by non-parapsychologists and opponents of psi, when brought face-to-face with a claim for significant results? It is a sad fact that failed replications are always a cause for rejoicing for at least some observers. Could not the problem of repeatability have come about, and be persisting, as a result of some highly skeptical audience (experimenter, colleagues, critics) "sabotaging" present and future research by needing or hoping that nonsignificant results will ensue, in order to remove the threat posed to the Paradigm by claims of psi? Could the "witness effect" be a special case of the sheep-goat effect? Is the sheep-goat effect better termed an "audience effect, " that audience sometimes being the subject, the experimenter, or outside observers? Whence, then, is the psi coming in our experiments? Such is the Pandora's Box that would be opened by extending the sheep-goat effect to persons outside of the well-defined experimental context. But such implications must, I suggest, be taken seriously if we are to appreciate the full ramifications of the sheep-goat effect (especially the "goat" part).

Most of these speculations rest on the assumption that the "agent" may paranormally influence an event in accordance with his sheep-goat attitude regarding the desirability of that event. The data upon which this assumption was made were the significant correlations between ESP score and Sheep-Goat Scale scores of the agents observed in the series of free-response studies cited above. This effect I called the "Active-Agent Effect." It is interesting to consider exactly what sort of psi process is going on in this effect. For in the case of the percipients, we can imagine the psi process as being analogous to the scanning of the environment by radar: in the case of a sheep percipient, the information is correctly acquired, and manages to manifest itself on paper as a response resembling the target; in the case of a goat percipient, the correct information is still apprehended at some level, but for whatever reason (our conjecture being that this reason is the desire to vindicate chance by producing a "low" level of resemblance), the information that finds expression in the response is quite the opposite of what is in the target.

But what is happening in the case of the agents? Presumably, one could imagine a sheep agent successfully "transmitting" the correct target-information to the percipient, like a radio signal, the percipient somewhat passively receiving the signal and reproducing the information on paper. But what of the goat agent? How does he or she bring it to pass that the percipient's response shows significant avoidance of the target-drawing's content? On an "information-transference" model, one would have to suppose that the goat agent was perverse enough to try to send a message which was diametrically opposite, in concept and form, that portrayed by the target! It seems to me unlikely in the extreme that such a process actually occurs. It is much more as if the agent thought "I expect that the response-drawings will show a low degree of resemblance to these targets," and that expectation somehow became translated into reality.

It may be, then, if this argument can be sustained, that the Active-Agent Effect points to the possibility that the psi process is a purely teleological one rather than an information-transference one. Empirical support for such a process would then make more plausible my postulated relationship between the sheep-goat effect and the problem of repeatability.

MISCELLANEOUS RESEARCH REPORTS*

ESP AND MEMORY: SOME LIMITING CONDITIONS

Gertrude R. Schmeidler (City College of the City University of New York)

Kreiman published in 1978 (abstract: JP, 1978, 340-341) an innovative theory about memory and ESP: (a) recall of well-learned material would show psi-missing, but (b) recall of less well-learned material would show psi-hitting. Thus, his summary hypothesis was that (c) psi scores would be higher for material hard to recall than for material easy to recall. His ingenious test significantly supported each part of his theory.

In 1980 three attempts at replication were reported: by Kreiman himself, by Weiner and Haight, and by me. Although all showed trends supporting the hypotheses, not one was significant. This was such an unsatisfactory state of affairs that I attempted two further (indirect) replications. The first was a false start. The second used an unorthodox criterion for selecting test subjects. Those selected subjects significantly supported Kreiman's summary hypothesis (described in RIP 1980, 118-120).

This still seemed unsatisfactory, especially because meanwhile I had thought of a counterhypothesis to explain the results: perhaps subjects were merely responding to the experimenter's suggestions. The present report describes two new series. One tested but failed to support the counterhypothesis. The other used different experimenters for a direct replication of my preceding series and found similar, significant results.

Kreiman's Method and My Rationale for Changes

Kreiman tested the 16 enthusiastic and eagerly hopeful stu-

---

*The papers and research briefs abstracted here comprise two sessions held on different days and chaired separately by Martin Johnson (Parapsychology Laboratory, University of Utrecht) and Mary Rose Barrington (Society for Psychical Research).

dents in his parapsychology class to find if precognitive ESP would help their memory. They were given a list of 50 words, with instructions to learn them in any order and to reread the list repeatedly during the five-minute learning period. Their recall period was 15 minutes; recalls were to be in any order and to include words of which they were uncertain. Twenty words were randomly selected for each subject as ESP targets. The first half of each recall list was taken as well learned; the second half as less well learned.

For my first subjects, precognitive targets seemed so remote as to be irrelevant as an aid to recall. Thereafter I used clairvoyant-type targets.

Few of my subjects seemed eagerly hopeful. Pretests indicated that the uncritically optimistic mood typical of Kreiman's subjects might be shown by affirmative responses to two vague questions about fortunate or unfortunate past experiences. If both responses described past experiences as fortunate, this would show that happy memories had surfaced; and when happy rather than unhappy memories surface, it implies that one's mood is happily optimistic. In the preceding and the two present series I restricted the experimental group to 16 subjects (following Kreiman) but (a) excluded goats; (b) perhaps mistakenly, excluded supersheep; and (c) excluded subjects who had not given affirmative answers to both questions about luck.

Most of my subjects wrote rapidly when they began recall, then paused, then slowly added a few more words. The initial spurt usually lasted beyond the first half of their recall lists and presumably represented the well-learned words. I therefore followed Kreiman in taking the first half of each recall as well learned, but discarded the third quartile and took only the fourth quartile to represent material learned less well.

Mean chance expectation for ESP success, following Kreiman, was initially .4 (20 ESP targets out of 50 words). For the fourth quartile, however, both target and response pools were smaller. I therefore computed mean chance expectation for the fourth quartile separately for each subject, as the ratio of ESP targets not yet recalled to words not yet recalled.

Series 1: Test of the Counterhypothesis

Rather than suggesting that ESP might aid recall, Series 1 suggested that ESP might influence learning. Subjects were told they would receive both a long list of words to learn and an envelope containing some of those words. They were to hope their ESP would help them learn the right words, the ones in their own envelopes. The method was otherwise identical with that of Series 2 (below). The hypothesis to be tested was that with these instructions, the best-learned words would show psi-hitting and thus ESP scores would be higher in the first half of the recall lists than in the last quarter.

When 43 subjects were tested, the experimental group was obtained: 16 sheep who answered both luck questions affirmatively. The experimental group's ESP scores were insignificantly below chance expectation for the first half of their recall lists (t = 0.44, 15 df) and insignificantly above for the last quartile (t = 0.97, 15 df); the difference was insignificant (t = 1.18, 15 df).

The data not only fail to support the counterhypothesis, but even show a slight trend in the opposite direction.

Series 2: Direct Replication of the Prior
Report with Different Experimenters

This series used the same method as the series reported in 1980.

Subjects. When 44 subjects had been tested, the experimental group was formed: 16 sheep who answered affirmatively both questions about luck.

Experimenters. Miriam Wollman, a parapsychologist, administered a group test to six students in the psychology class she taught; two were in the experimental group. A graduate student with only a mild, peripheral interest in parapsychology tested 23 students individually (eight in the experimental group) and 13 in a group test at another college (six in the experimental group). He did initial scoring of subjects he tested. I tested him to familiarize him with the procedure and also tested a volunteer; neither was in the experimental group.

Learning List. Fifty familiar, nonthreatening words were randomly selected from a small dictionary and typed in a column in random order.

ESP Targets. For each subject to be tested, 20 words from the learning list were randomly selected, typed in the order they appeared on the learning list, wrapped in aluminum foil, and sealed in an envelope.

Questionnaire. Question 1 asked if, in little things or big ones, subjects had been lucky or unlucky. Question 2 asked if, in studying for a test, they "unconsciously" selected appropriate areas. Question 3 asked about attitude toward ESP in this experiment.

Procedure. Subjects were told the experiment would study whether ESP could help them remember. They would try to learn words from a long list, in any order, by rereading the list repeatedly. When they tried to recall the words they would have an envelope which held some of the words. Their ESP might help them recall the words in their own envelopes. They were to write in a single column, in any order, any words that might have been on the list.

After five minutes with the learning list, subjects were given a recall sheet and the ESP envelope; instructions were briefly repeated; the learning list was removed. Subjects who seemed inattentive during the recall period were briefly encouraged. After 15 minutes they were asked to answer the questionnaire.

Results: Series 2. In the last quartile of their recall lists, the experimental subjects' ESP scores were significantly higher than in the first half (t = 2.48, 15 df, p < .05). ESP scores were negligibly below chance expectation in the first half and only suggestively above in the last quartile (t = 1.93, 15 df, p < .10).

Of the other subjects, the two goats and two supersheep who answered both luck questions affirmatively had scores similar to the experimental group. The 19 sheep who did not answer both luck questions affirmatively showed a negligibly small trend in the opposite direction.

Discussion. Data of Series 2 are remarkably close to those previously obtained with the same method (t_{diff} = 2.66, 15 df, p < .05). The two indirect replications give strong support for Kreiman's summary hypothesis that ESP scores will be higher for partially learned than for well-learned material.

The effect seems robust because different experimenters administered the two series and did almost all the initial scoring. Null results in Series 1 let us disregard the possibility that the effect is due entirely to the experimenters' suggestions.

Three limiting conditions must be noted. (1) After their initial spurt, many subjects wrote many incorrect words. Thus ESP aids memory only when the advantage from a few true positives outweighs the disadvantage from many false positives. (2) Without direct suggestion from the experimenter, data were insignificant. Expectation of success seems important. (3) Subjects whose questionnaire response implied they were not in a happily optimistic mood failed to show the effect. Mood seems important.

The data suggest two conclusions. The substantive one is that ESP can aid the retrieval of partially learned material in persons happily expectant that their ESP will be helpful in this.

The methodological conclusion seems more important. It is that psi research should build into the experimental design an examination of the subjects' moods, should segregate scores according to mood, and should make different predictions for different mood states.

EXPLORING THE FUNDAMENTAL HYPOTHESIS OF THE OBSERVATIONAL THEORIES USING A PK TEST FOR BABIES (RB)

Dick J. Bierman (Research Institute for Psi Phenomena and Physics)

Two babies of about ten months of age were subjects in a PK experiment. Each subject was seated in front of a visual display that was controlled by a computer with a Random Number Generator (RNG). Before the experimental session started a target number was generated and also a series of numbers from the RNG were prerecorded in the memory of the computer (prerecorded condition). During the session additional numbers, instantaneously generated by the RNG, as well as the prerecorded numbers were compared with the target numbers. When a hit (p = 1/256) occurred the nonsense blockpattern display was replaced by a display of a laughing face and a melody played for a few seconds. However, for the even "trials" the hits were only counted and the display was not changed (no-feedback condition).

The results of the 24 sessions were split in two parts and analyzed by two different analyzers. There was an overall missing in the data analyzed by analyzer 1 (z = -2.01, p < .025, one-tailed) and overall missing in the prerecorded condition (z = -2.12, p < .020, one-tailed). A comparison of the two subjects showed that subject 1 especially was responsible for the missing in the prerecorded condition (z = -3.08, p < 0.0015, one-tailed).

The results fit within the observational theories because the main contribution of the analyzer 1 effect came from the no-feedback data while the main contribution of the subject 1 effect came from the data actually observed by the subject.

LEARNING TO USE PSYCHOKINESIS: THEORETICAL AND METHODOLOGICAL NOTES

Charles T. Tart (University of California, Davis)

In 1966, I proposed that if we provided immediate trial-by-trial feedback of results to initially talented percipients who were motivated to learn, they might increase their ESP performance, rather than showing declines (JASPR, 1966, 46-55). Given the expanded model of this process published later (JASPR, 1977, 375-408), this was a matter of discriminating relevant experiential characteristics of successful ESP responses so that a percipient could respond only on trials that were associated with such relevant, psi-hitting characteristics and/or deliberately induce such characteristics.

Any multiple-choice type of ESP test, where the probability of a hit is p, has p proportion of chance hits. This proportion of hits will be associated with irrelevant experiential characteristics and so constitutes inherent noise and an extinction procedure. Thus, a percipient must bring some higher-than-chance level of ESP performance to the task initially if learning is expected.

A review of the empirical research on ESP (JASPR, 1979, 151-165) provided strong support for the prediction that immediate feedback would usually eliminate decline. The rarity of talented percipients working in immediate feedback situations, however, leaves the prediction that learning can occur largely untested. An empirical estimate of the level of ESP talent that needs to be brought to the feedback training situation for learning to occur is that it requires a psi coefficient (Timm, JASPR, 1973, 282-294) of about 10%.

Although the original presentation of the learning theory focused on ESP, almost all aspects of it apply directly to the possibility of teaching improved PK ability through immediate feedback training. If initially talented PK agents who are motivated to learn are given immediate, trial-by-trial feedback on their efforts, decline should be eliminated and improved performance should occur. The agent should be able to discern experiential qualities associated with successful PK use and either wait to try until these qualities are present and/or induce these qualities deliberately.

At first glance, the learning hypothesis seems contradicted by the PK literature. In the ESP test literature, immediate feedback has been rather rare, but immediate feedback has been almost universal in PK studies. The agent sees how dice fall or sees the indicator on the electronic random number generator (RNG) move one way or another. Yet Stanford notes (in Wolman, Handbook, 1977, 324-381) that decline effects are common and incline effects rare in PK work.

Recalling the need for strong initial talent, however, due to the inherent noise level and extinction procedure caused by chance-produced hits, I reviewed the PK literature to see if the theory has been adequately tested. It has not. (I am indebted to Barry Boatman for his library research for me on mechanical PK studies, and to Ed May for use of his review data that he collected for an SRI International report on electronic RNG PK studies.)

I have reviewed 33 successful (psi-hitting with p less than or equal to .05) studies of PK on mechanical systems (usually dice) and 35 similarly successful studies of PK effects on electronic RNGs, and computed psi coefficients for their most successful conditions. As distributions of psi coefficients did not differ significantly between the two types of studies, I then looked at the combined results. The majority of psi coefficients fall in the 1% to 3% range, with 90% of all studies showing less than 10% psi coefficients. If the 10% psi coefficient I empirically estimated as necessary for learning ESP performance is a reasonable estimate of learning the rather similar multiple-choice PK type of task, it is clear that there has been little chance for learning to occur in the vast majority of PK studies. The learning theory application has not been adequately tested, and the prevalence of declines is not surprising.

I would like to have seen whether learning had occurred in the few PK studies with high psi coefficients, or declines eliminated in those with moderate coefficients, but frequent lack of analyses for decline/incline effects and/or great variation in style of analysis precluded this analysis. Overall, the possibility that improved PK performance might be possible through immediate feedback training is still with us, but untested.

It should be noted that my learning theory application to both ESP and PK is about instrumental or operant conditioning, where we take a behavior that exists in poorly developed, unreliable form (initial psi functioning) and try to increase and stabilize it by informational feedback. The percipients/agents must be motivated to learn, otherwise they won't expend the effort needed. Because of this motivation, the information that one is right also acts as a reward, a positive reinforcer.

Recently Broughton, Millar, and Johnson (EJP, 1981, 317-344) applied an aversive conditioning procedure to try to increase PK. Using an electronic RNG PK task, they applied very strong, unpleasant electric shocks to their four would-be agents when they did poorly. No significant indications of PK were found in the data, much less signs of learning. Although these researchers connected their approach with my learning theory application, this connection is mistaken. Aversive conditioning is applicable to an already well-developed behavior whose frequency we want to decrease. When the task is to try to discriminate subtle experiential correlates of a poorly developed and unreliable talent like psi, however, the physiological activation and anxiety resulting from aversive stimulation would only increase the noise level and make learning more difficult than ever. Thus, there is no use for aversive conditioning procedures at our present level of development.

In conclusion, the provision of immediate feedback of results to motivated percipients or agents in ESP or PK tasks may lead to improved levels of performance on theoretical grounds. The rarity of talented agents in PK experimentation to date has not allowed adequate test of this possibility. If immediate feedback training can allow high level, stable ESP or PK performance, however, parapsychology will move on to much more fruitful research.

INFRARED MEASUREMENTS OF HEALER-TREATED WATER

Douglas Dean (Ph. D. candidate, Saybrook Institute)

In 1964 Grad published results suggesting a healer effect, that is, saline from a healer-held bottle poured on barley seeds in pots of soil produced plants 55% taller than saline from a non-healer-held bottle. He then passed infrared light (IR) through both bottles and found a difference of absorption of the light. He repeated this in four double-blind studies. Due to the fact that the difference was at the edge of the scale of his instrument beyond the manufacturer's range of accuracy, he assigned the effect to artifact.

The author had this repeated on an instrument with much wider scale and the absorption difference was present when not attributable to this artifact. Along with a spectroscopist (specialist in spectrum chemistry), who worked out the technique, the author repeated this IR test double blind using distilled water (not saline). An MIR (multiple internal reflection) cell is required to separate the 2.7 micron band (healer associated peak) from the nearby massive hydroxyl bond peak at 3.0 microns.

The IR ratio was used as a unit (intensity or size of the 2.7 band or peak divided by the intensity of the 3.0 band). IR ratios below 0.035 were controls; ratios above 0.035 and up to 0.080 were obtained from healers.

The healer, Olga Worrall, produced increasing IR ratios when she held bottles for 5 minutes, 15 minutes, and 30 minutes. Then these IR ratios showed a slow decline in value with time after she held them for periods of 1 day, 7 days, and 21 days.

The author was given equipment to try to repeat these results at Kings College, University of London. He found the effect first in $2\frac{1}{2}$-year-old bottles of tap water held by the English healer Rose Gladden. Holding for 5 minutes averaged 0.043; 15 minutes, 0.053; 30 minutes, 0.058; well above the control limit of 0.035 for IR ratio. Then he went to Rose Gladden's house to get bottles freshly held by Rose and her husband, Peter, acting as a control. The water was distilled. When Rose held a bottle for 2 minutes the IR ratio was 0.052; for 5 minutes, 0.053; for 15 minutes, 0.056; and for 30 minutes, 0.060. Peter's values were around the control (same water--not held): 0.026.

Then the author tried a new concept, that of partly full bottles. First, a full 2-oz. bottle with 2 ounces of distilled water in it, second a half-full 4-oz. bottle with 2 ounces in it, and third a 35-oz. bottle with 2 ounces in it. Rose Gladden held all three bottles at once for 30 minutes. The IR ratio values of partly full bottles were much higher than those of full bottles, but there was an approximately 12-hour delay in reaching the high values. Thereafter the IR ratio values slowly declined with time. A repetition of this result was carried out with healer Peter Higginson.

Rose Gladden tried placing a 2-oz. bottle of distilled water for 5 minutes at her solar plexus (IR ratio 0.043) and at her thyroid (IR ratio 0.079). The latter was the second highest healer peak obtained. Further, holding a 2-oz. bottle in her hand, she imagined healing with her body energy (IR ratio--control); while imagining healing by "higher consciousness," she recorded 0.074.

Next it was hypothesized that the healer effect would be boiled out by heating high IR ratio water into steam and condensing back into water. This did not appear to be the case. Boiling 0.055 water into steam and condensing still produced 0.053 water. Rose Gladden placed her hands around the steam from control water (IR ratio 0.020) and the condensate water was 0.053, suggesting a healer effect with steam.

Finally, Rose Gladden held her hands around heavy water (D_2O). The massive hydroxyl band is shifted 0.9 microns up the scale. Measuring a healer band in the same proportionate position for normal water seemed to show a healer band which was not present in the control (not held) heavy water. The results showed a five times more rapidly decaying IR ratio than normal water.

The results are speculative because of the small body of data and the short time allowed for use of the equipment free of charge. Further research would be worthwhile.

LABORATORY PK: FREQUENCY OF MANIFESTATION AND RESEMBLANCE TO PRECOGNITION

Charles T. Tart (University of California, Davis)

Advancement of understanding in most science depends on quantification of the magnitude of phenomena. Parapsychologists usually test the statistical significance of findings, but seldom quantify them. As part of a theoretical modeling of whether immediate feedback training might improve PK performance, the bulk of the successful laboratory studies of PK were reviewed and quantified.

Criteria for selecting a study for this review were that the results showed above-chance PK scoring at at least the .05 level of significance, and that it have all-or-none type outcomes on each trial that could be clearly labeled as hits or misses. Studies published in JP since 1943 and JASPR since 1961 were reviewed, as well as studies of PK on electronic random number generators (RNGs) from a recent review by May, Humphrey, and Hubbard. If a study had several a priori conditions, the one yielding the highest magnitude of PK was used to represent the study outcome. Thirty-six studies of mechanical PK (usually rolling dice) were reviewed and 30 studies of electronic RNG PK. For each study, the psi coefficient (Timm, JASPR, 1973, 282-294) for the best condition was computed by this formula:

$$\Psi + = \frac{H - Np}{Nq}$$

This coefficient, conveniently expressed as a percentage, indicated the percentage of time PK was being used after hits expected by chance were subtracted.

The distribution of psi coefficients for mechanical and electronic RNG PK did not differ significantly from each other For the combined 66 studies, PK manifests itself less than 3% of the time in the majority (56%) of the studies, with occasional higher frequency manifestation pulling the mean psi coefficient up to 4.7%. The highest psi coefficient was 17%.

This low frequency of manifestation of PK reminded me of the low frequency of manifestation I found for laboratory precognition (RIP 1981, 10-12). Thus, the psi coefficients of the 66 PK studies were compared with those for 32 precognition studies and 53 present-time ESP studies.

The proportion of times that PK is manifested in laboratory trials does not differ significantly from the proportion of time laboratory precognition is manifested. Just as precognition manifested far less frequently than present-time ESP in the previous comparison, laboratory PK manifests far less frequently than present-time ESP (Z conversion of Mann-Whitney U-test, $Z = -5.45$, $p < 10^{-7}$, two-tailed). Many present-time ESP performances are in far higher ranges than those ever seen for PK or precognition.

Given the excellent evidence for occasional manifestations of macro-PK, I am disinclined to take the above data as any sort of ultimate limit on PK per se. However, there may be more than one kind of PK, viz., macro-PK and a weaker kind that manifests as weak proportional shifts in laboratory random test situations. Following a suggestion by Ingo Swann, one way of accounting for the above findings is to hypothesize that laboratory PK affects the future rather than the present state of an object and thus is subject to the limitations of manifestation reported earlier for laboratory precognition. Another hypothesis is that laboratory PK tests inherently involve some precognition as part of their "guidance" mechanism, and so are again subject to the stronger limitations of laboratory precognition. Another line of investigation worth pursuing is the hypothesis that precognition and PK may be different manifestations of some more basic factor.

THE MOBIUS PSI-Q TEST: PRELIMINARY FINDINGS (RB)

Stephan A. Schwartz† and Randall J. De Mattei (The Mobius Group)

There have been several precognitive tests conducted at the mass level. None were positively significant, although the Rhine test in 1961 did report some evidence of psi-missing (JP, 1962, 244-51). In 1981 Mobius proposed to Omni magazine a precognition test which would also seek correlates with other measurements, particularly brain hemisphere dominance.

The precognition portion of the experiment was couched in a story format for reader appeal, and to avoid the usual dry numerical nature of psi tests. Previous mass-test results using straight number- or card-guessing had produced nonsignificant results. We wanted to test the effect, if any, of the invocation of visualization. Readers were asked to make a forced choice: locate five "golden discs" in a circular field of 12 circles. Embedded commands suggested relaxation and allowed the respondents permission to be precognitive. Consideration was given only to correct predictions, not to displacement, or psi-missing. A number of psychological variables were also tested as follows.

Style of Learning and Thinking. We decided to look for a psychological correlate with psychic functioning. We chose the 40-question, forced-choice SOLAT instrument developed by Torrance. This instrument, primarily oriented towards students, was modified to reflect a more general audience. The Torrance SOLAT questionnaire has been well correlated with a wide range of other established instruments, and it has been used and reported on in 45 earlier studies. Also, the Torrance test was designed to study the relationship between high I.Q., creativity, and apparent learning style. Torrance and Reynolds report in the SOLAT manual, "The right hemisphere seems to relate consistently to measures of creative ability...." Previous studies have suggested that psi-functioning seemed to be similarly oriented. If a connection between parapsychological studies and Torrance and Reynold's work could be established then there would be a link between two fields of research.

Holland Occupational Scale. We felt that job category might provide a possible correlate with precognitive skills and lateralization. The Holland Scale was selected because it has been widely reported and because Torrance had already used it in relation to the SOLAT.

Handedness and Writing Posture. Several studies discuss the relationship between handedness, writing posture, and brain hemisphere dominance. Such questions might establish a possible bridge between the psychological and physiological hemisphere models.

Time Perception. Schmeidler (JP, 1964, 93-101) and Dean (Executive ESP, 1974) have both reported studies in which the Time

Metaphor Test of Knapp and Garbutt positively correlated with precognitive skills. Since time perception had been advanced as the only existing correlate with precognition, we included these questions.

Procedure. The experiment produced a test population of approximately 18,000, of which 15,470 were properly filled out and usable as our data base. Incoming answers were split into two groups by simple alternate selection of incoming responses. Targets were generated utilizing a feedback shift register, pseudorandom number generator suggested by Edwin C. May. An individual target was generated for each respondent from a total target pool of 792 (5 combinatorial 12). Feedback was provided to each respondent. We sent an individualized follow-up report to each test-taker within four to six weeks. Our goal was to create a two-part visualization in which test-takers were first asked to precognize an event and then, upon receipt of their feedback, to post-cognize themselves at the time they took the test--sending back the correct answer. We believe that a key to precognition lies in emotional connections. The moment being precognized, we felt, was the test-taker's exposure to their feedback, rather than the actual computer target generation.

Hypotheses and Preliminary Findings. It was hypothesized that there would be a significant number of significantly scoring precognitive individuals. The odds of successfully choosing 5 out of 5 correct locations were 1 in 792; 4 hits = 35/792; 3 hits = 210/792; 2 hits = 350/792; 1 hit = 175/792; 0 hits = 21/792. The number of significantly scoring individuals was within the range predicted by the null hypothesis. The results showed odds of 16 to 1.

Pop.	4&5 "Hitters"	Ch. Exp.	Z-Score
15,470	743	704	1.54

It was also hypothesized that individuals defined as Dynamic on the Time Metaphor Test would score significantly higher than individuals defined as Nondynamics. The Dynamics did not attain higher scores than the Nondynamics, and Neutrals scored higher than Dynamics.

Pop.		4&5Hit.	Ch. Exp.	Z-Score
Dyn	4213	176	192	-1.15
NonD	9728	483	443	1.99
Neut	1529	84	70	1.78

It was predicted that the group of individuals identified as Extreme Right, in terms of the SOLAT, would contain a significantly higher number of significantly scoring individuals--on the precognitive part of the test--than the Extreme Left group. Extreme Rights did not score significantly higher than Extreme Lefts. They did, however, score higher, and we will explore this trend using a stepwise approach of discriminant analysis. Through the use of an item analysis we will isolate the strongest indicators defining lateralization.

In comparing Groups A and B we found no major variances between the two.

Our next lines of inquiry will address post hoc possible correlations based on occupation, sex, age, lateralization, writing posture, handedness, and precognition.

RECORDING OF SUDDEN PARANORMAL CHANGES OF BODY WEIGHT (RB)

John B. Hasted,† David Robertson (Birkbeck College, University of London), and Ernesto Spinelli (Richmond College)*

Experiments have been conducted on the changes of body weight that might be recorded by psychic subjects and meditators. A metal bed 200 cm x 77 cm, of 37 cm in height has been designed by Geoffrey Blundell, operating as follows. Each corner is suspended by a tensioned wire; the wires pass round pulley wheels and are all attached to a single load cell. Lateral movement is minimized by pivoted horizontal constraint ties.

The load cell, Transducers Incorporated type T62H-1K-10PI, consists of a 350-Ω thermally compensated strain gauge bridge mounted on a steel bar held rigid at the end opposite to the one to which the four tensioned wires are attached. For a 1000-pound weight the output of the bridge, excited with 10 V D.C., is 10 x 2.0005 mV; this is fed to the amplifiers of a Yokogawa-type 3047 chart recorder. Electronic controls enable a high sensitivity suppressed zero output to be recorded, after adjustment to the body weight of the subject who is seated or lying on the bed. Calibration of the recorded output, carried out by adding weights, is found to be linear within $\pm 4\%$. Natural oscillations of the loaded couch are of the order of 10 grams.

A metal frame chair is placed on one end of the levelled couch and the subject invited to sit upright thereon. The couch is positioned so that fixed objects, such as the walls of the room, are out of his or her reach. The subject's feet normally rest on the couch, and it would not be possible for them to touch the floor. By reaching sideways with one foot it would be just possible for the

---

*We would like to acknowledge the support of the K.I.B. Foundation and the participation of Deborah DuNann and Ruth West.

subject to touch the screen covering the load cell, but observation is maintained in case he or she should ever attempt this maneuver. We are confident that no subject has ever attempted it; thus, there is no normal method by which he or she can produce an apparent change of body weight, other than by expelling material objects, for example from his or her pockets.

On the other hand, dynamic effects can readily be recorded by body movement, rocking, bouncing, etc., and these can be as large as one kg. They oscillate about a mean value which is the subject's normal body weight. When the seated subject is motionless, there remains a dynamic signal which is his or her ballistocardiogram, produced by the body-shaking caused by the operation of the heart and the motion of the blood. The mean value of ratio of height of first peak to height of second peak ("I/J ratio") may possibly be related to cardiac condition, in that for the three post-myocardial infarct subjects monitored the mean ratio was 1.08 ± 0.15, whereas for ten normal subjects the ratio was 1.83 ± 0.26.

For recording of a "levitation session" the chart speed is slowed down, so that the ballistocardiogram appears as noise (-100 grams). The subject is carefully watched at all times.

More than 20 subjects have been monitored for periods of up to 50 minutes. With the following exceptions, the apparatus has behaved perfectly; that is, no levitation or anti-levitation signals have been recorded.

In two of the sessions, with subjects G.H. and G., four sharply peaked weight-increase signals were recorded in otherwise quiet sessions with apparent body tranquillity. The longest of these corresponded to a weight of 0.8 kg. Although we can find no physiological or physical reason for these signals, and therefore consider them to be paranormal in origin, we do not regard them as essentially due to a levitation or anti-levitation phenomenon because of the short time durations (less than one second).

In the only session with erstwhile (Enfield) poltergeist subject, J.H., in the presence of Maurice Grosse and the authors, more interesting data were recorded. Instructions had just been given to the subject to rock the body slowly forwards and backwards, but the normal signals obtained when this maneuver is carried out do not depart from the mean value for any appreciable time.

The J.H. data show two sudden five-second weight-increase signals of about one kg and a minute gradual weight increase which eventually returns to normal. We can find no explanation of these data in physical terms.

Preliminary experiments have been done with a complete table-lifting group and table supported on the bed.

SOME ATTEMPTS TO DETECT THE HUMAN AURA (RB)

G. Karolyi, D. Nandagopal, H. H. Wigg (University of Adelaide)

Many people claim the ability to see an "aura" surrounding the human body, extending approximately 10 to 20 cm from the skin surface. The authors felt that if such an aura existed and were of physical nature it ought to exhibit physical properties, such as absorbing light passing through it, reflecting light falling on it, or being perhaps self-luminous to some extent. It was also considered a possibility that self-luminosity possessed by the body surface could be the primary source of the aura. Experimental procedures were devised in order to test each of these hypotheses.

Procedure. The experimental setup essentially consisted of a double dark room, a monochromator from which a narrow light beam could be passed into the room, a photomultiplier tube, and associated equipment for monitoring the light originating from the monochromator, or from a subject inside the dark room. The authors acted as subjects.

The monochromator was a prism-type instrument, Beckman Spectrophotometer Model DUR, and the photomultiplier was the EMI QB 9659 tube with a wavelength range extending from 200 to 900 nanometers (nm). The tube was cooled to $-15°C$ to minimize the dark current. At the maximum permissible anode to cathode voltage the tube gain was 6.76×10^6. The anode current was passed into a current to voltage converter with a transfer gain constant of 10 nanoamperes per volt. The output of the converter was then integrated typically for 10 seconds with an integrator gain of 10.

Readings were taken with the subject in position, and the subject away (background only), the difference of these readings yielding the net integrator output voltage. The net cathode current could then be calculated from the net integrator output voltage, the tube, converter and integrator gains, and the integration period.

Absorption and Reflection. A narrow beam of light originating from the monochromator was passed into the dark room and allowed to fall on the cathode of the photomultiplier tube. The beam passed between the prongs of a fork. Various parts of the subject's body were then placed in contact with the prongs. The distance between the skin and the beam was determined by the position of the prongs relative to the beam, and could be varied from 5 mm to 150 mm.

Light beams of various intensity and wavelength were passed at different distances from parts of the body such as the head, palm, and abdomen. In no case could any change in the light signal be detected resulting from the body being placed in the proximity of the beam. It was therefore concluded that the aura did not exhibit any detectable absorptivity in the 200- to 900-nm wavelength range.

Next, the photomultiplier was placed adjacent to the entry point of the light beam into the room. A nonreflecting collimating tube was mounted in front of the cathode window of such length and diameter, and so directed, that the photomultiplier could respond to scattered radiation from the region where the beam passed adjacent to the body, but was not able to pick up any radiation originating from the skin.

Once more various intensities and wavelengths were tried for different distances from parts of the body. In no case could any scattered light be detected, leading to the conclusion that the aura had no detectable reflectivity, or scatter effect, in the 200- to 900-nm range.

Self-luminosity. In order to test for self-luminosity of the aura, nonreflecting flat horns were mounted in front of the photomultiplier tube. A typical horn aperture was 50 x 250 mm. The long side of the aperture was positioned parallel to the body and 10 to 50 mm away from it. This enabled radiation to be gathered from a rather large volume of space adjacent to the body, but to exclude any direct radiation from the skin surface.

Once again the results were negative; the aura did not exhibit any detectable self-luminosity in the 200- to 900-nm wavelength range within the sensitivity of the apparatus.

Emission from the Body Surface. Various body surfaces were found to emit measurable radiation. Since the fingers yielded by far the largest output, it was decided to determine the spectral distribution of the radiation from these using a set of filters.

A 50-mm diameter collimating tube was mounted in front of the photomultiplier. The distance between the aperture of the collimator and the photomultiplier window was 130 mm, with provision for the insertion of filters in front of the window. Typically sets of 10 readings were taken with the subject away, then with three fingers bunched together in front of the aperture both with and without a filter, and finally the subject away once more. The net cathode current was then obtained by subtracting from the average of the "in front" readings, with or without a filter, the weighted average of the before and after "away" readings. This would allow for any small constant drift in the background readings.

The maximum number of wavelength subranges into which the overall tube range of 200 to 900 nm could be divided was limited by the minimum signal reliably determinable by the apparatus.

The compromise arrived at consisted of nine subranges of approximately 80-nm width each. Net cathode current readings for each of the subranges were obtained either using a band pass filter alone, or using pairs of long wavelength pass filters sequentially to obtain cathode currents that were differenced.

The body surface radiation was found to be considerably time dependent. Consequently, normalization of the net cathode current was carried out with respect to the unfiltered average of a particular experimental run, typically 10 minutes per filter, 90 minutes total.

The emitted radiation density for the various subranges was calculated from the normalized net cathode currents, the filter attenuation characteristics, and the radiant sensitivity of the photomultiplier cathode material on the assumption that the subranges were small enough for the radiation density to be regarded constant within any given subrange.

The finger radiation spectral distribution curves deduced this way indicate that most of the radiation occurs in the 600- to 700-nm region. The total radiation collected by the cathode is the area under the distribution curve and was found to be typically 3×10^{-16} watts. It must be remembered that this is only a fraction of the total emitted radiation by the three finger source. If one regards the latter as a point source radiating with equal intensity in all directions, then the radiation collected by the cathode needs to be increased by approximately 150 for the setup used, leading to a total radiation from three fingers of approximately 5×10^{-14} watts.

Radiation from other parts of the body was found too low for the spectral distribution to be determined. However, if one assumes the spectral distribution to be similar for all parts of the body with most of the emission concentrated in the 600- to 700- nm range, and if one approximates the distribution curve by a constant in that region and zero outside that region, then the radiation collected by the cathode is estimable from the net cathode current and the radiant sensitivity of the cathode material.

It appears that after the fingers the palm and the nose are the most effective radiators, while flat surfaces, such as the abdomen, are the least effective, with typically 2×10^{-17} watts from a circular area of 50-mm diameter.

One might anticipate a fingertip to approximate a point source, in which case the emitted radiation may be expected to obey the inverse square law. In order to test for this, collimator tubes of various lengths were mounted in front of the photomultiplier window, enabling the fingertip to be positioned at known distances from the window.

The radiation was found to fall off more rapidly with distance, in fact, approximately in accordance with an inverse cube relationship, which, perhaps, is attributable to atmospheric absorption at the low levels of radiation involved.

Finally, the question arises whether the radiation detected is the black body radiation one would expect from inanimate objects at the temperature of the human body. The possibility was tested for using internally heated metallic cylinders to simulate the human fingers. No radiation from such models could be detected within the sensitivity of the photomultiplier, even when the temperature of the model was raised to 100°C, which is well above the human body temperature. It was therefore concluded that the radiation emitted by the various parts of the human body is a property of the living organism.

In conclusion, the aura was not found to exhibit any reflectivity, absorptivity, or self-luminosity within the sensitivity of the apparatus, which could detect 10^{-17} watts change in radiation collected by the cathode. However, the body surface was found to emit a time-dependent low level radiation, mostly in the red region of the spectrum. Whether this radiation is within the threshold of human vision, and could be the source of the aura, requires further investigation.

SOME OBSERVATIONS ON THE PHANTOM LEAF EFFECT (RB)

P. C. Kejariwal (Jadavpur University), A. Chattopadhya (Sitaram Bhartia Institute of Scientific Research, Calcutta), and J. K. Choudhury (Jadavpur University)

Since the introduction of Kirlian photography to the Western world by Sheila Ostrander and Lynn Schroeder in Psychic Discoveries Behind the Iron Curtain (1970), the phantom leaf effect (PLE) has often been mentioned as an interesting falsehood or an uninteresting fact. Although high voltage, high frequency discharge photography (popularized as Kirlian photography) is not new (Bose, Proceedings of the Royal Society, 1902) nor is the phantom leaf effect, which was first obtained in 1966 (Adamenko and Vilenskaya, Technika Molodezhi [in Russian], 1974), details of a repeatable PLE experiment were published only recently by us (Journal of the Institution of Engineers [India], 1979).

In Kirlian photography, a high voltage pulse is normally applied across the top earth electrode and the bottom high voltage electrode. The pulse may be unipolar or bipolar, single or multiple. The pulses are usually modulated by a carrier frequency. The leaf is kept next to the high voltage electrode with or without intervening insulation and the film is placed on a mylar sheet which is used to cover the leaf.

It was first reported by Adamenko that even after a part of a leaf is cut off and removed the Kirlian photograph of the rest of the leaf can show the full leaf, the cut-off portion appearing as the "phantom." The experimental conditions we used for obtaining the PLE are briefly reported here.

Identification of the Parameters to Obtain the Effect. To obtain the PLE we found that the internal frequency of the high voltage pulse should be maintained above 100 kHz. The air gap distance was not absolutely critical but controlled the brightness of the picture. The peak voltage between electrodes was maintained around 15 to 20 kv. But it was the pulse repetition rate (PRR) that showed the most interesting variations. By varying the PRR the phantom could be made to appear or disappear. In the majority of our attempts to obtain the effect the most favorable value of the PRR was within a frequency band of 20 Hz. The phantom appears at less than Hz, also; but beyond 50 Hz the phantom was rarely found. We have taken large numbers of PLE photographs and our standard method is to vary the PRR (keeping the pulse modulating frequency above 100 kHz) and then to visually observe the appearance of the PLE through the transparent electrode system. The sharpness of the image and the clarity of the "phantom" can be regulated by changing the air gap distance in between the sandwich and by varying the amplitude of the hv pulse. The phantom portion appears in unpredictable details in different leaves, as can be seen clearly from the slides accompanying this paper.

It is only on rare occasions that sufficient internal details of the phantom portion of the leaf can be seen, although an overall outline of the phantom may be found most of the time. We have also observed that it is more difficult to get a top-cut phantom than a side cut. It seems that the PLE is connected with the growth phenomena of the plant leaf, the growth rate being reported to be highest at the bottom portion of the leaf and least at the top (Scientific American, May 1980). We have also found that about 15 to 20% was the maximum extent of the cut area possible for PLE as was previously reported by Soviet scientists.

Phantom Leaf and Life Force. Despite all attempts to reach a comprehensive theory to explain this phenomenon, we have no working hypothesis. The theories of Inyushin and Andrade are not clear to us. We have found that the PLE is highly sensitive to magnetic fields and it can only be obtained 5 to 10 minutes after the cut and not later. It seems that the phenomenon is connected with the life force of the leaf. As long as this force is there, the coordination and organization of the leaf exists, and the phantom is available. As soon as this organization is lost, the power of the leaf to produce the phantom is also lost.

We have observed that a leaf after being plucked from a plant loses weight slowly at first, but after a few minutes the weight loss becomes faster. The time interval for this is close to our observations regarding the disappearance of the phantom portion. We tried to correlate the two effects and found that the phantom can be obtained only when the weight loss is slow. Once weight loss is accelerated the phantom cannot be obtained. This shows that the phantom leaf effect is connected with the life force of the leaf and can be used to study this elusive subject.

MACRO-PK: THREE NEGATIVE REPORTS*

A TEST OF PSYCHOKINETIC METAL BENDING: AN ABORTED EXPERIMENT (RB)

James Randi (Committee for Scientific Investigation of Claims of the Paranormal)

In October of 1975 Professor John Taylor of Kings' College and Professor John Hasted of Birkbeck College, London (among others), were testing children who claimed to be able to bend metal by psychokinetic (PK) powers. One method was to provide metal specimens in closed containers and to require that the metal be deformed while so controlled.

Skeptical investigators had shown that the methods used were less than secure against tampering and outright cheating. Denys Parsons, a CSICOP associate, had demonstrated that glass globes with small holes, containing paper-clips to be "skrunched" by the children, were easily defeated. I myself had discovered that certain plastic tubes closed with rubber stoppers were also unsatisfactory. Then, too, the children were usually allowed to take these specimens home, where no observation or control could be exercised. Since cheating was thus possible, by parsimony it became probable.

I designed what I believed to be a foolproof system to perform similar tests of my own. With the assistance of Mr. Len Pitches of Kings' Instrument Development Department, and with the approval of Professor Maurice Wilkins of Kings' Department of Biophysics, I made a set of five acrylic cylinders, each containing a thin, easily bendable aluminum rod. These varied so that no length was a simple multiple of any other.

It had been claimed that access to the outside atmosphere was essential, so "blind" holes were provided in each tube. A rectangle of nitrocellulose paper was enclosed with the specimen, so that an attempt to raise the temperature of the metal considerably above normal would result in destruction of that paper, which was distinctively marked. Duplicates of all rods, identifying objects, and substances were kept.

---

*Chaired by Charles Honorton (Psychophysical Research Laboratories)

Each tube was closed by chemical "welding" which provided stress patterns in the acrylic (shown by polarized light) that were as distinctive as fingerprints. Each tube was carefully weighed and photographed. Each had identifying enclosures cemented into the end plugs as well, and there were fluorescent markings on each that showed up under medium-wave ultraviolet radiation. I was satisfied that these tubes could not easily be duplicated.

Protocol required that all five tubes be given to any subject in any test. All tubes were to be returned to Kings' College within two months of submission. A report was to be made on who had accepted or rejected the test. Professor John Taylor was given the specimens on October 3, 1975.

The tubes were never returned. There were rumors that they had been seen, singly, in various places, and Professor Z. W. Wolkowski of the Institut de Paraphysique in Paris even reported that Jean-Pierre Girard, a reputed metal-bender, had "modified" one of the specimens (that term was never explained) in the presence of Professor Taylor. This was denied by John Taylor.

Wolkowski had asked if I was prepared to provide a thorough analysis of these specimens, and I had replied that I was ready to do so. I never heard from him again about the matter, in spite of requests for information.

In the opinion of those at Kings' College who approved my protocol, the test was a fair and proper one, with good control measures. Since I was not present at any tests that might have taken place, it could not have been claimed that I inhibited any success by "negative vibrations" or a skeptical attitude. Other tests, done under circumstances that allowed possible cheating, have not been satisfactory as proof that PK powers of this nature have been demonstrated.

I am prepared to offer assistance in designing cheat-proof tests and by supplying similar test objects for use by investigators, and I encourage all interested persons to ask for my participation.

AN ATTEMPTED REPLICATION OF THE COX FILMS OF PK

Peter R. Phillips and Michael K. McBeath (McDonnell Laboratory for Psychical Research)

At the PA convention in August 1981, W. E. Cox presented a film of alleged psychokinetic (PK) events occurring spontaneously inside a sealed transparent glass box. The camera was triggered by an electrical signal produced when target objects moved off microswitches on which they were set. The events all happened in

Rolla, Missouri, in the home of J.T.R., whom Cox believes to be the PK agent, though J.T.R. himself makes no such claim. The filmed events are spectacular if we can be sure they are the result of PK and not fraud.

As the closest professional parapsychology laboratory to Rolla (100 miles distance) the MacLab undertook a replication. We agreed to keep our equipment in J.T.R.'s home for about six months (September 1981 to March 1982). During this time Cox removed his filming equipment and did not participate in our experiments until near the end when we asked him to prepare some targets for us. After the equipment was installed visits were made by one or both of the authors every week or two. J.T.R. was always informed about the current state of the equipment. We set no traps to try to catch him in fraud although we were urged last year to do so. While attempted fraud is always a possibility we felt that our equipment was secure enough that complex and delicate events occurring in it would almost certainly be due to PK.

Our sealed box (minilab) was an inverted aquarium tank; the rim of the tank fitted into a groove in the Plexiglas baseboard. The tank was secured by a steel bar running diagonally over its top. This bar passed through two aluminum posts and could be withdrawn only when two independently keyed padlocks had been opened.

The camera recorded the direct view of the box and also an orthogonal view by means of a 45-degree mirror. In the Cox experiments the camera was accessible to anyone. We mounted our camera inside a wooden box which was secured like the minilab. Light entered the box through a glass window. To obtain better resolution we used 16 mm film rather than 8 mm. Our camera was a clockwork one and would run about 30 seconds on one winding. The shaft was extended so that the camera could be rewound without opening the box. J.T.R. accepted the task of rewinding the camera and resetting the electronics when necessary. The film lasted about five windings, at which point one of the authors drove to Rolla to open the box, reload the camera, and arrange new targets.

Seven 100-foot rolls of film were obtained. Many times the camera was triggered without a switch indicator light going on. We were never able to locate the origin of the spurious electrical pulses. In the end we were obliged to slow down the equipment so that it would respond only to signals longer than about 1/3 second.

Results are categorized according to the strength of the evidence we feel they provide for PK.

Interesting but evidentially weak are simple movements of objects outside the minilab, such as a box and a letter. No clearly paranormal events were seen outside the minilab.

Weak also are two events involving magnetic objects inside

the minilab. One was caught on film, the other was not, but both could be simulated by using external magnets.

Somewhat stronger evidentially are simple motions of nonmagnetic objects inside the minilab. These were sometimes accompanied by slight shaking of the whole equipment as if the table had been suddenly moved. This could have been done by a person outside the field of view of the camera.

Strongest of all are a few events involving simple motions in the minilab (such as the sliding of a cardboard box and the vertical movement of a piece of paper) which occurred while the rest of the equipment seemed steady.

AN INVESTIGATION OF MACRO-PK: THE SORRAT (RB)

George P. Hansen and Richard S. Broughton (Institute for Parapsychology, FRNM)

There have been numerous claims of paranormal events occurring in the presence of various members of the Society for Research on Rapport and Telekinesis (SORRAT) (SORRAT: A History of the Neihardt Psychokinesis Experiments, 1961-1981, Scarecrow, 1982). G. P. H. visited Dr. and Mrs. J. T. Richards in June and November 1981 and spent a total of five nights as a guest in their home. It was reported that cards in sealed boxes had sorted themselves into suits.

Experimental Attempts. Three identical boxes of ESP cards were prepared by G. P. H. and R. S. B. in accordance with the methodology proposed by Hansen (JP, 1982, 53). The boxes were taken apart and marked with fluorescent paint and writing to prevent substitution. The decks were placed inside and the boxes reglued with epoxy. Hairs, threads, and fine wires were embedded in critical locations in the glue to detect surreptitious opening. A number of the security precautions were done at a microscopic level. G. P. H. prepared photographs and notes to document these precautions which were checked and verified by R. S. B. Stamped, self-addressed labels were placed on the outside of the ESP card boxes. These were then placed in stamped, self-addressed corrugated cardboard boxes. Also in the corrugated boxes was a note requesting the opener to telephone R. S. B. or G. P. H. (and reverse the charges) should the box be inadvertently opened. After all this was complete, one box was randomly selected and sent to Dr. Richards and placed in his home. If the cards were successfully sorted, it was planned to contact skeptics and to ask them to attempt normal duplication of the feat with one of the remaining decks. This would provide an empirical test of the security precautions.

The box disappeared from the Richards' home and there was a message left in alleged direct writing indicating that the box had been sent to Z. Mr. W. E. Cox reported that while in the presence of Dr. Richards there were ostensible paranormal raps that confirmed that the cards had been sorted and sent to Z.

A few days later the box arrived in the mail at the FRNM post office box; apparently it had never reached Z. A paper-glue remnant was attached to the corrugated cardboard, suggesting that there had been a label which came off the clear plastic tape on the outside of the corrugated box, thus exposing the FRNM address. It was also noticed that the clear plastic tape had been carefully cut and there were several small knife or razor marks in the cardboard.

The outer box was then opened in the presence of Debra Weiner, W. E. Cox, R. S. B., and G. P. H. It was found that the warning message was no longer in the box. The address label on the ESP box had been completely removed; in fact, there was no trace of it at all. After checking the documentation it was quite clear from the outer appearance that the ESP card box itself had also been tampered with. The examination was halted until all FRNM research staff could witness further examination.

The next day the box was examined further. It was found that the sealing tape on the ESP card box had been carefully extracted from beneath the glue seals. The tape had been placed back in approximately the original position. In other places the cardboard beneath the glue had been carefully cut and replaced.

Discussion. It was clear that the box had been tampered with by normal means. Whoever undertook the task spent considerable effort to enter the box without leaving any trace. The layered security precautions forced the person to proceed through a gradual unwrapping of the packet. It appears that unusual care had been taken at the early stages of this operation but that when the final security measures resulted in the obvious destruction of the box, the opener gave up in frustration, and, after entering the box, resealed it with rather less care than at the start. The fact that all warning and precautions against accidental openings were removed suggests that someone deliberately intended the box to be opened innocently by a third party. Thus, it was quite fortuitous that the address label apparently fell off. This scenario suggests a convenient "laundry" operation for botched jobs.

This is by no means the only failed attempt. Various FRNM staff members have prepared eight different test items. None provided any evidence for paranormal effects. Five have been sent to third parties for opening.

SURVIVAL RESEARCH*

THE PSI STRUCTURE THEORY OF SURVIVAL

William G. Roll (Psychical Research Foundation)

A survey of ostensible apparitions of the dead, rebirth memories, and mediumistic communications, including drop-ins, indicates to me that for the first few years after someone's death, evidence for survival is interwoven into the social and physical environment where the person lived, and further, that after a few years the constellations can no longer be identified with a previous personality. This leads to my proposing a "psi structure" theory of survival.

The concept of psi structure is congruent with many prior theories. William James (PSPR, 1909, 2-121), for example, suggested that after death, memory traces may exist "psychometrically" in the physical objects associated with a person while he or she was alive. If this "system of physical traces" should be activated during a mediumistic session, it would simulate what the individual recollected and also how the individual tended to act. Experiments by Gustav Pagenstecher (PASPR, 1922, 1-136), Eugene Osty (Supernormal Faculties in Man, 1923), and John Björkhem (Det Ockulta Problemet, 1951) suggest support for this "psychometric" thesis, i. e., if an object was frequently associated with emotionally intense events, gifted sensitives who handled the object could become aware of those events.

A theory with considerable explanatory power emerges if we combine these ideas of James et al. with concepts developed by Whately Carington and Gardner Murphy. Carington (PSPR, 1944, 155-228) proposed that an individual mind or personality is nothing but a cluster of psychons, that is, ideas, images, and sense-impressions which have been formed in the course of the experiences of the organism. Psychons are connected with each other to form a mind or "psychon system" following the laws of association, such as recency and frequency. (Current thinking supplements these laws with others, but this can readily be integrated with Carington's thesis

---

*Chaired by Gertrude R. Schmeidler (City College of the City University of New York)

and does not demand a basic change in it.) The central thesis is that in psi the same psychological processes occur as within a single person's mind, but in psi they connect psychons between minds, including minds separated in space.

Murphy (JASPR, 1945, 67-94) used the Caringtonian approach but employed the metaphor of a field to describe interpersonal relationships. He suggested that interpersonal fields are more than a sum of their parts and are likely to have their own organizational structure. The interpersonal field, either with its original or its new organization, may emerge into awareness or expression during altered states of consciousness. If there is survival after death, it may consist of the continuation of the interpersonal field rather than of any self-contained individual personality.

The psi structure theory accepts the postulate that individual minds need not be separate and adds the postulate that mind and matter need not be separate. This brings clairvoyance under the umbrella of association theory. If the extended personality of the experimenter encompasses the laboratory where the target for a clairvoyance test is located, this target could be integrated into the experimenter's personality. The various laws of cognition, including laws of association, could apply to the target.

The theory pictures the objects, images, and ideas that make up everyday experience as connected with objects, images, and ideas that are distant in space or time. Psi is the expression of relations both between people and between people and things. The relations are formed in the same way as the cognitive structure within a single person.

The theory differs from psychological theories in that it does not assume a sharp distinction between person and environment. A person who moves from one location to another may, in a parapsychological sense, remain "in" the old environment (although there may be changes in the course of time). Similarly, people remain "psi-contiguous" with places and people they have encountered in the past. They are part of the psi structure which includes these places and people.

Because psi processes have been regarded as primarily mental, few contemporary studies have explored the type of theory outlined here, although pilot tests by Martin Johnson (P. of the PA, 1965, 60-61) and myself (JASPR, 1966, 363-379) tend to support it. Marsh (Unpubl. Ph.D., 1958), Kirby (JP, 1959, 290), and Osis (JASPR, 1945, 67-94) have conducted similar studies. Research with Pavel Stepanek (M. Ryzl and J. G. Pratt, JP, 1963, 227-241; and Pratt and Roll, JASPR, 1966, 91-124) is also relevant because it raises the possibility that Stepanek responded to "psychic traces" on the cards, left there by his previous guesses.

The psi structure theory describes how an ESP percipient connects with his or her "target" and it dovetails with my earlier theory for the reception end of the ESP process. In this theory an ESP response is the result of an activated memory trace, which is triggered into awareness or expression by the target. (As Irwin [JP, 1979, 31-39] points out, the process may apply only to long-term memory.) The present theory extends the picture from the receiving to the transmitting end but avoids the concept of trace. It describes the complete target-to-response process as occurring within a structure of which the percipient is a part.

The views of some earlier theorists are similar. Hans Driesch (PSPR, 1935, 1-14) suggested that "the brain is a psychometric object [and the] proprietor of the brain is the one who used this rapport object, namely, his own brain, in order to get information about his own past history." Raynor Johnson (The Imprisoned Splendour, 1953) also gives an account of memory as a form of ESP and of ESP as a form of remembering.

This approach can readily be integrated with Karl Pribram's (Journal of Indian Psychology, 1978, 95-118) theory of memory and with David Bohm's (Wholeness and the Implicate Order, 1981) concept of physical reality. Bohm proposes that the sensory ("explicate") world is to be understood as a manifestation of an implicate, higher-dimensional order where matter and consciousness are indistinguishable. Memory is a familiar example since mental contents are here "enfolded" within the physical brain. This is a special case of a general process where previous moments leave an implicate trace in material objects from which it may be possible to "unfold" an image of the past. Psychometry may be an example. An analogy to the implicate, enfolded order is the hologram, where each part contains information about the whole object. Pribram used holography as an analogy to the brain process whereby memories are encoded in the brain as a whole rather than in any distinct part.

As a survival hypothesis, the psi structure theory argues that memories, dispositions, and other aspects of human personality remain in implicate form in the environment of the organism after it has died. There are continuous changes in the psi structure as persons come and go, just as the individual person changes with new encounters and experiences. The theory thus accommodates the decline effects that seem to affect some of the material suggestive of survival. The theory explains why memories of deceased persons may be evoked in the presence of their survivors or their personal belongings, or near the place where the person lived.

Tests for the theory might begin with ESP studies. If psi contiguity does not facilitate ESP, the theory is falsified. Another series of tests would determine whether, in fact, the images, memories, and dispositions of people become ingrained in the environment of those persons. The laws of association should be tested as predictors of psi, though we would expect to modify the early ones and find relationships consistent with more recent psychophysiological descriptions of cognition.

I will suggest here one other test among the various possible ones. This is based on the principle of psi contiguity which leads us to expect that in order to establish a close relationship between the living and the dead, there must first be a close relationship between the living and the living. There should be two procedures. Both call for mediums, subjects, and researchers who follow the same method except in one procedure the individuals have no contact with each other beyond the experimental session, while in the other procedure the individuals consist of a tightly knit group of people. (The study would use proper experimental safeguards against normal sources of information.) For the strangers, the theory predicts weak and erratic results. For the group of friends, it predicts more evidential communication--and it also predicts apparent autonomous behavior that could not be fully explained in terms of the desires of the individual members of the group.

SOME VIEWS ON SURVIVAL

T. N. E. Greville (Psychical Research Foundation)

1. The Psi Structure Theory.

W. G. Roll's "psi structure" hypothesis occupies an important place in current theorizing about the mechanisms underlying psi phenomena. The most recent and the most complete exposition of his views with regard to the bearing of this hypothesis on the survival question is contained in a long chapter, "The Changing Perspective on Life After Death" (Advances in Parapsychological Research, edited by Stanley Krippner, 1982). This chapter includes a wealth of interesting material on the history of survival research and the various kinds of evidence and observations that have been adduced in support of survival theories. Roll argues that there is no individual, personal survival of physical death; what survives is the "psi structure," which is a matrix that includes both the deceased individual and all those persons, places, and things with which he or she has been associated during physical life.

In expounding a theory that is novel to most of us and not always easy to understand, terminology is important, and in my opinion Roll uses some unfortunate terminology. An example is the term "mental entity," which is used to characterize all survival theories that postulate any form of personal, individual survival. It is mentioned early in the chapter that others once used the term "incorporeal personal agency." Here "incorporeal" is undesirable because it unnecessarily rules out the possibility that any kind of "body," even a "subtle" one, might be involved. However, "personal" is appropriate, as it represents the one common thread running through all the diverse theories that Roll rejects. On the contrary, the word "mental" seems restrictive. I am not convinced that the categories "physical" and "mental" are exhaustive: that anything that is not physical is necessarily mental. Ramakrishna Rao, in his 1978 PA presidential address (RIP 1979, 174), postulates that reality has many layers. He does not specify the number, but I suspect he had in mind more than two.

While "mental" is too specific, "entity" is too vague. An "entity" is anything that exists; most theories of personal survival suppose that the surviving entity is capable of "acting" in some way on some level, as the word "agency" suggests. A totally passive entity would not be able to make its existence known to us. Thus, I would prefer the term "nonphysical personal agency" (which could be abbreviated as NPA).

For each of various categories of psi phenomena, with particular emphasis on those that have been cited as evidence for survival, Roll tries to show (in my opinion, with varying degrees of success) that they are better explained by the psi structure theory than by the "mental entity" (or NPA) theory. It is taken for granted that an unequivocal choice must be made between the two hypotheses. Nowhere does he entertain the possibility (a likely one in my opinion) that both might have some degree of validity.

In a paragraph summarizing his objections to the "mental entity" theory he says:

> Even without Catch-22 [the so-called Super-ESP hypothesis], the mental entity paradigm is in trouble. It seems doubtful that apparitions of the dead, mediumistic communicators, and reborn personalities exist apart from the people and places where the deceased spent their lives. The decline effect and the ways in which the identities of the deceased merge with the living, and with other communicators, make it difficult to sustain the concept that they exist as long-lasting autonomous and independent entities.

Presumably the two arguments chosen for inclusion in this summary paragraph (the decline effect and the merging of personalities) are those that he considers his strongest arguments. However, the diligent reader of the chapter will find that he acknowledges that there are other plausible explanations for the fact that purported communications from a particular deceased person tend to taper off and eventually cease several years following death. The argument for merging of personalities is based on a few instances (in my opinion, isolated, sporadic cases) in which there was some confusion as to the identity of the communicator. There is not time for further details, but I think he has not made a strong case, except with regard to psychometry and mental robots like Philip (I. Owen and M. H. Sparrow, Conjuring Up Philip, 1974).

Though the survival question was responsible for much of the original impetus that led to the beginnings of psychical research, interest in the subject on the part of parapsychologists was at a low ebb for many years as they perceived the formidable difficulties in devising ways to arrive at any definitive conclusions. In recent years there has been a marked resurgence of interest, largely due to the attention focused on near-death experiences through the work of Moody, Osis and Haraldsson, Ring, Sabom, and others, and to the publication of well-documented cases suggestive of reincarnation, primarily by Ian Stevenson. With all due respect to Roll's very important contribution, I think that if indeed one can speak of "the changing perspective on life after death," it owes more to these latter developments than to the psi structure theory.

2. Reincarnation Studies

I believe that a majority of parapsychologists reject the philosophical doctrine of materialistic monism, the notion that the physical universe is the sum total of all reality. It is one of the strangest developments in the annals of human thought that most establishment scientists have come to accept this bizarre hypothesis, for which there is no hard evidence, and which is contradicted by the daily experience of every human being. Among many others, John Beloff (JSPR, 1980, 263-272) has offered a persuasive argument that psi phenomena cannot be adequately explained in purely physical terms. Recently Jule Eisenbud in his book Paranormal Foreknowledge (1982) has expressed himself very forcefully:

> If mind and mental events are conceived of as emergent from material processes, which is the assumption defended by most scientists today, then it goes without saying that paranormal phenomena do not exist and that only malobservation, delusion, or poor experimental design can give the impression that they do.

If then, there is a realm of nonphysical reality, it is logical to suppose that the human being is not synonymous with the physical organism, but includes a nonphysical part, and it is at least conceivable that this nonphysical part might survive physical death. I commend to your attention the interesting paper of Frank Dilley "What Is Wrong with Disembodied Spirits?" (Research Letter, 1981, 31-42).

If you are willing to entertain, for purposes of further discussion and investigation, the notion that some part of the human being might survive physical death (and I am far from saying that this has been demonstrated), then is it really inconceivable that this detached part might then attach itself to another physical organism? Grosso (JASPR, 1979, 367-80, and 1980, 419-424) has raised important semantic questions about the sense in which personal identity can be regarded as continued from one incarnation to the next. There is a tendency in some quarters to regard the idea of reincarnation as something so preposterous and absurd that it should not be taken seriously by intelligent persons. If some of you are inclined to take this view, I invite you to ponder seriously how much of this attitude has a rational basis, and how much of it stems from preconditioning by the particular cultural milieu in which most of us have grown up. Of course, in this area, as in all aspects of the paranormal, there is much sensationalism, embellishment, and outright fraud. On the other hand, all of us, as parapsychologists, have suffered because of the closed-mindedness of establishment science. It therefore ill behooves us, when the shoe is on the other foot, to rule out of bounds certain areas of investigation merely because we find their subject-matter distasteful. I invite your attention to two readings that I think may help to make the idea of reincarnation more palatable. One is an article by Ian Stevenson, "The Explanatory Value of the Idea of Reincarnation" (Journal of Nervous and Mental Disease, 1977, 201-208). The other is a book, Reincarnation in World Thought by Head and Cranston (1967). I think some of you may be surprised at the number of eminent Western personalities who have expressed themselves favorably toward the concept of reincarnation. In the brief time available, I cite only two. German philosopher Arthur Schopenhauer says, "We find the doctrine of metempsychosis, springing from the earliest and noblest ages of the human race, always spread abroad in the earth as the belief of the great majority of mankind." Thomas Carlyle, Scottish essayist and historian, says, "Death and birth are the vesper and matin bells that summon mankind to sleep and to rise refreshed for new advancement."

ASSUMPTIONS AND RECURRENT FEATURES IN SURVIVAL RESEARCH: A PRELIMINARY ATTEMPT AT INVESTIGATION (RB)

Arthur S. Berger* (Survival Research Foundation)

J. G. Pratt (JASPR, 1978, 127-139), observing that parapsychological research was not advancing as rapidly as might be hoped, invited a debate over some of the assumptions that influence parapsychologists to see if change might be required.

Research on the question of survival after death is also charged with assumptions that influence investigators. The pace at which this research is moving might be increased if some of the assumptions held were not merely debated but scrutinized. One of these assumptions is that, supposing survival, every human being will survive. Another is that human beings will survive with the same psychical powers and capacities, i.e., abilities to remember experiences and communicate them, posthumously as they possessed when living.

---

*I wish to express my appreciation to the Psychical Research Foundation for a grant to support this study.

If these assumptions are wrong, they may be misleading and retarding many present methods of research. For example, current efforts by some researchers to obtain evidence of survival from tests such as those devised by Thouless and Stevenson may be undermined because the participants in the tests may not survive death or, if they do, will not be as able as others to remember key words or sentences or to communicate them after death. Investigations into mediumship are foredoomed if the dead persons from whom messages are sought are not survivors for one reason or another or are incapable of sending a message through a medium.

Aims of the Project. These two assumptions (that everyone survives and survives with equal psychical capacities) have never been systematically and empirically investigated to determine their correctness. One of the aims of the research project reported here (done in consultation with Dr. Gertrude R. Schmeidler) is to make such an investigation. If it turns out that the assumptions are not warranted, the further aim of the project is to discover those special features and circumstances which appear to recur in the cases of those who have survived death with seemingly unimpaired psychical capacities, of those who have survived with limited ones, and of those who either have survived death with none or may not have survived death at all. These features and circumstances may distinguish one class of survivor or nonsurvivor from another and may be related to or may influence postmortem survival and faculties.

Methodology. To start the study by attempting to detect the peculiarities distinguishing one class of survivor or nonsurvivor from another by the investigation of people with dissimilar aims, interests, social stations, educational levels, and intellectual abilities seems impossible. Methodologically, it appears better to hold such a group in reserve and to start with a homogeneous sample consisting of persons of similar social class, education, and intellect and who had common interests and aims, even ties of friendship. In such a group the factors based on these elements would be controlled and minimized and the search for distinguishing variables would be less complicated. Moreover, these variables would be more sharply defined.

In addition to homogeneity, the lives and backgrounds of the people in this sample should be open to public inspection so that as much as possible can be known about them. It would be best therefore to study prominent people about whom much information can be obtained either from what they did or wrote or from material published about them that concerns their lives, deaths, and possible survival of death.

For this preliminary investigation six persons have been selected. Logically, if the assumptions that all people survive death and do so in the same degree and manner are correct and one of the six survives death with full capacities, then all should; and if one falls into a different class of limited survival or none at all, then all should. If, however, members of the group fall into different classes, the assumptions influencing survival research will be shown to be invalid, and the search will then go on to try to discern the special features that distinguish one member from another.

A second sample of six persons with different values and backgrounds, with no interests in common, and who were strangers to one another will then be studied. This heterogeneous sample will be representative of the general population. Its members will have been selected at random, the only qualification being that they were all conspicuous people so that what they said or what was written about them will provide information relevant to their lives, deaths, and possible survival.

This sample will be used for cross-reference. It will allow the data obtained from the study of the special homogeneous sample to be compared to the relevant data from the unselected sample to see if they mesh and confirm or clash and contradict. If they mesh, a basic pattern may emerge which is normative and characteristic of survival or nonsurvival. Having made the comparison, the researchers can then draw conclusions that may result in hypotheses or criteria requiring more research in a larger and confirmatory review.

Confirmation of a pattern would help survival researchers predict which human beings may be able to survive death and be good communicators. Thus, when these researchers design or conduct investigations or experiments, not only would much time and expense be saved but also the chances of survival research advancing and of research efforts reaching successful outcomes would be greatly enhanced.

THE FORLORN QUEST

George Zorab (Zoetermeer, The Netherlands)

Modern spiritualism, directly resulting from a case of poltergeist in 1848 in the village of Hydesville, New York, was the first religious movement to regard paranormal phenomena as proof of human survival after death. At the spiritualists' séances it was believed that the spirits of deceased persons communicated with the living, and proved their presence by the manifestation of ESP and PK phenomena.

Within a couple of decades spiritualism spread all over the Christian world at a time (the second half of the 19th century) when the advancements of the natural sciences (e.g., the evolution theory) seriously undermined the authority of the Bible, and when many people started to have doubts concerning the truth of the tenets of the Christian religion. Modern science was also evoking an ever-rising tidal wave of a materialistic view of life among the educated classes that compelled them to turn away from the conception that man was a spiritual entity capable of surviving the shock of death and existing for all eternity.

This state of affairs greatly distressed a number of Cambridge scholars who were much afraid that a materialistic way of life, if not halted, would soon bring about the complete collapse of Christianity and all it stands for. One of these scholars was the highly talented Frederic Myers, who was very much distressed that he was losing faith in the truth of the ideas of the Christian faith in which he was brought up. In his desperation Myers turned to his friend and former tutor, Prof. Henry Sidgwick, for help (December 3, 1869) and asked him, "almost with trembling, whether he thought that when Tradition, Intuition, Metaphysics, had failed to solve the riddle of the Universe, there was still a chance that from any actual observable phenomena--ghosts, spirits or whatsoever there might be --some valid knowledge might be drawn as to a world Unseen." Sidgwick thought that such a possibility did exist, pointing to the claims of the spiritualists who presumed to be able to communicate with the spirits of the deceased by experimental means.

Several years passed but no results were obtained that could satisfy their quest to find sound evidence of humanity's spiritual nature and the hope for the existence of a world of spirits. The turning point came when the physicist W. F. Barrett (later Sir William Barrett) read a paper during a meeting of The British Association for the Advancement of Science (1876). In this paper he described his experiments with a mesmerized servant girl who in that condition could produce telepathic phenomena. She could correctly guess playing cards Barrett presented to her in such a manner that she remained ignorant of the nature of the card. She also could answer Barrett correctly if sent on a trip of so-called travelling clairvoyance. If, for instance, Barrett sent her to London, where she had never been, and directed her to a certain square or building, she, without hesitation, could give a correct description of the place she "mentally" visited. But if Barrett, whom we may indicate as the agent, was himself ignorant of the playing card to be guessed or of the place to be visited in London, the girl, the percipient, was no longer correct in her answers.

The results of Barrett's experiments permitted the conclusion that human beings are able to communicate with other humans without the assistance of sensory organs. The meaning of this is also that a purely mental contact is possible between people. This experimentally evidenced thought-transference or mind-reading pointed to the presence in humans of a purely mental, spiritual something that could act independently of the material body. The latter raised the hopes of those who were seeking for scientifically based evidence of humankind's spiritual nature--a nature that was necessary to enable personality to survive in a spiritual world.

There is little doubt that in more than one respect Barrett's experiments gave an important impetus to the founding of the (English) SPR. For here already we have a beginning of the fulfillment of Myers' ardent hope that "Science in our time would open the spiritual gateway leading into the vestibule of an Unseen World." Science, represented by Barrett, seemed already on its way, while Belief was represented by the clergyman Stainton Moses, who was a well-known medium, constantly in communication with the spirits of the dead, and prepared to have his spiritualistic phenomena investigated by Science. It was this combination of Science and Spiritualism that formed the basis on which the SPR was founded in 1882. More than 70% of the first members of the SPR were spiritualists, while the rest were those who wanted to approach the problem of human survival in a scientific manner without any religious bias.

The results of Barrett's telepathic experiments greatly influenced the conceptions of the SPR founders concerning paranormal phenomena. These founders were specially interested in discovering a method to penetrate the gateway leading to a world of spirits mentioned above. The greater part of the SPR's researchers concentrated on telepathic communication, meaning mind contacting mind. Hardly any attention was given to what was known as clairvoyance, that is, mind contacting matter. During several decades after the SPR's foundation clairvoyance was deemed impossible, since allegedly mind (a spiritual entity) could only contact another mind, and not a material object. Contacting material objects, so it was believed, was only possible by means of the sensory organs.

Successful dowsing experiments are sound indications that mind can contact matter, that is, that the phenomenon of clairvoyance does exist. In England Barrett was one of the first to point out that "before we could hope to arrive at any definite conclusion as to the origin of spiritualistic phenomena, we must ascertain whether such a thing as the transfusion of thought between sitter and medium really existed, and its extent; and secondly, whether such a thing as clairvoyance or a transcendental perceptive power had any foundation in fact." Barrett wrote this in 1876. More than forty years later he declared: "Both these questions have been answered in the affirmative, and this renders the above caution the more necessary."

The SPR investigators of the survival problem, headed by the Sidgwick group, approached the question of human survival by bringing--so to say--the evidence supplied by trance mediums before a jury that had to decide whether telepathy had something to do with the matter. If this was not the case, the only explanation left was that some discarnate entity was responsible for the communications received through the medium.

It is curious to note how during the early 1920s the controls (one of these was claimed to be the deceased F. W. H. Myers) of the medium, Mrs. Gladys Osborne Leonard, also known as the English Mrs. Piper, suddenly started to attempt proving their identity and presence in the séance-room by the phenomena of clairvoyance (the so-called book-tests). The idea was that not only telepathy could thus be eliminated as an explanation of the phenomena produced, but also the alleged superhuman origin of clairvoyance would emphasize that the communicating entities were superhuman beings, that is, spirits of the dead.

When it was found that these clairvoyant phenomena could not bring about general conviction of the reality of human survival after death, Mrs. Leonard's controls, who probably should be regarded as secondary personalities of the medium, switched over to the phenomenon of precognition (the so-called newspaper-tests). Just as was the case with regard to clairvoyance in those days, so also precognition was believed to be completely beyond the possibilities of living human beings. So if sound proof of precognition was obtained, there would also be good evidence for the presence in the séance-room of some superhuman entity.

However, general conviction of human survival brought about by the phenomena of the Leonard sittings was not obtained, although in clerical circles many believed that new evidence for human survival had been advanced.

We now arrive at the 1930s when a last attempt to find proof for the survival of human personality was made by Whately Carington, who still believed that there existed such a possibility. He concentrated upon finding evidence pointing to the reality of a spiritual world by submitting both medium and the alleged spirits communicating through him or her to word association tests in order to trace differences between the two that might lead to the conclusion that the medium and the communicators were different entities. Significant results in Carington's investigations were not obtained. The SPR's quest for survival practically came to an end at the beginning of World War II.

Forty years have passed. Whether the quest for human survival will be resumed, we cannot tell.

AFTER ONE HUNDRED YEARS: TIME FOR A CHANGE IN APPARITION RESEARCH

Karlis Osis (American Society for Psychical Research)

Over the past one hundred years, interest in apparition phenomena has dwindled considerably. Parapsychological Association Convention proceedings from 1971 to 1980 list only eight reports and one symposium with apparitions referred to in the title. Why have apparitions become such an endangered species in RIP?

Could scarcity of apparitions be the reason for this decline? Not according to the statistics (Audience Selection Poll, 1980; Gallup Poll, 1982). Palmer and Dennis (RIP 1974, 130-3) surveyed one county in Virginia and 17% of respondents claimed apparition experiences. Haraldsson (RIP 1980, 3-5) found that visual apparitions were reported by 9 to 17% of populations surveyed in the U.S., Britain, and Iceland. Therefore, apparition experiences are frequent. Could reasons for the decline be found in the researchers themselves? This paper explores several wrong turns we might have taken over the century.

Polarized Apparition Theories. The study of apparition experiences was a focal point of early SPR and ASPR researchers, who produced brilliant work and powerful theories concerning them. Gauld (in Wolman, Handbook, 1977, 577-630) summarized Gurney's apparition theory: "Extrasensory perception operates at unconscious or subliminal levels of the personality, which then dramatize the information received and transmit it to consciousness in the form of a hallucinatory quasi-perception." According to Myers (Human Personality and Its Survival of Bodily Death, 1903) the appearer's presence invades the observer's surrounds, localizes itself at that area, and acts as a "phantasmagenetic center," which creates the basis of a percept. Both theories assert an apparition is not a physical entity but is accessible by paranormal means.

While Myers' and Gurney's theories both contain successful preformulations of the underlying processes in apparition experiences, some researchers mistook them as mutually exclusive: if one were considered true, the other must be assumed false. Ideological camps with passionate allegiances to one or the other of these two theories thus emerged and persisted over decades. Stevenson and I proposed that the Myers-Gurney controversy is not irreconcilable: each theory accounts for a different kind of apparition--one ESP-based and the other caused by the appearer's presence external to the observer (Osis, RIP 1980, 1-3; Stevenson, RIP 1980, 1). I presented a model which accommodates, without friction, the major theories and their later offshoots. Embracing theoretical convictions too passionately seems to have impeded the whole process of research, touching data collection, evaluation, and interpretation.

Data Collection. Pre-SPR accounts of apparitions lacked efficient data collection methods, and therefore often failed to extract the facts from malobservations, storytelling, and superstitions. Criteria for authenticity, veridicality, and credibility of observers were sorely needed and established. However, these high standards also misled researchers as data collection became biased because less clearly perceived, verifiable, and consistent apparition experiences were rejected. Case collections bulge with lifelike, articulated percepts, although in reality less clearly defined apparitions occur more frequently. Perception itself is a process wherein signals from external stimuli merge with internal resources (memory, fantasy, expectation). In paranormal perception, internal resources play a much larger part, even in collectively seen apparitions. An investigator could easily mistake quite customary cognitive noise for intentional embellishment or fabrication, and so reject such cases, thus again biasing data.

An evaluation of the full range of apparition experiences can tell more about their roots than can dealing with only a portion of the variations, the "good cases." The greater the number of phenomenological subgroups we have to compare with each other and to correlate with other factors, the richer the information will be. Modern analyses necessitate the accumulation of more data on the varieties and frequencies of apparitional images between different observers, and of the same observer on different occasions and under varied environmental and psychological conditions. Inconsistency may compel a judge to throw a case out of court, but variability allows a psychologist to find answers to many questions.

Do apparitional images differ depending on their source, be it psychophysiological (hallucinations), ESP, or caused by an external presence? Are collectively experienced apparitions more consistent and clearly articulated than those with only a single witness? Do perceptual characteristics vary according to whether the appearer is alive and aware (out-of-body experience) or unaware of appearing; has died recently or long ago; and has died suddenly or gradually? Are factors conducive to apparition experiences different from those affecting ESP processes or hallucination formation? These are just a few questions. Other determinants of apparitional experiences might involve location effects, as well as time and its relation to the occurrence of phenomena. Do experients' perceptual styles matter or are advanced imagery skills necessary? Are similarities regarding the interpersonal situations of percipient and appearer important?

The dominant view that apparitions are hallucinations may bias researchers against gathering data on physical effects that accompany phantasms: temperature changes, sounds, kinetic disturbances. An aversion to spiritualism might lead to neglecting reports by psychics brought in on cases. Records should be kept of any attempted intervention with the phenomena and the outcome should be carefully studied: whether the phenomena increased, remained the same, stopped, or was altered; and whether changes exceed suggestion effects. Basic questions like these can be answered only if unbiased samples containing a wide variety of apparitions are collected. Analyses will be hampered if a large part of these variations are suppressed by inadequate data-collection standards.

The Evaluation of Data. Qualitative and quantitative methods have been used in case studies. One advantage of quantitative methods is in their greater resistance to researchers' theoretical biases. In the late sixties, statistical designs were introduced in single case studies of hauntings (Schmeidler, JASPR, 1966, 139-149), but they emphasized ESP rather than apparition experiences. Moreover, the results of such studies have been meager, perhaps because they do not focus on the core processes of apparition experiences. An in-depth study of a good case can be extremely informative but could become sterile if isolated from the larger context and regarded only as a unique, self-contained unit.

Qualitative analyses are powerful but vulnerable to researchers' strong theoretical biases. Pet ideas are often "supported" by citing a few rare cases, while the bulk of the collected data points in the other direction. Whether employing a quantitative or qualitative technique, we should be aware of the adage, "one swallow does not make the spring," especially when the "spring" is one's own preferred hypothesis.

Interpretation of Findings. Philosophical views and beliefs are hidden variables which influence our thought processes to a surprising extent, even when we are trying to be objective when interpreting scientific results. In a scientific treatise, alternate explanations should be considered in addition to the main or preferred one. Ideally, a scientist should carefully compare the support each alternative receives from his or her data and other sources, and then honestly report the outcome. In practice, however, this model works only if the alternate hypotheses are reasonably concordant with the scientist's own belief system. As long as we are human, and neither abstract ideals nor computerized robots, we function within our belief systems, for no one exists in a cultural vacuum. When scientists outside parapsychology reject psi without any signs of having properly assessed the evidence for it, we become outraged. But how do we ourselves behave when confronted with some parapsychological hypothesis that is discordant with our own personal beliefs?

The hypothesis that explains apparitions by ESP is concordant with a belief system that accommodates ESP. However, the external-presence hypothesis might be violently discordant with the belief systems of many who accept ESP with ease. I have encountered a number of colleagues who feel about the out-of-body hypothesis as some outsiders do about ESP: that it is impossible. Can we expect fair treatment from them for this "impossible" hypothesis?

What is the way out of this trap of subjectivity? The judicial system deals with disruptive effects from deep-seated beliefs, convictions, and tacit knowledge by having lawyers probe prospective jurors and disqualify them if there is reason to suspect prejudice, while judges are supposed to disqualify themselves. Perhaps we, too, should scrutinize our own beliefs and philosophical convictions: if we find strong biases in us regarding a competing hypothesis, then avoid that research area by not theorizing, engaging in polemics, or serving as referees for papers about it. Therapists and philosophers give as their prescription for this situation the task of becoming aware of our underlying beliefs and philosophies: make the tacit explicit, they say, and it will lose its power and, it is to be hoped, diminish its effect upon research processes evoked in the pursuit of apparitions.

Conclusions. Two basic theories on apparitions have competed for dominance in the field for nearly one hundred years: the "ESP theory" and the "external presence theory." The tension between these two theories and other beliefs has exerted bias on research (influencing data collection, evaluation, and interpretation), slowing progress and discouraging researchers from investigating apparitions. Endurance over time and through crossfire is the mark of a good theory, and both the ESP and presence theories have withstood the test for nearly a century. Each theory can accommodate observations and has explanatory power, so it is most likely that philosophical reasons, not empirical ones, are responsible for keeping both theories (and their later reformulations) apart, thus impeding empirical work. A model was previously proposed which would integrate both perspectives (Osis, RIP 1980, 1-3). In this paper, measures were suggested for improving data collection, evaluation, and interpretation of apparition experiences. The ground is being cleared and the time is ripe for a new, less biased turn in the research to gain understanding of the apparition experience.

A HAUNTING-TYPE RSPK CASE IN NEW ENGLAND

William G. Roll and Steven Tringale (Psychical Research Foundation)

Mr. and Mrs. Berini and her two children by a previous marriage--John, 15, and Daisy, 11 (assumed names)--moved into their home in May 1979. They reported apparitional and RSPK occurrences which lasted until August 28, 1981. Our interviews with the family and visitors on September 13 (ST) and October 3-6 (ST and WGR) suggested that the case might include genuine effects. The main events, until August 9, 1981, were recorded by Mrs. Berini and a friend of the family, a Catholic priest.

The Apparitions. About six times the Berinis heard a voice at night which seemed to belong to a girl, Serena, crying for her mother. Mrs. Berini heard it first. They knew nobody of that name but Mr. Berini's father recalled that his sister, Serena, had died in the house at the age of five. Three of the incidents were followed by a death or illness: in May 1979, the night before Daisy's tonsillectomy when she had cardiac arrest; in June, the night before Mr. Berini's grandmother had a stroke; and, finally, in November, the night before she died. The stroke was unexpected, her death was not.

On March 19, 1981, Mrs. Berini woke up and saw a figure in the hall of a boy eight to nine years old, dressed in white. Mr. Berini thought it might be Giorgio, a brother of his father who had died at eight. A neighbor recalled that the boy was buried in his white communion suit. On March 23, Mr. Berini also saw the apparition. It seemed to try to pick up the hallway rug. Mr. Berini later removed this and the floor boards and found a medallion of the Virgin. The boards were interlocked so it had probably been left during the construction of the house. The apparition came two or three times a week making short statements, sometimes in response to questions. Mr. and Mrs. Berini did not always both see it. The figure occasionally seemed to cause physical movements. The Berinis are Catholics and a priest suggested they ignore it. When it returned May 27, Mrs. Berini did so. The closet door in the bedroom then opened and slammed shut some 20 times, she said. On June 3, two other priests performed a ritual and placed holy oils on the outer walls of the house. The apparition was back the next night and Mr. Berini, as instructed by a third priest, commanded it to leave in the name of Christ.

The visits tapered off but on June 5 another figure, caped, black and with a hump on its back, was seen by Mr. Berini, and, a few nights later by Mrs. Berini. Sometimes during the seven nights this unidentified figure was seen it spoke in a gruff male voice saying "really disgusting things," usually when Mrs. Berini was praying. When they asked it who it was, it said "I am a minister of God." Once when Mr. Berini and his mother were in the bedroom, he saw it twice but she observed nothing.

The RSPK Disturbances. The night after the appearance of the black figure the bedside phone "kept flying across the room" and the bedside lamp fell on Mrs. Berini's head several times. The incidents continued with movements and breakage of dishes, crosses, and religious figurines. A china cupboard turned over four times, a bookcase on the top landing moved downstairs twice, and Daisy's desk moved out of her room and down the stairs once. The most frequent occurrence was the opening and slamming shut of the retractable staircase to the attic, causing the ceiling in the hall to crack. The incidents continued until August 28, Daisy's birthday, when the family found a carving knife stuck in the kitchen table. They moved out until September 24, when a priest performed an exorcism. The family reported no further incidents.

Observations by Visitors. Ben Alcantro, 15, a tenth-grader and a friend of John's, was visiting in late August. While seated in the kitchen by the doorway to the living room talking to Mrs. Berini, who was standing in the living room by the main entrance, he saw a candle in the window sill on the other side of the entrance take off, moving towards him. Mr. Berini was in the kitchen behind Ben. Daisy and John were away.

Mrs. Lisa Jardin, a 70-year-old neighbor, was with Mrs. Berini in the living room during the latter part of August 1981 when a table lamp moved about four feet, breaking on the floor behind them. Mrs. Berini was about six feet from where the lamp had stood. There was no one else in the house.

Miss Mona Berini, 21, Mr. Berini's sister, works as a secretary/receptionist at a Catholic community center. On June 13,

1981, she was in the bathroom with her mother, John, and Daisy. Mrs. Berini was in the hallway (Mr. Berini was away). Mona saw a large comb, placed in a hairbrush on a dresser, move up into the air and fall down on the dresser. Hearing the sound, Mrs. Berini came in. While all were in the bathroom, they heard a loud crash and found the bookcase from the top landing standing upright halfway down the stairs.

"Attacks" on Persons. Mrs. Berini was hit several times by moving objects, Mr. Berini was hit twice, and John once. One night, when Mrs. Berini was asleep, Mr. Berini watched as she was moved out of the bed into the room where she was released, dropping to the floor. This happened three more times. Another time she had a burning sensation and they found three bleeding scratches on her chest and an upside down cross scratched on her back. She was scratched two other times, once on July 11 when Mona Berini was present and phoned one of the priests. When she hung up, she had a burning sensation on her own face and discovered a scratch on her left cheek.

Psychological, Interpersonal and Medical Aspects. Mrs. Berini was the center for the RSPK events. Nearly all took place when she was home and she was usually the person closest to the object involved. She was the one who experienced the first two apparitions. She filled out the Wilson and Barber Inventory of Childhood Memories and Imaginings (ICMI), which measures the extent to which a person is "fantasy-prone." She checked only two of the 48 items. However, she had two or three dissociative episodes during the RSPK period. One time her husband saw her prepare a house plant for dinner and "had to snap her out of some kind of trance." Mr. Berini also had no previous apparitional experiences but scored 19 on the ICMI. Perhaps his experiences were triggered by his wife's.

Mrs. Berini had suffered from migraine headaches and vomiting since a child and regularly sought medical relief. These disappeared during the disturbances. To determine if there might be a connection between the medical problems and the occurrences we examined the times she sought medical help in relation to the active RSPK periods. During the first 11 weeks of 1981, she spent 15 days at her doctor's or the hospital. The RSPK incidents came during the next three weeks, March 16-April 5, when she had no medical problems. The RSPK incidents then ceased during seven weeks, April 6-May 24 when she spent six days seeking medical attention. During the eight weeks from May 25 to July 19, there were numerous RSPK incidents but no headaches. She had a migraine attack the week beginning July 20 and the RSPK occurrences ceased for two weeks. August 3 to 28 there were many RSPK disturbances but no migraine attacks. As of this writing, these have not returned.

If the substitution of the migraine attacks by the RSPK disturbances is not coincidental, both could be symptoms of the same underlying condition. If so, this apparently goes back to Mrs.

Berini's childhood since this is when she said her headaches began. She had an unhappy childhood, feeling alienated both from her family (her mother is now in her fifth marriage) and her Jewish religion. Her relations to Mr. Berini's parents and grandmother were also stressful. The latter blamed the fatal heart attack of one of her sons on Mrs. Berini's marriage to Mr. Berini and vowed "to get" Mrs. Berini.

If the occurrences were related to Mrs. Berini's interpersonal problems we might expect the latter to be reflected in the events. The little girl who seemed to call for her mother and the first words of the white apparition ("Where do all the lonely people go?" and "Where do I belong?") seemed to match Mrs. Berini's inability to reach the attention of her own mother and the rejection she experienced from her new family.

The anti-religious theme represented by the black figure and by the breakage and desecration of crosses could be related to feelings of conflict engendered by Mrs. Berini's conversion to Catholicism.

One of us (see pp. 270-73) has speculated that RSPK may be related to disturbances in the central nervous system similar to those which result in epileptic symptoms. In some cases of epilepsy, the attacks are preceded by "auras" of recurrent hallucinations. In the Berini case, when apparitions and RSPK occurred in succession, the apparitions came before the RSPK incidents on five of six occasions.

The development of this case over time may provide another clue to its nature. The first apparition was an example of rigidly repetitive haunting. The voice was heard at night, a period which may be conducive to such experiences because the percipients may be in a hypnogogic or hypnopomic state and also because of the reduction of sensory imput. The same conditions may be ESP-conducive so it makes sense that the ostensible ESP aspects should be interwoven with the nocturnal visitations. The second apparition was also a repetitive haunting but with increasing signs of autonomy. The Berinis' acceptance of this as a real entity may have paved the way for further phenomena. When the family and the priests decided to suppress the apparition, it retreated (as might be expected from a boy in his communion clothes), but the underlying problem seemed to remain and another apparition took over. This was explicitly sacrilegious and thus immune to religious injunctions. With this change, other restraints seemed to fall away and the phenomena became increasingly violent.

Haunting Versus RSPK Features. Like other haunting ghosts, the apparitions seemed to represent both actual and imaginary persons: they were restricted to a limited area, they were nocturnal, and their behavior was repetitive. The physical effects were often "imitative" (A. Gauld and A. D. Cornell, Poltergeists, 1979), i.e., suggestive of such human activity as footsteps, banging on walls, articulate speech, disturbance of bedclothes, and the opening of room and wardrobe doors.

The case also showed RSPK features. There was an RSPK "agent." This person had psychological or medical problems; the incidents were concentrated during waking hours; and there was focusing on special objects, types of objects, and areas.

Discussion. The evidence for RSPK in this case and, to a lesser extent, for veridical apparitions, is sufficiently suggestive for us to look for the underlying process. Though it seems that Mrs. Berini played an important role in providing or directing the energy that animated the contents of her home, the incidents cannot be understood in terms of her personality alone. A larger structure seems to have come into being where the distinction between person and environment was replaced by direct interactions that included individuals and objects separate in time or space which were associated with the Berini house and family. This structure changed over time and may have been personified by the three apparitions.

Some of the events in the house seem difficult to understand either in terms of the personalities of living or deceased members of the Berini family but may reflect this larger and more complex organization.

The issue of whether apparitions, particularly of this quasi-autonomous type, are conscious may be approached by comparison with multiple personalities. The latter, which seem to be conscious at least when they are in control, may offer the closest familiar analogy to some apparitions and may suggest that the latter too represent conscious personalities during the periods when they are in evidence. If this analogy is valid, it may apply to apparitions of persons who once lived as well as to imaginary apparitions.

MISCELLANEOUS CONTRIBUTIONS FROM THE CONTINENT*

SOME RECOMMENDATIONS FOR THE FUTURE PRACTICE OF PARAPSYCHOLOGY

Gerd H. Hövelmann (Philipps University)

A few strategies parapsychologists should take into consideration in their future attempts to obtain legitimacy and recognition by "normal" science are recommended.

First Recommendation

Parapsychologists should instantly give up their revolutionary outlook upon their field and upon themselves.

Comment. For a long time many parapsychologists have pleased themselves in calling their field revolutionary and themselves revolutionaries. Aside from the fact that I cannot see any revolution here at all, this self-assessment reveals a grave misconception. It is not enough to commit oneself to research in a frontier science to be called revolutionary. As has been pointed out by sociologists Collins and Pinch, parapsychology has many characteristics of orthodox scientific disciplines. One of these characteristics is the rigid application of scientific research methods in many parapsychological investigations. Parapsychologists cannot at the same time loudly propagate revolutionary slogans.

Second Recommendation

Parapsychologists frequently seem to feel urged (or even entitled) to express themselves in more or less learned words on the problem of survival after bodily death. They should stop this habit.

Comment. In fact, as I have tried to show elsewhere (ZP, 1982, in press), strict repeatability of our laboratory experiments

---
*Chaired by Carroll B. Nash (Parapsychology Laboratory, St. Joseph's University)

(a) is impossible to obtain for theoretical reasons and (b) cannot reasonably be postulated to be a condition sine qua non to establish parapsychology as a science. The results of our experiments are still far too unreliable, ambiguous, and inconsistent to draw firm conclusions from them. Even the most cautious inferences we draw from our experiments very often turn out to be essentially premature and invalid. On the other hand, conclusions drawn from thanatological research or from other examinations aiming at support of the survival hypothesis to date are even more arbitrary and speculative than those drawn from experimental laboratory tests. Moreover, they often are widely open to various kinds of alternative explanations, be they normal or paranormal.

When applying scientific standards, survival cannot be regarded as proved, of course, as long as there are reasonable counter-explanations possible. As for me, in the foreseeable future I do not see even the slightest chance of getting conclusive evidence of survival in the sense of a definite scientific proof excluding any other alternative explanation. No matter what our personal attitudes toward the survival problem may be, in a scientific approach to that problem we should realize that Occam's razor is still sharp. Therefore, we responsibly ought to avoid provoking treacherous hopes and expectations among the lay public by holding back our more or less poorly founded speculations for the time being.

Finally, we should afford to ask ourselves whether investigating the survival question is important and desirable at all. Would we profit in one way or another by finding out whether we will survive? Would this knowledge be useful to meet our vital interests and the requirements of our everyday lives? Would it relieve our mortal dread?

In connection with this second recommendation it must likewise be postulated that parapsychology should be kept free of any kind of ideological or cosmological speculations on the nature of man, of the world, of the universe, and of the meaning or purpose of life. Speculations of this kind should be reserved to aging Nobel laureates.

Third Recommendation

Parapsychologists should (a) cease to pretend that they are able to explain anything by means of their present terminology, which is merely descriptive and (b) build up a standardized, methodically constructed terminology as soon as possible.

Comment. (a) Occasionally one can notice that parapsychologists use their technical terms in a way that seems to suggest that these terms have considerable explanatory properties. So, on several occasions I have come across statements in the parapsychological literature saying, for example, that certain phenomena can be explained as effects of a PK force or other phenomena as results of an information transfer independent of the recognized channels of sense. This manner of speaking is grossly negligent. In fact, nothing is explained by making reference to a "PK force" or to an "information transfer independent of the recognized channels of sense," respectively, as long as we do not know what a "PK force" is or how the "information transfer" operates. One may well label certain unusual phenomena as, let us say, "extrasensory" or "psychokinetic," but we should realize that this is only a descriptive classification. The limits of all these terms, and of many others as well, are so poorly specified that they could almost be used at random.

(b) As a norm, scientific statements have to be intersubjectively understandable and verifiable. We cannot observe this norm using the vague terms that presently are at our disposal. It is a matter of great urgency, therefore, to methodically construct a standardized parapsychological terminology. By "methodical" I mean that each technical term has to be introduced explicitly, progressing from the most basic to the peripheral ones. Circular definitions must, of course, be avoided. By means of an adequate terminology it will be possible to guarantee the intersubjectivity of our statements.

Fourth Recommendation

In view of the frequent inconsistencies of their experimental findings, parapsychologists should not resort to the fatalistic conception that these inconsistencies are constitutive of paranormal events.

Comment. Obviously, some parapsychologists are troubled or even discouraged by the fact that very many of their experimental results are notoriously inconsistent. However, it is neither admissible nor logically self-consistent to conclude from this unpleasant fact that these inconsistencies must be, so to speak, constitutive of paranormal events. This conclusion is all the more questionable as it is by no means clear whether it is just our methods and conceptualizations that are not yet sophisticated enough to allow a water-tight explanation of psi functioning. We should, therefore, not overhastily abandon the concept of lawfulness in our field.

Final Recommendation

Parapsychologists should strictly separate themselves from all those pseudoscientific claimants who put forward frequently untestable ideas often full of supernaturalism and metaphysics and who refuse to adopt rigid scientific methods.

Comment. Unfortunately, despite the rigid use of orthodox scientific methods which I have praised in the comment upon my first recommendation, many parapsychologists evidence an alarming inclination to flirt with occult or antiscientific ideas and to ogle bizarre, esoteric, mystic, or--as Martin Johnson pertinently named it at an earlier PA convention--"parapornographic" groups and periodicals. These researchers occasionally show such an uncritical tendency to accept questionable pseudoscientific claims that sometimes one is under the impression that the critics of the field are not entirely wrong when they reproach parapsychologists for lacking critical judgment and intellectual self-discipline.

If we really want our field to be accepted as a science, we should act accordingly and, in methodological respects, be more papal than the Pope. Arbitrariness of our methods and statements, on the other hand, would open the door to all kinds of pseudoscientific speculations and lead to the field's vulgarization in the worst sense of that word. Thus, we would badly risk the still low degree of academic integration parapsychology has achieved to date. Therefore, it must be emphasized again that we should rigorously dissociate ourselves from obstinate occultists and from credulous and thoughtless supernaturalists of whatever shading they may be. Those parapsychologists who are worried about the financial support which these organizations and private persons currently give to our research should consider John Beloff's recent proposal that a scientific committee be established which (under the auspices of the PA and the AAAS) would evaluate once and for all whether there are valid clues to the existence of ESP and PK. Whatever the committee's conclusions might be, in any case they would be of considerable influence on the attitude of the "scientific community" toward parapsychology and, consequently, on the funding of our research.

Finally, to turn back to the relations of parapsychologists to the occult, I must strongly emphasize that--like Rao (Parapsychology Review, 1982, 1, 3)--"I have little sympathy for those among us who are bothered by the methodological 'scientism' in our field. A return to hermetic contemplation may give one a more satisfying picture of psi, but such will not constitute a scientific endeavor." No matter whether we regard science as the most recommendable way to "approach the truth" (to speak like a Popperian, for once) or whether we think of science as just another ideology or tradition having no more rights than others (as Paul Feyerabend does), in any case we will have to adhere to the methods and standards which are held to be scientific in orthodox science, provided that we want to substantiate our claim to be scientists conducting scientific research. Note that I am not saying that the scientific methods are particularly sound and recommendable per se. All I am saying is that if we regard ourselves as scientists we have to use them. We cannot have it both ways. Either we adopt the methods and methodological standards provided by science or we should cease to desire and expect favorable recognition by the scientific profession. It's for us to decide!

THE RULE OF IMPROBABILITY, OR WHAT TO DO IF PSI RESULTS LOOK "TOO GOOD" (RB)

Ulrich Timm (University of Freiburg)

I propose an explorative rule as an aid in the evaluation of reports and data from all areas of psi research. The development of the rule is based upon the following facts:

1) The experience of a century of parapsychological research has shown that many reports about supposed psi effects are incorrect or falsified. The phenomena themselves may, for instance, be fraudulently manipulated. Nonpsi-effected phenomena may be misinterpreted as psi effects. Experiments may be intentionally or inadvertently misevaluated. Reports, protocols, even numerical data may be more or less altered.

2) The apparent reputation of the source of information does not always insure the correctness of the reports. Concrete events have shown that not only politicians and popular columnists, but also qualified scientists occasionally falsify facts, alter data, or simply make colossal mistakes. Furthermore, scientists, just as other people, may be deceived by their expectations and led to unconscious misinterpretations. This especially applies to parapsychology, in which expectations play a great part with both followers and opponents.

3) There are, however, a few features of genuine psi effects which do not agree with typical forms of falsification, and therefore may be used as a more reliable criterion of truth. By this I refer to the rarity, unreliability, uncontrollability, and instability of psi phenomena, whose discovery is to be considered as one of the surest results of empirical parapsychology. These fluctuations of psi are commonly felt as an annoying flaw and contradict all expectations one has of an ideal psi effect. Therefore, spurious or incorrectly reported psi effects should seldom show such features.

4) On the basis of the preceding considerations, the following rule may be formulated: Reports of extremely high or extremely stable psi performances are in contradiction to general experience and warrant the conclusion that they are most probably due, at least in part, to error, delusion, or deception. I have named this the "rule of improbability."

It should be pointed out that here we are dealing with a rough empirical rule. It permits only unsure probabilistic inferences, which in individual cases might be erroneous. Accordingly, the theoretical assumption is not made that exceptional psi-performances are impossible in principle. It is only claimed that they usually do not occur and, therefore, are at least not probable. A real "high-scoring subject" or "high-scoring experimenter" would have no special difficulties in overcoming the initial skepticism because of his or her phenomenal performances: thus, the person would be presented as the famous "exception to the rule."

The possibilities of practical application of the rule are more numerous than one may initially think. Here only the most important categories will be mentioned:

1) Application on professional tricksters, who claim to command psi abilities and exhibit their performances, before the public, regularly and over long periods of time. Possible example: Uri Geller.

2) Application on a variety of methods of spiritualistic communication up to the modern taped-voice-technique, which, in the eyes of their advocates, are distinguished by an unusually high success rate.

3) Application on most classical physical mediums, which does not exclude the possibility that some of them have occasionally produced genuine PK effects.

4) Application on all too successful clairvoyants, psi-healers, etc., which again does not exclude the possibility that they occasionally produce genuine psi results.

5) Application on the qualitatively and quantitatively enormous psi performances that are reported about magicians and shamans of primitive cultures and also about Indian gurus, Philippine psychic surgeons, etc. Possible example: Sai Baba.

6) Application on especially regular and persistent apparent RSPK events. An example of this is the case of the later exposed "ghost" named "Chopper," which appeared this year (1982) in Germany.

7) Application on extremely high results of qualitative and quantitative psi experiments. Possible example: The famous Soal-Goldney experiments, for which an astronomically low error probability of 10^{-31} has been calculated.

8) Application on the exaggerated presentation of assumed psi results in certain popular-science books and magazines, including most instructions to train or to utilize one's own or others' psi abilities.

Finally, I caution against blindly trusting this rule of improbability and using it without careful consideration. Nevertheless, after many years of observation in the field of psi research, I feel that this rule, with appropriate application, would avoid more errors than it would produce. I believe the proposed rule could be highly useful for maintaining critical scientific rationality in a sphere where this is constantly threatened.

MEANINGFUL CLAIRVOYANT MISTAKES (RB)

Hans Bender (Institut für Grenzgebiete und Psychohygiene)

"Meaningful Clairvoyant Mistakes" (MCMs) presuppose that there are clairvoyant hits. Thus I think an adequate frame for my report on mistakes could be two hits--one at the beginning and one at the end.*

This [the film] was only an extract from a 30-minute TV film which is a very impressive documentation of a clairvoyant success with such a complex structure of corresponding details that it cannot possibly be attributed to mere chance. One wonders which arguments professional skeptics could bring forth to invalidate this hit. It poses the question of the evidential value of qualitative findings (see the Presidential address of Henri Bergson in PSPR, 1912). In an open controversy with Piet Hein Hoebens on the genuineness of an early pilot chair experiment with Gerard Croiset (in a workshop) I will show why I and other judges, including the subjects, are convinced of its authenticity.

The following Croiset case, documented by a BBC television film, features a clairvoyant mistake. It's the Pat McAdam case which has been thoroughly investigated by my friend Colin Godman on whose report my summary is based. The repetition may serve as a stepping-stone for recent analogous cases which I am going to demonstrate to you.

Scottish journalist Frank Ryan visited Croiset in Utrecht in February 1970. He asked for help to find a girl, Pat McAdam, who was reported missing in February 1967. Ryan was told to search for a bridge with tubular metal railings and a house with advertising signs, a white wooden paling-fence, and tree-roots. At a later visit Croiset gave more details of the area, which proved to be correct. As indicated by Croiset, articles of clothing were found nearby, but not the body of the missing girl. The dress was not that worn by Pat at the time of her disappearance. It was that of an older woman and one must conclude that it just happened to be

---

*At this point the author presented a film from Japanese TV featuring an outstanding clairvoyant hit by Gerard Croiset. This is a particularly well-documented case.

in the small area clairvoyantly "chosen" by Croiset. Thus he "found" the wrong article of clothing--a meaningful clairvoyant mistake: meaningful because a complex "gestalt" of correct clairvoyant impressions was brought forth by Croiset in the service of his wrong supposition that tree-roots sticking out of the bank would hold Pat's body in a sort of cave. The remains of the girl, who is thought to have been murdered, were never found. This clairvoyant mistake shows once more that a sensitive has no criterion to recognize when his impressions point directly to the fact which is searched for, or when they are misleading. Anyhow, the clairvoyant's impressions can certainly not be rejected as pure coincidence. Colin Godman ends an article on the Pat McAdam case with this appeal to the skeptics: "One must calculate the odds against finding a cottage with a particular garden containing an old car with a wheelbarrow leaning against it" (one of Croiset's statements).

Analogous cases of meaningful clairvoyant mistakes have been observed by Dr. Serge Jacquay, Maître-Assistant of electronics at the University of Upper Alsace in Mulhouse in collaboration with the Freiburg Institute. In his experiments with a group of radiesthesists, including the specially successful teacher, Jean Hurter, this MCM-pattern appeared time and again. In one case the radiesthesists were asked to search for a lost ring in a snow field covering an area equivalent to that of about three football grounds. Using a special technique, Jean Hurter indicated a spot of one square meter. There, with the help of a metal detector, a ring was found, but it was not the lost one. Apart from the blue stone, the ring which was found was identical to the one searched for. Another MCM case.

More complicated is the case in which the radiesthesists were asked to locate a grey-beige Citroën DS 19 car with the license-plate number 34 22 QK 68 in the Mulhouse area. Indeed, the point indicated by means of a search with a pendulum on a map led to the immediate discovery of a parked grey-beige Citroën DS 19 car, but with the license-plate number 47 22 QH 68. Since the psi-detectives had obviously encountered another case of MCM they decided to try it out once again in the suburb of Riedisheim, where the original car was thought to be. There, by means of a pendulum and a rapidly sketched map again a grey-beige Citroën DS was located. It was the same car they had located before and which in the meantime had moved to the new psi-detected place. Other cases show the same pattern, though the Mulhouse radiesthesists could also produce quite remarkable psi hits, as in the case of finding a precious necklace that Mr. Hurter's sister-in-law had lost somewhere in or around her house, 500 kilometers from Mulhouse. During a trial under deep hypnosis, Mr. Hurter indicated a spot in the garden on the basis of a sketch of the property, where the necklace was not expected to be, but where it was found nonetheless.

With this hit, I conclude the report of clairvoyant cases. My main purpose was to present the MCM-pattern, or practical

ESP-trials where the desired target was missed and replaced by an analogous object. Most of these cases do not show an analogy to normal sensory awareness. But there are some cases of meaningful clairvoyant mistakes which can be compared with errors in the realm of normal perception.

For example, if one is searching for a car with certain characteristics, one might believe it to be found, but a closer examination reveals that the registration number is slightly different from that of the car in question. It seems difficult to construct an analogy with the second part of the Citroën experiment where the same car was detected again after having been removed to another distant parking place.

The case of the black dress, erroneously detected in a region where Pat McAdam disappeared, and where Croiset was searching for traces, and the case of the lost ring seem to have a more enigmatic background. To attribute these happenings to mere coincidence is hardly convincing. There seems to be something more behind them. In terms of the theories of Carl Gustav Jung, the renowned depth psychologist, and the physician Wolfgang Pauli, one is tempted to speak of a synchronistic event. The archetype involved may be the famous "trickster," but in suggesting this, I fully realize that we can never think of putting the concept of archetypes, nor that of synchronicity, to a critical test of refutation. Perhaps we need new paradigms to cope with these rather bewildering events.

AN EVALUATION OF HANSEL'S CRITIQUE OF HELMUT SCHMIDT'S EXPERIMENTS (RB)

Kaare Claudewitz (University of Copenhagen and Danish Society for Psychical Research)

In his book ESP and Parapsychology: A Critical Re-evaluation (1980), Professor C. E. Hansel devoted a chapter to Helmut Schmidt's psi experiments with quantum mechanical random number generators and cited four major points of criticism: (1) The exact numbers and types of trials to be undertaken by each subject in Schmidt's original experiments were not specified in advance before the tests were started. (2) The allocation into high-scoring and low-scoring runs, or into high-scoring and low-scoring subjects, provided obvious loopholes. (3) Schmidt's subjects practiced on some occasions and carried out experimental runs on others using the same machine. (4) There was no control of the experimenter.

Hansel is quite right on the first point, since the numbers of trials to be undertaken were only prespecified within certain limits in Schmidt's first experiments carried out in February to May 1967.

One can especially wonder why only one subject (K.R.) stayed within the prespecified number of trials while the two others, O.C. and J.B., undertook, respectively, 2,570 trials more and 3,749 less than prespecified. Although, of course, it can be difficult to force a subject (here J.B.) to do an exact number of trials, one may ask why Schmidt did not stop O.C. when he had reached the prespecified 20,000 trials. The total number of trials stayed, however, within the prespecified number (55,000 < N < 70,000), but it is interesting to note that if J.B. and K.R. had stayed within the prespecified number (20,000 < N < 25,000) and, for example, had undertaken 24,999 trials each, then they would have exceeded the total number of trials prespecified with no fewer than 3,567 trials! However, Hansel's critique is probably more serious as regards Schmidt's second experiment with high- and low-aim trials; it is not clear why the subjects here undertook 1,344 more high-score trials than low-score trials and in his later clairvoyance tests 818 more low-aim trials than high-aim trials. Hansel probably here implies that Schmidt had discontinued testing with each of his subjects at a time when the score was slightly above or below the chance level, thereby artificially inflating the group score (the "optional stopping hypothesis"). However, even if Schmidt had used such a method it would have little effect, provided the RNG worked satisfactorily, since it has been shown by the mathematician Greville that changing subjects or conditions can only affect the score if there is some difference (either temporary or permanent) which operates selectively in the direction of high or low scores (i.e., ESP or PK).

Regarding (2), there is no doubt that Hansel with this criticism implies that Schmidt first, after, or during the experiments could have decided the allocation of the results of the tests into the two categories, high or low scores, since the machine was not involved in this allocation. Hansel suggests that instead Schmidt should have used two machines, one for high-aim trials and one for low-aim trials, but if Schmidt really wanted to cheat in this way it is difficult to see how the use of a second machine with certainty could have prevented him from manipulating both.

Regarding (3), it is obvious that it is more appropriate to include all attempted trials--even training trials--in the final assessment, especially if they have been conducted in the middle of a session. However, this can hardly be of any crucial importance; we are here arguing about small statistical arguments.

As for (4), even in the early fifties both Rhine and Pratt emphasized the importance of the presence of at least a second experimenter as a controller in ESP experiments; in spite of this Schmidt worked mostly alone and Hansel's criticism of this point cannot be said to be unjust. A second experimenter could have insured that all the scores for high- and low-aiming runs were kept separate from the start, that they were not changed during the experiment, and that all records were included in the final assessment.

The critical reader may with Hansel wonder why Schmidt's

experiments were not confirmed by experimenters using the "VERI-TAC" machine, which was a pseudorandom-number generator. It should be pointed out that the U. S. Air Force Cambridge Research Laboratories experiment may not have succeeded as a consequence of inexperienced experimenters, subject selection, or geographical factors, and does not demonstrate any holes in Schmidt's protocol. On the contrary, other experimenters (Honorton, Tart, Haraldsson) using either Schmidt's machine or another similar to it have been successful and therefore replicated Schmidt.

Finally, I would mention that Hansel's claim that the "dead time" in the reset circuit could affect results is not correct: it only limits the maximum rate at which trials can be registered-- about two per second. No extra trials are registered when the buttons are blocked.

A DERMO-OPTIC PERCEPTION TEST (RB)

Yvonne DuPlessis (Institut Metapsychique International)

In 1980-1981, we tried to find out whether the subjective impressions by which certain people expressed unconscious dermo-optic sensitivity reactions could be quantified.

All human beings are sensitive to visible as well as invisible radiation from colored surfaces surrounding them. Objective methods consisting either of physical measurements or of recording physiological responses have proven that the unconscious reactions of dermo-optic sensitivity distributed themselves in an order analogous to that of the prism and that certain factors such as lighting conditions can reverse these findings.

Analogous results have been obtained by using a subjective method of dermo-optic perception training, in other words developing an awareness of the different impressions perceived by the hands of the subject in contact with colored surfaces he or she cannot see. They are either enclosed in a special box or are placed beneath opaque screens which act as thermo-absorbent filters. Hands are capable of making a distinction between impressions felt within a few centimeters distance from the colored stimuli.

These subjective impressions are not visual; they may be based on temperature, weight, or other factors. A subject may feel one color as hotter or colder than another. After a few trials, the experimenter will tell the subject what results have been obtained so that the latter can learn to associate a given colored surface with the corresponding subjective impression. The subject eventually succeeds in differentiating between three, four, or even five colors. These exercises require very concentrated attention and cannot be carried out over long periods of time. They must constantly be varied. It has been estimated that only one out of six subjects is capable of achieving this awareness of the interactions between colored surfaces and his or her hands.

In an attempt to quantify these impressions, one of my collaborators, Jean-Paul Bailly, developed a procedure involving a code to be analyzed statistically by computer in the form of histograms. The subject must make five successive classifications of five different colors, the results of which are not relayed. This may be described as a "mixed" procedure since the subject remains in ignorance of the results as in an objective method while he or she is asked, as in a subjective method, to differentiate by conscious, nonvisual impressions, between the various colored surfaces.

We thought it would be of interest to utilize this procedure (thanks to the support of the Parapsychology Foundation Inc.) in selecting subjects who, despite the monotony of this test, might experience impressions significantly differentiated between at least two colors in order to be able to train them later using the same color contrasts, the same screens, and the same lighting conditions. Screens may be in the form of aluminum cases or opaque black and white envelopes.

Procedure. A deck of 25 cards is used which contains five cards of each of the following colors: blue, green, red, yellow, and white. The 25 colored cards are placed under screens in aluminum cases $\frac{1}{2}$ mm thick, of which one series would measure $16\frac{1}{2}$ x 11 cm and the other 10 x $7\frac{1}{2}$ cm. The remaining opaque materials used consisted of black ESP cards and envelopes and white envelopes lined with a piece of white cardboard.

The closed pack is then divided into five parts, each consisting of the five different colors. Each part is marked with a geometrical symbol pasted on the back of the envelope. Five symbols, therefore, are used five different times and underneath them are five letters of the alphabet: A, C, D, E, and F, coding the colors in five different ways for each part of the deck. These codes have been established randomly by computer. The cases or envelopes thus coded are then sealed and presented to the subject by an experimenter to whom they have been handed.

The subject then proceeds to classify them according to one and the same type of impression by spreading them out from his or her right to left, for example, according to the graduated impression of cold to hot. The five impressions are marked on the test sheet by figures from one to five under each of which the experimenter marks whatever letter appears on the envelope. In this way the subjective impressions of the subject are numbered making it possible for the computer to compute the five means of 25 trials.

The test sheet also bears a code in numbers of the experimental conditions of the test including the type of screen used, the type of subject response (whether thermal or according to weight), the program corresponding to the code letters of the colors, the subject's number, the experimenter's number, and the date of the experiment.

The place, the time, the type of lighting used must all be described plus information as to whether the subject has normal vision or is blind. All the test sheets are given to J. P. Bailly to be decoded by computer, statistically analyzed, and graphed. The statistical evaluation, the standard deviation, and the means of the impressions induced by each of the five colors are then computed.

Preliminary Statistical Results. A total of 9,200 trials were made in 368 series of 25 trials each, using 34 subjects and 16 experimenters. To date we have only examined the results of 26 subjects each of whom made 10 series of trials, or 50 classifications of five colors each under the same conditions, i.e., same place, lighting, and screens. Several of them made 10 series of trials with different screens but under the same kind of light and in the same place in order to compare the results with the different screens used in each of their 10 series.

The differences between the maximum and minimum impressions induced by colors were evaluated according to Students' t criterion. It should be pointed out that these differences refer not to the intensity of the impressions but to qualitative differences among them (from hot to cold, from rough to smooth, etc.). A total of 11 subjects were tested under incandescent electric light. When aluminum cases were used, two subjects out of three obtained significant results. For one subject white as compared to blue was associated with $p = .04$, and compared to green, $p = .02$. For a second subject white compared to blue, as well as to yellow, $p < .01$. With black envelopes one subject (blind from birth) of a total of five obtained significant results. Again, for white as compared to yellow, $p = .03$. Using white envelopes none of the three subjects tested achieved significant results.

A total of 19 subjects were tested by daylight. With aluminum case, one subject out of seven had significant results: for red compared to green, $p < .01$. With black envelopes one subject out of 10 achieved significant results: for blue as compared to green, as well as to yellow, $p < .01$. Using white envelopes one subject out of two had significant results: for green as compared to red, $p = .02$.

These results would seem to show that the aluminum cases under incandescent electric light induced the most significant results differentiating two colors. The aluminum cases as well as the black envelopes under incandescent light produced the most significant results for white as compared with blue, green, or yellow, whereas in daylight, it was red and blue as compared with green and yellow.

SCREENING FOR GOOD ESP SUBJECTS WITH OBJECT-READING (RB)

Jan Kappers (Amsterdam, The Netherlands)

In the early sixties I explored with two co-workers the possibilities of inducing psi in subjects by giving them hallucinogens. One of the methods to test this was object-reading (OR). The subject, handling something belonging to a target-person unknown to him, was asked to describe as many data as possible that entered his mind, on the supposition that they could be related to the owner of the object. In 500 trials it became evident that persons, not known to be sensitives, could sometimes give detailed and peculiar descriptions for which only a paranormal explanation seemed possible. Since then I have used this method to get a preliminary impression of the psi abilities of persons claiming to be clairvoyant.

The ability for OR proved less subject to decline than the ability for good card-guessing. This led me to consider the possibility of using OR to screen for good ESP subjects. In a pilot experiment, I used as objects six rags of textile cut out of pieces of cloth carried with them for a month by each of six future target-persons (three male, three female). The six rags were put into slip-in cards and distributed among the subjects, with written indication of the sex and age of the target-persons. Seven returned a description for every rag; two of them gave such interesting details that they were invited to participate in additional OR. Both had an almost nonexistent "paranormal anamnesis," but their performance was promising.

The pilot experiment stimulated me to try a more sophisticated experiment with six new target-persons in the autumn of 1981. This time the subjects were members of courses in astrology, chosen as potential sheep because they already believed in the possibility of a mantic practice and were used to verbalizing traits of personalities and circumstances. This time only the sex of the target-persons was indicated.

Of a total of 90 subjects 74 handed in handwritten descriptions to a co-worker; 53 gave a description of every target-person. The descriptions were sent to a second co-worker who did not know the subjects nor the target-persons. He coded them and had them typed, leaving out remarks identifying the rags as such. The typed specimens were sent to the target-persons for blind matching, the "womenrags" to the females, the "menrags" to the males. They had to divide the descriptions into five categories of increasing similarity to their own personality and circumstances: a rating of one meant there was no resemblance, to a five, which indicated a perfect fit.

The results can be judged in two ways, for the group as a whole and for each subject. If ESP is operating it can be expected that the target-persons found the statements pertaining to their own rags more fitting than those connected with the rags of the other target-persons. Further, good subjects should make better judgments for right combinations of rag and target-person than for wrong combinations. The group as a whole did not give sufficiently recognizable descriptions to the target-persons. Only two males rated their own rags better than those of the others, but not significantly so. The three females rated the others better than themselves, but this was not significant either.

The experimenter himself rated the descriptions in the same blind way as the target-persons themselves had. The outcome was not very different. However, the results of both judgings enabled me to select the subjects who had done best, and by judging the quality of their verbal statements, to decide which would be the most interesting prospects for further experimentation. Four subjects were selected and six more possible subjects as well. With the first four, further OR experiments have been done by a panel of three experimenters, each supplying three objects for each sitting, arranged in random order on a tray. The objects are so chosen that in themselves they give no important cues, e.g., used ballpoints. Generally five objects are used per session. The results again are promising. To illustrate this with one example: Subject 38, in describing the characteristics of a male target-person, said-- as an isolated impulse--"Stekelenburg," a rare family name in the Netherlands (13 entries in the telephone directory of Amsterdam of a total of 294,000 names). It turned out that a former colleague of the target-person had this name, a man who evoked strong negative feelings. None of the three experimenters knew anything about this; it was the only name mentioned by the subject during the entire sitting.

COMPUTERS AND REGS*

A PRELIMINARY STUDY WITH A PK GAME INVOLVING DISTRACTION FROM THE PSI TASK (RB)

Ephraim I. Schechter, Pat Barker, and Mario Varvoglis† (Psychophysical Research Laboratories)

This pilot study combined a computer-controlled video game ("Psi Ball") with a PK task involving a noise-diode random number generator (RNG). The player moved a lever to keep a "ball" on the TV screen away from the screen's "walls" for as long as possible. About five times each second, a ten-event RNG trial was taken. If there were fewer than five hits in the trial, the game's difficulty was increased by making the ball slightly more sensitive to small lever movements; the difficulty did not change if five or more of the RNG events were hits. There was no direct PK feedback; individual changes in difficulty were too small to be detected and game length did not necessarily reflect PK since sensory-motor skill was also involved.

When the game ended, the player rated the degree to which attention had been focused on the game; then game and PK scores were displayed. Ten players participated and each played ten five-game sessions, half of which were "RNG-Contingent," with RNG hits affecting the game's difficulty level. The other sessions were "RNG-Noncontingent"--RNG output was monitored, but hits did not affect the game. The difficulty level in Noncontingent games increased at approximately the same rate as in Contingent games. Contingent and Noncontingent sessions occurred in individualized random sequences, and neither players nor experimenters knew which sessions were which until after all the data had been collected.

Control games, without a player, were run each day; their number and length were the same as those of the day's "real" games. As a further check on the RNG, four sets of ten million RNG events each were gathered. Z-scores and Komolgorov-Smirnoff analyses indicated no significant departures from chance performance.

*Chaired by Robert G. Jahn (Princeton University)

Before playing Psi Ball, each player took two multiple-choice inventories. One consisted of the 30 Absorption Scale items from the Tellegen Differential Personality Questionnaire plus 34 items from other DPQ scales. The other was the Myers-Briggs Personality Indicator, which yields scores on Jungian continua of Extraversion/Introversion, Sensing/Intuition, Thinking/Feeling, and Judging/Perceiving.

We predicted only that RNG behavior during "real" Psi Ball games would be significantly different from its performance during the Control games and that extraversion would be significantly related to PK hitting.

A program artifact (eliminated for the next Psi Ball series) resulted in significantly longer games in the Contingent condition. Since the Contingent/Noncontingent comparison is confounded by game-length, no conclusions about the effects of RNG-contingent game difficulty can be drawn.

Mean number of RNG-events per session was 14,053; mean proportions of hits per session in Contingent/longer (C/L), Noncontingent/shorter (NC/S), and Control conditions were 49.9%, 50.06%, and 50.04% respectively. The proportions were normalized by z-transformation; the Z-scores and an analysis of variance indicated no significant differences between conditions or deviations from MCE. Absolute values of the Z-scores were used to evaluate nondirectional deviations; there were no significant differences among conditions or deviations from MCE.

RNG hitting was, as predicted, related to some of the psychological factors. Extraversion was significantly related to directional scoring in the C/L games (Pearson $r = -.58$, 8 df, $p < .05$, one-tailed; low scores on the Myers-Briggs E/I scale indicate high extraversion). Players who tended to evaluate perceptions in terms of feeling-tone (high Myers-Briggs T/F scores) had significantly greater absolute deviations from chance performance in the NC/S games (Pearson $r = +.65$, 8 df, $p < .05$, two-tailed).

Attention-rating was significantly related to PK hitting in C/L games (Spearman rank-order $r = +.16$, 248 df, $p < .01$, two-tailed), which could conceivably have resulted from subtle PK feedback in contingent games affecting the players' attention-ratings. Attention-ratings were significantly higher in C/L games than in NC/S games (post-hoc Mann-Whitney U-test: $Z = -2.706$, $p < .003$), which supports this interpretation. On the other hand, this interpretation also suggests that attention-ratings should be positively related to game-length in C/L games, since RNG-hitting affects game-length in this condition; the attention-ratings, however, were inversely related to game-length in both C/L and NC/S games (C/L games: Spearman rank-order $r = -.18$, 248 df, $p < .004$, two-tailed; NC/S games: $r = -.13$, 248 df, $p < .025$, two-tailed).

There were no other significant correlations. It is possible, of course, that the patterns that appeared in this pilot study may be artifacts of multiple analysis; the next step is to see whether a second pilot study confirms these findings.

AN REG EXPERIMENT WITH LARGE DATA BASE CAPABILITY, II: EFFECTS OF SAMPLE SIZE AND VARIOUS OPERATORS*

Brenda J. Dunne, Robert G. Jahn,† and Roger D. Nelson (Princeton University)

Electronic random event generator (REG) experiments of large data base capability reported previously (RIP 1981, 50-51; Proceedings IEEE, 1982, 136-170) have been extended to investigate the effect of larger and smaller numbers of binary samples per trial, and the performance of several operators.

Protocol. The experimental protocol requires the operator to be seated in front of the REG with its remote initiation switch in hand and its LED indicators and computer terminal display clearly visible. The operator attempts to distort the trial counts either toward higher or lower values than the theoretical mean. The direction of effort is determined either by random instruction based upon a separate number generated before each 50-trial run or by the operator's preference which must then be pursued for a minimum of five runs, or 250 trials. The options of initiating each trial manually or of generating a run of 50 trials automatically, and the selection of a counting rate of 100 or 1000 samples per second, are also left to the operator's discretion.

These options, along with the direction of effort, are recorded before each run, but are so far considered secondary parameters in the analysis of the data. A full series for a given operator consists of a minimum of 25,000 experimental trials (or 5,000,000 samples) and half as many interspersed baseline trials, all of which are generally accumulated over periods of many months. No prescreening of operators, special training, preparatory exercises, or instructions regarding strategy are employed. Operators are encouraged to perform their experiments whenever and for as long as they choose, and to select their own preferential environmental conditions such as lighting level or background sound.

Sample Size Effects. An extensive initial series of over 25,000 trials, carried out by a single operator employing only 200-sample trials, was reported previously (RIP 1981, 50-51). Briefly, the 13,050 high-instruction trials (PK+) yielded a mean of 100.223,

---
*This work was supported in part by grants from the McDonnell Foundation and the John E. Fetzer Foundation.

and the 12,100 low-instruction trials (PK⁻) yielded a mean of 99.709, compared with a baseline mean of 100.045. The combined probability of this direction of effort split (ΔPK) was p = 3 x 10⁻⁹. The average yield of these data was tantamount to directed inversion of about one or one and one-half bits per thousand in the basic noise pulse train, or alternatively, of about 0.2 or 0.3 bits per trial.

In an effort to distinguish whether this magnitude of effect correlates more directly with the total number of bits processed in a given PK experiment, or with the number of trials, this same operator has since performed a second 25,000 trial series, all consisting of 2,000-sample trials rather than 200, under the presumption that if the PK process functions at the bit level, the yield per trial should increase correspondingly, whereas if the effect functions at the trial level, the yield should remain the same. The results of this series are curiously ambiguous. As before, there is clear and significant separation of the means of the PK⁺ and PK⁻ efforts. The 12,200 PK⁺ trials have a mean of 1000.386 (p = .026); the 13,100 PK⁻ trials, a mean of 999.598 (p = .018); compared with the baseline mean of 1000.08 (p = .358). The combined probability of the split in the direction-of-effort, ΔPK, is p = .002. Although these values are larger on a per-trial basis by a factor of about 1.7, they fail by a factor of 6 or 7 to endorse any simple bit-level hypothesis for the PK mechanism.

In an attempt to illuminate this issue further, the same operator has performed yet another 25,000 trial series composed solely of 100-sample trials. The results further confuse the issue in that they fail to reach significance, with a mean for 12,350 PK⁺ trials of 50.022 (p = .311); a mean for 13,300 PK⁻ trials of 49.980 (p = .318); compared with the baseline mean of 50.028 (p = .342). The direction of effort probability for ΔPK is .250.

At this point in the experimental logic, it seems important to ascertain whether this operator's performance characteristics have been changing along with, or independently of, the machine settings. For this purpose, a series has been undertaken in which the three sample sizes are randomly intermixed in each session. These results are not yet complete enough to allow further comment on the implication of the sample-size experiments.

Other Operators. Yet more pressing at this stage than attempting to localize the PK mechanism through variation of the machine parameters is to acquire some sense of the degree of generality or peculiarity of our original operator's performance, i.e., whether the results above are primarily characteristic of this operator's interaction with the machine, or of the device itself. Given the magnitude of the data base required to extract definitive results from the inherent statistical noise, this is a major task which has become feasible only by virtue of recent refinements in our on-line data acquisition and processing equipment and algorithms, and the development of a sophisticated data base management system.

At the present time we have a number of other operators in the process of generating REG data, only six of whom have exceeded the minimum of 5,000 trials which we regard as necessary for the extraction of any trend from the noise, and only one of whom has completed an entire 25,000 trial series. The results are much more informative when viewed in graphic form where the cumulative deviations from the mean are plotted relative to theoretical and baseline references, but briefly these can be described as follows:

Operator B's PK$^+$ trials are indistinguishable from baseline while the PK$^-$ trials show a clear and significant linear trend in the instructed direction, which inverts where the instructional mode was changed from random to volitional.

Operator C shows a consistent separation of PK$^+$ and PK$^-$ efforts, with both trends linear in the instructed direction, but neither significant in this small data base.

Operator D's full data base shows an inversion under both instructions, with the PK$^-$ efforts proceeding linearly in the positive direction to a significant degree.

Operator E shows a successful PK$^+$ trend in the early half of a data base accumulated in two major series. In the second half, both trend lines show strongly negative slopes, and the net deviation is quite small.

Operator F accumulates data in parametric clusters, and in some of the conditions, e.g., volitional instruction and manual operation, achieves strongly significant deviations. The net combined series, however, though clearly separated in the intended directions, does not reach significance.

Operator G's data tend in the negative direction for both instructions, and although the data base is small, both relatively linear trends approach significance.

With the understanding that many of these series are still incomplete by our large data-base criterion, we can make some provisional generalizations regarding the performance of these seven operators:

1) Each operator appears to display a characteristic "signature" of achievement with this device which usually varies more from operator to operator than from within the individual operator's temporal profile.

2) In most cases there is a clear separation of PK$^+$ and PK$^-$ efforts which display essentially linear gross characteristics over long periods of effort. The slopes of these gross trends are different for the PK$^+$ and PK$^-$ efforts, and in some cases are contrary to the instruction.

3) Subjective reports from the operators of their impressions of their interactions with the REG, such as strategic preferences, overall attitude, degree of enthusiasm, etc., show some correlation with their patterns of performance. For example, Operator E, whose results showed the least regularity, admitted, "I really don't like this experiment," but felt an obligation to continue, whereas Operator D, whose results were negatively significant, observed, "it was necessary to stop trying so hard (to imitate others' results) and start to have a good time and do my own thing."

4) Beyond these general characteristics, it appears that several of these operators, unlike the original operator, are sensitive to the secondary experimental options mentioned earlier. Even though their data bases are insufficiently large to permit quantitative correlations of these parameters with their performance, provocative differences in their yields under various experimental conditions are beginning to emerge. These are being explored further.

In summary, this REG experiment continues to provide instructive data on low-level PK, but also continues to display the importance of very large data bases, protocols of minimum complexity, and the individual characteristics of the operators which essentially preclude the compounding of their data.

FEEDBACK AND PARTICIPANT-SELECTION PARAMETERS IN A COMPUTER RNG STUDY (RB)

Charles Honorton, † Patricia Barker, and Nancy Sondow (Psychophysical Research Laboratories)

We report a computer-based RNG study comparing immediate versus delayed feedback on RNG hit rates. The study comprises three concurrently run experimental series and one control (i.e., no intended influence) series. The three experimental series differed only in method of participant selection: Series 1 consisted of participants who passed a moderate scoring criterion (Z > 1.0) in a five-trial screening series. Series 2 consisted of participants who failed the screening criterion. Series 3 consisted of unscreened laboratory visitors.

Our only formal hypothesis, derived from previous RNG studies, was that there would be a statistically significant overall RNG effect combining feedback (FBK) and silent (SIL) binary hits for Series 1. No predictions were made concerning Series 2 or 3, nor were any predictions made concerning the superiority of FBK or SIL sources. Since RNG effects are often bidirectional, we set a two-tailed 5% significance criterion (binomial Z). Since decline effects are a frequent characteristic of experimental PK reports, we also planned an analysis for within-participant declines, though we did not predict a decline effect.

Series length was set in advance to 100 trials (10,000 events) per series. The number of participants per series was not specified though each was limited to a maximum of 25 trials.

Two independent noise-diode random sources were simultaneously sampled in 100-event trials by a Cromemco Z80 microcomputer programmed in BASIC. Event by event feedback was available to participants for only one of the two RNG sources (FBK source). Feedback to the second RNG source ("silent" or SIL source) was limited to an end-of-trial statistical summary. FBK and SIL sources were assigned randomly at the beginning of each trial.

A target byte (0-255) was selected at the beginning of each trial by computer RND function. Binary hits were counted when RNG byte values were within the target nybble (upper or lower half of the byte). Direct hits were counted when the RNG byte value was the same as the target byte. The FBK source was displayed to participants via a thermometer-style computer graphics display showing a bar rising and falling in relation to the current FBK source byte value. Centered horizontal lines on either side of the bar demarcated target/nontarget areas of the display. Arrows on either side of the bar displayed the vertical target location.

Bar color provided feedback on cumulative performance within the trial. Above chance scoring was associated with a white bar, below chance with red, at chance with a yellow bar. Verbal messages were displayed at the end of each 10-event segment, with content determined by the cumulative Z-score. Feedback was also provided for direct hits, and a special "Jackpot" display was activated at the end of the trial if a preset scoring threshold was met.

The data generated for each trial, consisting of session ID, target value, FBK/SIL RNG assignments, FBK/SIL hit counts, raw byte values, and associated statistics, were stored in individual disk files and on a hardcopy printout. The data were subsequently transferred to a commercial database file for analysis.

Participants were adult volunteers, recruited from PRL staff and acquaintances, area residents responding to ads in a local newspaper, and drop-in visitors. Five participants passed the screening criterion, and went on to complete 12-25 trials each in Series 1.

A total of 310 control trials (31,000 events) were taken on each RNG source at various points during the experimental series. Means and standard deviations closely approximated expected binomial values. The overall control Z was -.46.

The 200 trials completed in Series 1 yielded a binary hit Z of 1.71 (p < .087, two-tailed). While close, this does not reach the 5% criterion specified by our design, and we therefore reject our formal prediction of overall significant scoring in Series 1. Stronger scoring occurred on the SIL source, which gave a Z of 1.68, than on the FBK source (Z of .76). Two of the five participants in Series 1 obtained significant scoring (p < .05) on the SIL source, while none scored significantly on the FBK source.

All five participants in Series 1 declined in scoring from first to second half of their trials. The decline was statistically significant overall (t = 2.73, 48 df, p = .0088) and for the FBK source alone (t = 2.44, 48 df, p < .017).

Series 2 and 3 yielded totally nonsignificant results (Z-scores of -.58 and -.65, respectively), no individually significant participants, and no declines.

Our results, though only suggestive, provide support for participant selection via screening. Overall scoring was higher in Series 1 than Series 3 (t = 1.61, 198 df, p < .105).

ANALYTICAL JUDGING PROCEDURE FOR REMOTE PERCEPTION EXPERIMENTS, II: TERNARY CODING AND GENERALIZED DESCRIPTORS*

Robert G. Jahn, Brenda J. Dunne, Roger D. Nelson, Eric G. Jahn, T. Aaron Curtis, and Ian A. Cook (Princeton University)

The course of research into the phenomenon known as "remote perception" or "remote viewing," wherein an individual (the percipient) attempts to obtain information regarding a remote geographical location where another individual (the agent) is situated at a prescribed time, without recourse to the normal modes of sensory communication, has led to a number of methodological questions regarding the reliability and quantifiability of data assessment by human judging procedures. In an effort to circumvent this difficulty, an analytical method for evaluation of the information content of remote perception or other free-response transcripts, based on a code of thirty binary descriptors, was developed as described in detail in previous references (JP, 1980, 207-231).

This method has now been extended to accommodate ternary responses to the descriptor queries, and to employ standardized or "universal" probabilities of these descriptors, rather than those

---
*This work was supported in part by grants from the McDonnell Foundation and the John E. Fetzer Foundation.

pertinent to the specific target pools, as the computational basis of evaluation. This standardization permits determination of the statistical merit of an individual transcript or a group of transcripts, without resort to intermediate ranking procedures.

Background. The heart of the original method, and of the refinements described here, is a code, or alphabet, of 30 simple descriptive queries which are applied to all targets and all perceptions, responses to which permit quantification and subsequent statistical analysis of the information acquired in remote perception efforts. In the original version, for example, each target and each perception was thereby represented by 30 binary bits (1/0), corresponding to the appropriate (yes/no) responses to these queries. The encoding of the target is normally performed by the agent at the time of visitation, although later reference can be made to photographs taken by the agent for verification. The perception is encoded by the percipient, but only after he has formed a free-response impression of the target in some form.

With the target and perception data thus encoded, a variety of scoring methods may be invoked for quantitative comparison of the perceptions with all of the targets in a given pool. Critical elements of these methods include the establishment of the a priori probabilities of all of the descriptors in the given target pool, in terms of which the correct responses are weighted, and the calculation of suitable normalization denominators, such as perfect scores and chance scores, with which the actual perception/target scores are compared.

Probably the most powerful attribute of the method is the capacity to process much larger numbers of perception/target comparisons than any human judge could handle, and thereby to score not only the proper matches, but all permutations of mismatched targets and perceptions in a given pool as well. With all these matched and mismatched scores in hand, it is possible to rank every matched perception against all improper targets in its pool, and then to employ rudimentary statistical criteria to establish the significance of the perception efforts.

Application of the original methods to a variety of precognitive remote perception data obtained previously yielded some highly significant statistical scores which were relatively insensitive to the particular scoring/normalization recipes, and in coarse agreement with more qualitative human judgings.

Ternary Descriptors. There has been some concern from the outset that the enforcing of a strict binary response to every descriptor query may be an uncomfortable aspect of the perception transcription, and in some cases, even of the target coding. Although ideally one would like to deal with targets and perceptions that are unambiguous in terms of the presence or absence of all of the descriptor features, in practice this is unattainable. For a number of reasons, such as imprecise definition of the extent of the target scene or region of focus, insignificance of a given feature in the overall context, uncertainty or obscurity of a detail, etc., it may be more comfortable for the participants to respond equivocally to a given descriptor query.

One method of addressing this problem is to employ ternary (1/0/2) coding, whereby a given feature may be specified as definitely present, definitely absent, or for some reason ambiguous. Inevitably this coding must complicate the scoring and normalization calculations to some degree, and it is not clear, ab initio, whether the problematic sharp distinction between the yes/no choice will not essentially be replaced by the two dichotomies of yes/unsure and no/unsure.

To explore whether the inclusion of an "ambiguous" or "unsure" category in the coding improves the quality of information quantification, we have recoded in ternary form all experimental series previously reported, along with more recent experiments performed specifically to test this version. In this study, the "unsure" category has been invoked specifically and only to cover aspects of the perception or target scene that are neither clearly present and significant in the scene, nor clearly and unequivocally absent. For example, for a scene which is essentially treeless except for a few minor bushes well off to the side, the descriptor query which asks, "Are trees, bushes, or major potted plants apparent in the scene?" would be coded "unsure." Similarly, for a scene whose central focus is an assortment of man-made and natural features, such as a zoo or a public beach, the query, "Is the central focus of the scene predominantly natural, i.e., not man-made?" would also be coded "unsure."

The alterations in the scoring/normalization procedures necessary to accommodate this ternary alternative are substantial in both their algebraic and digital form. Seven different scoring methods, retaining the essence of the original five binary methods, have been developed and applied to 35 trials from several different series, the results of which have been compared with those obtained via binary codings and human judging. In general, there appear to be few major changes in the assessment of the quality of the transcripts, and on the basis of these comparisons, we have concluded that any relative functional advantages or disadvantages of the various coding or computational recipes are outweighed by the coarseness of the descriptor net itself. Hence, it would not be unreasonable to select a particular method on the basis of its appeal or comfort for the percipient, agent, or experimenter, rather than for any intrinsic superiority of calculation.

Universal Target Pool and Generalized Descriptors. A substantially more consequential alternative involves the assignment of fixed or generalized descriptor probabilities, as opposed to those existent in the limited pools of targets for individual experimental series. By compounding the descriptor probabilities extant in a broad range of over 200 targets (local, national, and international) assembled from several previous and ongoing series, it is possible to identify a set of "universal" probabilities by which all or any perception transcripts may be weighted. The results of rescoring on this basis all of the data previously scored against their specific target pools display somewhat less variation over the five binary methods and average to very nearly the same mean ranks. This leads us to conclude that the vulnerability of the process to disparities between the characteristics of the small pools and those of the universal pool is minimal, and permits us to move to a more powerful and discriminating analysis which bypasses the ranking steps altogether and assigns statistical significance to each perception effort on its own merits.

Assignment of individual statistical values to the matched target scores can be achieved only if some reference distribution has first been established. To provide this, we take advantage of the capacity of the computer program to score each perception not only against its proper target, but against all other targets in its pool as well. All such mismatched perception/target scores for all series are computed using the same generalized descriptor probabilities and the same scoring method, and these are then concatenated into one grand empirical distribution function, which is regarded as a universal "chance" expectation for scores by that method. With reference to this empirical "chance" distribution, in our case compounded from over 1,400 mismatched targets and perceptions, the individual matched scores are converted to Z-scores and the statistical significance of each then calculated.

We have applied this procedure to all of our formal precognitive remote perception data, totaling 146 trials, nearly all of which followed protocols whereby the targets were not selected until well after the perceptions were completed, in several instances more than 24 hours later. Comparison of the distribution of actual scores against the empirical "chance" distribution shows that the former is clearly displaced positively with respect to the latter. For each of the five binary scoring methods, this matched target score distribution can reasonably be decomposed into three components. The major component is a scaled similarity of the reference "chance" distribution, and presumably is descriptive of the pattern of all unsuccessful trials. The second component, displaced well to the positive side of the mean, epitomizes the pattern of successful trials and comprises approximately 20% of the data base. The third and smallest component, representing about 5% of the data base, is displaced far to the negative side, and may indicate some significant "psi-miss" efforts.

The overall significances of these total precognitive remote perception data base distributions may be calculated from the displacement of their means from those of the reference "chance" distributions. Using the standard t-test within the approximation of quasi-normal distributions, these values range from $p = .025$ to $p = .0007$ for the five binary scoring methods.

<u>Further Refinements</u>. The analytical judging procedure as

modified herein provides a powerful tool for assessing the information transfer in remote perception experiments. Among its advantages are an ability to process large numbers of experimental trials each of which results in a relatively robust statistically derived score, and a capacity to evaluate the significance of each individual effort. Of most importance, this method provides a vehicle for replicable and quantitative analysis of free response remote perception data. Our continuing effort in this area will be toward refinement of the descriptor set to reduce its ambiguity to a minimum.

PSI TESTS WITH ALGERNON, A COMPUTER ORACLE (RB)*

William Braud and Winona Schroeter (Mind Science Foundation)

In two experiments, we attempted to upgrade the motivational conditions of the laboratory psi experiment by providing feedback which we hoped would be more meaningful than the lights, tones, and other indicators of "correctness" typically employed. We sought to accomplish this through the use of a specially designed computer program, ALGERNON, which provided meaningful information and answers to important personal queries if psi were manifested.

ALGERNON is a BASIC program written by W. B. and inspired by a similar program, ALICE, conceived at the Maimonides parapsychology laboratory by Michael Luthman, written by Keith Harary and Larry Tremmel, and further developed by Charles Honorton and his co-workers at Maimonides and later at the Psychophysical Research Laboratories in Princeton, N. J. Stored in ALGERNON's memory are 512 statements judged to be meaningful, albeit brief, commentaries on the problems and significance of life. Some items are selected from ALICE's original pool, others from philosophical, literary, and popular sources, and still others were invented by the authors. The items varied widely in their degree of abstractness, specificity, seriousness, and humor. It was hoped that ALGERNON's statements would provide useful answers to the subjects' queries or suggest new points of view from which to approach areas of concern.

Experiment 1: Lability Tested via Indirectly Assessed Psi

When one asks a question, one may already have the answer to that question, or at least a preferred answer. ALGERNON might provide a means of accessing these answers via psi, a means of "talking to oneself." The opportunity to obtain meaningful information via ALGERNON might provide sufficient motivation, incentive,

---
*Not presented due to the absence of the authors.

and reinforcement for psi performance. The subject types a meaningful question on the keyboard, then waits for an answer to be displayed on the screen. It was hypothesized that the subject might clairvoyantly scan the computer memory for the most appropriate answer, then psychokinetically influence the answer-selection process to increase the likelihood of obtaining that answer. At the end of the session, the subject's 16 questions, ALGERNON's 16 answers, and a rating form are printed out, and the subject is asked to rate the degree of relevance/meaningfulness/appropriateness of each answer. If suitable answers had been obtained through psi, consistently high ratings would be expected. Such ratings are subjective and cannot provide a direct assessment of psi. However, by varying the way in which answers were selected, an indirect assessment of psi could be made. It was hypothesized (see Braud in B. Shapin and L. Coly, eds., Concepts and Theories in Parapsychology, 1981, 1-36) that more labile (characterized by free variability) processes would be more susceptible to psi (in this case, PK) influence than more inert (more deterministic) processes. Therefore, four "degrees of randomness" of answer selection were possible. The greatest randomness was obtained through the use of a radio activity-based random generator ("truly random" condition). The next greatest randomness was obtained through a pseudorandom algorithm seeded 16 times (once for each question) by key pushes which varied randomly in time ("pseudorandom-multiple" condition). The next degree of randomness was provided by the same algorithm seeded only once by a key press early in the session ("pseudorandom-single" condition). The least random (most inert) condition provided no degrees of freedom for selecting one's own answers; answers for these subjects were retrieved from a disk record of the answers obtained by a predetermined previous subject ("fixed" condition). It was hypothesized that these four selection processes would be decreasingly susceptible to psi (PK) influence in the order given, and would yield meaningfulness ratings of the corresponding order. Subjects were randomly assigned to conditions, both subject and experimenter were blind with respect to condition, and nonpsi factors were expected to contribute equally to the four conditions as error variance and any consistent rating differences could be attributed to psi.

Sixteen subjects contributed to each randomness condition. Mean meaningfulness ratings were determined for each subject and the scores of the four groups were analyzed by analysis of variance. The order of the mean ratings of the four conditions was almost exactly as predicted (truly random > pseudorandom-multiple > fixed > pseudorandom-single), but the group differences did not reach significance. Thus the lability prediction was not confirmed.

Experiment 2: A Directly Assessed Psi Effect

Psi was directly assessed in this experiment in which thirty-two subjects participated. Again, each subject asked 16 meaningful questions and wished effortlessly for "good answers." The random time at which the RETURN key was pressed following a question was used to seed a pseudorandom algorithm which produced a string of 100 ones and zeros. If the number of ones exceeded chance (50%), then a "real" answer was randomly selected from the pool of 512 possible responses and displayed on the screen. If the number of ones fell below chance, a "nonanswer" (e.g., "Would you please ask another question") was displayed. A printout at the end of the session listed the information described earlier, as well as the number of randomly generated hits (ones) for each of the 16 questions, and the subject's overall Z score for the session. It was hypothesized that subjects would be motivated to obtain answers to their questions, and would manifest psi in order to meet the answer-yielding contingency.

A single-mean t test comparing the 32 Z scores with the chance expectation of zero yielded significant evidence for a missing effect ($\overline{X}$ = -.32, t = -2.16, 31 df, p = .036, two-tailed). Nearly all subjects spontaneously mentioned becoming quite frustrated when several "nonanswers" appeared, and this negativity may have influenced the direction of scoring. The results of 32 randomness tests interspersed with the experimental runs did not differ significantly from chance.

A NEW COMPUTER-CONTROLLED DEVICE FOR TESTING DIFFERENT PK HYPOTHESES (RB)

Walter von Lucadou and Johannes Mischo (University of Freiburg)

The Computer System and Its Components

The computer used here is a special model used to control industrial processes, thus it works very reliably and is resistent to mains and other transients.* It is a SIEMENS 310-16-byte system called Sicomp 10C with a 64K-byte memory (solid state RAM) containing 16 byte-words. The peripherals of the system consist of a video monitor with keyboard (SIEMENS 3974), a printer (SIEMENS 8106), and a paper tape read- and punch-unit (SIEMENS 38/203, FACIT 4070). The external storage consists of two floppy-disk units (SIEMENS 3974) with 255K-bytes and a cartridge disk drive (SIEMENS 3941) with 2 x 4.98 megabytes storage. The external process is controlled by a digital TTL-input-output-interface (SIEMENS 3661/A) with 22 input possibilities and 18 output possibilities.

---

*It is gratefully acknowledged that the computer system is a gift of the SIEMENS Company, Munich, West Germany.

Hardware Structure of the Components Concerning the PK Experiment

There are several possibilities for presenting a PK task to a subject:

1) Programmed figures can be displayed to the subject on a video screen.

2) It is possible to give tones with different pitches to the subject by headphones.

3) A string of lamps can display random events which are produced simultaneously or pre-recorded.

The subject can interact with the system by pressing five different buttons.

The random event generator (REG) is binary, thus it produces strings of 0 and 1 digits. The random source is an SR^{90} source about 0.045 mCi which is centered in a circle of 5 Geiger-Müller (GM) tubes (Valvo 18509 [ZP 1310]). The pulses coming from the GM tubes are amplified and transformed to TTL-norm-pulses. Afterwards they are counted by a counter which gives a handshake-signal when a certain number of counts is reached. This signal stops a flip-flop which is switching with high speed (triggered by a 5-MHz clock). The random event is given by the output of the flip-flop after it has stopped running. This is similar to the REG used by Helmut Schmidt (JP, 1970, 219-24; JSPR, 1977, 171-6), who has shown that "0" and "1" are equally distributed. The handshake-signal, however, is used additionally to produce another random event. The time difference between the start pulse coming from the computer and the handshake-signal is a measure of the decay rate of the SR^{90} source detected by the GM tube. This time Δt is measured by a fast counter programmed in the computer which makes, for instance, Z_i counts. This number Z_i is compared with the previous number Z_{i-1} and the random event is calculated by a simple algorithm:

"0" for $Z_i < Z_{i-1}$

"1" for $Z_i > Z_{i-1}$

For $Z_i = Z_{i-1}$ the procedure will be repeated. Thus every starting pulse from the computer will yield a set of 10 simultaneous random events which are stored in one computer word that consists of five events from the Schmidt-type generator and five events from the algorithm. One of these 10 random events can be selected arbitrarily to be displayed simultaneously on the string of lamps of the display. Both the REG and the display functions can easily be utilized by built-in call routines of the BASIC interpreter. Thus it is possible to get an arbitrary rate of random words up to 70 events/sec containing 10 random events.

It can easily be shown that the events "0" and "1" produced by the algorithm are equally distributed independently of the distribution of Z. Nevertheless, the resulting sequence is no pure random sequence but a Markoff-chain. It can be shown that it is approximately a Markoff-chain of the first order with the eigenvalue $\lambda = -1/3$ and the transition matrix

$$\begin{pmatrix} P_{00} & P_{01} \\ P_{10} & P_{11} \end{pmatrix} = \begin{pmatrix} 1/3 & 2/3 \\ 2/3 & 1/3 \end{pmatrix}$$

Although it is not possible in principle to evaluate a Markoff-chain g(t) used as a PK target with the usual CR method, this method will yield conservative results if one starts with the asymptotic ergodic probability p = 1/2 as hit in the CR formula. Thus the error probability p will be overestimated.

A better method for evaluating such sequences is the autocorrelation function

$$\phi(\tau) = \int_{-\infty}^{+\infty} g(t) \cdot g(t-\tau) \, dt$$

which is explicitly known under the null hypothesis. The measured autocorrelation function

$$\phi_j = \frac{1}{n} \sum_{i=1}^{n} g_i \cdot g_{i+j}$$

of a PK experiment can be compared with the theoretical curve by the chi-square method.

At first glance such techniques seem to be more difficult and complicated in relation to the usual method with pure random sequences. But with such a Markoff-chain there is a momentary one to one correlation between the decay rate of the SR^{90} source measured by the GM tube and a PK hit. Thus it becomes possible to test several hypotheses on the location of influence of PK.

Since we have displayed only one Markoff-sequence to the subject we can correlate it with the four others which are stored simultaneously. If the cross-correlation function

$$\phi_j^{kl} = \frac{1}{n} \sum_{i=1}^{n} g_i^k \cdot g_{i+j}^l$$

of all Markoff-sequences g^k g^l looks similar it is highly probable that the effect is due to a fluctuation of the decay rate. The same method could be used to reveal angular dependencies. However, if there would be only zero cross-correlations-functions but still a deviation in the autocorrelation function of the displayed sequence, this would indicate that most probably the effect was due to a fluctuation of the sensitivity of the single GM tube.

Finally, if only pure Schmidt-type random sequences would

show a deviation within a double-blind experiment this would indicate that neither the decay rate nor the sensitivity of the GM tubes shows any anomalies. In such a case the deviation can only be produced by some goal-oriented jitter in the synchronization between the Poisson-distributed GM-pulses and the fast-running five MHz clock.

OUTLINE OF A MULTIVARIATE PK EXPERIMENT (RB)

Walter von Lucadou and Johannes Mischo (University of Freiburg)

Experimental Setting. The subjects are not selected and first have to fill out a questionnaire at home. Before the experiment starts the subject has to fill out a second questionnaire. Then the subject is asked to influence a random generator connected with a string of lamps in such a way that the light will rise to the top, similar to the rise of a thermometer. Every subject has to do four runs with 600 trials, with a trial rate of approximately 10 trials per second. Before every run the subject has to press one of five buttons in order to start the run and simultaneously to give his or her estimation on the success in the subsequent run. After each run the subject has to estimate the success based on the observation of the string of lights during the run. Before the next run can be started there is a pause of one minute when the results in terms of standard deviations from chance expectation are displayed to the subject. The subject is given four categories of success: normal (CR < 1), interesting ($1 \leq$ CR < 2), good ($2 \leq$ CR < 3), and very good ($3 \leq$ CR). During the pause a nonfeedback run of the same length is running.

Physical Variables. The random event generator can produce 10 independent random events simultaneously, one being displayed on the string of lamps. Five of these events produce normal random sequences (like Schmidt's random event generator, or REG) and five produce Markoff-chains. Thus we get 10 different sequences at once. With the present experiment a pseudo-random number generator decides which of these 10 sequences will be displayed, but a single subject will always get two normal random sequences and two Markoff-sequences under both the feedback and nonfeedback conditions. The physical variables are due to the scoring differences among different random sequences and their intercorrelations. Since the whole system is working in real time in regard to the SR^{90} decay process the duration of the run is an additional variable.

Psychological Variables. The psychological variables consist of trait and state variables. The trait variables are derived from the questionnaire filled in at home which is composed of three parts: a sheep-goat scale, the IPC scale, and the FPI scale.

For the IPC scale three factors have been found: "internality," which means that the subjects believe in their ability to control their own fates; and two kinds of "externality": "powerful others, external control orientation" (powerlessness), and "chance control orientation" (fatalism).

The FPI scale includes the dimensions of "extraversion," "aggression," and "neuroticism." The state variables are measured with the EWL scale, which has six dimensions. Additionally, we get at least two state variables from the self-estimation of the subject before and after each run.

Data Evaluation. The randomness and distribution of the REG used was tested by a set of different computer programs.

It is obvious that an experiment which contains such a great amount of variables can be evaluated under quite different aspects, thus several variables can be regarded as predictive variables from one aspect and criteria variables from another.

It is planned to search for an effective "measure of PK" within an independent set of data. Thus two or three alternative "measures" could be found and correlated to independent variables. From the parapsychologist's point of view it is interesting to correlate all the psychological variables with the physical ones. But it could also be important to regard the self-estimation before and after the run as criteria variables and to correlate it with the sheep-goat variable, for instance. Furthermore it will be interesting to look for time dependencies during the session of both "PK measure" and self-estimation. It is clear that different trait variables, such as sheep-goat and other personality variables, can be correlated with each other.

It is highly probable that nonlinear dependencies between the parapsychological criteria variables and the psychological predictive variables will be found based on such an evaluation. Therefore it is necessary to begin the data analysis with nonlinear models similar to the approach of Mischo and Wittmann (ZP, 1980, 23-50; ZP, 1981, 27-57, 95-110). In our case it is planned to perform a variance analysis with nonlinear regression models. In order to avoid the problem of multi-collinearity an additional evaluation by dummy-coding and subsequent orthogonal factor analysis will be carried out. These dummy variables will be evaluated by a stepwise regression analysis. Finally, a canonical correlation analysis will be performed to get a relationship between predictive and criteria variables which can be tested in future experiments. The efficiency of this method can be checked by a discriminant analysis.

AN INEXPENSIVE ELECTRONIC CLAIRVOYANCE TESTER/TRAINER FOR PARAPSYCHOLOGISTS (RB)

Charles T. Tart* (University of California, Davis)

The unreliability and low level of manifestation of psi are the major problems of the field. If my 1966 theory that the provision of immediate feedback of results to talented percipients can increase psi ability is correct, a major step forward can occur. Given the apparent rarity of the talented percipients needed to test the theory, and the rarity of laboratories that can provide feedback training, an inexpensive way of providing such training would be quite helpful. This paper presents a software program, developed by Harold Puthoff and myself, that turns a high quality, relatively inexpensive hand-held computer, the Hewlett-Packard model 41C, into a quality clairvoyance testing and feedback training device. Thus any interested individual can have an ESP tester/trainer for about two hundred and ten dollars, the cost of the HP-41C and one memory extender module. Researchers who wish to use a printer with this device and supervise testing can also use it for formally testing percipients. If a zero for (no) is entered when the program prompts the user as to whether "Feedback?" is wanted, the program will provide a pure clairvoyance test, giving summary results, but no individual target identity data.

The following use instructions will be clear after you have familiarized yourself with the manual provided with the HP-41C.

Enter the program, given below. Once entered, it will be permanently stored in the HP-41C. Now make the following key assignments: "PESP" to the summation key; "PASS" to the 1/x key; and "RESULTS" to the square root of x key. Switch to the USER mode of the HP-41C and start the PESP program by pressing the summation key. Respond to each prompted query by entering the desired information on the keyboard and then pressing the R/S (run/stop) key. You will be prompted for the number of the month, day, and year, then for the number of choices. You may choose any number between 2 and 10^{99} choices, but 10 choices (keys 0 through 9) are usually plenty. The "RN LN?" prompt wants the number of trials in the run before automatic summary of results. If you want feedback just press the R/S key when prompted with "FEEDBACK?"; otherwise enter a zero for no feedback.

When prompted for "TIME?" look at the second hand of your watch immediately and read it, then the minute and hour. As the exact time is part of the seed for the pseudo-random number generator (PRNG) subroutine that generates targets, following this rule eliminates conscious control over the targets. Enter the hours and minutes as integers, and the seconds as decimals.

---

*I wish to acknowledge support from the Parapsychology Foundation and the McDonnell Foundation that greatly assisted in this work.

The PESP program will now alert you with a double beep tone and flash "READY" on its display. Enter an integer number in the chosen target range as your response, then press R/S. You will get a low tone and target identity feedback if you are wrong, or a fanfare of sound if you are correct. If you wish to pass on a given trial, push the 1/x key that was assigned to "PASS." You will get feedback on target identity but it does not count as a trial. If you wish to review results to date at any time in a run, push the square root key that was assigned to "RESULTS" and you will see the number of passes, hits, and trials, and the percentage of hits displayed. The review of results takes place automatically at the end of each run. The review of results cannot take place during a run if you have selected the no feedback option: it acts as a pass, but pass does not provide target information in the no feedback condition.

The PRNG subroutine has been thoroughly tested, as described in the paper to follow. Good randomicity is achieved by entering a new time seed for every run.

At the end of a run ("END OF RUN" displayed), another run with the same choice parameters may be had by pressing the R/S key. Wait for the "READY" display before entering a new response, otherwise you just accumulate errors.

```
01♦LBL "PESP"              28 PROMPT
 02 CF  00                 29 X=Y?
 03 FIX 0                  30 SF 00
 04 0
 05 STO 00                 31♦LBL 04
 06 STO 03                 32 "TIME=?"
 07 STO 04                 33 PROMPT
 08 STO 05                 34 LN
 09 STO 07                 35 ABS
 10 SF  02                 36 ST+ 02
                           37 CF 01
 11♦LBL 00                 38 CF 02
 12 "MONTH?"
 13 PROMPT                 39♦LBL 05
 14 "DAY?"                 40 PI
 15 PROMPT                 41 RCL 02
 16 STO 02                 42 +
 17 "YEAR?"                43 5
 18 PROMPT                 44 Y↑X
 19 ST* 02                 45 FRC
 20 "CHOICES=?"            46 STO 02
 21 PROMPT                 47 RCL 01
 22 STO 01                 48 *
 23 "RN LN?"               49 INT
 24 PROMPT                 50 STO 06
 25 STO 00                 51 CLX
 26 0                      52 SF 11
 27 "FEEDBACK?"            53 "READY"
```

```
     54 TONE 6
     55 TONE 6
     56 PROMPT
     57 FC? 11
     58 GTO 02
     59 RCL 06
     60 X=Y?
     61 GTO 06
     62 GTO 03

     63♦LBL 07
     64 1
     65 ST+ 03
     66 RCL 03
     67 RCL 00
     68 X=Y?
  69 GTO "RSLT"
     70 GTO 05

     71♦LBL 03
     72 1
     73 ST+ 07
     74 FS? 00
     75 GTO 07
     76 TONE 0
     77 XEQ 01
     78 GTO 07

     79♦LBL 06
     80 1
     81 ST+ 04
     82 FS? 00
     83 GTO 07
     84 SF 12
     85 BEEP
  86 "CORRECT"
     87 AVIEW
     88 CF 12
     89 PSE
     90 GTO 07

  91♦LBL "PASS"
     92 FS? 01
     93 GTO 08
     94 FS? 02
     95 GTO 00
     96 1
     97 ST+ 05
     98 FS? 00
     99 GTO 05
    100 XEQ 01
    101 GTO 05

102♦LBL "RESULTS"
    103 FS? 00
    104 GTO "PASS"
    105 FS? 02
    106 GTO 00

107♦LBL "RSLT"
    108 TONE 3
    109 TONE 2
    110 RCL 05
111 "NR PASSES="
    112 ARCL X
    113 AVIEW
    114 RSE
    115 PSE
    116 RCL 04
117 "NR HITS="
    118 ARCL X
    119 AVIEW
    120 PSE
    121 PSE
    122 RCL 03
123 "NR TRIALS="
    124 ARCL X
    125 AVIEW
    126 PSE
    127 PSE
    128 RCL 04
    129 RCL 03
    130 /
    131 100
    132 *
    133 "%HITS="
    134 ARCL X
    135 AVIEW
    136 PSE
    137 PSE
    138 RCL 03
    139 RCL 00
    140 X=Y?
    141 GTO 08
    142 GTO 05

    143 LBL 01
    144 FS? 00
    145 GTO 07
146 "TARGET WAS"
    147 ARCL 06
    148 AVIEW
    149 PSE
    150 RTN

    151♦LBL 08
```

```
152 CF 11               161 ADV
153 SF 01               162 GTO 84
154 "END OF RUN"
155 AVIEW               163♦LBL 02
156 STOP                164 "POWER OFF"
157 0                   165 AVIEW
158 STO 03              166 GTO 05
159 STO 04              167 .END.
160 STO 05
```

A RANDOMICITY TEST PROGRAM FOR PSEUDO-RNG ROUTINES ON THE HP-41C (RB)*

Charles T. Tart (University of California, Davis)

In the preceding paper, I described a way of turning a Hewlett-Packard model 41C programmable scientific calculator into an ESP testing/training instrument. This paper describes another program for the HP-41C, TESTRNG, which will test the pseudo-random number generator (PRNG) subroutine of that program or any other PRNG subroutine you wish to test, or test numbers from any other source that you wish to input by hand.

Basically the TESTRNG program generates integer PRNG outputs in runs of any selected length and then prompts for a new PRNG seed for the next run. Integers zero through nine can be handled and tested by chi-square test for equal frequency of appearance. Because of limited memory capacity, integers zero through four (five choices) can be tested by chi-square for equal frequency of sequential doublets, but not higher integers.

The TESTRNG program requires extended memory in the HP-41C and connection to an appropriate HP printer. Required SIZE is 061. The present PRNG subroutine has the local label 05 and occupies steps 056 through 066. You can delete these steps and substitute your own PRNG subroutine, as long as it is called LBL 05, starts at step 056, draws its seed number from register 09, and draws its scaling factor from register 08. That is, it should produce an output between .0000001 and .99999999; multiply it by a scaling factor representing the number of choices, and use the INT function of the HP-41C to then produce an integer output.

After clearing tally registers, the TESTRNG program will prompt you for various inputs. Enter each one from the keyboard

---

*This project was greatly assisted by support from the Parapsychology Foundation and the McDonnell Foundation.

and then press R/S. "TOTAL N?" is the number of trials in a single run, before you change the seed number. "CHOICES?" is the number of integer outputs, two through ten. When "PRINT RAW?" appears, just press R/S if you want the raw outputs printed out, otherwise enter "N" for no if you want only summary outputs. When "ANALYZE?" appears, press R/S if you want chi-square analyses performed, "N" if you don't. The program will then prompt for "SEED?"; after your seed number has been entered it will generate a run of outputs. Because we are dealing with a hand-held computer, this is slow: it can take four minutes to collect a hundred PRNG outputs.

After each run is completed, a new seed is prompted for, and the total number of trials in all runs to date is printed. After any run you may instruct the HP-41C to XEQ CHI, which will initiate and print the results of a chi-square analysis on the total accumulated trials to date. This analysis is always done for singlet frequencies, but is automatically deleted if more than five choices have been chosen. The chi-square analysis does not affect the accumulation registers, so you can add more runs of outputs after a chi-square analysis. Note also that if the expected value in any chi-square cell is less than five, a warning to that effect will be printed.

The following sample problem will allow you to check your programming. Run 20 trials of a three-choice output, using the PRNG subroutine as given. The seed number is 935.54. The raw output from the PRNG will be printed as follows:

    2 1 2 0 1 2

    1 1 1 0 1 0

    1 2 1 2 0 2

    2 1

Upon executing CHI, we see

    4 9 7

    S CHI SQ = 1.900

    0 3 1

    2 2 4

    2 4 1

    D CHI SQ = 7.053

    E < 5

indicating the frequencies of appearances of the three singlets (4 zeros, 9 ones, 7 twos) with an associated chi square of 1.900 and the frequencies of appearances of zero-zeros (0), zero-ones (3), etc., with an associated chi square of 7.053, and a warning that the expected frequencies in each doublet cell were less than 5.

To test an externally generated series of numbers, delete the current steps 058 to 067 in the TESTRNG program and insert instead

    58 "NUMBER?"

    59 XEQ PROMPT

Now when the program prompts you with "NUMBER?" give it the first of your integer numbers in the zero to nine range, the next number when it again prompts you for "NUMBER?", etc.

Randomicity Test Program

```
01♦LBL "TESTRNG"          31 SF 02
  02 CF 00                32 "N"
  03 CF 01                33 ASTO Y
  04 CF 02                34 AON
  05 CF 03             35 "PRINT RAW?"
  06 0.05901              36 PROMPT
  07 STO 60               37 AOFF
                          38 ASTO X
  08♦LBL 02               39 X=Y?
  09 0                    40 SF 00
  10 STO IND 60           41 "N"
  11 ISG 60               42 ASTO Y
  12 GTO 02               43 AON
  13 FIX 0             44 "ANALYZE?"
  14 "TOTAL N?"           45 PROMPT
  15 PROMPT               46 AOFF
  16 STO 05               47 ASTO X
                          48 X=Y?
  17♦LBL 07               49 SF 01
  18 "CHOICES?"
  19 PROMPT               50♦LBL 01
  20 STO 08               51 TONE 6
  21 1                    52 "SEED?"
  22 -                    53 PROMPT
  23 STO 46               54 LN
  24 10                   55 ABS
  25 RCL 08               56 STO 09
  26 X>Y?
  27 GTO 07               57♦LBL 05
  28 5                    58 PI
  29 RCL 08               59 RCL 09
  30 X>Y?                 60 +
```

```
 61 5                    110 RCL 06
 62 Y↑X                  111 ST+ 07
 63 FRC                  112 RCL 07
 64 STO 09               113 "ΣΣ = "
 65 RCL 08               114 ARCL X
 66 *                    115 AVIEW
 67 INT                  116 0
 68 STO 16               117 STO 06
 69 FS? 00               118 GTO 01
 70 GTO 04
                         119◆LBL "CHI"
 71◆LBL 03               120 0
 72 ACX                  121 STO 26
 73 1                    122 STO 35
 74 SKPCHR               123 50
                         124 STO 27
 75◆LBL 04               125 RCL 46
 76 1                    126 +
 77 ST+ 06               127 1 E3
 78 FS? 01               128 /
 79 GTO 06               129 1 E-5
 80 RCL 16               130 +
 81 50                   131 ST+ 27
 82 +                    132 STO 28
 83 STO 17               133 RCL 07
 84 1                    134 RCL 08
 85 ST+ IND 17           135 /
 86 FS? 02               136 STO 25
 87 GTO 11               137 5
 88 RCL 06               138 X>Y?
 89 1                    139 SF 03
 90 X=Y?
 91 GTO 06               140◆LBL 08
 92 RCL 18               141 RCL IND 27
 93 RCL 16               142 ACX
 94 +                    143 1
 95 STO 19               144 SKPCHR
 96 1                    145 RCL IND 27
 97 ST+ IND 19           146 RCL 25
                         147 -
 98◆LBL 06               148 X↑2
 99 RCL 16               149 RCL 25
100 10                   150 /
101 *                    151 ST+ 26
102 STO 18               152 ISG 27
                         153 GTO 08
103◆LBL 11               154 FIX 0
104 RCL 06               155 PRBUF
105 RCL 05               156 FIX 3
106 X>Y?                 157 RCL 26
107 GTO 05               158 "S CHI SQ= "
108 FIX 0                159 ARCL X
109 PRBUF                160 AVIEW
```

Computers and REGs

```
161 PSE
162 CLA
163 FIX 0
164 FS? 03
165 XEQ 13
166 CF 03
167 FS? 02
168 GTO 12
169 RCL 07
170 ENTER↑
171 ENTER↑
172 RCL 05
173 /
174 -
175 RCL 08
176 X↑2
177 /
178 STO 25
179 5
180 X>Y?
181 SF 03
182 RCL 46
183 1 E3
184 /
185 1 E-5
186 +
187 STO 27
188 STO 29

189♦LBL 09
190♦LBL 10
191 FIX 0
192 RCL IND 27
193 ACX
194 1
195 SKPCHR
196 RCL IND 27
197 RCL 25
198 -
199 X↑2
200 RCL 25

201 /
202 ST+ 35
203 ISG 27
204 GTO 10
205 FIX 0
206 PRBUF
207 10
208 RCL 08
209 -
210 .01
211 +
212 ST+ 27
213 ISG 29
214 GTO 09
215 FIX 3
216 RCL 35
217 "D CHI SQ= "
218 ARCL X
219 AVIEW
220 PSE
221 CLA
222 FIX 0
223 FS? 03
224 XEQ 13
225 CF 03
226 GTO 01

227♦LBL 12
228 "NO DBLT ANAL"
229 AVIEW
230 PSE
231 GTO 01

232♦LBL 13
233 SF 12
234 " E<5"
235 AVIEW
236 CF 12
237 RTN
238 .END.
```

MENTAL STATE VARIABLES*

POSSIBLE PSI-MEDIATED PERCEPTUAL EFFECTS OF SIMILARITY OF REG ALTERNATIVES TO THE PK TARGET: A DOUBLE-BLIND STUDY

Rex G. Stanford (St. John's University)

The major purpose of this study was to learn whether similarity to the target of nontarget alternatives selectable by the random event generator (REG) has a negative effect upon PK performance. This question was to be studied in the context of full feedback to each subject, such that whatever was the REG outcome--target or nontarget alternative--the subject immediately observed the outcome. Thus, we were not attempting in this study to distinguish between effects related purely to perceptual similarity and those related, possibly, to the effects of that similarity on incentive value of the nontarget alternative. In the first case (perceptual similarity) the imperfectness of the psi process could result in the erroneous selection of a nontarget similar to the target, rather than in the selection of the target itself--a form of psi-mediated confusion. In the second case, the immediate feedback concerning the outcome could favor erroneous selection of the similar nontarget alternative because such an alternative, due to its similarity to the target, would have considerable incentive value. If either or both factors were operative, a reduction in the frequency of selection of the target should occur. Therefore, the hypothesis of this study was that the presence of a nontarget alternative which is perceptually similar to the target reduces, at least with full feedback, the probability that the REG will select the target. The psi-mediated character of any observed effects of such similarity was to be insured by the fact of both subjects and experimenter being blind at the time of the REG running concerning the nature of the nontarget REG alternatives.

Another objective of this study was to compare the rate of REG selection of specific nontarget alternatives when those alterna-

---

*The papers and research briefs abstracted here comprise two sessions chaired separately by John Palmer (University of Utrecht) and K. Ramakrishna Rao (Institute for Parapsychology, FRNM)

tives are embedded in the context of varied other nontarget alternatives. This allowed detection of possible contextual response to the nontarget array.

A total of 180 St. John's University students participated voluntarily and without pay. They were recruited for a PK study which would last only about 10 minutes and would involve psi communication with a machine. Each subject participated in only one PK trial of the type discussed below. Two experimenters each tested 90 subjects. One, Ray Angelini, is a doctoral student in clinical psychology and is a research assistant for the author. The other, Robert Guarcello, is a special student taking graduate psychology courses; he volunteered to test subjects because of his interest in gaining research experience.

The task required the subject, first, to observe the target slide in an illuminated slide viewer. This target slide was the same for all subjects and had been preselected by the author as a visually striking, perhaps even exciting, scene. It showed a group of horses, possibly wild ones, running left to right in front of the camera with manes and tails flying. The horses were more or less silhouetted against a backdrop of snow and mountains with a few bushes in the foreground. The subject viewed the slide for as long as he or she wished, and it was then removed from the viewer and from sight. The goal of the single-trial PK task was for the subject to cause the REG to select this slide for viewing once more, rather than any of the other slides it might select randomly.

Though the target slide was the same for all subjects, this was not the case for the nontarget alternatives which were potentially selectable. Birgit Stanford, my wife, used the RAND table of random digits on a one-third probability basis to assign each subject to one of three nontarget arrays. (A nontarget array consists, in this case, of the slides, in addition to the target, which can potentially be selected, through the running of the REG, for the subject to view.) The subject at the time of testing had thus been assigned to a gradient similarity array (G), a high-only similarity array (H), or a low-only similarity array (L). The G array consisted of three slides each bearing progressively less similarity to the target slide (see below). The H array consisted of the slide from the G array which was most similar to the target, plus two blank slides. The L array consisted of the slide from the G array which was least similar to the target, plus two blank slides.

Pretesting with two groups of 10 subjects each had shown very clearly that the assumed gradient of similarity to the target of the slides in the G array was shared by the subject population and was not idiosyncratic to the experimenter. (Details are available upon request.) The most similar slide showed a large, brown monkey running across a green background from left to right, near the camera. The monkey's tail was out behind it in a slightly curled position, somewhat reminiscent of the tails of the horses in the target slide. The second most similar picture also showed a brown monkey; this one was sitting near the center of a large fan-shaped palm leaf and was peering straight into the camera; similar leaves were in the background. The least similar picture was an aerial view of Angel Falls in South America which showed the falls for its entire length and, in the foreground, a small image of a single-engine aircraft maneuvering in the chasm around the falls.

At the beginning of the session the subject read a one-page sheet of instructions which emphasized a mind-machine communication set, rather than mind-machine manipulation. (Copy available upon request to the author.) He or she then observed the target slide, and when the subject was ready, the experimenter removed that slide from the viewer and from view. The subject then started the REG by pressing a button.

The REG ran for about 60 seconds before stopping. As it ran, a digital counter on its front showed the rapid accumulation of pulses entering one of its registers. (The register increments were too rapid for visual tracking, and, in any event, the subject did not know the exact significance of what the REG was doing, except that its running would determine which slide would later be seen.) At the end of the run the experimenter hand-recorded the last digit on the right of the number then displayed on its digital register. This digit represented the last digit in the total number of pulses which had accumulated in the register. A pulse had entered the register, causing it to increment, each time the REG (with a 1/8 probability) made a decision in favor of such a pulse. The REG made random decisions at a rate of about 5,000 per second--producing a total of 299,997 decisions in the approximately 60 seconds of running time --and, of course, about 7/8 of these decisions resulted in no pulse being sent to the register and about 1/8 resulted in such a pulse. The random timing of the pulses, coupled with the rapid decision (sampling) rate and the relatively long running time, meant that the final digit of the register rapidly and repeatedly cycled through the digits 1-9 and stopped on one of them, with an essentially equal probability for all digits.

However, since there is always some conceivable possibility of REG bias, which slide the subject actually saw at the end of the run was determined, not by the REG-produced digit alone, but by a combination of this digit and a digit obtained (prior to the session) through the use of the RAND table of random digits. (For example, the register digit "4" resulted in the selection of the target slide only when the RAND digit was "0.") If the REG produced either the digit "8" or the digit "9," the experimenter considered that no decision had been made, and the machine was started again for a rerun. (This was because with four slides only eight of the digits could be used.)

After the experimenter hand-recorded the (usable) REG digit, he opened a sealed, opaque envelope which had been prepared by Birgit Stanford, who was not involved in the testing. This envelope contained both a randomly determined letter (based on the RAND table) representing one of the three nontarget arrays (G, H or L) and a digit (see above) to be used in combination with the REG digit to determine which of the slides (target or one of the three from the designated nontarget array) the subject would see. Thus, prior to completion of the running of the REG, both experimenter and subject were blind as to the nontarget array and as to which REG outcome would designate the target (or a given nontarget). (Subjects, indeed, did not even know that different nontarget arrays were possible.) After the subject had seen the selected slide, the experimenter briefly discussed the study with him or her and the session was concluded. Each subject was later mailed a letter describing the purposes and outcomes of the study.

In accord with the experimental hypothesis, the hit rate was significantly higher for the condition (nontarget array L) which provided low target-nontarget similarity than for the combined conditions (nontarget arrays G and H) which provided high target-nontarget similarity because of the presence of the high-similarity slide (hit rates of .304 and .193, respectively; Z for the difference of proportions = 1.65, $p = .05$, one-tailed). None of the arrays showed hit rates which were significantly different from mean chance expectation of .250. Because of the use of the RAND table to assign subjects to the three arrays, 64 subjects were tested with nontarget array G, 60 with nontarget array H, and 56 with nontarget array L.

Generation rates for the most similar slide did not differ significantly for nontarget arrays G and H, so this contrast provided no evidence of a contextual effect. Nor did the generation rates for the least similar slide differ according to the nontarget array (G and L), so, again, there was no evidence of a contextual effect.

The first outcome discussed above provides some evidence in support of the hypothesis that the presence of a nontarget which is highly similar to the target can, in a PK task, reduce the probability that the REG will select the target. Before any conclusion can be drawn, however, this work should be replicated, since the statistical outcome is not strong. Further work is certainly warranted because the existence of such effects in "blind" contexts could have major theoretical importance. Future work should also manipulate the feedback variable in order to disentangle "pure" perceptual-similarity effects from the enhanced incentive value associated with a nontarget which is very similar to the target.

PSI FUNCTIONING AND ASSESSED COGNITIVE LABILITY*

William Braud, Donna Shafer, and Judith Mulgrew (Mind Science Foundation)

Two experiments were conducted to test a prediction from a recently proposed "lability/inertia" model of psi functioning (Braud, in B. Shapin and L. Coly, eds., Concepts and Theories of Parapsychology, 1980, 1-36) that psi performance would be positively correlated with degree of assessed cognitive lability (degree of free variability of the mental processes of percipients).

Experiment 1: Lability Assessment Involving Ambiguous Auditory Stimulation

If one is presented with an ambiguous auditory stimulus, one may "project" into that stimulus a variety of "meanings." The stimulus functions as an "acoustic Rorschach," eliciting a variety of possible responses. We assumed that individuals with more labile nervous systems would project into the ambiguous stimulus a greater number of meanings and more qualitatively dissimilar meanings than would individuals with more inert nervous systems. Thus, during an initial laboratory session, we exposed 32 individuals to this material. The ambiguous stimulus was a 16-minute presentation of the word "cogitate" presented over and over by means of a tape loop to which the subject listened with headphones. The subject was instructed to verbalize what he or she heard in the sound. The verbalizations were tape recorded and later transcribed. For each subject, a list of the different words or phrases heard in the stimulus tape was prepared, in proper chronological order. The number of different words or phrases perceived in the ambiguous stimulus by a subject was used as that subject's lability index.

In a second laboratory session, several days or weeks later, the subject again listened to the identical ambiguous auditory stimulus and was again asked to verbalize whatever he or she heard in the sound. The subject's responses were again tape recorded and later transcribed. This second session was a psi session in which the aim was to influence the subject's perceptions of the content of the ambiguous stimulus so that a randomly selected target meaning was verbalized more quickly than a matched control meaning. For each subject, the two middle-most responses were selected from the response list generated during the first session; one of these two responses was randomly selected as the target meaning, the other as the control meaning. This method assured that the two meanings were approximately equal in likelihood of occurrence, and were neither excessively dominant (early in the list) nor excessively rare

---
*Delivered by Rex G. Stanford (St. John's University)

(late in the list). While the subject listened to the ambiguous stimulus and verbalized his or her responses, an agent in an isolated distant room listened to the same ambiguous stimulus at low volume through a loudspeaker, and attempted to "project" the target meaning into the stimulus, mentally repeating the target meaning over and over while intending for that meaning to be quickly perceived and verbalized by the subject.

In order to study the influence of Ganzfeld stimulation upon both psi performance and cognitive lability, half of the 32 subjects were both lability assessed and psi tested during Ganzfeld exposure (uniform visual stimulation only, auditory Ganzfeld stimulation omitted because of the auditory nature of the assessment and psi tasks), while half were assessed and psi tested under nonGanzfeld control conditions. Ganzfeld stimulation began four minutes before the "cogitate" tape began, and continued throughout the 16-minute tape, thus providing 20 minutes of visual Ganzfeld exposure.

Due to limitations of space, only the major lability prediction and analysis will be discussed here. It was predicted that across all 32 subjects there would be a significant positive correlation between lability index and psi score. The lability index was simply the number of different words or phrases reported by the subject in response to the ambiguous auditory stimulus (for both sessions combined). The psi score was a difference score: the signed difference between the ordinal positions of reporting target vs. control meanings during the second (i.e., psi-testing) session. For example, if the subject's third response was the target meaning, and his or her eighth response was the control meaning, that subject's psi score would be + 5. The scores of 13 subjects had to be eliminated from this analysis. Ten scores were eliminated because neither the target nor the control meaning was mentioned by the subject in the second session and therefore no psi difference score could be calculated. The remaining three subjects were eliminated because they failed to complete their second session before the deadline required for submission of this paper. The Pearson r correlation between lability score and psi score for the 19 subjects with valid psi scores was significantly positive ($r = +.39$, 17 df, $p < .05$, one-tailed).

Experiment 2: Lability Assessment Involving
Ambiguous Visual Stimulation

The rationale and protocol of this experiment approximated those of Experiment 1. In Experiment 2, an ambiguous visual stimulus, a Necker cube, was substituted for the ambiguous auditory stimulus of Experiment 1. Additionally, a measure of degree of control of percepts was substituted for the more spontaneous "flow-of-percepts" measure of Experiment 1.

In the first (assessment) session, 32 subjects were confronted with a slide-projected Necker cube figure and reported (by means of a button press which marked a polygraph in a distant room) the rate at which the perspective of the figure reversed during two one-minute epochs in which the cube was simply observed ("spontaneous" epochs), and two one-minute epochs in which the subject attempted to reverse the cube's perspective as frequently as possible ("control" epochs). The four assessment epochs were presented in an SCCS order to minimize progressive error, and were separated by 30-second rest periods. Polygraph tracings were later blind-scored to determine the subject's lability index. This index was a measure of the subject's degree of control of perspective and consisted of the ratio of the total number of figure reversals (pen deflections) during the control exposures (sum of deflections for exposure periods 2 and 3) to the total number of reversals during the spontaneous exposures (sum of deflections for exposure periods 1 and 4).

As in Experiment 1, half of the subjects were assessed and tested under Ganzfeld stimulation, and half under nonGanzfeld control conditions. In Experiment 2, Ganzfeld stimulation was lengthened to 23 minutes duration and included both visual and acoustic (white noise) components. Lability and psi measuring periods occurred immediately following Ganzfeld stimulation, because of the visual nature of the Necker cube task, rather than during stimulation as in Experiment 1.

The second session psi-measurement task required that the subject passively observe the rate of spontaneous perspective reversals of the Necker cube figure during four one-minute epochs (separated by 30-second rests) in which each reversal was signalled by a polygraph-marking button press. During the middle two epochs (periods 2 and 3), an agent in a distant room herself viewed a similar Necker cube and attempted to reverse the figure's perspective as frequently (during one randomly selected period) or as infrequently as possible (during the other period), while intending for the subject's reversal rate to match her own. Polygraph tracings were later blind-scored to derive a psi score consisting of the signed difference between the frequency of target (increase) and control (decrease) deflections, a positive difference score indicating hitting.

As in Experiment 1, it was predicted that a significant positive correlation would obtain between lability index and psi difference score. This prediction was not confirmed in this experiment (r = +.09, 30 df, p = ns).

In spite of the absence of overall psi hitting in the experiments, there did occur significant evidence in support of the lability hypothesis. This evidence took the form of a significant positive correlation between assessed cognitive lability and psi hitting in Experiment 1. Subjects who reported many new meanings in the ambiguous auditory stimulation evidenced higher psi scores than did the subjects whose response patterns were more "inert." Whether the psi effect obtained might best be conceptualized as telepathy, clairvoyance, or psychokinesis (by the agent upon the mental activity of the subjects) is irrelevant to the lability hypothesis in this instance, since in all three cases, the lability/inertia model predicts greater psi manifestations in the more labile participants. An important feature of these experiments is that lability is experimentally assessed in the very systems in which psi is later measured. This maximizes the likelihood that the assessment is a valid one and capable of generalization to the psi-indicating system.

Additional hypotheses, analyses, and discussions regarding the absence of a significant effect in Experiment 2, and the absence of a significant effect of Ganzfeld stimulation in either experiment may be found in a greatly expanded version of this paper which will be published in due course.

THE NOISE-SILENCE AND TARGET-ENCODABILITY VARIABLES IN A GANZFELD WORD-ASSOCIATION ESP TASK: THE APPLICATION OF METHODS BASED UPON SIGNAL-DETECTION THEORY (RB)

Rex G. Stanford and Raymond F. Angelini (St. John's University)

This is a methodological report; results are not yet available. Our primary objective is to test the hypothesis that pink noise used during Ganzfeld has, as contrasted with no special noise ("silence"), particular value in reducing the cognitive constraints believed to interfere with ESP. We are thus examining both the cognitive and extrasensory consequences of pink noise as contrasted with silence during Ganzfeld. We are also studying whether target encodability (i.e., the nonpsi probability of a response corresponding to a target class) influences extrasensory sensitivity. This study of encodability is preliminary in that encodability is manipulated by varying target type, so encodability is potentially confounded with target type. A final objective is to learn whether the trait of Absorption (A. Tellegen and G. Atkinson, Journal of Abnormal Psychology, 1974, 83, 268-277) is correlated with the cognitive and extrasensory consequences of Ganzfeld stimulation. The Absorption scale measures the inclination "for having episodes of 'total' attention that fully engage ... representational ... resources" (p. 268).

Subjects are 100 unpaid volunteers, mostly university students, who fill out the Absorption scale (34 items mixed, in this study, with 40 buffer items) before coming for the experimental session. The experimenter, Ray Angelini (RA), is blind to subjects' Absorption scores when they are tested.

The subject reclines in a recliner chair while alone in a

commercial, acoustically shielded chamber; a ping-pong ball half is over each eye and light from a 150-watt incandescent bulb with foil reflector and red filter shines onto the face from six or seven feet away. Through a headset the subject hears taped instructions and word-association stimuli (87 concrete nouns, the first three of which, unknown to the subject, are buffer words), as well as the "live" experimenter when appropriate. Sound level for instructions and stimuli is approximately 81 dB; for the noise condition, taped pink noise is mixed at about 77 dB with the output of the aforementioned tape, beginning at the end of the instructions.

Instructions state that subjects will hear everyday words at 15-second intervals and that they should say the first word to come to mind on hearing each. RA will aid their giving the correct response by sending a message on each trial concerning that response. They will get feedback about performance at the session's end. Relaxation will aid their receptivity, so they are given brief relaxation instructions near the end of the instructions. They are to let the relaxation deepen during the three-minute interval following instructions and preceding the first word. Word association lasts 22 minutes; total Ganzfeld, 35 minutes.

Unknown to the subject, some stimuli (selected with one-third probability, RAND table) have no target. (Responses to these stimuli allow uncontaminated cognitive measures and computation of false-alarm rates.) The remaining stimuli each have as a target either the category "concrete noun" (CN) or "concrete adjective" (CA) on an equal probability basis (RAND table). The target sheet has been prepared by an assistant and is not seen by RA until he is outside the experimental chamber; it indicates which words have target responses and which do not; it also indicates, for each of the former, the target category and gives an example of an appropriate such response to that word. RA "sends" that example, though he is aware of the category also. (ESP is scored only for category, not specific response.) RA via one-way intercom hears and transcribes the responses and at session's end unofficially scores them to aid in giving feedback to the subject. (Official transcription and scoring is done from a session tape by a person unaware of the subject's targets.)

Just before ESP feedback, the subject answers a questionnaire on subjective time estimate for Ganzfeld, liking for Ganzfeld experience, liking for background auditory stimulation (noise or silence), relaxation during word association, and subjective estimate of average inter-stimulus interval.

The official scorer derives hit and false-alarm rates for both CN and CA categories for each subject. These measures allow computation of separate extrasensory sensitivity measures (d') for the CN and CA targets for each subject. (Concerning d' and related concepts, see J. A. Swets, Science, 1973, 182, 990-1000.) CN targets are considered high encodable and CA low encodable because subjects tend to produce responses of the same form class as the stimulus.

Space limitations prevent discussion of our planned nonpsi analyses, but they are available upon request. Planned ESP-related analyses include the following: (a) between-within subjects analysis of variance to assess whether the noise-silence and target encodability variables or their interaction influenced d'; (b) Pearson r to assess the correlation of d' for CN and CA targets for noise and silence conditions separately; and (c) Pearson r to assess the correlation of Absorption scores with d' (for the two target types separately) for noise and silence separately. Two-tailed tests are used for (b) and (c).

PROLONGED VISUALIZATION PRACTICE AND PSYCHOKINESIS: A PILOT STUDY (RB)*

William Braud (Mind Science Foundation)

Elsewhere I have suggested (in B. Shapin and L. Coly, eds., Concepts and Theories of Parapsychology, 1980, 1-36) that the likelihood and/or magnitude of a psychokinesis effect may be proportional to the degree of free variability (lability) of the target system, and also proportional to the degree of structure (inertia) of the intention of the PK agent. The degree of target-relevant structure of an inert system is defined as the proportion of the organization of that system which is devoted to or representative of the target event. Stated otherwise, degree of structure is determined by how completely the PK agent's brain or mind is permeated with the target intention or goal. An inert system structure which would be optimal for the occurrence of PK would be one in which the agent's intention is strong, clear, well-defined, persistent, and undistorted by competing mentation. Training in concentration, meditation, and visualization would be expected to aid in the maintenance of a well-structured intention.

This research brief describes a pilot investigation of the usefulness of prolonged visualization or imagery training in facilitating psychokinesis. Seven well-motivated participants attempted to psychokinetically influence a random event generator which provided colored light feedback for hits. The participants then experienced intensive imagery training which emphasized visualization of colors. After daily imagery practice for a period of six weeks, a PK posttest was administered. Several self-report and performance assessments of imagery were also administered.

The procedure involved weekly group meetings as well as daily at-home practice. During the first group meeting, pre-test assessments of imagery and of PK were made. Imagery was

---

*Not presented in the author's absence.

assessed by Paivio's Individual Differences Questionnaire, Marks' Vividness of Visual Imagery Questionnaire, and Gordon's Test of Visual Imagery Control. A performance measure of the degree to which imagery succumbs to verbal interference (the Stroop test) was also administered. The final psychometric assessment was of the number of spontaneous and controlled reversals that occurred while the subject viewed an ambiguous stimulus, a Necker cube. The PK assessment (administered individually) involved five 100-trial runs in which the aim was to influence a thermal noise-based binary random event generator. Hits were indicated to the subject by diffuse red illumination; no feedback was provided for misses.

The visualization exercises were adapted from an imagery enhancement training program originally developed by Leonard George at the FRNM. George's imagery exercises were tape recorded by W.B. (with some slight modifications) and were mixed with appropriate musical backgrounds. Each exercise was preceded by an abbreviated (nine-minute) progressive relaxation exercise. The taped imagery exercises involved predominantly guided visualizations of color and colored objects. Early exercises were simple and static, while later exercises were more complex and dynamic. In addition to the taped exercises, which were experienced in weekly group meetings, there were daily homework assignments of exercises which were done individually.

Following six weeks of imagery training, a post-test session was held in which PK and imagery assessments identical to those of the pre-test were administered. It was predicted that there would be significant improvement on the PK task. The goal of the PK task was to keep the red feedback lamp illuminated for as long as possible. Subjects were instructed to visualize the lamp burning constantly. It was expected that the intensive training in color visualization would facilitate this goal image and result in a more structured "agent template" or inert system to which the more labile random generator might conform.

The prediction regarding improved psychokinesis scoring was confirmed. Before training, there was a 50.51% hit rate, which did not differ significantly from chance. However, following training there was a 53.91% hit rate, which significantly exceeded chance expectation (1,887 hits, $Z = 4.63$, $p = 3.66 \times 10^{-6}$, two-tailed). The difference between pre- and post-test PK scores was significant ($Z_{diff} = 2.84$, $p = .0044$, two-tailed). Moreover, there was a significant positive correlation between PK performance and amount of visualization practice ($r = +.84$, 5 df, $p < .02$, two-tailed). This Pearson r correlation coefficient was computed for PK improvement (signed difference between pre- and post-test PK scores) vs. self-reported total number of minutes of imagery practice during the six-week period (W.B. obtained the time measures by examining the participants' practice logs).

All imagery scores changed in the expected direction, but the only imagery measure change to reach significance was the Gordon Test of Visual Imagery Control (t = 2.93, 6 df, p = .026, two-tailed). These preliminary findings are consistent with the hypothesis that prolonged visualization training may facilitate psychokinesis performance.

ESP AND SP IN TM AND NON-TM GROUPS (RB)

P. V. Krishna Rao (Andhra University) and K. Ramakrishna Rao (Institute for Parapsychology, FRNM)

Rao and Puri (RIP 1976, 77-79) studied the relation between extrasensory perception (ESP) and subliminal perception (SP) among subjects who were initiated into transcendental meditation (TM) and found a negative correlation between the two phenomena. The interpretation of this relationship was complicated because of the problem of the likelihood of the occurrence of the differential effect (DE). The present research attempted to replicate the Rao-Puri study. It was carried out in two parts. The first part, which consisted of two series each with 50 subjects, attempted to control for the DE; but only chance results were obtained in both series. The second part of the study, reported here, was designed to test the influence of TM on ESP, SP, and their relationship.

The study was comprised of two series, one control and one experimental, each consisting of 50 subjects. All the subjects were students of Andhra University. Rao's subsensory psi test (SPT), which has provisions for testing SP and unintentional ESP at the same time, was used. This test involves the tachistoscopic presentation of 30 picture slides to test SP and 30 blank slides with designated ESP target pictures to test ESP. These picture and blank slides are mixed randomly and each one is presented to the subjects for 1/100 of a second. In the control series the subjects were administered SPT individually. In the experimental series another group of subjects was initiated into TM by two trained TM instructors and they practiced TM twice a day for one week. On the eighth day the SPT was administered to these subjects individually, just after they had practiced TM for about 20 minutes. (We used subjects who had practiced TM for only one week because we wished to investigate the effect of the presumed state of mind/consciousness produced by TM on ESP, SP, and their relationship, rather than the trait changes that occur in long-term practice.)

The control data and experimental series were analyzed to test the hypotheses that there would be a significant relationship between ESP scores and SP scores and that the TM group would obtain significantly more hits on both SP and ESP targets than the control subjects. Only chance results were obtained with the control subjects. In the case of the TM group the SP and ESP scores correlated positively and significantly (r = .34, df = 48, p < .05, two-tailed). When the subjects were divided into psi-hitters (those who scored more than 3 hits, which was the mean chance on the ESP part of the test) and psi-missers (those who scored fewer than 3 hits), the psi-hitters obtained more hits than psi-missers and the two groups differed significantly (t = 2.13, df = 40, p < .05, two-tailed). The division of subjects into high-SP subjects and low-SP subjects, taking the group mean as the cutting point, indicated that the former group scored better than the latter on the ESP task (t = 2.71, df = 48, p < .01, two-tailed).

When the two groups were compared, it was found that the TM group obtained significantly better SP scores than the control group (t = 1.80, df = 98, p < .05, one-tailed). The TM psi-hitting subjects also performed better than control psi-hitters (t = 1.90, df = 37, p < .05, one-tailed) on the SP task. The TM high-SP subjects also scored better than control high-SP subjects (t = 1.69, df = 45, p < .05, one-tailed) on the ESP targets. A post-hoc analysis of the variance of the ESP scores of TM high-SP subjects (Av. = 3.78 hits), control high-SP subjects (Av. = 2.92 hits), TM low-SP subjects (Av. = 2.44 hits), and control low-SP subjects (Av. = 3.03 hits) yielded an F of 5.45 (p < .05), indicating an interaction of TM and SP on the ESP performance of the subjects.

Thus the significant findings of this study indicate a positive correlation between SP and ESP only in the TM condition, suggesting that to the extent that both phenomena are influenced alike by TM they may be processed in a similar way, and that the relation between SP and ESP may depend on the strength of the subliminal conditions and of the state of mind/consciousness of the individuals.

TWO SERIES OF VOLITIONAL STUDIES WITH COMPETITION SET

K. Ramakrishna Rao (Institute for Parapsychology, FRNM), Carl Sargent† (Cambridge University), and Marilyn J. Schlitz (Mind Science Foundation)*

In the studies we have done earlier on the volitional effect the subjects competed or cooperated in pairs, guessing ESP symbols printed on a record sheet by a computer in a random order. Sometimes they guessed the same target sequence and at other times they guessed different target sequences. The findings suggested (a) that subjects' scores tend to vary significantly when the two participants seek opposite outcomes; (b) that such an effect does not seem to occur when they seek the same outcome; and (c) that

---

*Thanks are due to Dr. H. Kanthamani (H.K.) and Ms. Debra H. Weiner (D.H.W.) for their help in these experiments.

there does not seem to be any consistency in regard to whether the volitional effect occurs in the same-target condition or the different-target condition.

The tendency for the subjects' scores to differ significantly from each other under conditions of volitional conflict is called the volitional effect. So far significant evidence for the volitional effect was obtained only in single-pair series in which the same pair of subjects competed in all the sessions of a series. Further, in most of the significant series of volitional studies K. R. R. himself was a subject.

The present report deals with two more series in which single pairs were repeatedly tested and K. R. R. was one of the subjects. The first series is a long distance study in which K. R. R. and Carl Sargent (C. S.) competed and in the second K. R. R. and Marilyn Schlitz (M. S.) participated.

Before the beginning of each series, targets for the whole series were generated by a Schmidt RNG interfaced with PDP 11/45 computer. The program generated 125 trials printed in five sequences of 25 trials. The targets also were stored for later computer analysis. H. K. in the first series and D. H. W. in the second series were in charge of the generation of targets and their safekeeping.

The number of sessions was preset at 20 per series. The response sheets were numbered 1 through 20. In the first series the response sheets were sent to C. S. by mail and he was asked to complete one sheet each day beginning on a predetermined date. K. R. R. was given the response sheets on the day he was to begin his first session. C. S. was instructed to send his response sheets to H. K. after completing all 20 sessions. After receiving the response sheets from K. R. R. and C. S., H. K. mailed photocopies of the target sheets to C. S. so that he could score his results. She also gave the record sheets to K. R. R., who first checked his results and later the record sheets of C. S. In half of the 20 sessions both subjects had the same target sequences and in the other half they had different targets. The order of the same- and different-target sessions was arranged by a pseudo-random procedure and the subjects were not aware whether a given session involved the same or different targets. In the second series K. R. R. and M. S. sat in K. R. R.'s office and did their guessing at the same time. Immediately after completing their guesses, M. S. made photocopies of their response sheets and gave a set to D. H. W. who in turn gave a copy of the target sheets to M. S. K. R. R. and M. S. then checked their response sheets against their respective target sheets. Thus the subjects in the second series had immediate feedback of results, whereas they had delayed feedback in the first series.

It was not necessary to give any instructions to the subjects as they were all familiar with the literature on this topic. In order to facilitate competition it was agreed that whoever obtained more

overall hits in the first series would be treated by the loser to the
PA Banquet at the 1981 Convention in Syracuse. In the second
series graded incentives were provided for each session as well as
for the overall scoring. It was agreed that if there was a significant difference in the overall scores of the two participants, the
loser would treat not only the winner, but everyone else connected
with the experiment to a lunch. If the overall difference was nonsignificant, the loser would take the winner to lunch. For individual sessions, if the difference between the two scores was 12 or
more, the loser would pay for the lunch of the winner at a place
chosen by the latter. If the difference was between 7 and 11, the
loser would take the winner to lunch at the place of the loser's
choice. If the difference was 6 or less the loser would give the
winner something for lunch, such as an apple or a granola bar.

After the completion of the experiment the subjects' responses were typed into the computer and compared with the target
file stored in the computer. The computer printed out the scores
for each session and these were then compared with the results of
the handscoring of the subjects.

The main purpose of the study was to replicate results obtained in our first study. Therefore the results were analyzed in
the same way as in the previous study to test the hypothesis that
subjects' scores tend to differ from each other significantly. The
planned analysis is one of obtaining the critical ratios for the difference in the scores of the two subjects in each session, squaring
them to obtain chi squares. The chi squares for all the sessions
in each condition are added to obtain the probability value separately for each condition. In the first series K.R.R. obtained 537 hits
(+37) and C.S. scored 512 hits (+12). In the second series K.R.R.
scored 517 hits (+17) and M.S. obtained 500 hits. In the RaoSargent series the sum of chi squares in the same-target condition
is 4.78. For the different-target condition the sum of chi squares
is 11.59. Neither of the two nor an F ratio between them is
significant. In the second series the respective chi squares are
5.19 and 11.40. Again they are insignificant. Thus neither of the
two series provided any evidence for the volitional effect.

Before the results were analyzed C.S. suggested that we
should look into displacement scores because he found some significant effects in the displacement data of his volitional study. Therefore the records were checked for +1 and -1 displacements. It
was found that there was significantly high variance in C.S.'s +1
data ($p < .002$). Also, there was a significant difference in the
scoring rate between +1 hits and direct hits in K.R.R.'s data. The
t of the difference is 2.271, 19 df, $p < .05$, two-tailed. For the
combined data of C.S. and K.R.R., the obtained t difference is
2.097, 39 df, $p < .05$, two-tailed. Even when we correct for the
17 different analyses done on the data, we find the results still
significant. Therefore, we made similar analyses of the RaoSchlitz data to test the hypotheses suggested by the post-hoc analysis of the Rao-Sargent data. None of the hypotheses are supported.

That neither of the series gave support to the volitional hypothesis was indeed disappointing. K. R. R. was very hopeful that the Rao-Schlitz series would turn out to be successful for it was as close to the original study as one could possibly come. These failures to replicate make us less optimistic of this line of research and indeed suggest that we may have overlooked something crucial here. Again, perhaps it would be imprudent to rush to any quick conclusion without further data.

RESISTANCE, BELIEF, AND REPLICATION (RB)

David Hess (Cornell University)

Studies of experimenter "psychology" effects and experimenter "psi" effects are similar since both interpret the experimenter as a static element, or independent variable, in the experimental setting. Under this view, the experimenter either "PKs" the data or triggers a psi-conducive syndrome in the subjects. An alternative view would see the experimenter as a psychologically dynamic entity who undergoes changes as the experimental situation unfolds. As a result, psychodynamic concepts such as the dialectic of resistance and belief in Batcheldor's theory (cf. Hess, RIP 1981, 72-75) may become important.

One way to try to measure the complicated psychodynamics centering on the experimenter's reaction to the experiment is suggested by Giesler's psi-in-process methodology (see p. 241). It is also possible that the structures of the experiment itself may consistently affect the psychodynamic status of the experimenter. For example, a strict replication may leave the experimenter feeling bored and less enthusiastic, whereas a conceptual replication would allow the experimenter to innovate and therefore maintain more interest and enthusiasm. Furthermore, if the experimenter suspects an experimenter psi effect, which not only undermines the credibility of the experiment but also might be ego-alien, then a strict replication would confirm this suspicion more clearly than a conceptual replication. Thus, resistance might arise more strongly in strict replications. In both cases, resistance and disbelief might negatively affect successful results in strict replications more than conceptual replications.

In a review study of 50 experiments (45 after five were thrown out), I asked five questions: (1) Is there any difference in the relative success rate of strict, close, and conceptual replications? A Kruskal-Wallis test showed no significant differences. (2) Is there any difference in the relative success rate of strict, close, and conceptual replications of unsuccessful original experiments? A Kruskal-Wallis test showed no significant differences. (3) Do more successful original experiments tend to be followed by stricter replications? A chi-square contingency test showed no significant differences. (4) Do replication experiments tend to be less successful than original experiments, regardless of replication type? A Wilcoxen Matched-Pairs test revealed no significant differences. (5) Do strict replications tend to be less successful than original experiments? A Wilcoxen Matched-Pairs test confirmed this question (+ = 1.5, n = 7, p < .05 after correction for ties, two-tailed).

Extreme caution is urged in interpreting these findings since multiple analyses of the data were made and the successful results of the last test could have been changed by two experiments (n = 13, = 7 after zero d-scores were dropped). While the tendency for strict replications to be less successful is consistent with the psychodynamic interpretation suggested here, it is also consistent with a regression-to-the-mean artifact. (That is, 5% of the replications would have a 95% chance of failure due to a type I error.) However, it is questionable whether this effect would apply more strongly to strict rather than conceptual replications. The artifact is possible if the new variables added in conceptual replications contribute to the success of the experiment; however, if this were the case, the second Kruskal-Wallis test should have been successful. A more likely artifact lies in judging bias.

In conclusion, the study does not clearly support the hypotheses presented here, and in addition several possible artifacts make interpretation difficult. It would seem that the next step in testing the hypotheses discussed in this paper would be through self-report scales or manipulations of the experimenter's resistance and belief. In either case, the experiment would have to study the dialectical relationship between resistance and belief, and not simply examine one variable and ignore the other. In this type of study, we may find that scientists are indeed becoming shamans.

PERSONALITY VARIABLES*

TARGET AFFECT, ANXIETY, AND BELIEF IN ESP IN RELATION TO ESP SCORING

John A. Ballard, Joseph C. Cohee, and Telena M. Eldridge (Purdue University)**

Two studies were conducted to examine performance on a clairvoyance detection task in relation to affect of the target, trait anxiety, beliefs/attitudes toward ESP, and self-report of psi experiences. Heeding Palmer's (JASPR, 1975, 333-39) advice that we pay more attention to our dependent variables, we decided to examine outcomes from both a one-factor model (Model I) and a two-factor model (Model II). Dependent measures were deviation scores (absolute differences from MCE) for Model I and number of hits for Model II.

The first study focused primarily on affect of the target and secondarily on individual differences. The procedure involved a clairvoyant detection task consisting of 60 trials in which the participant stated "yes" or "no" as to whether or not an envelope, not in view, contained a picture. Participants were 40 students enrolled in an introductory psychology course. Targets for the psi task were 30 pictures from magazines such as Time and Sports Illustrated, 15 of which were positive affect (e.g., forest, mountains) and 15 were negative affect (e.g., war, death). A five-item ESP questionnaire assessed beliefs toward ESP and the participants' prior psi experiences. A relaxation tape prepared the participant for the psi task. Spielberger's State-Trait Anxiety Inventory assessed trait anxiety and state changes. The participants' task on each of the 60 trials was to say "yes" if he or she thought a picture was in an unseen envelope, or "no" if he or she thought the envelope contained blank paper. Procedure was basically the same for each of the students.

(In the following hypotheses we have introduced a new term,

---
*Chaired by Erlendur Haraldsson (University of Iceland)
**The authors express their appreciation to the Parapsychology Foundation, New York City, which provided partial support for this research.

"telospond." It is roughly equivalent to the term "respond," as in stimulus-response or mediational models of the individual, and the humanistic term "telosponse," which implies an affirmation of a prediction or premise by which meaning is extended to the environment.) Hypotheses in the first study were as follows: (1) Participants will telospond differentially to the presence or absence of a picture even when that picture cannot be perceived via classical perceptual systems. (2) Participants will telospond differentially to pictures depending upon whether the pictures have been positively or negatively assessed. (3) For the pictures, participants high in trait anxiety will telospond differently from participants low in trait anxiety.

Confounding by calling predispositions yielded the results of hypothesis 1 uninterpretable. Hypothesis 2 received only marginal support ($p < .1$) from both models. Hypothesis 3 was supported by Model I deviation analysis ($p < .05$) but not by Model II. Participants higher in trait anxiety tended to have smaller deviation scores than participants low in trait anxiety. Sheep-goat analysis by a high-low break on attitude indicated that both sheep and goats hit significantly more on pictures of negative affect ($p < .03$).

Hypotheses in the second study were as follows: (1) People will telospond differentially to the affect of the pictures. (2) People who report having had psi experiences will telospond differently from people who report having had no psi experiences. (3) On the pictures, people high in trait anxiety will telospond differently from people low in trait anxiety. (4) Male participants will score higher with female experimenters and female participants will score higher with male experimenters.

None of the hypotheses were strongly supported in the analyses of variance. It appears that people who were more relaxed going into the experiment and who believed ESP was possible in the experiment tended to have higher overall deviations from MCE.

A post hoc sheep-goat analysis indicated no differences by Model I but large differences by Model II. Sheep had significantly larger deviations from MCE than goats ($p = .004$).

The studies suggest that additional research on affect trait anxiety, state anxiety, and belief toward ESP is warranted. In the two studies effects of individual differences were associated with magnitude whereas effects of the target appeared to be associated more with direction. Furthermore, these studies demonstrate that the operationalization of the dependent measure can be of major consequence in parapsychological research.

RETEST RELIABILITY OF ESP AND SHEEP-GOAT SCORES

Erlendur Haraldsson (University of Iceland)

The Defense Mechanism Test (DMT) developed by Ulf Kragh and associates to measure perceptual defensiveness has been particularly successful in predicting ESP performance in an experimental setting. Six out of a total of nine experiments (EJP, 1978, 104-114; RIP 1980, 106-108) have shown a significant relationship between ESP and DMT scores in the way that low defensive subjects tended to score above mean chance expectation and high defensive subjects below, thus revealing a negative correlation between DMT and ESP scores. Four of these experiments have been conducted in Iceland with a total of 170 male subjects.

The question of retest reliability is closely related to the problem of replicability in ESP research. Since the experiments conducted in Iceland had been fairly successful and there were reasons to expect a real ESP effect in them, it seemed a worthwhile effort to retest all the available subjects with the same ESP task to test the constancy of their ESP scoring. For a meaningful testing of the retest reliability of ESP scores it must be essential that the experimental situation has proved psi-conducive.

No data are available on the constancy of belief in ESP. Therefore the second purpose of this experiment was to find the retest reliability of the sheep-goat variable by readministering the three-item "Icelandic Sheep-Goat Scale" (RIP 1979, 100-104) to the subjects since most of them had filled out this questionnaire in the previous experiments.

Procedure. The same basic procedure was used as in the previously reported DMT-ESP experiments by the author. (For further details see EJP, 1978, 104-114.)

A total of 170 male subjects, all university students, participated in the previous experiments. At the beginning of the present experiment three years and three months had passed since the first Icelandic DMT-ESP experiment, and one year and three months since the fourth experiment had been conducted. We succeeded in retesting 98 of these subjects. The rest had either left the university or could not be traced.

Subjects were tested individually and given two ESP tasks during one session:

In the first there were 40 trials of a paper-and-pencil precognition test in which the subjects had to guess which of four letters of the alphabet (B, N, O, V) the university computer would select for 40 boxes depicted on a sheet of paper that was handed to each subject. When all the subjects had filled in their 40 guesses ($p = 1/4$) the computer randomly produced the targets for each subject. The ESP score was the number of correct guesses.

The second task was a precognition computer game giving a feedback of hit or miss after each of 40 trials (p = 1/5). The trials were divided into four runs of 10 trials each. To further a playful spirit each subject and his experimenter alternated their runs in a competitive way. A toss of coin determined which of the two would start the first run. Calls, targets, and number of hits were automatically recorded by an Apple computer that was used for this game. The subjects seemed to enjoy the computer game. If they obtained 12 or more hits they were rewarded with a hardcover book.

The computer game had been administered to subjects participating in the fourth DMT-ESP experiment, but not to subjects in the first three experiments, who instead were tested by a pushbutton machine for clairvoyance. In that way the ESP tasks were different for a part of the subjects.

The "Icelandic Sheep-Goat Scale" consists of three forced-choice questions dealing with (1) belief in telepathy, (2) belief in precognition and psychic dreams, and (3) frequency of reading articles and books on psychic phenomena.

Results. For all 98 subjects the retest reliability for the total ESP scores was only $r = .13$ ($p = .095$, one-tailed). For the paper-and-pencil test this correlation was .04 and for the computer game it was .08. None of these reliability coefficients are significant so this experiment failed to demonstrate any reliability of ESP performance over time.

We also analyzed the relationship between the new ESP scores and the old DMT scores. As a five-point scale had been used in the first DMT-ESP experiment and a nine-point scale in the other three, we had to conduct two analyses instead of one. For those participating in the first DMT-ESP experiment the correlation between the new ESP score and the old DMT ratings was .11 ($n = 18$, n.s.) but was .49 ($p = .02$, one-tailed) for the same subjects with their old ESP scores. For the 80 subjects participating in the other three experiments the correlation was .03 with the new scores .00 with the old ESP scores of the same subjects. It therefore seems that the majority of the subjects whom we retested had contributed rather little to the DMT-ESP correlation in the original experiments. This may possibly reduce somewhat the value of our present finding regarding the retest reliability of the ESP scores.

The retest reliability of the Icelandic Sheep-Goat Scale was $r = .78$ ($n = 63$, $p < .01$). For individual items the reliability was .74 for belief in telepathy, .71 for belief in precognition and psychic dreams, and .69 for reading of articles and books on psychic phenomena, findings which indicate that belief in psychic phenomena is a fairly constant attitude.

SOME FURTHER TESTS OF THE EXTRAVERTED SHEEP VERSUS INTROVERTED GOATS HYPOTHESIS (RB)

Michael A. Thalbourne† (McDonnell Laboratory for Psychical Research), John Beloff, Deborah Delanoy (University of Edinburgh), and Janet Jungkuntz (McDonnell Laboratory for Psychical Research)

At the 1981 PA Convention, the first three authors reported the results of two attempts to test the so-called "extraverted sheep vs. introverted goats" hypothesis, i.e., the hypothesis that subjects who are both extraverts and sheep should obtain higher ESP scores than do subjects who are both introverted and goats. In both studies the direction of the scoring difference was confirmed, but in neither case was the difference significant. The authors surmised that the difficulty in achieving a significant difference was in part due to the measure of extraversion used (viz., the E-Scale from Eysenck's Personality Inventory): this scale does not have as good a psi-predictive record as do alternative scales, and also fails to correlate consistently with the sheep-goat measure used (whereas part of our enthusiasm for the hypothesis derives from previous findings that extraverts tend significantly to be sheep and introverts goats). The authors therefore decided to use new measures of extraversion: in the United States, M.T. and J.J. employed the Social Introversion Scale derived by Drake from the Minnesota Multiphasic Personality Inventory while in the United Kingdom, J.B. and D.D. used various extraversion-relevant primary factors taken from Cattell's Sixteen Personality Factor Questionnaire (viz., A, F, H, and M). In this brief we report the results of four more tests of our hypothesis. (Following on from the original two studies, these new ones will be designated as the "Third" through "Sixth.") As in the previous experiments, all subjects were administered (1) the ten-item Australian Sheep-Goat Scale; (2) a test of extraversion (as described above); and (3) the Beloff "Consumer's Choice" ESP test--a ten-trial, four-choice paper-and-pencil test of precognition.

Third Study. In this study, conducted by J.B. and D.D. at the University of Edinburgh, 135 naive psychology students were tested. The 55 sheep scored nonsignificantly lower on the ESP test than did the 80 goats. Again, the 69 extraverts scored nonsignificantly lower than the 66 introverts. And the 28 extraverted sheep scored nonsignificantly lower than the 39 introverted goats. There were no signs of psi in the study. However, sheep were significantly more extraverted than goats $r = +.20$, $p = .012$, one-tailed).

Fourth Study. This experiment was conducted by M.T., assisted by J.J., at Washington University in St. Louis. There were 152 subjects, mainly students and for the most part naive. The 89 sheep scored nonsignificantly higher than the 63 goats. The 61 extraverts scored nonsignificantly lower than the 91 introverts. And the 42 extraverted sheep scored nonsignificantly lower than the 44 introverted goats. However, sheep were marginally more extraverted than were goats ($r = +.12$, $p = .069$, one-tailed).

Fifth Study. There were 246 subjects in this experiment, mainly volunteers from the St. Louis metropolitan area who were naive. The 219 sheep scored nonsignificantly lower than the 27 goats. The 151 extraverts scored nonsignificantly higher than the 95 introverts. And the 137 extraverted sheep scored nonsignificantly higher than the 13 introverted goats. Again, sheep were significantly more extraverted than were goats (r = +.24, p = .00007, one-tailed).

Sixth Study. Fourteen persons otherwise eligible for the Fourth or Fifth Studies were aware of the hypotheses being tested, and it was therefore thought prudent to analyze their results separately. These people were volunteers from the St. Louis area. The 11 sheep scored nonsignificantly lower than the 3 goats. The 7 extraverts scored nonsignificantly lower than the 7 introverts. And the 6 extraverted sheep scored nonsignificantly lower than the 2 introverted goats. Sheep were significantly more extraverted than were goats (r = +.49, p = .038, one-tailed).

Conclusions. Excluding the Sixth Study, we have now tested a total of 721 naive subjects over five studies. In the majority of these experiments there has been a positive, generally significant, correlation between the Sheep-Goat Scale and the extraversion scale used. However, the attempt to improve our psi-predictive ability by comparing just those sheep who are extraverted with just those goats who are introverted has yielded results scarcely better than chance. The use of a different sort of test of psi may prove more successful.

AN ATTEMPTED REPLICATION OF SEX DIFFERENCES IN VOLITIONAL STUDIES

K. Ramakrishna Rao[†] and Beverly Norwood (Institute for Parapsychology, FRNM)

In a previous study of the volitional effect with pairs of unselected subjects (JP, 1979, 101-112) it was found that when subjects of the same sex competed against each other in an ESP test, they tended to score alike, but the scores of subjects of opposite sex in competing pairs tended to differ significantly. The present study is an attempted replication of this finding, namely, the difference between the scores of competing subjects tends to be greater in boy-girl pairs than in same-sex pairs.

The subjects were 84 students of two high schools in Durham, N.C. They guessed, in pairs, the sequence of ESP symbols generated by a computer and presented to them on concealed target sheets under competition and cooperation conditions. Each pair was tested in only one session. Both subjects of each pair had the same targets in half of the sessions, while in the other half each subject had a different target sequence. The order of the conditions was determined randomly. In the competition condition, the subjects were told that if one of them obtained seven more hits than the other, he or she would be given a prize (L. E. Rhine's Psi: What Is It?). In the cooperative condition the subjects were told that they would each be rewarded with a copy of the book if together they obtained seven hits more than mean chance expectation (MCE).

Out of the 42 pairs of subjects tested there were 20 in the competition condition and 22 in the cooperative condition. In the former condition the subjects obtained a total of 1,006 hits (+6), with a mean of 25.15 where the MCE is 25. In the latter condition the subjects scored 1,087 hits (-13), with a mean of 24.71. Though the scores are in the expected direction, the mean difference in the performance of competing and cooperating subjects is not statistically significant (t = .43, df = 82).

The analysis of the data for sex differences confirmed the findings of the previous study. The sum of chi squares of the opposite-sex pairs in the competition condition is 17.77 (df = 9), p < .05. For the same-sex pairs the sum is 5.61 (df = 11). The F ratio for the opposite- and same-sex pairs is 3.17 (df = 8, 10), p < .05. Thus there is evidence that when subjects of opposite sex compete their scores tend to vary from each other significantly. Secondly, the difference in the scores of competing subjects of the opposite-sex pairs is significantly larger than the difference in the scores of competing subjects of the same-sex pairs.

Analyses of data to test for the volitional effect gave essentially chance results. It appears that the single-session testing is unlikely to bring about the kind of results obtained when single pairs were repeatedly tested as in some of our previous studies for a variety of reasons: It is possible that the effect observed in our previous studies, in which a single pair was tested over a number of sessions, may not have really reflected the influence of volitional conflict such as we assumed. The method we used to produce a competition set among high school students in the present study may not have had the desired effect. Practice in competing on a psi task or continuation of intentional set--competition or cooperation--over a period of time may be essential for manifesting the differential scoring and the volitional effect. The nature of social interactions among participants--subject pairs and the experimenter--may be a more powerful determinant of psi scoring than mere intentionality. Further studies on the role of psychosocial variables in determining psi scoring seems to be very much in order.

SHEEP-GOAT EFFECT AND THE ILLUSION OF CONTROL (RB)

Tom Troscianko† and Susan J. Blackmore (Brain and Perception Laboratory, University of Bristol)

Introduction. There is evidence that when people are presented with a random sequence of events they may feel that they have exerted some influence over the outcomes, i.e., there is an illusion of control. There is also evidence that they remember higher scores than those actually obtained. In a random sequence of events, apparent control or prediction of outcomes could be attributed to psi. So it can be argued that an illusion of control underlies some belief in psi.

Our previous experiments (SPR Conference, 1981) suggested that sheep and goats differ on some tests involving decisions about randomness and probability. This experiment uses a task in which subjects have to decide whether or not they have control over a sequence of events. The main hypothesis is (1) that sheep are more prone to an illusion of control. Secondary hypotheses are (2) that goats are better able to differentiate between conditions in which control was or was not exerted, and (3) that sheep are more prone to remember their performance as better than it was. A truly random condition can be used to look for psi effects, including any differences between sheep and goats.

Method. One hundred subjects--students and employees in the Medical School--were tested. The tests were presented as a computer game in which a coin was tossed (an alternating display of heads and tails was seen) and the subject had to try to influence the outcome using a pushbutton.*

Each session consisted of 10 practice tosses followed by four runs of 20 tosses each. The computer instructed the subject to try for heads or tails before each trial. The subject then pressed the button to start the coin flipping and let go to stop it, trying to get it to "land" on the correct face (i.e. target face shows last). A delay was introduced after the button release to produce two types of run: two controlled and two random. In the former, the delay was 2 or 4 half cycles so that the coin returned to the same face and the subject potentially had full control. In the latter the delay was 1, 2, 3, or 4 half cycles, determined by a random number generator, which produced equal numbers of each digit in randomness checks. The order of runs was randomized.

After each run the subject was asked to rate, on a 1-7 scale, how much control he or she thought the pushbutton gave him or her. After all four runs the subject was asked to try to recall the num-

---

*We are grateful for the assistance of François Dupre in programming and running the experiment.

ber of hits in each run, and to answer three questions on belief in psi (ESP, PK, and their demonstration in the laboratory). The data collected were (1) hits per run (MCE = 10); (2) subjects' ratings, for each run, of degree of control; (3) subjects' estimates of the number of hits per run; and (4) total ratings of belief in psi.

Results. The main hypothesis was confirmed. Sheep gave higher overall ratings of control than goats (t = 1.93, 98 df, p = .028, one-tailed). The effect was also independently significant in both controlled and random conditions (t = 1.78, 98 df, p = .039 and t = 1.75, 98 df, p = .042, one-tailed).

The second hypothesis was not confirmed. Sheep and goats did not differ in how well they differentiated between the two conditions either by ratings (t = -.11) or by estimates of scores obtained (t = -1.8). Altogether, subjects differentiated between the two conditions both by ratings (t = 5.37, 99 df, p < .001) and by estimates (t = 2.08, 99 df, p = .04, two-tailed). Scores were much higher in the control condition ($\bar{X}$ = 26.8) than in the random condition ($\bar{X}$ = 20.5, t = 8.11, 99 df, p < 0.001, two-tailed).

The third hypothesis was not confirmed. In fact, in the random condition, goats estimated that they had scored at about chance while estimates of sheep were much lower, even though they too scored at about chance. This could be caused by sheep falsely estimating what to expect by chance. To test this, subjects from number 48 onwards were asked how they thought they would score (out of 20) if they did the test with their eyes shut. The difference was surprisingly large. Sheep guessed well below 10 ($\bar{X}$ = 7.86) while goats guessed around 10 ($\bar{X}$ = 9.55) and the mean difference from 10 was much larger for sheep than for goats (t = 3.37, 51 df, p = 0.0014, two-tailed). Possibly sheep thought they were scoring well when they got 10 hits!

There were no psi effects. Overall scores were close to chance ($\bar{X}$ = 20.47, t = 1.47, 99 df, ns) and sheep did not score differently from goats (t = -.71, 99 df, ns).

Conclusion. Sheep are more susceptible to an illusion of control than goats. They also underestimate the number of hits to be expected by chance so that when they score at chance they may erroneously believe that they have done well. These factors may contribute to their belief in psi.

SPONTANEOUS CASES AND REAL LIFE PHENOMENA*

SPONTANEOUS SIGHTINGS OF SEEMINGLY AUTONOMOUS HUMANOID ENTITIES: A COMPARATIVE STUDY IN THE LIGHT OF EXPERIMENTAL AND CONTRIVED ENTITY FABRICATIONS

Hilary Evans (Society for Psychical Research)

Experiences in which percipients claim visual encounters with entities (human-like in appearance but clearly other than living, physical human beings) include not only the apparition or "ghost," but religious and demonic visions, hallucinations, hypnagogic and hypnopompic images, extraterrestrial beings, and many others. Traditionally it has been customary to treat each of these categories as a distinct phenomenon, the manifest differences between them seeming to offer sufficient justification. The religious vision, for example, is unique in being always of an identified and widely-known figure, is typically repetitive, is often shared, and generally involves response to the percipient(s) on an individual basis. The hypnopompic image, conversely, is typically unidentified, rarely recurrent or communicative, and so forth.

At the same time, characteristics are often shared with other categories in varying combinations. The similarity may be visual: what starts as "a ball of light" may resolve itself into a bodhisattva, an extraterrestrial entity, or the Virgin Mary. Again, a percipient may receive a personal warning either from the apparition of someone familiar, or from an archetypal entity from religious teaching or folklore.

Such correspondences support the possibility that we are dealing not with a diversity of phenomena, but with a single phenomenon in a diversity of forms. This possibility is confirmed when the range of study material is extended to include <u>nonspontaneous cases</u>:

    ● Hypnotized subjects, selected for minimal interest in unidentified flying objects (UFOs), when asked to fabricate an account of an encounter with extraterrestrials, did so in

*Chaired by Anita Gregory (North London Polytechnic Institute)

terms that corresponded with allegedly real encounter experiences, not simply in general outline but in minute detail. Even if we suppose that the percipients went no farther for their material than the mind of the hypnotist, this is evidence for a mental process of selection and story composition of a very remarkable kind.

● Psychiatrist Morton Schatzman's subject "Ruth" demonstrated that the unconscious mind has the capability of creating an entity which will proceed to conduct itself in such a way as to convince the conscious mind of its autonomous reality (The Story of Ruth, 1980).

● Several seemingly successful experiments by individuals to project an image of themselves at a distance, capable of being seen by others, are on record; and some of these clearly involve the ability of the projected entity to act in an autonomous manner relative to the environment in which it manifests, and to respond to the percipient.

● Under the influence of drugs, sex, ceremonial practices, or other stimulants, some persons have claimed to summon up by magical conjuration an entity, generally of a demonic character though sometimes defined as an "elemental."

● Occasional individuals have claimed to have willed into existence, by power of thought, an entity which is thereafter capable of autonomous action. Alexandra David-Neel's creation of a tulpa (Magic and Mystery in Tibet, 1932) remains tantalizingly unique, though she alleged that such practices were not uncommon among Buddhist initiates. In 1912 a society of Russian occultists allegedly brought into being an egrigor by united thought-power.

● Séance-room manifestations, whether or not the entity is what it or its impresarios claim it to be, provide a further instance in which certain people, in an appropriate psychological state, can construct short-lived entities that seem capable of some autonomous activity.

● Bertrand Meheust demonstrates that many alleged encounters with extraterrestrial beings replicate, in detail which defies coincidence, incidents that can be found in science fiction stories, often from another country and epoch. In the absence of any direct link, this implies that both "true" percipient and avowed fiction-writer have access to a common stock of "material."

● In many cases of supposed UFO sightings, the percipient claims to see, say, a metallic cigar with windows through which occupants can be seen, yet is subsequently shown to have seen the Moon or Venus. The implication is that certain people, under appropriate conditions, will experience a hallucinatory event whose form is dictated by their sociocultural background.

● Piddington in 1901 (PSPR, 1905, 19) compared hallucinations occurring as a side effect of disease with those spontaneously reported to the SPR, and established that the two categories, however similar in their mode of perception, were markedly distinct in content. This implies that we should think in terms not of a single undifferentiated hallucinatory state, but of a capability, when such a state has been induced, to experience different kinds of hallucination according to, inter alia, the percipient's physical and psychological condition.

● In a wide variety of cultures, selected persons have ceremonial recourse to hallucinogens, leading to a state in which entities are perceived. Harner has noted how the form of such entities is modified or even dictated by the percipient's sociocultural circumstances.

Taken together, these findings suggest that, over a wide range of often disparate experiences, there are many correspondences in the mental and perceptual processes involved, in the conditions requisite for those processes to occur, and in the nature of the experience resulting from those processes. They support the hypothesis that we are dealing with variant forms of a single, if complex, phenomenon and justify our seeking to construct a model for the basic process.

Such a model can at this stage be speculative only; though some of its "components" are known to exist, others must be employed for whose existence the evidence is only circumstantial. In particular, the notion of some kind of "image bank," from which the subconscious mind may draw the raw material for its fabrications, is entirely suppositional. Jung's archetypes are of course the classic form of the hypothesis, but it is doubtful whether they are adequate to explain the highly circumstantial character of some of the accounts.

The machinery whereby the unconscious mind presents the material to the conscious mind is, on the other hand, known to exist: the classic case is Morton Prince's study of Miss Beauchamp (Dissociation of a Personality, 1905), one of whose dissociated personalities was in the habit of fabricating hallucinations with which to confuse the conscious personality. We may suppose some such process to be the "power unit" of our model.

As for motivation, there is ample justification for deriving this from the percipient's psychological situation at the time, whether spontaneous or brought about artificially.

We may therefore conclude by hypothesizing that all entity sightings are variants of a single model whose modus operandi is as follows: Under suitable circumstances the percipient, having induced or been induced into an appropriate altered state of consciousness, has the illusion of seeing an entity, seemingly externalized and autonomous, which has in fact been constructed by his own subconscious from a combination of subjectively derived and externally obtained material, the selection and form of that material being dictated by his individual physical, psychological, and sociocultural situation.

Such a model, in this over-simplified form, accounts only for those sightings in which the percipient is also the agent. A more sophisticated model will be required for those cases, whose existence is hard to avoid, in which an external agency is involved. It may be that in such cases the percipient's subconscious is not the ultimate source of the illusion, but simply a relay station transmitting a program of external origin. If so, the implications are far from reassuring.

CRYPTOMNESIC AND PARANORMAL PERSONATION: TWO CONTRASTING EXAMPLES

James F. McHarg (University of Dundee, Scotland)

Introduction. The term "personation" is here used in the sense of an unconscious process (in contradistinction to the conscious process of "impersonation") whereby an individual comes to behave, to speak, to remember, and to feel as if he or she were some other person.

Two contrasting examples of transitory personation are presented: the first, a case of post-traumatic personation apparently on a cryptomnesic basis; and the second a case apparently having a paranormal, or "synchronistic," basis.

Case 1. Transitory Cryptomnesic Personation

Clinical Summary. Robert G., an unmarried, 29-year-old Dundee man of unexceptional background, sustained a moderately severe head injury in a motorcycle accident on December 10, 1962, and was admitted to neurosurgical care. On returning to clear consciousness, he repeatedly and consistently spoke, for a time, about being a major in the Confederate Army of the American Civil War.

On psychiatric examination he gave a clear account of his upbringing in Dundee but continued to reassert his other identity, giving his claimed name (not recorded) and describing how he had been sworn-in on a train in South Carolina. He gave other circumstantial detail which, unfortunately, in the ward setting, was also not recorded.

This peculiar state of personation persisted only for three or
four days and, after it, he was perplexed by his experience, averring that he had never had any special interest in, or knowledge of,
the American Civil War.

The Puzzle. The clinical diagnosis was not in doubt. It was
that of the not very uncommon condition known as a "post-traumatic
Korsakoff state." One essential feature of this is gross impairment
of short-term memory. The other is "confabulation," which is not
lying, designed to cover up the memory defect, but the voicing of
coherent, sincerely believed, pseudomemories. Usually, such
pseudomemories are very plausible and the puzzle, here, was that
the pseudomemories were those of a person from another time and
place who was quite other than the patient himself. For a year and
a half it seemed as if the puzzle would remain unsolved.

The Apparent Solution. The apparent solution began to
emerge a year after the last contact with the patient. On one of
his "Tonight" programs on BBC-TV Cliff Mitchelmore reported
a group of people in Maidenhead, England, who had become so fascinated by the American Civil War that they had banded themselves
together to identify themselves with the Confederate Army and to
wear its uniforms. It was the fact that this movement was said to
have been started eighteen months earlier which drew attention to
the fact that the patient's post-traumatic personation had also been
almost eighteen months previously. After managing to get into touch
with "Major General" Hinton of this movement, it became possible
to track down, eventually, the one and only item of national publicity
which had come out prior to the patient's head injury. This had been
a one-page article in the magazine Weekend, which was published
just two or three weeks before the patient's head injury. The expatient himself was then traced once more, and a copy of the magazine shown to him. With some surprise, he recognized it, although
he was at first unable to say where he had seen it before. At a
later date, he remembered that he had seen it in his dentist's waiting room. It thus appeared that normal cryptomnesia was the solution to the puzzle.

Lurking Doubts. And yet, some lurking doubts remained.
Why, if personation is not a usual feature of the pseudomemories of
post-traumatic Korsakoff states, had there been a process of personation at all? And how to explain the circumstantial detail which
had no counterpart in the Weekend article? As if to encourage consideration (at least) of a paranormal explanation, a colleague of the
writer passed to him an undated cutting from the magazine Fate
which contained an account of the alleged investigation of a 15-year-old boy called George Field, in New Hampshire, who, under age-regression hypnosis in 1965 (three years after the present case),
had experienced and expressed what purported to be the memories
of a man, Jonathan, who had been killed in the Civil War in 1863.

Doubts Resolved. However, ten years later still, such lurking doubts about cryptomnesia as remained were diminished to vanishing point. On August 20, 1977, there was a BBC-TV showing of the film The Red Badge of Courage, which had first been issued in 1951, when the patient would have been 18. The film was about a young hero of the American Civil War, also aged about 18, with whom the patient could well have identified if he had seen the film at that time. It then seemed that this could have been the source of such detail as would not be found in the Weekend article of 1962. In short, the cryptomnesia could have had a double basis in elements taken both from the 1951 film and the 1962 article.

Case 2. Transitory Paranormal Personation

Clinical Summary. While in a psychiatric hospital Mrs. Margaret D., a married lady of 44, had a curious experience on August 4, 1967, in relation to the sudden death of her father, to whom she was greatly attached. Mrs. D. had had several admissions because of recurrent psychotic illnesses of the manic-depressive type. The admission on that particular occasion had been for no more than a mild to moderate depressive attack.

The Transitory Episode. On the Friday of the experience, Mrs. D. had been settled comfortably early in the day. Even in the evening when, at about 6:15, she had set off with her husband for a walk in the hospital grounds, she had been feeling quite well. However, at about 7:25, when they were at a certain point in the hospital grounds, the husband noticed a change in her manner. Some ten minutes later, at about 7:35, when they had reached another point in the grounds on the way back to her ward, she had passed rather suddenly into a very disturbed mental state, shouting and swearing, insisting that she wanted to go to her father's house, and saying "I think there's something wrong." Mrs. D. was due back at her ward at 8 p.m. and sufficiently close to it for her husband to summon the help of nurses who dissuaded her from leaving the hospital and persuaded her to return quietly to her ward.

The Discovered Correlates. It subsequently emerged that Mrs. D.'s father had died that evening, probably about the time of Mrs. D.'s outburst. He had gone to bed early and, at 9 p.m., when the patient's mother had taken a drink in to him, she had found he had died. They were told he had died of a stroke. No word of his death had been sent to the patient in hospital. On the following day, Mrs. D. had left the hospital with her husband for her customary weekend at her own home. When they then visited her parents' home that day, the mother was out. Eventually, of course, Mrs. D. learned that her father had died.

Retrospective Inquiry. The objective account of the disturbed episode in the grounds was obtained from the husband, and from the nurses who had been called to see her. The subjective account, from Mrs. D. herself, I obtained on August 16. She reported that, at the first point in the grounds, she had begun to feel very tired and to have "a floating feeling." At the second point, she had rather

suddenly developed a severe headache, had felt the compulsion to
go to her father's house, and had felt resentment at her husband's
resistance to this idea. Next, it had seemed to her as if she were
actually in her father's house. She had looked round the familiar
setting, expecting to see her father, but could see no one. She was
asked if, as had been supposed, she had had the feeling, at the
time, that her father had died. Her immediate reply was a firm
negative. She said that, on the contrary, she had felt that it was
she herself who had died.

Discussion. Three facts suggest that the transitory paranormal "personation" of the dying father was primary, rather than
secondary, to extrasensory perception of him. First, the sudden
severe headache, which would correspond to the sudden severe
headache the father would have had before dying of a cerebral
hemorrhage; second, Mrs. D.'s feeling that it was she herself who
had died; and third, the fact that, although she felt herself to be in
her father's house expecting to see him, she could not see him.
This would have been because, presumably, at the time she, in
some sense, was him.

TOWARD A MODEL FOR MENTAL HEALING STUDIES IN REAL LIFE SETTINGS: A TRIBUTE TO THE WORK OF DR. F. W. KNOWLES

Gerald F. Solfvin (Parapsychology Laboratory, University of Utrecht)

This paper is an outline of a model for mental healing in
real-life settings that has emerged from my studies during the past
two years at the Parapsychology Laboratory of the University of
Utrecht. Much of this model was anticipated some years ago by
the mental healer and physician Dr. Frederick W. Knowles, in three
articles published in JASPR during the 1950s (1954, 21-6; 1956, 110-
17; 1959, 62-5). Knowles' writings have been all but ignored by
parapsychologists. His experimental work, though impressive in
volume, is not adequately reported for it to be included in most
reviews. However, from these studies, taken together with his
clinical observations of the effects of his mental healing treatments,
he was able to draw several conclusions which since then have
gathered some empirical support. These observations led directly
to the model proposed here so I would like to present it against the
backdrop of Knowles' work.

I will begin with Knowles' observation that his clinical results
with mental healing treatments applied to his own patients in pain
were quite good, while his experimental attempts to affect artificially induced pain or injury always failed. It may be that the very
methods that we use to gain control over the phenomena are adding
unwanted noise to the system that drowns out the phenomena themselves.

Worse yet, the noise created by the extraneous influences in the experimental situation may conceal whatever lawful relationships or regularities the phenomena may have in real-life settings.

There is an example of this in the attempts to establish a relationship between hypnotic susceptibility and placebo response. In a review of these mixed results, Shapiro (in A. E. Bergin and S. L. Garfield, eds., Handbook of Psychotherapy and Behavior Change, 2nd ed., 1978) has concluded that the problem lies in the setting of the studies. Apparently, the relationship has been hidden by administering the placebo as therapy and the hypnotic susceptibility measure as a gullibility test. The psychological atmosphere, as Knowles points out, changes from clinic to laboratory. But even in studies conducted entirely in a clinical setting, the very presence of an experimenter or administrator who has particular attitudes (enthusiastic, skeptical) concerning the treatment under test may affect the eventual outcome of the test.

Apparently we need to carefully evaluate our specific goals before embarking on a treatment effectiveness study. If our goal is to find a 100% (or nearly so) effective treatment which is not dependent upon the administering physician, then we would certainly want a tightly controlled experimental test to determine if the treatment is "effective" in this restricted sense. However, if our interest is to study a particular form of treatment (e.g., mental healing) and to understand under what circumstances it may operate, the limitations of its effectiveness, and how it interacts with patient, doctor, and setting variables, then we would chose a different testing procedure. Perhaps a longer series of careful observations under a variety of controls and conditions would be called for here.

But even more essential in a scientific investigation is the kind of conclusions that we draw from our data, which depend on whether these were gathered experimentally or clinically. We have a duty to ourselves and others to be aware of the limitations of our methods, whatever they are, and to draw our conclusions accordingly. This is one of the reasons I find Knowles' work so valuable.

Another conclusion reached by Knowles is that the patient's belief in mental healing per se is not essential for the treatment to be effective. However, when he treated a patient in pain without his knowledge of Knowles' intention to help him, the treatment nearly always failed. Knowles gives examples of occasions when this "intent" was present but the treatment omitted and this also resulted in failure. Thus, the patient's knowledge of the intent to help seems to be a facilitating factor allowing the treatment to work, regardless of whether the patient is a sheep or a goat. Indeed, one is hard pressed to find a single solid example of a successful mental healing treatment when the patient was unaware of the healer's intention to help. According to Knowles, this tells us less about the efficacy of mental healing than about the facilitating environment that is necessary for it.

There is experimental evidence to support this view from the studies of a minor tranquillizer, meprobamate (Miltown). Apparently, if this drug is administered by an enthusiastic, therapeutic physician it is measurably effective (over placebo). When administered by a skeptical, experimental physician it is not. (Uhlenhuth et al., Psychopharmacologia, 1966, 392-418). These results give clear and direct support to Knowles' contention that the patient's knowledge of the intent to help is important. If this is a facilitating factor for a drug treatment, it must also be so for mental healing treatments, since these are certainly weak and variable in their effects.

As for the belief of the patient in mental healing, the studies with animals (Grad, JASPR, 1965, 95-127; Watkins and Watkins, JP, 1971, 257-272) seem to support Knowles' idea that it is not important per se. However, the question is rather ambiguous until we can adequately operationalize it. Belief is a nebulous concept in the healing situation, being influenced by the actual course of the treatment, the practitioner, the quality of the healing encounter, and the host of events (e.g., side effects) that are subsequent to the actual treatment. Belief, in any static sense of the word, is almost certainly not essential for successful treatment by a mental healing technique. A more communicative, dynamic, and interactive extension of the concept may be. Both Knowles and I have noted that the concept of expectations may be such a concept.

Knowles also addressed the question of what is at the core of the mental healing treatment. Through trial and error, he concluded that the procedural formalities (special actions or words) were not essential for success. For him, the mental concentration seemed to be the key. And since there was sometimes sensory screening between the healer and patient, he concluded further that there must be a parapsychological process operating between patient and healer. This he guessed to be a telepathic one. Apparently, as a clinician, Knowles was aware that it is not necessary to hypothesize a direct psychokinetic influence upon the patient's illness. It is only necessary to hypothesize a communicative process between the patient and the healer.

To see this more clearly, consider the near miracles that have been brought about by a skillfully (and therapeutically) administered sugar pill. The placebo, as it is called, may be medicine's most potent drug. It has relieved functional and organic disorders (Evans, in Advances in Neurology, vol. 4, 1976), has brought about objective changes in physiological and biochemical processes (Wolf, Journal of Clinical Investigation, 1950, 100-104), and even produced a wide variety of side effects (Honigfeld, Diseases of the Nervous System, 1966). It is as if each person comes equipped with his or her own internal "doctor," as Albert Schweitzer put it, and the physician's job is to stimulate this inner "doctor" into service (Cousins, Anatomy of an Illness, 1979). Thus, the psi aspects of the mental-healing situation can be most parsimoniously viewed, as Knowles implies, as a communicative process between patient and healer, with the patient's own inner doctor doing the rest of the job.

This view is more realistic since it integrates the psychological and social-psychological factors that are known to be of importance in healing encounters (e. g., placebo effects) and it views the patient as an active participant in the process rather than as a passive object for the mental healer's psychokinesis. It also has heuristic value in suggesting questions concerning the form of the healer-patient interaction to be researched.

Knowles made it quite clear that the mental concentration that he felt was essential for his own success may not be essential for others. Any technique that establishes in the healer's mind a vivid expectation of benefit for the patient would be adequate. It was on this pin, what we might call "psi-potent expectancies," that Knowles hung his model of mental healing. By this Knowles implies that the ability to produce positive effects in patients may not be restricted to a few "gifted" persons, but is probably widespread in the population, particularly in those who are already involved in the health-care fields. These persons may be able to apply these procedures to their own patients with good results.

The hypothesis that vivid mental expectations of a healer may have measurable effects upon the course of illness in the patient has considerable support from the literature. In medicine, the doctor's attitudes and expectations are clearly related to the success of treatment (see reviews by Shapiro, op. cit., and Frank, Persuasion and Healing, 1973). In psychology laboratories it is also well-known that the experimenter's expectancy is not independent of the outcome of the experiment (Rosenthal and Rubin, Behavior and Brain Sciences, 1978, 377-415). Indeed, the similarities between the effects of persons' expectancies in the clinic and in the laboratory cannot but lead us to wonder whether there is a general principle concerning human expectations and outcomes of certain events which might be the basis for both of them. We wonder further, as Knowles did, whether there is a parapsychological factor sometimes involved in the operation of these expectancy effects.

Recently, I have reported (EJP, 1982, 159-197) experiments designed to directly test Knowles' hypothesis that the expectations of a healer or helping person may exert an influence on the course of an organic illness in a living organism. In these experiments, a total of eight veterinary students each cared for one cage containing 12 mice during nine days of the incubation of babesia rhodaini, a parasite, in their bloodstreams. Each student was told that half of the mice in each cage received a high dosage of babesia which would produce grave illness, while the other half received a low dosage (or none at all) and were not expected to be very sick during the experiment. They were further told that half of each group would be receiving distant healing from a well-known healer who had shown very strong results in pilot series. In fact, all the mice received the same dosage of babesia and there was no healer. The results confirmed that both expectations showed significant effects on the actual spread of the parasite in the mice (assessed by hemoanalysis). For the healing expectancy effect, the handlers did not know which mice were supposed to be receiving the healing, nor did anyone else. Thus there was apparently a parapsychological factor involved in the operation of this effect, just as Knowles would have predicted.

In summary, it seems that Dr. Knowles, through his experimental and clinical observations, has arrived at some conclusions that have since gathered experimental support. The central core of the model that is implied by Knowles, if we can call it a model, is that there is a communicative process that occurs between patient and healer (all types of healers) in real-life settings. This communication may be verbal or nonverbal, sensory or nonsensory, or a combination of several communication channels. The communication of the healer's intent to help the patient may facilitate the action of whatever treatment is administered, while its absence may suppress this action. In addition, the communication may exert a therapeutic influence of its own upon the patient, stimulating, so to speak, the patient's own inner "doctor."

The positive expectations of both patient and healer are probably important elements in the process, but the belief of the patient in the healing treatment per se is not. The effects of this communication process, even when it involves psi, can be seen in operation in a wide variety of real-life health care situations with a wide variety of "healers." It is not restricted to a few persons who have a special gift. The real-life clinical, therapeutic situation is probably important in maximizing the possibility of such effects.

Although far from conclusive, the evidence at hand supports the idea of a common thread running through health care and other situations that can be summarily described as persons affecting other persons and processes with which they are the most involved and interested by the establishment in their minds of certain vivid expectations for the outcomes of these processes. So far, too few experimental studies have been conducted under such a communicative model to determine the extent of its value. It is hoped that this paper might stimulate some.

A REVIEW AND ANALYSIS OF "UNSOLVED" CASES OF THE REINCARNATION TYPE

Emily Williams Cook,† Satwant Pasricha, Godwin Samararatne, U Win Maung, and Ian Stevenson (University of Virginia)

Introduction

The statements of children who claim to remember a previous life differ to a great extent in the amount, specificity, and accuracy of detail. Thus, many such cases are "solved," meaning that we have identified a deceased person corresponding to the subject's statements, whereas other cases remain "unsolved," since the child's statements have been insufficient to enable us to identify a corresponding deceased person.

Some persons assume that unsolved cases of the reincarnation type can be attributed to fantasies on the part of the child subjects; but many unsolved cases resemble in important features those cases that have been verified, or solved, and thus cannot be exclusively fantasies. This suggests the possibility that both types may belong to the same genus. For this paper we examined some of their similarities and differences by analyzing some data from 856 solved and unsolved cases in six cultures. (For some analyses the sample size was smaller because of insufficient information about some features of the cases.)

Results

The Proportion of Unsolved Cases in Different Cultures.
The percentage of unsolved cases among all cases is low in Burma, India, Lebanon, and Thailand, but it is high in Sri Lanka and the United States (nontribal cases only). The percentage ranged from 8% in Thailand to 80% in the United States, with an overall average of 33%.

A case is more easily solved if the subject seems to be referring to a relative or an acquaintance of his or her family. The proportion of unsolved cases in a culture might therefore be related to the frequency with which the previous personality is identified as someone already known to the parents. In 70% of all the cases, the two families knew each other before the development of the case; in 30% they were total strangers. Only the data of India and Sri Lanka showed significant deviations from this average. Among all the cases there seemed to be no unvarying relationship between the solving of cases in a culture and the frequency in that culture with which the two families concerned are related or acquainted.

Comparison of Some Features of Solved and Unsolved Cases.
In both types of case, the subjects usually began to speak about the previous life at about three years of age ($\bar{X}_{solved}$ = 37.1 months, $\bar{X}_{unsolved}$ = 36.7 months; F = .47, df = 1, p < .50). On the other hand, among the unsolved cases, subjects stopped talking about the previous life at an earlier age (70 months) than in the solved ones (90 months) (F = 22.79, df = 1, p < .00001).

The subject mentioned the mode of death of the previous personality with about the same frequency in solved and unsolved cases in all but one of the cultures X^2 = 2.15, df = 1, p < .82). The exceptional culture was the United States, where subjects of both types of case mentioned the mode of death significantly less often.

Phobias related to the previous personality's mode of death occurred with about the same frequency among subjects of both solved and unsolved cases ($X^2 = .25$, df = 1, $p < .00001$).

Mention of the name of the previous personality by the subject may contribute importantly to the solution of a case. Our data show that the subject was reported to have mentioned the previous personality's name significantly more often in solved cases than in unsolved ones ($X^2 = 64.39$, df = 1, $p < .00001$).

Looking at solved cases for which we had information about the actual mode of death of the previous personality, we found that subjects mentioned the mode of death more frequently when the previous personality had died violently than when he or she had died a natural death ($X^2 = 100.17$, df = 1, $p < .00001$).

One of the most significant differences observed between solved and unsolved cases is in the previous personality's mode of death. Among the solved cases, the rate of violent death ranged from 41% in the cases of Thailand to 69% in the Lebanese cases. Among the unsolved cases in which the subject mentioned a mode of death, the rate of violent death ranged from 85% in India to 100% in Thailand. The difference between the two groups of cases was significant ($X^2 = 91.23$, df = 1, $p < .00001$).

Discussion

Shorter Duration of Speaking About Previous Lives in Unsolved Cases. Subjects of unsolved cases did not speak about the previous lives for as long as did subjects of solved cases, but this difference almost certainly derives from the comparatively small amount of attention that subjects of unsolved cases receive from their parents and other persons. Such persons may rapidly lose interest in the statements of a child that cannot be verified. Moreover, the two families concerned in solved cases usually meet and exchange visits, and such visits provide stimuli for subjects to continue talking about the previous life when they might otherwise forget it.

Incidence of Violent Death in Solved and Unsolved Cases. There are several possible explanations for the higher incidence of violent death among unsolved cases. If unsolved cases derive from children's fantasies, such fantasies might include the feature of a violent death. Texts in child psychology and psychiatry often claim that violence is a frequent theme of children's fantasies, although we have not yet found any statistical evidence in the literature supporting this claim. The explanation that unsolved cases are nothing but children's fantasies seems inadequate, however, since it does not address the question of the high incidence of verified violent death (as well as other verified details) among solved cases.

The high incidence of violent death in unsolved cases may result from a tendency to remember a violent mode of death more easily than names, which are usually essential for positively identifying a person. Two features in our data support this conjecture. Among solved cases, subjects mentioned the mode of death more often when the previous personality had died violently than when he or she had died naturally, indicating that a violent death is indeed more memorable. Also, subjects mentioned the previous personality's name more often in solved cases than in unsolved ones, and the name undoubtedly contributed to the solution of the cases.

A third possible explanation is that unsolved cases may consist of a mixture of real previous life memories and fantasies. Children who recall a real life that ended violently would be likely to remember and talk about that death, as our data indicate, but children who recall a life that ended naturally would frequently not remember the mode of death; such children might then supplement real memories of a previous life with fantasies about a violent death, thereby inflating the incidence of presumed violent death. The subjects of solved cases do not seem to have substituted fantasies of a violent death in cases in which the previous personalities actually died naturally; but such a process may occur among subjects of unsolved cases who do not recall the mode of death and are pressured to give more details that might help identify the previous personality.

Verified Information in Some Unsolved Cases. Subjects of unsolved cases do occasionally make accurate statements about information apparently not learned normally. These statements cannot be attributed to fantasy and also apparently not to cryptomnesia, and so, as with solved cases, an adequate assessment of unsolved cases must address the issue of how the subjects acquired the accurate information they did in fact have.

Conclusion

Many unsolved cases may derive from fantasies. Nevertheless, our data show that unsolved cases closely resemble solved ones in three important features. Moreover, unsolved cases frequently have still other features that resemble those of solved cases: these include birthmarks that the subject relates to the previous life, apparently untaught skills, claims of having changed sex from one life to another, and turmoil in the family caused by the subject's rejection of his or her parents. We are therefore justified in supposing that some unsolved cases may derive from memories of a real previous life that are too few in number or too lacking in detail to permit verification.

Unsolved cases may consist of at least three types: some may be pure fantasies; some may consist of real memories of previous lives that are unverifiable because of a lack of sufficient information needed for verification; and some may be an assortment of real memories of previous lives mixed with irrelevant and incorrect details or with normal memories of events in the child's present life.

PHYSIOLOGICAL MEASURES*

PSI SOURCES AND BRAIN EVENTS: AN EXAMINATION OF CORTICAL EVOKED POTENTIALS AT THE MOMENT OF OBSERVATION IN A SCHMIDTIAN PK TASK

Jeffrey Owen Katz (University of Lancaster)

Schmidt (JASPR, 1975, 301-320) suggests the critical moment in PK occurs when the subject receives feedback which activates his "psi-source." Are there distinct brain events associated with those observations which may effectively activate the subject's psi source? Experimentally testing this could produce confounding of observed feedback (Hit/Miss) with the presence or absence of psi: observing "Hit" flash on a screen would elicit a different EEG pattern than observing "Miss"; confounding arises from inferring the presence of psi from this feedback. Independent variables are needed for comparison between psi-hits and no-psi-hits, as well as psi-misses and no-psi-misses; however, this cannot be achieved by occasionally giving incorrect feedback since that would alter the trial's essential contingency, thus altering the meaning of the "Hit" which was displayed as a "Miss." In the present experiment, partial independence was achieved by using true (quantum mechanical) and pseudo-REGs, and a pseudo-random selection scheme to determine the REG (either quantum or pseudo) for each trial. The intrusion of psi in selecting seed numbers of pseudo-REGs was prevented by minimizing such selections.

Method. This experiment basically involved computerized recording of the subject's EEG while attempting to influence REG outcomes. Target generation and display were controlled by the computer. The subject only received feedback on whether each trial was a "Hit" or a "Miss"; no information was given about whether the targets were generated by the true (quantum) or pseudo-REG. Data were automatically placed on magnetic disk for later analysis.

Subject. Because of convenience and prior success at Schmidtian PK tasks, J.O.K. served as his own subject. Since

*Chaired by Martin Johnson (Parapsychology of Laboratory, University of Utrecht)

the computer essentially served as experimenter, J.O.K. remained blind to all data (except that presented as feedback) until all trials and analyses were completed.

Apparatus. A Nova 820 (Data General) with a 12-bit, 16-channel analogue-digital converter connected were the basis of the data acquisition system. The EEG amplifier had low noise and drift characteristics (noise < 0.5uv, p-p), and exceptionally high input impedance (> 100 megohms); gain was set at 2000, with time constant set at 10 seconds. The noise source consisted of a screened FM transistor radio (antenna input shorted) tuned between stations, resulting in noise from random thermal agitation, tunneling, and shot effects in the transistors.

Electrodes were homemade Ag/AgCl disks, attached to the scalp with Bechman electrode adhesive paste; occipital (between O_1 and O_2) to right temporal (T_4) placement was used. Electrode contact resistance was kept below 4 kilohms.

Procedure. This experiment was completed in one session of 600 trials, mainly because exact timing of average evoked potentials (AEPs) differs between occasions as a function of body temperature, dietary variables, the diurnal cycle, and other factors.

Once electrodes were attached and the computerized systems properly adjusted, J.O.K. typed in a command to begin the data acquisition program, whereby the computer took over all experimental and record keeping tasks. The author then made himself comfortable and began attempting to influence the REGs so that psi-hitting would be obtained.

Each trial consisted of a two-second interval. Targets were generated internally (no display) at the 2/3 second mark and placed in the computer's memory. At the 1+1/3 second mark, the target was partially displayed, i.e., either "Hit" or "Miss" was typed out, and the bell rung on the display terminal at 2400 Baud; no feedback on the True/Pseudo variable was given. During each two-second trial, the EEG was sampled every 60th of a second, resulting in 120 EEG values for each trial.

Targets were generated by sampling a pseudo-REG and then the FM radio noise source. Converted, truly-random noise values were transformed to one of four numbers (1-4) with equal probability. Pseudo-REG output could be one of eight values (1-8), also with equal probability. If the pseudo-random number was ≤ 4, it was compared with the result derived from the FM noise source: if the two values matched, a "True Hit" had occurred and was recorded; if the two values did not agree, a "True Miss" was recorded. If the pseudo-random REG result was 5-8, then a "Pseudo" trial had been generated: the trial was a "Pseudo Hit" if a 6 had occurred, otherwise it was considered a "Pseudo-Miss." The total time required for target generation was 50 microseconds and occurred between the 40th and 41st EEG samplings. The target's hit/

miss aspect was displayed (sent) between the 80th and 81st EEG samplings and constituted the "observation" for the trial.

Data anlysis occurred several weeks after the experimental session. AEPs were computed for each of the four possible trial outcomes (True Hit, True Miss, Pseudo-Hit, Pseudo-Miss). Trials with at least one EEG value larger than five times the Root-Mean-Square (equivalent to a standard deviation) amplitude were eliminated from the calculations as likely due to artefact. A two-sample t^2 test (multivariate analogue of the t test) for comparing mean vectors (or curves) was computed for each of the six possible comparisons of trial outcomes. The vectors compared were those formed by the series of EEG values which followed feedback (36 values were used: the 82nd-117th samplings of the EEG). These tests were intended to provide an evaluation concerning the differences (or their absences) between the evoked potentials associated with different trial outcomes.

Results. The Root-Mean-Square rule resulted in the elimination of 29 trials (< 5%). All further discussion concerns the remaining 571 trials.

It was hypothesized that different feedback would elicit different AEPs. This hypothesis, which does not imply psi but merely distinct brain responses to discriminable observations, was strongly confirmed: Hits (True or Pseudo) differed from Misses at very high levels of significance (True Hits-vs-True Misses: t^2 = 115.7, 36/246 df, p < 0.000002; Pseudo-Hits-vs-Pseudo-Misses: t^2 = 162.4, 36/251 df, p < .1x10^{-9}; True Hits-vs-Pseudo-Misses: t^2 = 152.9, 36.249 df, p < .1x10^{-8}; Pseudo-Hits-vs-True-Misses: t^2 = 110, 36/249 df, p < .00001). It was thought that brain events might also differ as a function of psi, that there would be significant differences in AEPs for True-vs-Pseudohits and True-vs-Pseudomisses, but no such differences were found: t^2 = 32, 36/111 df, p < .91; t^2 = 49.3, 36/386 df, p < .16, respectively.

Responses elicited by feedback have one pattern for both True and Pseudohits, and another pattern for both varieties of Misses. A graph of AEPs associated with True Misses placed atop one for Pseudomisses and then aligned for maximum coincidence in their initial phases, would indicate overall similarity (in accord with the nonsignificant t^2), but a peak of great amplitude at 108/60 seconds for the Pseudomisses would be noted. Similarly, when comparing True and Pseudo-Hits, the major peak occurring at 95/60 seconds seems of significantly greater amplitude for the True Hits. Whether these differences are stable or merely statistical error artefacts must be determined in further experiments.

AEP curves before feedback (1-80/60ths of a second) show a steady trend towards negativity (upwards) for True Hits, but a trend in the opposite direction for Pseudo-Hits. While this difference seems to be of apparent statistical significance, since this was not the hypothesis, no tests were performed. The curve for True Hits also indicates presence of alpha waves which appear to block around the time of target generation (40/60ths second), which also coincides with the beginning of a rapid incline that continues until around 50/60 seconds when alpha waves again become apparent. This seems to suggest that the brain was responding to the "stimulus" of target generation, despite the absence of sensory input. Could this be a cortical effect elicited by a psi-perceived stimulus, since such alpha blocking is well known to be associated with visual attention and perception? This will have to be answered by some future experiment.

Conclusion and Summary. An experiment was performed to determine whether brain events at the time of observation of the result of a PK trial differed as a function of psi involvement. Statistical tests suggest that there are no discernible differences in the average evoked potentials when trials in which psi may have played a part were contrasted with trials from which psi had been excluded. However, visual inspection of graphed AEPs indicates that differences may indeed be present, and tend to occur not at the time of observation but rather around the time of target generation. Further studies are required to determine whether these are real effects or merely statistical artefacts.

PHYSIOLOGICAL CORRELATES OF PSI RECEPTION: SOME METHODOLOGICAL CONSIDERATIONS

Charles T. Tart (University of California, Davis)

From the perspective of the tiny science of parapsychology, significant effort has been devoted to searching for possible physiological correlates of psi reception. Results have shown some promise, but fall far short of conclusively showing that there are such correlates. From the perspective of mainstream psychophysiological research, these parapsychological studies are very few in number and are often inefficient, so lack of clear physiological correlates of psi is hardly surprising. This paper discusses what efficient experimentation in this area would be like, using as examples an older, but methodologically efficient, experiment which found apparent physiological correlates of psi (Tart, IJP, 1963, 375-386), and a recent, but methodologically inefficient, experiment (Hearne, JSPR, 1981, 87-92) which did not.

When we deal with responses to intense stimuli, such as a sudden and startling noise, physiological responses are much larger than ongoing physiological background variation, so detection is no problem. The small literature on physiological responses to psi reception suggests that such responses, if they exist, are small at best, so only efficient experiments can detect them. Efficiency calls for precise temporal definition of the psi target, tightly controlled reactions by agents in GESP designs to further insure precise target definition, percipients and agents with known psi talent, sensitive and appropriate physiological monitoring apparatus, and sensitive and appropriate data scoring and analysis techniques. Main points concerning each of these factors will be illustrated by comparing the Tart and Hearne studies.

Temporal Definition of Target. Both studies were GESP procedures, with the agent's reactions an integral part of the target, so agent factors will be considered here. Detection of weak physiological responses to stimulation requires precise time-locking of the analysis epoch to the onset of the stimulus. In the Tart study, the stimulus was a two-second duration electrical current, sometimes delivered to an agent (Tart) where it constituted a severe electrical shock, sometimes to a resistor where it was undetectable to the formal agent. To eliminate agent anticipation of forthcoming shocks, highly variable intervals were used to eliminate discernible rhythms, and the agent forced himself to concentrate on a book he was reading at all times other than when he was shocked. Thus the pain of the shock, the psi target, had a sudden and precisely defined temporal onset. Offset was fairly rapid because the agent forced himself to again concentrate on his book as soon as the shock stopped.

Hearne also used a mixture of agent-shock and resistor-shock trials, but in the regular and psychologically salient rhythm of every minute through a series. Thus agent anticipation of possible shocks at minute intervals could constitute powerful psi targets. Shock intensity in Hearne's study was also of a momentary pulse type and of lower intensity than in the Tart study, so the psi target stimulus was temporally blurred and less intense.

Psi Talent of Percipients and Agents. The percipients in both studies were, unfortunately, not selected on the basis of psi talent. Tart, as both agent and chief experimenter, was very confident that physiological correlates of psi would be found. He has since proven to be a psi-conducive experimenter and occasionally scored well on self-tests of psi ability. Hearne, by contrast, reported himself as "moderately doubtful" about even the existence of ESP.

Apparatus. The Tart study measured a channel of electroencephalogram (EEG), galvanic skin response (GSR), and finger pulse volume (relative blood pressure) responses. The EEG was automatically analyzed by period analysis. All these measures are widely accepted as very sensitive in detecting reactions to weak sensory stimulation. All three measures showed either statistically significant or suggestive results. Hearne used only a mean heart rate measure, counted from an EKG recording over a 30-second analysis epoch. As standard psychophysiological texts state, however, measures of mean heart rate are appropriate when dealing with long term effects, but any attempt to average heart rate over time necessarily obscures short term responses. Heart rate responses to stimulation are also biphasic, an initial acceleration lasting about four beats followed by a more erratic deceleration. Averaging thus obscures, "averages out," genuine biphasic responses. Heart rate is also considered less sensitive to stimulation than measures like EEG or GSR. Thus Hearne's averaging techniques insured that even if genuine physiological responses to his psi target occurred, they would be unlikely to be detected.

Analysis Techniques. Physiological responses to sensory stimulation have known characteristics which must be adhered to for efficient detection. GSRs, e.g., have a latency of one to four seconds following stimulus onset, so GSRs occurring before or after this period should not be considered responses. In the Tart study the standard response latency times were used to select data epochs for analysis. Hearne, by contrast, measured mean heart rate over a 30-second epoch that began 15 seconds before the psi stimulus, to allow for "precognition." As we have no empirical data to suggest that physiological responses to psi stimulation would regularly begin 15 seconds before stimulation, this completely blurred the temporal definition of the target stimulus and thus destroyed the essential time-locking of the analysis. Further, the use of a 30-second epoch, when heart rate responses last 5 to 10 seconds at the most, added 20 to 25 seconds of irrelevant heart rate data to each response measure, losing possible responses in irrelevant noise.

Finally, Hearne only compared agent-shock periods and resistor-shock periods. Standard psychophysiological research technique compares possible responses to stimulation with control periods chosen some time after the stimulation period, a "rest period" of no known stimulation. This procedure was followed in the Tart study. Contrary to the original expectation that percipients would respond to the event of the agent's being shocked but not to the resistor being shocked, significant responses (compared to control periods) were found in both types of events, possibly because of too wide a psychological set of percipients. Given this empirical background, Hearne should have evaluated his two types of target periods against control periods.

Given the above and other considerations, it is possible that psi-mediated physiological responses to the agents' being shocked occurred in Hearne's study, but methodological inefficiency made their detection impossible. A reanalysis of this data, using appropriate methods, might find meaningful relationships, although it does not seem possible to compensate for all of the above problems.

The above discussion models psi reception and subsequent internal processing as being generally like that occurring with weak physical stimulation. We could widen the parameters of such modeling considerably if we had vast resources available for physiological studies of psi reception, using brute force empirical searches, but since we don't, it is important that research be efficiently designed, given the only reasonable model we have at this time.

TRANSMISSION OF EMOTION BY PSI UNDER HYPNOSIS AS MEASURED BY GALVANIC SKIN RESPONSE (RB)

Cambridge University Society for Psychical Research (CUSPR)*

The frequent occurrence of strong emotion in spontaneous cases involving ostensibly paranormal transmission of information led to the suggestion by one of us (A. D. Cornell) that using emotion as a target in a GESP task might be a fruitful line of research. Two experiments were undertaken to follow up this idea: one by the CUSPR group of 1970 (unpublished) and a more sophisticated version, the subject of this report, now (August 1982) nearing completion.

In order that the experimental conditions might better resemble those appearing in spontaneous cases, hypnosis was used both to establish an emotional or psychic rapport between agent and percipient and to induce strong emotion in the agent. Both received hypnotic suggestion--in the case of one pair, from each other.

A psychogalvanometer was used to measure the percipient's skin resistance (galvanic skin response, hereafter GSR) throughout the experiment, since the level of activation of the autonomic nervous system, of which GSR is an indicator, provides a good index of emotional changes (see Schouten, EJP, 1976, 57-71). This method is capable of greater sensitivity than verbal reporting and also avoids the disturbance consequent upon the latter, enabling the percipient to adopt a passive, receptive state during the experiment.

In view of the success achieved in psi tasks that have used hypnosis (see review by Honorton, in Wolman Handbook, 1977, 435-472) or autonomic responses (see Beloff, JSPR, 1974, 403-420), it was felt that a combination of the two, under conditions designed to mimic a spontaneous case, might enhance psi performance considerably.

Procedure. Data collection takes place over a 24-minute period, comprising two 10-minute "trials," together with short rest intervals, so that the whole period becomes partitioned as 1/10/2/10/1. The agent is asked to "transmit" emotion during one minute (randomly selected from the 10) for each trial, while the percipient's GSR is monitored throughout the 24 minutes. Each member of a percipient-agent pair goes through 20 trials--10 as agent and 10 as percipient. A total of three such pairs took part in the present study.

Before measurements begin, the pair receive hypnotic instructions--identical for the two subjects, each 24-minute experiment always repeated immediately, but with the two roles reversed. Each

---
*Delivered by Bernard Carr (Cambridge University)

is told that when acting as percipient he will feel relaxed, but nevertheless receptive to the emotional state of his partner and that when acting as agent a blank state of mind will ensue and time appear to pass quickly, except during the periods that emotion is required of him, when the emotion will be intense and time will appear to pass slowly.

Data Analysis. The problem here is to evaluate the percipient's response in any given one-minute interval using the information provided by the psychogalvanometer chart record. The GSR electrodes are placed on the hands, and a decrease in skin resistance (which should correspond to emotional arousal) shows up as a pulse in one direction. Hence it was decided to use the area under the curve, measured from an arbitrary baseline and with increasing area denoting decreasing skin resistance, as a measure of the amount of "emotion" present in each one-minute interval. The method described can cause the significance of the results to be underestimated--more sophisticated techniques are under consideration.

The area values so obtained were used to rank order the 10 intervals, and then two main analyses were performed: direct hit rate and sum of ranks. The latter statistic (Solfvin, Kelly and Burdick, JASPR, 1978, 93-109) was used as a secondary measure, guarding against various sources of noise obscuring a probably weak signal. Separate analyses were planned for each percipient-agent pairing, as large differences in hypnotizability across subjects were expected.

Preliminary Results. One percipient-agent pair has completed their series of 20 trials and achieved no significant results.

A second pair has completed 16 trials and managed five direct hits so far; assuming that they have no more direct hits in the remaining four trials, the (exact) binomial probability of achieving this score by chance is $p = .043$, one-tailed.

DREAMS AND ALTERED STATES*

DEJA VU: A PARAPSYCHOLOGICAL APPROACH (RB)

Vernon M. Neppe (South African Society for Psychical Research and University of the Witwatersrand)

The author has examined 50 definitions of déjà vu and developed the following conceptualization of the phenomenon: "a subjectively inappropriate impression of familiarity of the present with an undefined past." The definition of déjà vu suggested above is deliberately broad, including more than just its literal translation from the French of "already seen." In this regard, the author has described 20 subtypes of déjà vu such as already met, visited, smelled, known, "sensed" (in the ESP sense), dreamt, read, and spoken.

Déjà vu has been explained in 40 different ways. However, to a large degree these can be subdivided into three broad categories: psychological, organic psychiatric, and parapsychological. In my doctoral research I show that the qualitative features of déjà vu in these three differ.

Thus, déjà vu in its most common form in the nonpsychic, ostensibly normal person is generally vague with no major changes at cognitive or affective levels. It is frequently associated with anxiety relief, but is a rare occurrence in each individual, although found in about 70% of the population. This kind of déjà vu is probably due to associating parts of previous, forgotten memories with the present. I have called this psychological phenomenon "associative déjà vu."

Déjà vu due to an organic mechanism may well be exclusive to "temporal lobe epilepsy (type) déjà vu." In this case, the déjà vu experience may vary in quality from being vague, infrequent, and associative in character to frequent and apparently bizarre, associated with typical complex partial epilepsy features. Alternatively, déjà vu may be the aura to a tonic-clonic seizure or automatism. The major distinguishing characteristic, however, is the presence

---
*Chaired by Susan J. Blackmore (University of Bristol)

of typical post-ictal features, such as headache, sleepiness, or clouded consciousness. This kind of déjà vu does not occur in other kinds of epilepsy or in nonepileptic temporal lobe dysfunction.

In "schizophrenic déjà vu" the major features relate to the eliciting of either formal or content thought disorder, or (less commonly) mood incongruous features within the déjà vu experience. I found that such features could be elicited in at least a minimal form in 95% of a schizophrenic outpatient sample who were apparently under control and working. This disorder was elicited even in patients who had not had déjà vu. Thus there are specific qualitative kinds of déjà vu experience.

Theoretically, a different kind of déjà vu of a paranormal kind could also exist. From a scientific perspective it is more important to develop operational criteria for establishing whether, in fact, a specific déjà vu of the psi kind possibly exists before hypothesizing its etiology. Where possible, it appears preferable to consider the defining criteria for déjà vu from a purely subjective paranormal perspective.

Déjà vu is as subjective a phenomenon as a dream or a hallucination. Consequently, such research should be concerned solely with whether a qualitatively different kind of déjà vu is experienced by those who allege that they had paranormal abilities.

Specific criteria for choosing subjects who claim to have had large numbers of subjective paranormal experiences of high subjective validity are therefore required. This would imply defining a group of "Subjective Paranormal Experients" (Experients) and a control group of "Subjective Paranormal Non-Experients" (Non-experients), who appear to be logical populations for differentiating the hypothetical "subjective paranormal déjà vu" type from "associative déjà vu."

In order to analyze the various components of such déjà vu, a thorough literature survey and pilot study of déjà vu in various nosological groups would be necessary. This, in fact, has been done with the consequence that I have developed two special questionnaires on déjà vu. The first, the "Screening Questionnaire," screens broadly for the various kinds of déjà vu; the second, the "Déjà Vu Qualitative Questionnaire," analyzes 56 major qualitative parameters of such experiences (e.g. affect, intensity, frequency, duration) in both a structured and nonstructured way. This is the only real measuring instrument for déjà vu that exists in the literature.

A method of approaching déjà vu of a special qualitative subjectively paranormal kind has been suggested. Early controlled research which I performed using these methods has suggested that Subjective Paranormal Déjà Vu is indeed a separate entity, the following qualitative features differing statistically significantly from Non-Experients' déjà vu. The experiences are frequent in each person; they are very or extremely clear; they are associated more frequently with "claimed" and "acceptable" Subjective Paranormal Experience, as well as time distortions; the familiarity is intense, and may give the impression of "reliving the whole"; the experience is never at its peak only at its start--it always seems to grow (all $p < .01$); finally, marked cognitive changes occur. At the $p < .05$ level, the déjà vu experiences were found to involve many perceptual modalities including "sensing" more often, were very clearly remembered, were associated with an intense environmental awareness, and the specific déjà vu experiences were frequently "mentioned to others."

This study was retrospective, and confined to a westernized South African cultural group. It requires replication, extension across cultural lines, and prospective replication. It nevertheless confirms that the methodology and operational criteria suggested can be a new worthwhile approach in parapsychological research.

DREAM STATES AND ESP: A DISTANCE EXPERIMENT WITH A SINGLE SUBJECT (RB)

Betty Markwick (Hornchurch, Greater London) and John Beloff (University of Edinburgh)

General. The experiment, comprising 100 trials, was conducted between Edinburgh and London (some 350 miles) during the period 1979-1982, with B.M. as subject. The manifestation of psi in dream imagery was explored in a variety of free-response/forced-choice designs under GESP and clairvoyance conditions. The target material included art prints ("A," three runs), "memory" cards ("M," two runs), household objects ("H," two runs) and five specially selected objects ("S," three runs). Each trial was based on a judging pool of five contrasted (or randomly compiled) options.

Experimental Protocol. (1) In advance of the run (or part-run) J.B. prepares pools of five pictures or object-specifications, and sends a duplicate set to B.M. (2) Prior to each trial, J.B. informs B.M. that a target is to be set up. (3) J.B. randomly selects--by electronic die or otherwise--an option from the appropriate pool, and places the target picture/object in a box. (4) B.M. records significant-feeling impressions obtained during one or more nights, unseals the duplicate judging pool and rank-orders the five options. The dream protocol plus response is posted to J.B. (5) J.B. informs B.M. of the result. (A strict rule of "no communication during a trial" was observed throughout the series, to exclude any possibility of sensory leakage.)

Nature of Impressions. To aid the imagination, B.M. set up a "twin" (but empty) target box. The original idea was to "open" the empty box in the translucid state (B.M.'s less question-begging term for out-of-the-body experience); secondarily, to invoke impressions in dreams. In the event, translucid impressions declined while hypnagogic imagery developed spontaneously. A number of features emerged as tending to be associated with psi-effects: auditory hypnagogic imagery, dream-meetings with J. B., "telephone" dreams, sudden awakening, bizarre or "surprising" imagery, "first impressions." Lucid dreams proved disappointingly psi-evasive, however. Two extracts from the dream chronicle are given in illustration:

Non-lucid dream: "Conference setting ... Attention was centered on a large screen, but my view of it was almost end-on. ... I could just discern a figure on the screen, black and white, and gathered that a brief extract was being shown from the third part of some historical drama about kings and queens." The target proved to be a black and white picture of Garrick as Richard III.

Translucid dream: "The translucid state developed during a spell of relaxation, and I reached over to the psi-box scooping out an object. It felt like a tangle of tape, partially unwound--I thought perhaps a tape measure...." The target was a typewriter ribbon, with end undone.

Analysis of Results. Above-chance scoring was predicted. The primary method of assessment is based on Morris' exact test for the rank-sum statistic in "open-deck" preferential-ranking, as described in Solfvin et al. (JASPR, 1978, 93-109).

The mean rank-scores for the ten 10-trial runs are (where A, M, H, S, are defined above, C denotes clairvoyance mode, and MCE = 3):

2. 2 (S)   2. 6 (S)   2. 4 (H)   2. 5 (M, C)   2. 7 (M, C)

2. 4 (A, C) 2. 9 (S) 3. 1 (A, C) 3. 2 (H)   3. 3 (A)

The half-way stage analysis yielded the following: rank-sum = 124 (14 rank 1, 12 rank 2, 14 rank 3, 6 rank 4, 4 rank 5); MCE = 150, deviation = -26, p = .0054, one-tailed.

The figures for the completed series are as follows: rank-sum = 273 (25 rank 1, 20 rank 2, 24 rank 3, 19 rank 4, 12 rank 5); MCE = 300, deviation = -27, p = .030, one-tailed.

The cumulative probability showed a steadily decreasing trend, reaching a minimum of .0015 at Trial 64; thereafter the scoring rate fell to chance level.

Discussion. The overall result is of modest significance. It was obtained by a skeptically minded subject working under an ultra-rigorous regime, with a reputed negative experimenter moreover. This augurs well for a simple (and inexpensive) approach to dream research. The rigor achievable with a postal protocol is specially recommended: for even astronomical odds are evidentially worthless unless experimental conditions are completely watertight.

The statistical net inevitably fails to capture the richness of the experience--e.g., that beautifully symbolic screen, inclined slightly out of "normal," revealing specific correspondences to the target. Some observations bearing on the psychodynamics of ESP may be noted. The fall to chance scoring during Run Seven coincided with a crisis in B.M.'s life (death of father); subsequently, B.M. got into a vicious circle of tension ... over-deliberation ... spoiled responses. Displacement effects onto "control" options proved troublesome: conceivably a free-response pool itself constitutes an ESP stimulus.

In conclusion, other researchers--and, more especially, skeptics--are challenged to gain first-hand experience by developing internal imagery and themselves playing the role of subject.

THE OBE AS A NEAR-BIRTH EXPERIENCE (RB)

Barbara Honegger (Washington Research Center)

Honegger (Parapsychology Review, 1979, 10[2], 24-26), LaBerge (Ph.D. thesis, Stanford, 1980), and Salley (JASPR, 1982, 157-165) have all recently proposed that out-of-body experiences (OBEs) are a special case of lucid dreams, due particularly to the strong association of both with phenomenological lucidity, physiological paralysis, and penile erection indicative of the REM state.

Identifying OBEs as lucid dreams, however, does not account for the phenomenological aspects of OBEs that distinguish them as a special species of lucid dreams: the separation imagery itself, vibratory sensations prior to separation, and common, but not universal, umbilical cord imagery.

I propose that these unique phenomenological aspects of OBEs can be accounted for on the hypothesis that the onset of physiological labor may trigger fetal OBEs, as the viable but unborn fetus fulfills two key conditions of OBE genesis. First, the fetus is in an almost-perpetual REM state (Science, 1966, 152, 604-619; see also ultrasound research on fetal eye movement by Jason Birnholz of Harvard Medical School). Second, LaBerge has found that the initiation of lucid dreams--and of OBEs as a special case of lucid dreams--is highly correlated with physiological and/or psychological stress in a situation where the dreamer does not awaken--a condition sure to be fulfilled by the physiologically stressful event of normal (as opposed to Cesarean) childbirth. Fetal OBEs, triggered by the onset of heavy labor, may therefore constitute a fetal strategy for reducing or avoiding labor-induced stress.

If we are correct, OBEs later in life would be expected to contain frequent associations to the primal OBE of birth: vibratory sensations associated with labor-induced, rhythmic oscillations of the amniotic fluid; umbilical cord imagery; and once-quite-literal out-of-body imagery. Such phenomenological content is, in fact, quite common.

This hypothesis is at least indirectly testable. It predicts that adult OBEs should be reported more frequently by subjects who were delivered by natural childbirth than by Cesarean childbirth, which reduces fetal stress. OBE reports of umbilical cord imagery, tunnel imagery, pre-separation vibratory sensations, and separation imagery per se should also occur more frequently for subjects who underwent natural childbirth.

IMAGERY AND THE OBE (RB)

Susan J. Blackmore (Brain and Perception Laboratory, University of Bristol)

Introduction. It has often been suggested that the world of the out-of-body experience (OBE) is a product of imagery or hallucination. If so, one would expect those people who have OBEs (OBErs) to have better controlled or more vivid imagery, or to be more likely to suffer from other kinds of hallucinations. Several previous studies have not found the expected relationships with vividness or control of imagery (H. Irwin, Parapsychology Review, 1981, 12[4], 1-6; S. J. Blackmore, Beyond the Body, 1982). However, the most appropriate tests may not have been used in these investigations. In most OBEs the experient seems to observe things from a location above his or her normal viewpoint. It may be hypothesized that OBErs should be more used to imagining things from such a viewpoint. Therefore subjects were asked about the viewpoint of remembered scenes.

In addition, if the OBE world is imagined, then the ability to "move" by changing the imaginary viewpoint should be important. Subjects were therefore asked to imagine changing viewpoints. In this process the manipulation of three-dimensional shapes is involved and so some subjects were given a Space Relations test to investigate this ability.

Method. A questionnaire was given to 98 psychology students asking them to imagine from memory six simple scenes. They were asked whether they imagined each scene as though from eye level (as they would have seen it at the time), as though from above eye level, or in some other way. They were also asked how easily they could switch from one view to another (easily, with difficulty, or not at all). Other questions included Palmer's OBE question

(JASPR, 1979, 221-252) and questions on visual distortions (see pages 232-234).

Those who volunteered were given the Space Relations Test from the Differential Aptitude Test battery. This 25-minute paper and pencil test measures ability to imagine the rotation of simple geometrical forms. There was no stated connection between this and answers to the OBE question. Nine OBErs and 28 non-OBErs took this test.

Results. Thirty, or 31%, of the students reported having had at least one OBE. Most of these (89%) had had more than one. There were no significant age or sex differences. The number of scenes imagined as though from above did not differ between OBErs ($\bar{X}$ = 2.57) and non-OBErs ($\bar{X}$ = 2.15, t = 1.23, 95 df, p = .22). However, there was a difference in reported ability to switch from one view to another (t = 2.02, 95 df, p = .046). On the Space Relations test OBErs ($\bar{X}$ = 46.2) scored higher than non-OBErs ($\bar{X}$ = 41.3) but the difference was not significant (t = 1.32, 36 df, p = .19).

Discussion. Two of the hypotheses were not confirmed and the tests failed to distinguish OBErs from others. The only significant difference lay in the reported ability to switch from one imaginary viewpoint to another. This could be important because if the OBE world is a mental construction then the ability to "move" about in it may be crucial to the experience. In order to establish this, better tests of this ability should be devised. Since all the differences were in the expected directions similar tests with larger samples are planned.

OBES AND PERCEPTUAL DISTORTIONS IN SCHIZOPHRENIC PATIENTS AND STUDENTS (RB)

Susan J. Blackmore and John Harris (Brain and Perception Laboratory, University of Bristol)

Introduction. It has been suggested that the OBE may be a form of hallucination or dissociation and that the reduction or distortion of sensory input may be a factor in its generation. Accordingly, it would be interesting to know whether OBEs are more common in people who have various types of hallucination or who regularly experience sensory distortions. To investigate this questionnaires were given to a group of schizophrenic patients and a group of students.

Method. John Harris and Oliver Philipson placed an advertisement in the Newsletter of the National Schizophrenia Fellowship asking for volunteers to give information about their experiences.

Nothing more specific was mentioned at this stage, but the aim was to investigate perceptual distortions, which have been considered an early symptom of schizophrenia.

Volunteers were sent a questionnaire on distortions in all modalities, but only visual distortions are considered here. They were of seven types: color, movement, brightness or contrast, depth, shape, size, and tilt. The OBE question first used by Palmer (JASPR, 1979, 221-352) was included along with questions about whether the frequency of OBEs changed with the onset of the illness or with treatment given. Those who claimed OBEs were sent a further questionnaire about their experiences.

Another OBE study was being carried out at the same time with 98 psychology students. Questions on visual and body image distortions were included and drug-induced experiences were asked about separately. This cannot be considered as a control group but provides an interesting comparison and allows for the relationships to be tested in a different population.

Results. A total of 71 completed questionnaires were received from the schizophrenic group, of whom 30 (42%) claimed to have had at least one OBE. Thirty of the students (31%) claimed OBEs. There were no sex or age differences between OBErs and others in either group.

The schizophrenics were asked whether they saw visions, heard voices, or suffered from thought interference, three typical symptoms of schizophrenia. All these symptoms were more common among the OBErs but the difference was only significant in the case of seeing visions (chi square = 4.74, 1 df, p = .03). Of the 30 OBErs, 18 said that the experience became more frequent with the onset of their illness, seven that they stayed the same (or they had too few OBEs to make the comparison) and five that they became less frequent. Drug treatment appeared to reduce OBEs. Three claimed that OBEs became more frequent, 16 that there was no effect, and 11 that they became less frequent after drug treatment.

For both groups the total number of visual distortions experienced was compared for OBErs and others. OBErs suffered more distortions in both groups, although this was only significant for the schizophrenics (students: t = 1.95, 93 df, p = .55; schizophrenics: t = 2.82, 67 df, p = .006). Among the students OBErs suffered more distortions of body image, excluding drug-induced distortions (chi square p = 4.14, 1 df, p = .04). The schizophrenics were not asked about these. Also among the students OBErs were significantly more likely to have taken drugs, such as cannabis, LSD, or opium derivatives (chi square = 8.84, 1 df, p = .003).

Discussion. The results indicate that a large proportion of schizophrenic patients have OBEs. Only a controlled comparison will show whether they are more likely to have them than other people, and such a comparison is planned. Most of the respondents associated the OBEs with their illness and many were frightened by them. However, we need more evidence before concluding that the OBE forms part of the pathology. The only symptom of schizophrenia found to be significantly related to OBEs was seeing visions, and this makes sense if the OBE is seen as a kind of (predominantly visual) hallucination. There also seems to be a relationship, in both students and schizophrenics, between perceptual distortions and OBEs. These results justify a more detailed study using a proper control group.

THE OLFACTORY HALLUCINATION IN THE PSYCHIC

Vernon M. Neppe (South African Society for Psychical Research and University of the Witwatersrand)

Olfactory hallucinations (OHs) refer to environmentally unexplained perceptions of smell. There appear to be no adequate studies of their incidence in the normal, nonpsychiatric population. This is because OHs have generally been regarded as pathological and suggestive of temporal lobe pathology.

Denis Williams (Brain, 1956, 29-67) stresses that the actual anatomical site of origin of the olfactory cortex is still uncertain. Unexplained smells probably, however, reflect pathology from anteromedial lesions of the hippocampus. Consequently, the cortical site of smell appears to be the mesial temporal area. Olfactory hallucinations have generally been regarded as due to temporal lobe pathology. Such OHs are usually unpleasant and of "burning" or "rotting" kind. Pleasant OHs of "flowery" or "perfumy" kind are not described in the neuropsychiatric literature: consequently their origin would be uncertain.

The possibility exists that not all hallucinations of smell derive from the temporal lobe and that not all are pathological. Two parallels may be drawn: first with the apparent non-temporal lobe origins of the pathological auditory hallucinations of the schizophrenic: these are regarded as "functional" and possibly secondary to the primary thought disturbance; second, hallucinations involving almost every sense have been reported in subjective paranormal experients (people who were functioning extremely well and who claimed psychic experiences). These hallucinations have been called "sane" by West as opposed to "insane" (Psychical Research Today, 1962). Neppe and Hurst (Parapsychological Journal of South Africa, 1981, 55-75) have stressed how the invariable self-reference or special idiosyncratic meanings associated with such hallucinations of "sane" and "insane" kind must be considered, and even abnormal hallucinations may not necessarily have definable anatomico-physiological origins.

This study attempted to clarify whether the olfactory hallucinations of the subjective paranormal experient were of a special kind, and, if so, what explanations existed for this. A starting point was structured so as to establish first whether there was a special kind of OH via a formal controlled trial.

The measuring instrument asked about smelling something when there appeared to be nothing to smell. Spontaneous descriptions were requested. It specifically inquired into smell modality, frequency, pleasantness degree, quality (e. g. burning), duration, circumstances of occurrence, and perception simultaneously by others. Reliability and validity tests were incorporated into the research. The actual research involved three phases. The first phase was the formal controlled trial: Seven Subjective Paranormal Experients (Experients) were compared with ten Subjective Paranormal Non-Experients (Non-Experients) from the same original population. Numerous reliability and validity stages were involved and the groups were demographically homogenous. The Experients operationally had had at least 16 nonsymbolic, nonintuitive, extremely well-validated spontaneous subjective paranormal experiences (SPEs) of at least four kinds (e. g., waking ESP, veridical dreams, seeing auras, and psychokinetic experiences); the Non-experients had never had any SPEs.

Results of Phase 1 confirmed the presence of a special kind of OH: Not one of the Subjective Paranormal Non-Experients had ever experienced olfactory hallucinations in his or her life; yet, all seven of the controlled sample of Experients had had unexplained smells. Moreover, all seven described olfactory experiences of a certain very specific quality: namely, pleasant and of the flowery or perfumy kind. Six of the seven had associated the simultaneous impression of the "presence" of someone specific, and five of the seven had experienced this quality of smell at the same time as others present. These findings are all highly significant (p < . 001, Fisher's test).

Because of the consistent results with the controlled sample of Experients, the question of whether these results could be generalized to other subjective paranormal experients uninterested in scientific parapsychology was raised. Phase 2 therefore extended this research to other Experients. A small number (three) of active spiritualist mediums who had never read any scientific papers in or attended any scientific lectures on parapsychology, and who conformed to the stringent criteria for admission as "Experients" were available. They therefore constituted an additional small group of demographically dissimilar Subjective Paranormal Experients who were looked at without direct controls, taking cognizance only of the ostensible rarity of olfactory hallucinations in the "normal" population. All three claimed to have had both pleasant and unpleasant olfactory hallucinations associated with "presences."

Phase 3 examined whether the experiences of a neuropathological population expected to have had olfactory hallucinations would be similar to the findings above. Only two of 18 temporal lobe epileptic and none of seven nonepileptic temporal lobe dysfunction patients had pleasant olfactory hallucinations. One of the two perceived "burning" smells as pleasant. The second described a "perfume" smell, but could not explain its origin. (She was the only Temporal Lobe Epileptic to spontaneously describe SPEs.) These patients were chosen to insure that the research instrument would differentiate the quality of olfactory hallucinations in temporal lobe patients from Subjective Paranormal Experients. It appeared to do so.

Considering the controlled sample (in Phase 1), the figure of $p < .001$, derived from comparing the ten control and seven experimental subjects, is extremely thought-provoking. Even more persuasive, however, is the following speculation: Even if one estimates the incidence of pleasant "perfumy/flowery" OHs to be one thousand times more frequent than it may be (i.e., one in a hundred) the probability of ten successive people (i.e., the seven "experimental" and three "other" Experients) having OHs by chance is 10^{20}! Consequently, an attempt must now be made to find a reason.

The following explanations of the results above suggest themselves: (1) <u>Temporal Lobe Firing with Group Influence</u>. The most conventional explanation here would be neuropathological: the olfactory phenomena never existed in reality; they were purely hallucinatory; they imply firing in the mesial temporal area; this firing may anatomically derive from a position somewhat different from the more well-known unpleasant olfactory hallucinations of burning or rotting quality. Supporting this explanation is the higher incidence of temporal lobe symptomatology in Subjective Paranormal Experients found by Neppe (JASPR, 1983, in press). The occurrence of unpleasant OHs in seven of the ten Experients supports a common pathology. The spontaneous occurrence of collective olfactory experiences (in eight of the ten), particularly in the nonséance, nonreligious situation, would require a further explanation, as it is unlikely to be due to simultaneous temporal lobe firing. Consequently, a second unconsciously motivated explanation, such as collective wish fulfillment (folie à deux) with a functional olfactory hallucination, group influences, or hypnotic suggestion would be required. Eight out of ten Experients reported collective olfactory occurrences in this study. At times, more than one other person was involved. Also, the psychodynamics were usually not obviously conducive to any of the above explanations. Nevertheless, one possible explanation could certainly be temporal lobe firing in the one subject, with secondary influence of the other(s).

(2) <u>Fraud</u>. This is a second major explanation. However, this study included a control group and subjects were interviewed independently. There is no reason to doubt the character of any of the subjects, who are all respected individuals, and the information obtained by the investigator can easily be confirmed by others. It is difficult to conceptualize how fraud could occur only in the experimental group, especially as all subjects were interviewed independent-

ly and individually, and the identity of the other subjects was not disclosed.

(3) Real Physical Occurrence. An allied and far more acceptable suggestion is the real physical occurrence of the smells due to easily explicable physical origins: the perfumy or flowery smells derived from perfume or flowers; they were smelled collectively because the smells actually existed.

(4) Common Personality or Sociocultural Factors. Alternatively, the olfactory hallucinations in the Experients may be similar due to common factors other than their SPEs; for example, personality features, needs, or sociocultural components. No formal personality inventories were used but the Experients did appear to have one common personality trait--the conviction that they were genuine psychics. This conviction may well have stemmed from a need. Sociocultural similarities could also be cited--the families of orientation were very accepting of psi phenomena in four of the ten; six were actively involved in meditation and Eastern philosophy and three others in spiritualism. For one or more of the reasons mentioned above, a strange smell could easily be interpreted by them as the "paranormal trimming of a presence." The sociocultural/ personality explanation appears more parsimonious than the genuine "psychic" explanation. It is not entirely satisfactory in all respects; for example, it does not explain one subject's early childhood experiences.

(5) Paranormal Experience. Several explanations have been cited to deal with a particular hallucinatory phenomenon. Like clairaudient and apparitional hallucinations these are entirely subjective and consequently extremely difficult or impossible to validate objectively. Nevertheless, they have been repetitively interpreted as paranormal. In that sense, even if they are not really paranormal, they must be classified as another kind of subjective paranormal experience (just as the visual [apparitional or visual aura] and auditory [clairaudient hallucinations] counterparts are).

The case for hypothesizing a unitary, ostensibly paranormal component for certain olfactory hallucinations is still very tenuous. No doubt the majority of unexplained olfactory smells can be explained pathophysiologically, physically, or dynamically. These cases do, however, provoke paranormal explanations as one of many possibly fruitful hypotheses. Replication of this study under prospective, non-hearsay conditions, may allow perspectives for controlled experimental research into this area of olfactory hallucinatory-type subjective paranormal experiences. A useful starting point may be the assessment of suggestibility as to particular smells in the laboratory situation.

A PHENOMENOLOGICAL APPROACH TO EXPERIMENTAL PARAPSYCHOLOGY (RB)

Ralph G. Locke (Experiential Learning Laboratory) and Marilyn J. Schlitz† (Mind Science Foundation)

In this paper, we suggest that a phenomenological approach may be useful in psi testing. In doing so, the question of just what this means and how one might approach experimental parapsychology from such a perspective arises.

Due to the short space available, we do not attempt to explain phenomenology in detail. Rather, we have used a brief example to illustrate the usefulness of such a pursuit in psi testing, hoping to show ways in which a phenomenological attitude may be helpful in yielding more comprehensive and appropriate data. To do so, we drew from an informal remote-viewing session conducted at the Institute for Parapsychology. The aim of this effort was not to discuss remote-viewing methodology, but to examine the role phenomenology might play in the psi-elicitation process. The focus of the materials concerned the interactions between a research participant and the two experimenters, M.S. and R.L., after completion of a remote-viewing trial.

Prior to the session, it was agreed that at a prearranged time the participant, A.P., would relax and attempt to visualize (or otherwise describe) the physical locale surrounding M.S. She was aware of the standard remote-viewing protocol and was shown examples from other experimental sessions--specifically, notations and drawings that were described as subjects' impressions of the previous target sites. A.P. was encouraged to do the same, making sketches and recording her impressions.

In describing her impressions to the two experimenters, A.P. began by reporting her initial experience as visual images appearing in different degrees of clarity, intensity, and recognizability. Following this brief flurry, there was a period in which she reported "seeing" nothing. After this came a period in which she "knew" something was about to happen. She could not see anything until a bright spot of color expanded in the center of her field of vision, followed by "seeing something burst out of this patch that seemed like a locomotive--just like in one of those old movie sequences." She went on to fill in that she knew it was not a train but an antique car, which did in fact match elements of the site. In addition to the car, she correctly described the site as an old farm, complete with a log cabin, lanterns, and an old-fashioned kitchen stove.

Now, this seems fairly straightforward, except that it is clearly incomplete as a record of A.P.'s experiences during the experimental period. In gaining a more complete picture of the situation, the authors dealt with one small part of the reported episode. A.P. stated that she saw "nothing" preceding the sighting and description of an antique car. She was asked what exactly she did see that amounted to "nothing." Her reply after brief reflection was that she saw "grayness and flecks of light." She was then asked how she knew something was about to happen. She hesitated and said she was uncertain. She was then asked how she felt--again, hesitation--and then how her body acted at the time. A. P. quickly and animatedly reported that she had felt tense (hands clenched, legs tense) and that she had feelings like butterflies in her stomach. She reported experiencing some kind of anxious arousal, "like you get when you are going to do an examination."

We then examined this reportage, attempting to give some flavor of a phenomenological perspective. In the first place, we would like to point out that phenomenology is concerned with the deceptively simple dictum, "Don't think but look" (Schau). This translates into a more complex approach to human experience and consciousness, which emphasizes perception--but in a particular way. A central part of this approach is made up of the process of suspension of assumptions. There is no possibility of absolutely cancelling out assumptions inherent in acts of perception. Rather, assumptions are made into data and resources--i.e., topics for investigation--in our assessment of how perception is constructed (built up) and reported. Where the perceptual field is concerned, we are clearly interested in what is focal and what is subsidiary, and why. In other words, what kinds of implicit structuring or editing occurs which may reveal the following?

1) Culture-specific categories and language habits (descriptive protocols).

2) Context-specific categories and language habits contained within a situation--subtended by 1.

3) The composition of the natural attitude which is the basic matrix within which perception and action (including language acts) occur.

4) The idiosyncratic organization of experience which reflects the biography of subjects and their situational adaptation, and the way in which these intersect with points 1, 2, and 3 in the situation being investigated.

In A. P.'s case, the experiment had been introduced with a pronounced visual orientation. In other words, the implicit assumption negotiated in the experiment was the overriding importance of information (impressions) gained from a visual mode. The subject, in preparing for the session, was encouraged by the experimenters to attend to the task in a specific fashion. This attitude on the part of the experimenter was based on certain assumptions coming from a cultural, contextual orientation. So, A. P.'s reportage of the focal, visual phenomena was partly subtended by the construction of the experimental situation in terms of what counted as "relevant data." Implicitly, although not totally, she was oriented away from a range of experiences, other than visual, while performing as "an adequate or competent subject," as she believed. The datum, taken from the phenomenological point of view, is not the primarily reported visual field content and changes which may or may not match with the actual target site. Rather, it is the from-to relationship that is expressed by the focal visual experience (the vehicle perception) to which the rest of the visual, kinesthetic, and other modalities--in this case, expressed symptoms of anxiety--were subsidiary.

Now, this is not to say that the anxiety-state of embodiment caused the visual phenomena or that it was necessary to them--these issues can be dealt with separately--but rather,

> What must be borne in mind is that the main function of a phenomenological description is to serve as a reliable guide to actual or potential experience of the phenomena. It is in this sense never more than ostensive, or better, directive. Its essential function is to provide unmistakable guideposts to the phenomena themselves (Spiegelberg, 1970).

Phenomenology, then, is a kind of uncovering process. In the case of A.P., the definition of "something significant occurring" included the context of psychophysiological events that were "signposts" and part of the field out of which visual events were the meaningful figure. So, part of the uncovering process is an examination of the part-whole relations in language and perception. What distinguishes a phenomenological approach from introspective reporting alone is the view of ourselves, the experimenters, in the process. Our language, orientation and bias are vital properties within the process of data collection. We cannot assume that we are passive observers, objectively monitoring the experience of our subjects.

By utilizing a phenomenological approach in experimental settings, we may further our ability to map the components of consciousness that make up the psi elicitation process.

ANTHROPOLOGICAL RESEARCH*

PARAPSYCHOLOGICAL ANTHROPOLOGY: MULTI-METHOD APPROACHES TO THE STUDY OF PSI IN THE FIELD SETTING

Patric V. Giesler (John F. Kennedy University)

There has been a growing interest in the interface between parapsychology and anthropology. The purpose of this paper is twofold: (a) to introduce the scope of the research potential in a parapsychological anthropology, along with what advances have been made through the associated experimental and ethnographic methods for studying psi in the field setting; and (b) to improve these historically one-sided methodological models by suggesting means for their refinement by proposing combinational and integrated, or "multi-method," approaches to the study of psi processes in their psychosocial contexts.

Progress towards anthropology or parapsychology embracing the other's theories, methods, and data has been painstakingly slow. Yet for each field the potential benefits are enormous. For anthropology, for example, the classical psychosocial theories of magic are challenged by parapsychological data, which imply that the ontological basis for magical practices rests in the individual experience of the paranormal. For parapsychology, there is the diversity across cultures in terms of genetic patterns, climate, varieties of trance states, child-rearing, etc. New experimental designs may be generated from folk theory explanations of psi. Further, the field's comprehension of "culturally shaped" manifestations of psi would be expanded. And, certainly, the strengths and weaknesses of current psychical theories could be illuminated by the testing of alternative culture-bound hypotheses.

In order to develop a "cross-fertilization" of the two fields, as Van de Castle put it, it is necessary to consider methodology, and what we have gained from it.

Since Lang's time, reports about psychic events from ethnographers have been for the most part anecdotal descriptions tangen-

---

*Chaired by Robert L. Van de Castle (University of Virginia)

tial to their research aims. Yet from those relatively systematic observations reported, and a few preliminary cross-cultural analyses of patterns, we find the following: (a) a large range of types or manifestations of psi phenomena across diverse cultures; (b) psi phenomena of great magnitude with relatively high frequency; (c) psi events portrayed in natural cultural or sub-cultural contexts; (d) descriptions of several behavioral categories related to the events including altered states of consciousness and their inductions, use of ritual paraphernalia, role of any assistants, chants and dances, etc.; and (e) a measure of the reliability in those reports in which the personal involvement of the researcher in the event is described, and in which the biases for or against the reality of the phenomena are given, including attempts at alternative explanations.

The merit of these accounts is diminished to the degree that they are susceptible to the kinds of counter-hypotheses hurled at the (British) Society for Psychical Research by D. J. West (PSPR, 1946-1949, 264-300) regarding its 50 years of work with spontaneous cases. Yet these fundamental considerations are further confounded by other epistemological and methodological issues inherent in many ethnographic approaches to the study of psi and psi-related activities. For example, it is not unusual to find ethnographers mixing, and somewhat obliviously, the native informant's "emic," or, beliefs, codes, attitudes and depiction of what is real, normal, and paranormal, with the researcher's own emic. And then, on top of the confusion of emics, the researcher's "etic," or scientific system of observation and data recording, is imposed. Singer and Ankenbrandt (Phoenix, 1980, IV, 18-34) point to such an informant-researcher emic mix under the guise of a reliable etic framework in the following excerpt from John Beattie's Witchcraft and Sorcery in East Africa (1963), in which he describes a Nyoro cult séance:

> The excitement and colour of these occasions ... may be presumed to have a strongly cathartic effect on participants, and so to provide at least a partial means to the release of inner tension. There is evidence, too, that "cures" by these means of quite serious conditions are not uncommon. [Emphasis added.]

Note that the "cathartic effect" Beattie proposes would seem to reflect Beattie's own personal interpretation or emic, yet in the next line, he says there is "evidence" and that there are "cures." Do the latter refer to the informant's beliefs? to factual "evidence" which Beattie has gathered through his etic approach? Then, what is this evidence, and which are the "quite serious conditions" cured? We are left uncertain as to what is reality, what is belief, and whose.

With the methodology of controlled laboratory experimentation, these arguments become less relevant or irrelevant altogether. Desiring this greater rigor of experimental control and the concomitant validation of statistical evaluation, a few anthropologists and parapsychologists have carried out ESP and PK experiments in diverse cultural contexts such as Manitoba, New Guinea, interior Australia, and the San Blas Islands. Overall, the data from the experimental methods, which relied heavily on Zener cards or some culturally adapted form of them, offer us statistical evidence for ESP abilities in non-Western societies under controlled conditions. However, compared with the field observational data: (a) the range of types or manifestations of psi phenomena are narrow and rigidly defined and dependent on statistics; (b) the phenomena are of lesser magnitude; (c) the settings are not of normal everyday life; (d) the experimental research is not related to activities or processes credited with psychic bases by the culture; and (e) personal beliefs, biases, and experiences of the researchers relevant to the experimental trials are rarely addressed, or mentioned only peripherally. Clearly, the merits of laboratory testing in the field setting, if it is to be well designed and the controls and manipulation of variables are to be adequately checked, diminish to the degree that sufficient ethnographic data are or are not collected.

Thus, what is clearly needed for a parapsychological anthropology are combinations of field and laboratory methods; combinations that would afford the researcher the range and magnitude of "field psi" and the control and validation of laboratory methods and statistical evaluation. Ideally, a researcher who combines the methods would (a) learn a particular culture's conditions for psi and psi-related activities; (b) comprehend the folk perspectives on psi and psi-related activities: what it means to them, and how they believe it occurs; (c) validate the psi of their activities with the rigor of experimental controls and statistical validation; and (d) contribute to a cross-cultural data base on particular experimental and ethno graphic designs, so that the variable of "culture" may be systematically evaluated.

An alternative, more integrated approach to the study of psi in the field setting is a new method I call "psi-in-process." The psi-in-process approach is akin to the "unobtrusive measures" method of psychology and cross-cultural anthropology. With the unobtrusive measures method, an experiment is carried out in particular cultural contexts in which the "subjects" of the study are being observed and "tested" without their awareness and without any apparent disturbance of the naturalness in the context. Elements of the context are manipulated, and the subject's responses to the situation become the dependent variable. In the case of an unobtrusive measures study of racial prejudice, for instance, a black man might be stationed at one of two doors to a supermarket in a white suburb. White residents of the suburb going to the market become the "subjects," and which door they choose becomes the dependent variable. The unobtrusive-measures design avoids both the extremely troublesome problem of subjects reacting to laboratory experimentation (that "reaction" functioning then as an added variable), and the lack of control mentioned earlier in the purely observational methods. In the psi-in-process design that I am proposing, the aim is also to experiment in a natural context, but the object of the study or of the experimentation is the psi process that may be functioning in the context. However, unlike the unobtrusive-measures method, this approach does not intentionally constrain or manipulate elements of the context in order to discover an unsuspecting "subject's" reactions. Psi-in-process examines variables that are already naturally evident in the context. It is not the appearance of naturalness that this method aims to sustain, as in the case of the unobtrusive-measures approach, but rather the naturalness itself.

A brief outline of a potential application should adequately illustrate the approach. Consider, for example, the divination consultation in an Afro-Brazilian shamanic cult. It is a natural event in cult life. People go to cult shamans regularly for help with love affairs, business, sickness, and to help locate lost objects or reveal the identity of a thief. The divination consultation is predominately free-response, and addresses problems analogous to those of Targ and Puthoff's remote-viewing task. In remote viewing, subjects attempt to describe the general characteristics of a distant target site; in the divination consultation, one of the tasks is also to describe the general characteristics of a target site or a target person--that is, the location of a lost object or the identity of a thief. Thus, the purpose of the divination and the diviner's description of the "target site" make the consultation a free-response GESP task which may be evaluated statistically. Native assistants, for instance, could be recruited to serve as "clients," who would consult the diviners about a "lost" object. The object, of enough monetary or sentimental value to the "client" to warrant a consultation, would have been "lost" (i.e., hidden) beforehand at a randomly selected target site by an independent party. The target sites and diviner responses would then be evaluated by independent judges, after the consultation, for significant correspondences.

When complemented with appropriate ethnographic data collected outside of the testing context, this integrative approach to the study of psi becomes a considerable advance over previous methods employed. For the standard ethnographic methods of systematic and participant observation offer solely qualitative data, and these are often flawed by the weakness inherent in the single observational instrument: the ethnographer. Whereas, with the psi-in-process method, both qualitative and quantitative data are obtained, and with the validating controls and statistical analyses of experimental research.

THE EFFECT OF SCHOOLING ON THE MANIFESTATION OF CLAIRVOYANT ABILITIES AMONG ISNAG CHILDREN OF THE NORTHERN PHILIPPINES

Diane M. Murray (John F. Kennedy University)*

    The experiment described in this paper was designed to examine the effects of socialization, measured by years of schooling, on the manifestation of psi abilities. It is an attempted replication of the first of a series of previous studies conducted by Michael Winkelman, designed to test the hypothesis that formal education inhibits the manifestation of psi abilities. I expected the participants to demonstrate clairvoyant abilities and, consistent with Winkelman's results, I expected to find a significant negative correlation between clairvoyant abilities and years of schooling.

    Participants. Participants were drawn from two locations in the Northern Philippines. The primary location was Dagara--a small, remote, village in the Kalinga-Apayao province. The secondary location was Kabugao, the capital of the same province. A list of all the children of Dagara, their ages, and years of schooling completed, was generated by the head teacher. Thirty-six children ranging from ages 8 to 16 were the participants in this study. There were four children per age category. As mentioned earlier, a crucial part of this experiment was to draw children, per each age category, who had the correct number of years of schooling, as well as children, per each age category, who had no schooling. For example, in that culture a child who is 12 years old would be in the sixth grade. Therefore, to meet the optimal conditions, the 12-year-old age group should consist of two 12-year-olds with six years of schooling and two 12-year-olds with no schooling. In the event that no participants could meet the latter requirement, then two 12-year-olds who had the least number of years of schooling would be chosen: With the population being relatively small, and with some families who had potentially eligible participants living some distance from the center, adjustments in the scheduling had to be made. In fact, it became necessary to draw participants from the Kabugao community, upon my return. In all, 15 participants from Kabugao took part in the experiment in order to fill in gaps within the age groups and within the educational levels.

    Math Skills Test. A math skills test was given to all participants in order to assess their abstract abilities with regard to mathematical problems. The test consisted of 18 problems of varying difficulty assessing the participants' addition, subtraction, multiplication, and division skills. It was designed in such a way that 8-year-olds would only be able to answer a few correctly, while 16-year-olds should be able to answer most, if not all, with accuracy.

---

*I would like to thank the Parapsychology Foundation, Inc. for its generous financial support of this project.

In order to determine its cultural relevancy, it was shown to the head instructor. Upon her approval of the form and content, it was included as part of the experimental design.

Procedure. The clairvoyance test consisted of 30 trials with three possible targets to choose from per trial. The target pool was an opaque bag containing 60 pieces of Brach's commercial candy of three different colors. There was an equal number of pieces per red, yellow, and green colors, each representing different fruit flavors. All candies were of uniform weight and shape and were machine wrapped in clear cellophane.

The testing center was the floor of my room in the home of the village captain. This was consistently adhered to throughout the experiment conducted in Dagara. A narrow curtain was hung at the entrance to my room, which gave those of us involved in the testing situation some semblance of privacy. However, on numerous occasions children who had already been tested, as well as those waiting to be tested, would peek between the curtain and the wall and laugh. They had been cautioned not to suggest colors for their friend being tested to choose, as that would ruin the experiment, and they might not get their turn to play the game. Consequently, I had minimal problems with this potential artifact.

In Kabugao, the exact same experimental design that is described in this section was used. The obvious differences were the location of the testing and the research assistant. The testing was conducted on the floor of my room in the teacher's dormitory. This offered more privacy than my room in Dagara because it had a solid door which could shut out the noise from beyond. My research assistant was a 27-year-old woman (E. L.) who was my right-hand partner throughout the entire research period and was completely familiar with every aspect of all the projects.

In Dagara, my research assistant (M. A.) was the nine-year-old daughter of the family with whom I was living. She had been one of the first participants in the experiment, was familiar with the procedure, and was especially fond of me. Each child who entered the room would sit on the floor opposite me, and M. A., who was to my left, would explain the task at hand. Three colored pens matching the targets were placed within easy reach of the participant. It was explained that when I signalled to the participant, he or she was to guess the color of the candy my hand held within the opaque bag, reach for the pen that matched the color of that candy, and mark an X in the appropriate box on the answer sheet which was placed alongside him or her. If the participant made the correct choice, a matching piece of candy from the reward bag was given. Three practice trials were allowed per child. The exact procedure demonstrated during the practice trial was used during the 30 trials per participant, from which the data were collected.

Prior to each trial, I shook the opaque bag with the targets to mix them up thoroughly. (A chi-square frequency test measuring

the randomnicity of the targets generated for the entire experiment
showed a nonsignificant deviation from randomness, p < .25.) I
then reached into the bag and, without looking, selected a piece of
candy and held it in my hand. I signalled to the participant, who
would then take as much time as he or she needed to make a choice.
Only after he or she had decided, and marked an answer with the
appropriate matching pen, would I remove my hand from the opaque
bag and show the target I had selected. Sampling was with immediate replacement. After returning it to the target pool, I would write
the first letter of the color of the target alongside the participant's
response on the answer sheet. As mentioned earlier, hits were rewarded by giving the participant a matching piece of candy from a
separate reward bag. The general atmosphere during the clairvoyance test was one of fun and excitement. At the end of the test,
we counted the total number of candies the participant received, and
congratulated him or her on doing such a fine job.

The math skills test was given to every participant immediately after the clairvoyance test. Instructions were given that they
should try and solve as many problems as they possibly could, but
that they should not worry or be embarrassed in the event that they
could not solve all the problems. It was emphasized that no one
would see the results of their test except myself, and that under no
circumstances would I show their tests to their teacher. When this
was understood, the participants moved a few feet away to the corner
of the room and began the test. They were given as much time as
they needed to complete the exercise.

Results. The original statistics used to analyze the data
were Pearson Product-Moment Correlation and Partial Correlation
programs incorporated in the Statistical Package for the Social Sciences (1975), a computerized package consisting of numerous types
of statistical tests. However, a Multiple Regression Analysis proved
to be a more powerful and appropriate statistical test to use since
it can simultaneously look at the relationship among all the variables.
Another advantage is that the obtained regression coefficient can be
used to promote estimates of the effects of change in the independent
variables on the dependent variable.

Prior to using the multiple regression analysis, a t test
demonstrated that the scores of the clairvoyance test were nonsignificant (t = .56, 35 df, ns). Following this, the multiple regression
analysis was initiated. The dependent variable, clairvoyance, was
regressed on the following independent variables using a forward
(stepwise) inclusion procedure: sex, education, age, and math.
Age entered the equation on the third step, after sex and education
had already been included. The regression coefficient for age was
positive and statistically significantly different from 0 (b = .69, t
= 2.16, 32 df, p < .05). However, this information is misleading
due to the problem of multicollinearity which enters into a situation
where one has highly intercorrelated independent variables. In the
case of extreme collinearity (interrelations in the .8 to 1.0 range),
not only is it difficult to determine the coefficients uniquely, but it

causes instability in the regression coefficients from sample to sample.

To deal with the problem of multicollinearity, clairvoyance was regressed on sex and each of the three highly intercorrelated variables separately. The results of these analyses indicated that sex had the only statistically significant coefficient among any of the regressions (b = -1.96, t = -2.02, 33 df, p < .05). This indicates that males had statistically higher clairvoyance scores than females (t = 2.14, 35 df, p < .05, two-tailed).

Discussion. The results of the analyses failed to replicate previous findings by Winkelman (Parapsychology Review, 1979, 10[5], 18-23) which supported the main hypothesis that formal education inhibits psi performance. Though the correlation between education and clairvoyance was in the same direction predicted and found by Winkelman, it was nonsignificant. However, akin to Winkelman's findings, math and clairvoyance were significantly negatively correlated (r = -.281, 34 df, p < .05, two-tailed). Age correlated positively but nonsignificantly with clairvoyance (r = .09, 34 df, ns), whereas in the Ozolco study Winkelman reported a significant negative correlation between age and clairvoyance (r = -.35, 27 df, p < .05, two-tailed).

The results seem to suggest that although in Winkelman's research math and education are negatively correlated with clairvoyance, they may not be so strongly correlated as to actually inhibit psi processes. Indeed, it is only when the influence of age upon education and clairvoyance is partialled out that education and clairvoyance are significantly negatively correlated (r = -.472, 34 df, p < .005, two-tailed). This finding supports Winkelman's more specific hypotheses of later studies in which formal education and clairvoyance are assessed independent of age. Further research is needed to examine the relationships between age, education, math, sex, and clairvoyant abilities. The crucial requirement stipulated in the beginning of this report--that is, to separate math, education, and age--failed to be achieved on the methodological level. Thus it was dealt with, as best as possible, on the statistical level. However, it would be a valuable contribution in terms of truly testing the main hypothesis if future research would succeed in this attempt.

RITUAL TRANCE CONSULTATION PRACTICES OF THE AFRO-BRAZILIAN UMBANDA CULT (RB)

Patric V. Giesler (John F. Kennedy University)

A multi-method investigation of the Afro-Brazilian Umbanda cult's divination practice is outlined in this brief. In the divination consultation a "possessed" shaman in the context of a public session is consulted on a variety of personal problems. The consultation is often much like a free-response ESP task, analogous to Targ and Puthoff's remote viewing. In the consultation, shamans are sought for information regarding a target site, namely the location of a lost object.

Several pilot trials were conducted in which my São Paulo co-experimenter and I served as consultation "clients." We sought information on a variety of personal issues of genuine concern, including the problem of a "lost" object of high sentimental value. While one of us consulted an entranced Umbanda shaman, the other selected four target sites, photographed them, and "lost" (hid) the client's object at one of the sites (selected with the aid of a random numbers table). The client was always blind to the targets. Evidence for psi was to be based on the statistical significance of the independently judged correspondences between site photos and the recorded site descriptions offered by the diviner (i.e., by the shaman's spirit).

These initial studies revealed certain psychodynamics in the client-shaman interaction which contradicted the assumptions of our research design, yet did elicit the target information. On a typical trial, for instance, an entranced shaman's possessing spirit would tell me confidently that I would find the object, that it was not lost, and that if I did a small ritual and would think of·him when I returned home, he would guide me naturally to the object. Thus, the diviners (or the spirits) did not offer target-site descriptions. Nevertheless, I did as instructed by the spirit, and upon returning home and thinking of him, I sketched the images which would come to mind regarding the location of the object, adding a clarifying comment or two. Three pilot trials were carried out in this fashion. For two of the trials, the correct target photos were awarded ranks of "1" when evaluated against the client's sketches and comments by independent judges. On the other trial, judging was not done; rather I tried "following" my impressions, and went directly to the hidden target site photos!

The Umbanda consultation psychodynamics appeared to be functioning more in accordance with Batcheldor's sitter-group principles, although in this case ESP rather than PK was being elicited. Most notable in this regard was Umbanda's way of taking on the responsibility for psi, thereby neutralizing the psi-inhibiting effects of ownership resistance, which refers to "that in-built reluctance to identify oneself directly as the source of paranormality" (Brookes-Smith, JSPR, 1973, 69-89). This is because the client leaves the consultation feeling that he or she has nothing to worry about, and that the spirit will take care of it, directing him or her to the lost object.

An experiment was then conducted to explore the hypothesis that psi-mediated information was being elicited in the client-shaman interaction through the operation of Batcheldorian principles. Since it is the client who literally finds the object, it was assumed that the Batcheldorian principles operating in the consultation served to stimulate the ESP of the client. The experiment aimed at testing the client's ESP ability alone, the ESP elicited by way of the client-shaman exchange, and the shaman's ESP ability alone. It was predicted that under the client-shaman consultation condition better ESP scores would be elicited than with the clients alone and the shamans alone.

Ten non-cult Brazilians from São Paulo were recruited to serve as "clients" in the experiment. Each supplied two objects which were subsequently "lost" (hidden), as in the pilot study. For one object, the client consulted a possessed Umbanda shaman, and for the second object, no consultation was made. Ten shamans from six African line Umbanda sects (São Paulo area) were consulted. In both conditions (with and without consultation), the clients made sketches and comments as in the pilot study. The order of the conditions was counterbalanced. Five Umbanda shamans from five São Paulo area sects not involved in the divination trials were tested on a standard remote viewing task. In sum, a free-response ESP task of "finding a target location" was administered to the shamans, to the clients, and to the client-shaman pairs in the ritual divination context.

Since the client's task of writing and drawing, as well as of judging his or her own responses, returns the responsibility for successful ESP back onto the client (or induces ownership resistance), both client and independent judging was carried out. Three independent judges evaluated all of the client responses, and their independent ratings for each trial were then averaged: one final Z-score/trial derived. The remote viewing transcripts, on the other hand, were only evaluated by independent judging (also three judges and one final composite Z-score), since shaman judging was not possible.

Full analysis of the data including both the quantitative and the relevant qualitative ethnographic data is still in progress. For the quantitative data emphasized here, the following analyses are being done: (a) interjudge Pearson correlations to determine the degree of judging agreement; (b) the Lilliefors test for goodness-of-fit to determine if the Z-scores are normally distributed; (c) a two-factor repeated-measures analysis of variance to assess the effects of the "context" variable (with and without consultation levels), the "judging" variable (client and independent levels), and their interactions; and (d) two between-groups t tests to evaluate the difference between the shamans alone and the clients alone, and between the shamans alone and the client-shaman consultations.

Part 3: Roundtables

THE FUTURE OF PSI RESEARCH*

THE FUTURE OF PARAPSYCHOLOGY

Rhea A. White (Parapsychology Sources of Information Center)

This is my view of what parapsychology could be when it comes into its own.

First, it will have a new name, one which will reflect both its integration with other fields and its transcendence of them. Second, and most basic, we will approach our subject from an entirely different angle. This will lead to theoretical and methodological changes, and these, in turn, will result in much more data than we now have, and more reliable data.

Data will be the direct result of theories, for we will understand that perception is dependent upon conception. We will be at the forefront of those scientists who act upon the knowledge that the universe is participatory. In fact, parapsychology will be the prototypical experimental science. Parapsychologists will be in demand as consultants in the laboratories of any science, as well as in art studios, classrooms, playing fields--any endeavor where the transcendence of limits is the activity of prime importance. We will be expert in understanding the processes involved in transitional states. We will understand the dynamics of transcendence, and that the process is the same regardless of subject matter. Faith will be seen as the bridge between the known and the unknown, and we will perfect the effects of acts of faith beyond present limits.

Having once been considered anomalous ourselves, parapsychologists will be called upon by all fields for advice in dealing with situations in which problems are created by the occurrence of something that does not fit in with accepted knowledge. We will be midwives to ideas and data wherever they are entering the world, and

---

*Organized by Keith Harary (Washington Research Center); chaired by Russell Targ (SRI International)

we will be called upon to insure a safe delivery. In sum, we will be at the leading edge in understanding the creative process and in applying our knowledge of it.

Because of this understanding we will also have made significant advances in our own subject. Experiments will be viewed as works of art, and emphasis will be placed on the creation of phenomena, not their measurement, although the proof will still be in the p value. Even in cases--of which there will be many--in which a p value is superfluous for purposes of "proof," it will still be highly valued as a pointer reading, an index of progress. A degree of repeatability will have been achieved. To a large extent we will be able to predict which experiments will succeed and which will not. There will be many new approaches to both spontaneous and experimental psi. A number of parapsychologists will be exploring psi at first hand and will serve as advisors to other parapsychologists. To a large extent the differentiation between experimenter and subject will disappear, and anyone involved in psi research will be regarded as an explorer. Parapsychologists will lead in understanding interpersonal relationships as they occur in any context.

However, for the future of parapsychology to unfold as I have outlined it, I also predict that we will have to let go of most--if not all--of what we now have in order to adopt an entirely different viewpoint. If we do not do this--if we do not take our rightful place at the forefront of science and art--I predict that we will not be able to gain any more of a foothold than we presently have. If, however, we can leave the old behind and set foot on the new land, we can have it all back again, but instead of viewing our subject from land's end we will see it from the farther shore. As soon as we can establish a beachhead there, it will immediately open up the possibility of communication with the world we left behind. A degree of commerce will then be possible between the two worlds which simply could not take place if we remained where we are now. So come! Let's give up the foothold we have, and gain a whole new world.

THE MARKETING OF SOCIALLY RELEVANT RESEARCH*

Keith Harary (Washington Research Center)

In the midst of serious political, social, and ecological problems which appear to have always confronted mankind, psi researchers have been officially conducting their experiments for the past hundred years. Many of us originally decided to enter into psi research because we believed that our experiments would provide vital

―――――――――
*Delivered by Russell Targ

The Future of Psi Research

insights that would help us to understand better and to improve significantly the human condition. Perhaps our research will have a positive impact upon the ways in which we human beings relate to one another, and to the other life forms with which we share this beautiful and tiny planet. Perhaps psi research will help our species to lift itself out of the confused and dangerous mess in which we have so often found ourselves, so that we may realize the hidden greater potential of humanity. Perhaps it will not.

An anti-nuclear weapons lecture and rally at Grace Cathedral in San Francisco recently drew an overflow crowd of thousands after only a few days of advance publicity. The subject matter was of great importance, even to those who were not technically competent in understanding nuclear warfare, because of its obvious social relevance and its clear impact upon the lives of all who attended the rally. Undoubtedly, more people attended that single lecture than have attended the combined Parapsychological Association Conventions of the past ten years. A great deal of money was also raised to support the anti-nuclear weapons movement--enough in that one evening to have comfortably supported at least one fulltime psi researcher for a year.

In contrast, developing a scientific understanding of psychic functioning is currently of interest to only a very small proportion of the human population. Psi research suffers from subsistence funding levels and a general shortage of creative and fresh ideas with which to carry our understanding of psychic functioning forward into the twenty-first century. Those of us who conduct experiments in this area are so often caught up in our private battles for scientific and personal recognition that we sometimes seem to have forgotten about the greater human and social relevance of the research that we are engaged in.

We sometimes behave as if we will only be able to afford to worry about the higher significance of psi research when the field itself becomes a better established and more respectable area to work in. We pretend that it is reasonable to spend time and money conducting experiments which do not promise to inform us, in a very specific way, about what psi is, what it tells us about ourselves, and how we may eventually hope to use it for the betterment of humanity.

We may say that we are conducting "pure" research for the time being, until we develop a better understanding of what we are actually dealing with. Yet the only acceptable justification for funding and conducting psi research in the first place, in the face of so many other serious and critical questions which confront humanity, is the potential immediate social relevance of work in this area. If we can not establish psi research as a socially relevant field of inquiry then we shall never achieve the funding levels which are needed to reasonably conduct work in this field. We must be able to prove that our work is necessary and important, and that it involves more than the satisfaction of our own idle curiosity about a handful of anomalies, or we will not be able to prove that our research really deserves to be funded.

Psi research must become more marketable if this field is ever to attract a reasonable level of funding and become more than a fringe area of human endeavor. We must, therefore, concentrate our efforts upon developing psychic functioning as a useful tool for humanity and for Western culture. This focus will help to attract more research funding, lead more mainstream scientists to commit themselves to this area, and assist us all in formulating meaningful research questions. Researchers who are reluctant to consider developing psychic functioning as a socially meaningful process could more profitably devote their professional efforts to some other field.

Our experiments must have more than purely statistical or philosophical implications. Psi research findings must influence not only the ways in which we experience ourselves as human beings, but also the manner in which we relate with one another and with other life forms. These findings must also directly influence the ways in which we gather information to conduct our daily business and our everyday lives.

It is not enough for us to merely inform the public about current research while we take care to not overstep the limitations and boundaries that cowards and critics have laid out for us. Instead, we must be willing to consider the future implications of our research at every moment. We must not be afraid to state clearly and without ambiguity just what those implications really are. Finally, we can combat the apathy and ignorance that has enshrouded public awareness of our work by conducting experiments that will lead to the development of techniques for bringing psychic functioning itself easily within the grasp of anyone who wishes to learn about and use it.

Psychic functioning must become less mysterious and more practically useful, important, and accessible to the general public if psi research is ultimately to evolve into something more than a curious footnote in the history of science.

MEANING AND FUTURE RESEARCH IN PARAPSYCHOLOGY

Patric V. Giesler (John F. Kennedy University)

We might view the general shift in our culture from pure to applied research as a drive toward more relevance or meaning for the public. And rather than drop pure research, we should regard the emphasis on meaning as a stimulant for an in-depth scrutiny of our pure research methods, theories, and findings. My purpose is not to define meaning, per se, in some absolute, universal sense.

Rather, my intention is to introduce, briefly, several areas of psi research in which different or varied senses of "meaning" have been implicit concerns begging for resolution. I also suggest future avenues of research that would be more directly or explicitly focused on elucidating the role of meaning, and its context-defining constituents, in psi processes.

Experimental parapsychology has pursued a variety of predictor variables which we could view as attributes of "meaning" for the subject: a meaningful testing experience, meaningful beliefs in psi and in the psi task, etc. But as "meaningful," those conditions are not generalizable to the greater population of subjects. For "meaning" is in the eye of the experiencer, in the eye of each particular subject. In future psi research, rather than assign subjects to experimental conditions, which are hypothetically meaningful, we must discover from the subjects which conditions are meaningful for them.

A new and original study of certain psychosocial variables and psi is very meaningful to the scientist who does the original research. However, that would not be the case for the replicator. If we assume that an experiment must be meaningful for the subjects, and it is for its designer, then it may also need to be meaningful for the replicators in order to elicit the psi processes being studied.

Increasing attention has been given to the meaning of chance, of randomicity, and of our very definitions of psi. Our "probabilistic science" has offered us postdictive analyses of patterns in the experimental data, whereas our aim is prediction. Rao (RIP 1981, 127-129) has challenged the status of this knowledge by proclaiming that if 50% of the previously conducted micro-PK studies, for instance, were significant, then we must hypothesize that 50% of all future micro-PK replication attempts will be significant. Rao's challenge must be answered for our present knowledge to be meaningful.

More crucial yet is the emerging question, What is psi? Is it a significant deviation from MCE over, say, 54 micro-PK experiments in a trend analysis? an "overall effect" over 1,000 trials? This is a far cry from one trial spontaneous case visions of fires, or of death in one's family! The assumption that psi is on a continuum, from "micro" to "macro" must be reevaluated, and new, more meaningful definitions proposed.

For future research in parapsychology, a more direct approach to the issue of meaning is in order, to comprehend its role in laboratory and spontaneous case work, and to resolve epistemological conflicts in the science. One line of inquiry in this direction would be Carl Jung's and Barbara Honegger's (RIP 1979, 19-21) various analyses and methodologies for investigating "synchronicities," or meaningful coincidences. The emphasis here would not be on the controversial issues of "acausality," but rather on the grouping of types of events and concomitant analyses of the depths of meaning associated with them for the experiencer. Another line of inquiry might involve the interpretive methodologies of symbolic anthropologists Turner, Geertz, and others, as outlined by Hess (RIP 1981, 39). These offer us the tools for systematically distinguishing the layers of meaning in the social contexts of the laboratory and of the spontaneous case setting. The science of sociolinguistics is yet another route. This field has developed analyses and methodologies for delineating the uses and meaning of language and other communication forms in any social interactions. Psi-communication "codes," "levels," "styles," and "grammars" may well play an equal and integrated role with that of the verbal and nonverbal forms, thus giving us a handle on where meaning and purpose are effecting interactions in the laboratory or in the poltergeist family milieu, for example.

THE PAST IS PROLOGUE: THE EXPLORATION OF A NEW CONTEXT FOR PARAPSYCHOLOGY

Stephan A. Schwartz (The Mobius Group)

The great documents of humanity--the Bible, the Bhagavad Gita, the Secret of the Golden Flower, and the Koran among them-- all contain examples of what today we would call psychic episodes. Clearly, the enigma of altered realities has compelled the attention of humankind at least from the beginning of culture. Uncontrolled, usually unbidden, and largely anecdotal, this body of experiences continues to grow to the present day and in historical terms could be considered the first epoch of parapsychology. Beginning 100 years ago, researchers from a range of disciplines banded together to begin a second epoch--the study of psychic functioning using the objective tools of science. Now, on the occasion of our centenary celebration, perhaps it would be wise to consider a new context for our work, one which builds on research that has gone before and uses that momentum to propel parapsychology into a third epoch-- the era in which psychic functioning returns to the mainstream of our culture, although this time not anecdotally but within the framework of science.

To do this will not be easy, and there are powerful forces both within and without parapsychology which work against it. The most obvious of these in both instances is the inertia of the status quo. Researchers within parapsychology tend to continue on the path of their greatest expertise (and, hence, least resistance), and critics sensing parapsychology's defensive mind-set, tenuous place at the table of science, and peripheral involvement in the mainstream continue to fall on it like wolves on a sheep, secure in the knowledge that parapsychology rarely attempts to make itself intelligible or relevant to society at large.

The Future of Psi Research

For several decades the juxtaposition of these forces has created a kind of stable tension, but there are now suggestions that a new factor has entered the equation in the form of extreme economic pressures to reduce scientific expenditures. While this pressure is not peculiar to parapsychology, there is small doubt that science as a whole will do little to protect or insure the psychologically isolated parapsychologist's already meager funding.

If parapsychology is to survive and grow, the impetus for this movement must come from the field itself. In the process of growing, however, we must be careful not to lose what has been gained. What is required is less a change in technique and more a change in philosophy. The same rigor and many of the same experimental methodologies should provide guidelines for the future. But serious questions must be answered.

Are we as researchers secure enough to examine why our experiments do not work? Are we, for instance, prepared to acknowledge the full import of the observer effect, and psi-mediated instrumental response? Is this Association really interested in developing psychic functioning as more than a laboratory curiosity? Do we believe it has a use? Are we prepared to expand beyond the narrow confines of statistical analysis--while still retaining its strengths--to actively seek out contacts with anthropologists, psychologists, and others whose work has tangency with parapsychology? Do we see it as nurturing and being nurtured by other disciplines? In the face of an enormous public interest in this subject area and the fact that there is great confusion and ambiguity surrounding the central issues attendant to psychic functioning, why has formal parapsychology abdicated its natural role as leader to the charlatans and speculators whose statements fill the public press and do so much to form society's impressions of what constitutes parapsychology? Exactly why does parapsychology eschew discussion about the implications of its research and what they have to say about the nature of humanity? These are not easy questions, and they will not be quickly answered, for addressing each raises yet further challenges. But address and answer them we must, and perhaps our greatest goal is this question: If parapsychology does not change will it celebrate a bicentennial?

We would recommend that a task force be established to examine these issues and to poll the Association's membership for their feelings, thoughts, and suggestions as a first step towards turning our present obstacles into strengths.

SOCIAL AND ETHICAL ISSUES IN PSI RESEARCH*

PARAPSYCHOLOGICAL EXCHANGE AS AN AVENUE TO WORLD PEACE

Stanley Krippner (Saybrook Institute)

In this era of international tension, it would appear wise to make the maximum use of any available resource for alleviating disharmony among the superpowers. It could be argued that parapsychological information-sharing represents a minor but by no means unimportant avenue to scientific exchange and cooperation between the U.S.S.R., on the one hand, and the U.S.A. and Western Europe, on the other.

During my three trips to the Soviet Union, I was besieged with questions on psi research from a wide variety of persons, many of them representing important scientific institutions. Although Soviet officials might deny that parapsychological experimentation is carried out in their country, informal contacts indicate that both nonofficial research and secret official research is being conducted.

A decade ago, that prestigious journal Questions of Philosophy acknowledged that "some so-called parapsychological events actually occur." But it was also stated that these phenomena should be studied by already existing fields of science, e.g., biology, physics, psychology. In other words, no new science of "parapsychology" or "psychoenergetics" was needed to investigate ESP and PK.

Soviet newspapers and magazines provide a great variety of opinions on psi research and related issues. The most highly publicized sensitive in the U.S.S.R. today is Juna Davitashvili, a healer from the Republic of Georgia. The attention given to her is in excess of what would be expected in the case of a similar person living in the United States, the United Kingdom, or most Western European nations.

Western parapsychologists travelling to the Soviet Union are

---

*Organized and chaired by Stanley Krippner (Saybrook Institute)

advised to make their contacts officially, if at all possible. The
U. S. S. R. is a monolithic, not a pluralistic, society; recognition of
this fact will make exchange and travel easier and will avoid problems for both visitors and their contacts. When Soviet scientists
and psychic sensitives are contacted informally, any exchanges of
information or materials should be open and nonsecretive.

Esalen Institute has recently inaugurated a Soviet-American
Exchange Program to facilitate world peace by encouraging (1) the
dissemination of information; (2) the sponsorship of seminars; and
(3) the promotion of dialogues among scientists in the area of human potential. This program has attained official status in the
U. S. S. R. through the office of the Academy of Sciences' Commission for the Development of Human Potential. Programs are currently being carried out with the cooperation of the Soviet Institute
for Psychiatry and Foreign Affairs, the Association for Humanistic
Psychology, and similar groups. The first two years of this program have been quite successful with scholars from both countries
receiving favorable receptions in their travels. Parapsychology is
one of the topics which is discussed; others include holistic health,
sports psychology, accelerated learning, and social transformation.

SUPPORT NETWORKS FOR RESEARCHERS WHO ARE INVESTIGATING MASSIVE PSI PHENOMENA

Janet Lee Mitchell (Brooklyn, N. Y.)

Exploring the unknown is sometimes frightening, especially
for those who choose to investigate massive psi phenomena outside
the laboratory. Many present-day researchers seem reluctant to
confront phenomena comparable to those reported by the early researchers. The PA, as a group, seems to look askance at independent researchers who examine massive phenomena and dramatic
phenomena are sometimes rejected. We worry about critics but we
should be more concerned about how hypercritical we are of each
other. We are the skeptics, remember, who have dedicated our
lives to investigating these matters. Those who question our findings without doing their homework should be correctly identified as
obstructionists.

Why is parapsychology plagued by the extinction paradigm?
One possibility is that researchers may be afraid of psi phenomena
but either not know or admit this. Repressed fear may manifest itself as denial or rationalization, in which massive psi may be explained as artifact or denied outright, while we intellectualize about
a repeatable phenomenon. If we suppress first perceptions of psi
for our comfort, it is unlikely we will ever witness its manifestation repeatably.

Or, what happens when a person in the lab demonstrates outstanding psi abilities? Do we pattern our experiments around their abilities or try to fit them into our theories? We need to be extremely careful to sustain their abilities as we try to discern how these abilities become operative.

Batcheldor introduced a psychological theory concerning suppression of massive phenomena. He states that whereas one could argue that phenomena which evade verification have no objective reality, it is also possible for a class of phenomena to exist that disappear when one attempts to verify them by altering their surrounding conditions. This is true of certain psychological phenomena, as well as of ostensible paranormal events. Batcheldor also points out that whereas mental psi phenomena can be conceived as a form of human behavior, we do not usually think of macro-PK as behavior. If we thought of it as an exceptional form of human behavior, we wouldn't be surprised to find that it is sensitive to critical observation. These seem to be important considerations because if one has never seen large-scale psi phenomena, there may be something wrong with the observational techniques.

We may be able to facilitate our work by establishing support networks based on our individual interests in massive psi phenomena. Research teams may be needed to view such phenomena from different perspectives of background and experience. Some researchers may not be suited to investigate certain cultural environments with which they are unfamiliar and anthropologists might be added to the team.

It may be much more comfortable to infer ESP via statistics, but should the wealth of information in large-scale phenomena go unexamined? It is unsettling to be involved with massive psi phenomena. Observations may shake one's long-held concepts of reality and one may wonder about self-delusion. One tries to maintain a critical balance while evaluating new perceptions. While under this stress, one may be driven back to statistical analyses of ESP if colleagues shun and discredit one's work.

Courage is the ability to confront what one can imagine. We imagine psychic phenomena to be real and frequent. Let's have the courage to observe these phenomena and report them without fear of our colleagues' disapproval, but with their advice and support on how best to do our job. And, if a finding is determined through diligent observation, let's have faith in one another's abilities and not invalidate the phenomena, discount the scientist's work, and ignore anything that isn't at a .01 level (two-tailed).

We need to ask ourselves if we are investigating psi phenomena or suppressing it? And if we are suppressing psi (because we're the ones in the best position to do so), why are we doing so? We need to understand why we aren't getting more information when massive psi phenomena occur. The original researchers apparently had each others' support in doing the work as accurately as possible and stating their opinions about their observations. We are many more now, but we should still feel a general sense of solidarity among PA members. We have a right to be afraid as we enter unknown regions of human potential; forming networks of advice and support would remove stress from independent researchers so that they could more efficiently investigate psi phenomena.

THE ESALEN INSTITUTE SOVIET-AMERICAN EXCHANGE PROGRAM

James L. Hickman (Esalen Institute)

Michael Murphy, co-founder of Esalen Institute, traveled to the Soviet Union for the first time in 1971; I went there initially in 1972 with Dr. Stanley Krippner. Many of the people we met during those early visits have been invited to the PA several times but have been unable to attend. The official restrictions on foreign travel by Soviet scientists have prevented their participation. Yet the travel and contact we have had there over the past several years have shown us that Soviet involvement and participation in future PA conferences is possible.

Recent international developments, particularly the rising threat of nuclear war and the deteriorating state of Soviet-American relations, have stimulated attempts to establish alternative, nongovernmental channels of communication between the superpowers. This approach to international relations is referred to as Track Two diplomacy. Two groups engaged in this activity are the International Physicians for the Prevention of Nuclear War and the Lawyers for Social Responsibility. The common theme in such initiatives is to create a dialogue within the context of each profession to address the critical issues that can guarantee a more peaceful world for the future.

At Esalen Institute, we have established a Soviet-American Exchange Program to encourage the dissemination of information, the sponsorship of seminars, and the promotion of dialogues among scientists working in disciplines which seek to develop human potentials that are neglected by mainstream science and culture. Among these neglected potentials are physical fitness, emotional health, sensory range and acuity, management of stress, creativity, imaginative problem-solving, flexibility, empathy, tolerance of ambiguity, paranormal perception, and spiritual understanding.

In a broad sense, there is a surprising overlap of themes in human development evident in both Soviet and American cultures. There is a remarkable symmetry between Soviet and American interests in this field. The Soviet phrase "hidden human reserves," for example, is almost identical to the American term "human potential" as a guiding idea. Mental training in sports, holistic health, esoteric religions, innovative psychotherapies, and parapsychology are actively being explored by the scientific and lay communities in both countries.

Resistance to many of these ideas surfaces in similar ways. Over the past several years, for example, there has been an open debate in the Soviet media about the scientific validity of psychical research and psychic healing. A special commission has recently been formed in the Soviet Academy of Sciences to prove that all such phenomena are unscientific and "a return to Lysenkoism." Yet, at the same time, the Ministry of Health has established a clinic in Moscow where people can be treated by psychic healers under the guidance of physicians. A recent issue of Ogonyok, the official magazine of the Communist Party, published a sympathetic discussion of parapsychology and related themes by respected scientists. Dr. Alexander Spirkin, a member of the U.S.S.R. Academy of Sciences and Chairman of the Department of Dialectical Materialism in the Institute of Philosophy, is preparing a synthesis of Marxist/Leninist doctrine and human potential theories.

It is difficult to judge how extensive officially sponsored psi research is, since most of the published reports in the open literature appear in the popular press. However, in my opinion, a main focus of Soviet research efforts is to identify the physiological and environmental conditions necessary to facilitate psi functioning. Soviet researchers emphasize the applications of such skills. Paranormal functioning is usually regarded to be a power that could enrich society and create a more positive future.

Our strategy in expanding our exchange program with the Soviet Union is to encourage and facilitate professional organizations like the Parapsychological Association to make contact with their Soviet colleagues. I believe it is important that such an endeavor be initiated by the PA at this time. Today there is increasing discussion in the military and intelligence communities about possible weapons applications for psychic skills. Whether or not this is a realistic view, it is being pursued actively by both the American and Soviet military communities. I encourage the PA to engage the world's scientists in a dialogue about the ethics of such a utilization of these skills. It is time for America and the Soviet Union to join together in a creative task such as this. Let us dramatize to all nations that parapsychology lends insight into the finest untapped resources of the human being and that these offer exciting alternatives to the many destructive relationships our two nations have pursued for so long.

Following appropriate guidelines for maintaining official contact in these areas, we can begin such a dialogue. It is time we help lead the world into an age marked by the human race instead of the arms race.

APPLICATIONS OF PSI*

ON THE QUESTION OF APPLICATION

K. Ramakrishna Rao (Institute for Parapsychology, FRNM)

References to "psychic" applications abound in antiquity. The alleged practices of psi in such endeavors as divining, scrying, healing, and black magic still exist in many of the nonliterate societies. For example, Melanesian islanders believe in and practice a force called mana, which Pierre Saintyves defined as "a kind of material fluid devoid of personal intelligence ... in which the intentions of men and spirits can be incorporated so that they can fulfill their aims."

Notwithstanding the age-old belief in psi practice and the claims of psychics all over the world, psi researchers in the past have evinced little interest in studying the practical applications of psi. This was so despite the fact that, as F. C. S. Schiller pointed out, such applications are important for establishing a widespread conviction in the reality of psi. In 1945 J. B. Rhine raised the question: "Can any practical use be made of these parapsychical abilities?" "The answer," he wrote, "has invariably had to be, 'NO.' No practical use can be made of them with our present state of knowledge. They are not reliable enough." Our pioneers were motivated more by psi's implications for discovering "a true philosophy by which men can live better and more happily" than the possibility of applying it for achieving our common needs.

Have we made sufficient progress since 1945 to warrant a more optimistic response? Is psi reliable enough now to render its applications feasible? I am afraid the answer has to be "No" again. It is not that we have not made much progress. On the contrary, important strides have been made during the past quarter of a century that give a reasonable hope for replicating psi in our experimental laboratories, even though we are still far from making any claim of producing the phenomena on demand. We are, however, still mystified by the enigma of psi's elusiveness and annoyed

---

*Organized and chaired by K. Ramakrishna Rao (Institute for Parapsychology, FRNM)

by the low signal and high noise in psi retrieval. Hence ethical questions continue to haunt us when we seriously contemplate writing a grant application for applied psi research. It seems to me that the matter of highest priority in this context is a reasonable demonstration that at least some psi effects are replicable in a predictive sense.

If it is the case that psi effects are weak but replicable, we would then be led into developing techniques and strategies designed to filter out noise and optimize the signal. Multiple calling and other redundancy techniques suggest themselves as possible methodological approaches for quality enhancement in psi detection.

Do we, then, need to shelve the question of application until the replication issue is favorably settled? Not necessarily so. First of all, whether or not there is valid justification for such practices, psychic practices for utilitarian purposes continue to exist even in Western societies. Systematic studies of these are necessary and important not only for determining the scope, range, and validity of these practices in the context of applying psi, but also for understanding the nature of psi itself. These field studies in a sense show that there is no hard line that separates applied and pure research in parapsychology.

Again, there are areas where judicious application of psi is not unwarranted. These involve low risk and high reward cases. For example, an oil executive who is unable to choose between four different sites for drilling on the basis of available information may seek the help of a parapsychologist, and the parapsychologist need have no ethical worries as long as he or she makes no false promises.

Finally, even if applied psi research is proven to be feasible, is it really desirable? Considering its potential for misuse in warfare and the possibility of creating social chaos by threatening the disruption of personal privacy, not a few among us are concerned that in unravelling the secrets of psi we might make the same but more regrettable mistake we made when we split the atom but had little control over those who would have access to its awesome power. But, then, we may wonder whether psi-missing and other self-obscuring aspects of psi, which are currently irritating because they stand in the way of psi control, may not be nature's defense against the misuse of psi after all.

PROPOSED APPLICATION OF ASSOCIATIONAL REMOTE VIEWING TO OIL AND NATURAL RESOURCE RECOVERY

Russell Targ (SRI International)

The purpose of this investigation is to increase the accuracy and reliability of remote sensing of geological and geographical sites through the use of novel targeting procedures. The goal of these efforts is to develop techniques that can describe and locate the specific position of distant, hidden, or underground items. We are seeking greater resolution than the general terrain and architectural descriptions that remote viewing (RV)* has provided in the past.

One approach to the location of hidden or distant targets is termed "associational remote viewing (ARV)." Using this nonstatistical technique, the area in which a desired item might be located is divided into a countable number of discrete locations (the number or size of these quantized locations does not alter the ARV procedure).

The essence of ARV is the association, or linking, of a laboratory-based token object or picture with each of the possible discrete locations in which the target object might be found. This associational method is used because there is strong and convincing evidence that paranormal perception is relatively unsuccessful at directly carrying out analytical tasks, such as determining numbers, or choosing among known targets. Once a viewer knows the actual nature of a target pool, e.g., numbers, letters, specific geographical sites, etc., he is then faced with an extremely difficult signal-to-noise problem: his subjective memory and association to these targets are a potentially stronger source of imagery than the paranormal effect from the target itself.

In the current assessment of location applications, we wish to obtain "address" information about the target site. Instead of asking the viewer for the numerical address of the target, he is asked to describe the associated target object, which has been previously linked to the target address, even though that specific address was unknown, at the time, by the viewer.

For example, in order to examine an electromagnetic description of psi several years ago, SRI attempted to send one of six possible numbers to two viewers in a submerged submarine. We did not believe that a number from 1 to 6 could be reliably sent to viewers in the submarine directly, because this has historically been one of the most unsuccessful types of tasks attempted by parapsychologists. Therefore, instead each of the six numbers carried aboard the submarine were associated with six different San Francisco Bay Area locations (e.g., Number 1 was associated with Hoover Tower, Number 2 was linked to the Golden Gate Bridge, etc.). Thus, at the appointed time for number sending, the "send-

---

*This phenomenon is the ability of certain individuals to access and describe, by means of mental processes, remote geographical locations up to several thousand kilometers distant from their physical location after being given only geographical coordinates or a known person on whom to target.

ers" positioned themselves at the location that had been previously linked to the message chosen for that day. The task of the viewers in the submarine was to describe that location (from a target pool that was unknown to them). They were then shown the list of possible locations and asked to be their own judge and select the one that most closely matched their descriptions. This location, keyed to a number, could lead to the successful receipt of the day's number. This one-in-six number coding technique was attempted on two consecutive days, with the correct number being received both times by the two viewers in the submarine.

Since these initial trials, there have been both successful and unsuccessful series. Two successful series were applied in the forecasting of the winners of horse races. The unsuccessful series were the victims of psi-missing, in which we had very accurate descriptions of an incorrect target. We believe that this difficulty can be overcome by using several viewers and several target pools.

These and other ARV trials suggest that associational remote viewing has potential for the discrimination and identification of missing or hidden targets and the answering of a large variety of other questions that lend themselves to formulation into discrete sets. We feel that this approach should be pursued with regard to the important questions of improved judging and new techniques to train viewers for improved reliability. The possibility should be explored of increasing the potential target pool from five objects toward 10. The potential power of this ARV approach for general information-gathering applications should not be underestimated.

THE POSSIBLE APPLICATION OF PSI TO HEALING

Marilyn J. Schlitz (Mind Science Foundation)

The notion of application has intrinsic appeal for most parapsychologists, and due to its obvious potential along these lines, psychic healing holds special interest.

Claims of seemingly miraculous cures are by no means new to parapsychology or even to our culture. In fact, such ideas have existed throughout human literary history. In the eyes of the lay person, the scope of "psychic healing" is broad indeed. However, much of what is discussed in this context can be attributed to a wide gamut of non-psi explanations. Included here are such things as placebo effect, suggestion, wishful thinking, and spontaneous remission. To a healing practitioner a clear distinction between these categories is not always useful--if the patient gets better, that's all that matters. Dealing with the issue from a parapsychological perspective, however, we are concerned with the genuine role which psi might play in the healing process.

Rao offered some clarity in addressing the problem, suggesting, as it were, three levels in which psi might enter the healing process. The first of these is diagnostic, in which the healer gains information about the state of the healee via nonsensory means. The second is prescriptive. In this stage, a nonmedical practitioner obtains information via psi in order to tell the patient what he must do to regain health. The third level involves a healer's ability to cause some direct physiological change in another living system, without physical intervention.

From an experimental perspective, each area has received some, albeit small, interest. Certainly the largest body of experimental work has addressed the ostensible role of psi in effecting change in another physiological system. This line of research might best be considered as psychokinesis on living systems. A review of this literature reveals over 70 published reports dealing with psi influence on living systems. If one considers the potential of a psi experimenter effect in anpsi experiments, the list is even greater.

Such a review strongly supports the need for careful consideration in drawing conclusions from the data. From an experimental perspective, work in this area is difficult for a number of reasons and the methodology is far from being perfected. Research with living systems requires a far different approach than psi tests with dice, cards, or other inanimate objects. First of all, living systems do not behave in statistically elegant patterns, giving discrete responses which have known theoretical distributions. Also, living systems possess sensory acquisitions which can cause changes in behavior and physiology due to variations in uncontrolled factors of very small magnitudes. These changes could well be interpreted as due to PK when in fact they represent artifacts. As such, it is necessary to shield the target organism from the participant healer just as one would shield a subject from an agent in a GESP experiment.

Because the dependent variable in healing experiments is a form of physiological response, different statistical methods are called for. Because of the variability of the response due to individual differences, it is necessary to use either carefully matched control groups or a high aim/low aim experimental design when appropriate. In addition to the problem of artifactual results, care should be taken to reduce error variance and to increase the sensitivity of the statistical tests employed. In many instances, the parameter being measured involves a partially subjective component. This can lead both to increased error variance in the case of random errors of measurement, and artifacts, if the measurer is not blind to the groupings of members into conditions.

Frequently the experimental reports are too informed and imprecise. Tests may consist of too few trials to conclude anything. Tools of measurement have been crude and adequate double-blind conditions have been lacking. Control and experimental samples have often been treated in very different ways, e.g., different rooms, shelves in an incubator, or handling circumstances. By and large, adequate baselines for comparison between control and experimental conditions is lacking.

In conclusion, it is obvious that a clear methodology for dealing with PK on living systems is needed. The implications for application of this line of research are straightforward. But before we can seriously discuss the possibility of psi applications to healing, we must be certain that our effects are robust, and not subject to some subtle artifacts of experimental design. In this sense, we must be sure not to put the application cart before the experimental horse.

THE MATTER OF REDUNDANCY

George P. Hansen (Institute for Parapsychology, FRNM)

Although psi abilities are currently being used in many practical applications (e.g., Hibbard and Worring, Psychic Criminology, 1982; Schwartz, Omni, March 1979, 94-99, 116), greater reliability will be needed before becoming more useful and generally accepted. Certainly progress has been made in understanding psi--it is not completely unpredictable. Nevertheless it is still too uncontrollable, and this can lead to potential problems (e.g., psi-missing in healing situations).

Of course, most research is oriented toward understanding psi so that it can be elicited more frequently. There has been some progress, especially with work on internal attention states as discussed by Honorton (in Wolman, Handbook, 1977, 435-472). Although scoring has been considerably better than chance, it does not approach 100%. Such methods are limited.

Redundancy techniques (repeated responses to the same target and then combining them to form a majority vote) may provide stronger results. There has been some notable work in this area. Thouless and Scott (IJP, 1960, No. 3, 21-45) discussed several issues involved with the repeated guessing technique. Taetzsch (IJP, 1962, No. 1, 35-66) proposed a psi communication system using repeated responses. Ryzl, working with Stepanek, was able to successfully transmit 15 digits accurately using thousands of trials (JP, 1966, 18-30). Carpenter (RIP 1981, 111), with unselected subjects, was able to transmit the word "Peace" by using index trials and mood scales to predict hitting or missing for each subject.

The studies mentioned above are extremely encouraging. Additional techniques might be utilized to strengthen the signal even further. For instance, L. Rudolph (in B. Shapin and L. Coly, eds., Communication and Parapsychology, 1980, 150-167) suggested that coding theory could be applied to similar situations to enhance the reliability. However, some caution is necessary. Because psi seems to be "goal directed" and may enter at various levels of an experiment, Kennedy (JP, 1979, 290-314) suggested that the focus of the psi source should be the individual trial for the majority vote technique to work as a signal-enhancement method.

Free-response procedures generally do focus on individual trials; however, relatively little work has been done with majority-vote techniques in these situations. Studies by Barker, Messer, and Drucker (RIP 1975, 165-167) and Whitson, Bogart, Palmer, and Tart (Proceedings of the IEEE, 1976, 1550-1551) support the idea that majority vote can be effective with free-response ESP while Weiner and McCain (JP, 1981, 156-157) were unsuccessful with it. To be more effective, response bias possibilities might need to be reduced. Procedures for this have received almost no investigation.

THEORIES FOR RSPK*

SIMILARITIES BETWEEN RSPK AND PSYCHOMOTOR EPILEPSY

William G. Roll and Elson de A. Montagno (Psychical Research Foundation)

Since the first years of the Society for Psychical Research, the poltergeist has been one of the most rewarding subjects for research. Physicist Sir William Barrett (PSPR, 1911, 377-412), one of the founders of the Society, made the point that if the observer arrives on the scene while the disturbances are still going on, he or she is likely to be in a position to rule out fraud or hallucinations as reasonable explanations.

Barrett spoke from personal experience--which by now has been shared by many others, including the participants of this roundtable. He made several other points. The occurrences are reported from all parts of the world and go back to early periods of time; they are usually though not invariably associated with the presence of a child or young person of either sex; this person sometimes simulates the effects if the real ones have abated; the occurrences are shortlived, lasting anywhere from a few days to several months; and they show intelligence. These observations have all been substantiated in recent studies.

Though the poltergeist is a worldwide phenomenon, the term makes us think of it as peculiarly German. It seems appropriate that the person who has pursued the poltergeist longer and more persistently than anyone else should be a German scientist. This roundtable is a fitting occasion to honor Hans Bender for his important work on the poltergeist.

Bender suggests that poltergeist effects, or RSPK (as we now also call these phenomena), are partially to be understood in terms of transpersonal structures, the archetypes of C. G. Jung. It seems clear to us, too, that the poltergeist performs on a larger scene than any single mind or brain could supply. It also seems

---
*Organized by W. G. Roll (Psychical Research Foundation); chaired by Hans Bender (University of Freiburg)

clear that some of the features of the poltergeist are related to psychological or physiological conditions in the central person or "agent."

Human brains are structured similarly, though their "contents" differ. We shall discuss the possibility that some of the characteristics of RSPK which are found in many of the cases may reflect similarities in the brain processes of the agents, and that some of the ways in which the cases differ may reflect the different cognitive and emotional characteristics of these individuals.

Ever since psychical researchers discovered a relation between RSPK occurrences and specific individuals, it has seemed possible that the human brain or mind may be involved in these incidents.

More recently, when it was found that the central person often suffered from organic or functional disorders (such as epilepsy, headaches, and hysteria), the possibility was enhanced that the secret of the poltergeist may in part may lie in the human brain. More specifically, W.G.R. (EJP, 1978, 167-200) has proposed that the recurrent neuronal discharges that result in epileptic symptoms may also play a role in RSPK.

As a result of an examination of RSPK characteristics, E.A.M. (see pages 272-273) has proposed that psychomotor epilepsy may provide a neurobiological model for RSPK and that the same brain structures and functions may be involved in both.

A comparison between the symptomatology of psychomotor epilepsy (PME) and RSPK shows suggestive parallels: the movements of objects in RSPK may be analogous to the convulsive body movements in PME; the visual and auditory apparitions sometimes associated with RSPK may be analogous to the visual and auditory illusions and hallucinations of PME; the knocking and rapping sounds frequently associated with RSPK may be analogous to the rhythmic tonic-clonic movements of PME; the emotions and memories reflected in RSPK disturbances may be analogous to the affective and memory disturbances of PME; the way in which RSPK incidents sometimes symbolize significant ideas may be analogous to the contents of the forced thinking and dreamy states of PME; finally the repetitive involvement of specific objects and areas in RSPK may be analogous to the recurrent, forced thinking, dreamy states, and automatization of PME.

Aside from these analogies we have noticed several features that seem to be the same for RSPK and PME: the two phenomena both peak in the early teens; they involve equal proportions of males and females; they are worldwide in distribution; they involve displays of energy; they consist in recurrent effects; they are triggered spontaneously or in response to arousal; they are often associated with altered states of consciousness; and they often express emotional states, particularly violence.

A NEUROBIOLOGICAL MODEL FOR PSYCHOKINESIS

Elson de A. Montago and William G. Roll (Psychical Research Foundation)

In the preceding paper we outlined some reasons for believing that RSPK may involve neurobiological processes. In particular, we observed that RSPK phenomena resemble the complex symptomatology known as psychomotor epilepsy (PME).

PME is primarily associated with disturbances in the limbic system, an intricate neural network which includes the neocorticolimbic connections, the higher brainstem, the reticular formation, and structures adjacent to these.

Neuronal disturbances in the limbic system may be associated with three features of the poltergeist: (1) the informational content of the occurrences, such as the way in which they seem to express the agent's memories and emotions; (2) the mode of expression of these emotions and memories in the agent's environment; and (3) the times in the circadian cycle when this expression is likely to occur.

The parts of the limbic system that may play a role in shaping these three characteristics of RSPK are the temporal lobes, the gray matter of the higher brainstem, and the reticular formation. The temporal lobes, we suggest, are intimately involved in RSPK because of their association with memories, cognition, and behavior which seem to be expressed in many RSPK incidents. The temporal lobes, you may recall, are the areas where Wilder Penfield activated long forgotten memories through electrical stimulation of the exposed cortex of 1,132 patients. More recently another world-famous neurosurgeon, Blaine Nashold, evoked feeling of fear and death and other strong emotions by stimulation of the gray matter peri-aqueductal in the higher brainstem.

In PME the site of epileptogenic focus determines the types of symptoms. For instance, a discharge in the temporal lobe or in the gray matter of the higher brainstem may result in episodes of unconsciousness during which highly skillful activities are carried out, while a focus in the sensory or motor cortices (spreading to the higher brainstem) may result in crude major convulsions. This same distinction may be reflected in two types of poltergeist occurrences which we may refer to as "crude" and "smart" poltergeists (Stevenson [JASPR, 1972, 233-252] has made a similar distinction in a different context). "Crude" poltergeists consist of phenomena that show little if any cognitive guidance, such as explosive sounds and indiscriminate movements and breakages of objects. "Smart" poltergeists are cases characterized by responsive sounds or lights and by moving objects which, for instance, avoid obstructions and settle gently on the floor instead of falling. According to the PME model, we should expect these two types of poltergeist cases to be associated with neuronal disturbances in different connections of the limbic system. There is at least one respect in which RSPK is clearly distinct from familiar forms of psychomotor activities: it occurs outside the body. In exploring for a process which transforms neuronal disturbances to RSPK disturbances it may be relevant that in several RSPK cases the onset of the phenomena is associated with the abatement of organic or functional disorders, such as epilepsy and hysteria. This suggests the existence of a switching mechanism which controls how neuronal disturbances are to be expressed.

Brainstem structures help to determine in which ways cortical activities, normal or pathological, are expressed by the body. These structures may also provide a role for psi. For instance, the gray matter at the higher brainstem and the reticular discharges which, say, might result in a psychosomatic disorder, may be inhibited within these structures and consequently seek other forms of release.

The reticular formation plays a central role in controlling the circadian rhythm. This function may affect RSPK because the phenomena usually occur when the agent is awake. During sleep, the reticular formation inhibits the nerve impulses from the sense organs to the brain hemispheres and it inhibits the nerve impulses from the brain to the body. The higher brainstem and reticular formation also help to inhibit the sympathetic nervous system during sleep and to activate the parasympathetic, while the opposite conditions prevail during waking hours. Since RSPK appears to be associated with arousal it is to be expected that the sympathetic system is dominant.

To summarize this preliminary sketch of a theory for RSPK, we suggest that the process involves neuronal discharges in the temporal lobes and brainstem. In this respect the process is the same as for PME. It further appears that RSPK depends on activation of the sympathetic nervous system and on inhibition of the neuronal pathways between the brain cortex and the body, as discussed before. It is beyond the scope of this discussion to speculate about the nature of the channels for RSPK outside the central nervous system. We may note, however, that the rotating beam theory (Roll, Burdick, and Joines, JASPR, 1973, 267-281, and RIP, 1974, 64-67) presupposes transmissions of energy from "antennas" on the two sides of the body of the RSPK agent. This seems consistent with our thinking that the temporal lobes and higher brainstem are involved in RSPK (note that a discharge in one lobe is often mirrored by one in the other).

As a final observation, it is interesting that these structures, which may play important roles in RSPK, have stimulated the imagination of neurobiologists more than any other part of the brain. Penfield has proposed that the higher brainstem mechanisms constitute the physical basis of the mind, and the central gray the area where mind acts on the body.

DIFFICULTIES OF INTERPRETATION AND THEORY IN MINOR HAUNTINGS

Alan Gauld (University of Nottingham)

Difficulties in interpretation and theory are illustrated by a sample case. The case (largely nocturnal) is a recent one of what may be called "minor hauntings." It took place in a house occupied by a young couple with three children (the eldest aged seven). The initial phenomena consisted of movements and displacements of an ornament and a cupboard. The movements of the latter were witnessed, and some took place while it was being held. There were also footsteps, rappings, and occasional trifling but unmistakable imitative noises. Witnesses included persons who were not immediate members of the household. On one occasion the figure of an unknown woman was seen standing at an upstairs window when the house was locked and empty. The family members were inclined to link the phenomena (which died out in a few weeks) to the recent and gruesome death of a former occupant of the house, an elderly gentleman of marked eccentricities.

This case is characteristic of ones that are often encountered, but not often written about, no doubt because of the trivial and debatable nature of the alleged phenomena. And yet it raises numerous problems of interpretation: (1) Can we dismiss the case on the grounds of the fallibility of witness testimony? We must not let the fact that most of the phenomena are of a trivial kind mislead us into supposing that the testimony (which was contemporary with the later phenomena) was not good. (2) Ordinary natural causes will not provide a satisfactory explanation unless combined with suppositions about the fallibility of testimony. (3) The case does not fit the mold of an ordinary person-centered poltergeist--there was no single person whose presence was essential to the phenomena, nor were there any indications of unusual "family tensions." Yet it is doubtful whether we can sharply separate such cases from poltergeists, for the phenomena overlap. (4) A spiritualist would probably associate the phenomena with the old man who died. But there were no signs of "intelligence" except insofar as imitative noises may be thought to imply it. A medium brought to the house (without prior knowledge of where he was being taken) stated categorically that there was no "spirit entity" in the house. (He then proceeded to confound things thoroughly by giving "just through clairvoyance" a remarkably accurate account of the peculiarities and death of the elderly gentleman mentioned above.)

None of the usual theories of hauntings and poltergeist phenomena cover this case satisfactorily, nor can I think of an alternative. I remain completely baffled. Yet such "minor hauntings" are in my experience the kind of case with which the investigator is most commonly confronted.

Part 4: Invited Speakers from the
People's Republic of China*

REPORT ON INVESTIGATIONS INTO "EXCEPTIONAL HUMAN
BODY FUNCTION" IN THE PEOPLE'S REPUBLIC OF CHINA

Harold E. Puthoff (SRI International)

Although interest in exceptional human functioning has historically been part of China's tradition, recent widespread interest was triggered by a report in the March 11, 1979, Sichuan Daily. In that report it was claimed that a young boy, 12-year-old Tang Yu, was able to read written material placed in physical contact with his ears. Although this claim was soon being criticized as unscientific in, e.g., The People's Daily, in May 1979, reports began to surface from all over China that children elsewhere were duplicating this feat.

These reports caught the attention of scientists, many of whom assumed that some form of rudimentary biological function was at cause, since the early reports typically involved "reading" through the skin. Thus the initial approach to the phenomenon appears to parallel in many respects the earlier work of Jules Romains reported in his book, Eyeless Sight (1924/1978) and similar Soviet investigations into so-called "dermo-optic perception" (Soviet Psychology and Psychiatry, 1963). From this beginning, such functioning in China goes under a rubric which translates as Exceptional Human Body Function (EHBF). This phrase has now been broadened to include the entire range of phenomena that in the West are called "psi," since it was not long before the reading of Chinese characters, numbers, etc., extended to experiments involving noncontact forms of the phenomena (e.g., use of sealed containers, long distances, etc.).

As a result of growing scientific interest, a conference on parapsychology was held in February 1980 in Shanghai, sponsored by one of China's major monthly scientific periodicals, Nature Journal (Ziran Zazhi). Participants from over 20 colleges and research institutes were in attendance, along with 14 children purported to

---
*Chaired by H. E. Puthoff (SRI International)

possess EHBF skills, which they demonstrated at the conference. As a result of these demonstrations, a number of observers returned to their institutes to set up research programs and rigorous investigations began in earnest. These efforts led to a second conference on the subject in May 1981, held in Chongqing, and a continuing series of papers published in Ziran Zazhi, some of which have been translated and are available in English (Nature Journal [selected articles], Document No. FTD-1DCRS, T-1766-80, 26 Jan. 1981, Translation Div., Foreign Technology Div., Wright-Patterson AFB, 0, 45433).

As in the West, such research activities, conferences, and reports are not without controversy. Some criticism of methodology and reporting has appeared in the literature (Bulletin of the British Psychological Society, 1981, 125-26), and in October 1981 the State Science Commission set up a special group to study the phenomena, some of whose reports have cited cases in which the possibility of deception could not be ruled out. Nonetheless, vigorous research efforts are continuing in a number of university and research institutes, and a National Society of Human Body Science (roughly equivalent to the SPR and PA) is in the process of being formed.

October of 1981 was also the month in which a group of American and Canadian scientists, physicians, and educators, including me, had an opportunity to visit the People's Republic of China (P.R.C.) specifically for the purpose of meeting with Chinese researchers working in the EHBF area. The tour, organized by Dr. Stanley Krippner, took us to the cities of Beijing (Peking), Xian, and Shanghai, where we met some of the "EHBF children," and talked to a number of investigators working with them. During our visit, altogether five formal technical meetings were held with the scientists, physicians, and journal editors working in the field. The first was at the Friendship Hotel in Beijing; the second at the Beijing Medical College; the third, at Beijing University; the fourth at the Chinese Academy of Science's Institute of High Energy Physics in Beijing; and the fifth at the Yanan Hotel in Shanghai with the editors and staff of Nature Journal.

Our first discussions, held at the Friendship Hotel in Beijing, brought us together with researchers and educators from the following institutions: Beijing University physicists and biologists; Institute of High Energy Physics (Ch. Acad. Sci.); Institute of Biophysics (Ch. Acad. Sci.); Institute of Automation (Ch. Acad. Sci.); Beijing Astronomical Observatory (Ch. Acad. Sci.); Institute of Semiconductors (Ch. Acad. Sci.); Institute of Physics (Ch. Acad. Sci.); Physics Dept. of Beijing Teachers' College; and Institute of Traditional Chinese Medicine of Beijing.

This was followed up by visits to Beijing Medical College, Beijing University, and the Chinese Academy of Science's Institute of High Energy Physics. It was at this latter institute that we had our first opportunity for somewhat in-depth discussion of specific experiments.

Their basic experiment, apparently replicated many times under widely varying conditions, consisted of the remote viewing of Chinese characters or numbers sealed in an opaque bakelite container, inside of which was also some form of detector to register possible physical effects associated with the perceptions. The detectors used in this format included X-ray, nuclear emulsion, photographic films, photoelectric tubes, thermoluminescence dosimeters, and biological detectors. The claim made (backed up by raw data materials shown us, motion picture film of the experiments, and published papers) was that physical effects were registered during perception, and absent in the absence of perception. These included fogging of the films, and pulses on electrical output devices of the various detectors. The individuals carrying out the experiments were physicists, well respected in their own fields, using standard techniques and procedures familiar to them, as far as apparatus and analysis are concerned. It also appears that their work has some degree of official sanction, in that work in this area is considered part of their official work schedule, and in our visit we were cordially received by two of the Institute's Deputy Directors. These factors lend de facto credibility to their claims.

Later in the trip we met at length over a two-day period with the staff and Editor-in-Chief (Mr. He Chongying) of Nature Journal, and from him obtained an overview of the experimentation, results, conferences, and publication of the Chinese efforts.

It is impossible, of course, for one to evaluate accurately a nation's progress in the scientific study of exceptional human functioning on the basis of a visit of less than two weeks and the exchange of a few publications. As in the West, the study of exceptional human functioning is an endeavor which has provided many questions and few answers. Since this type of research continues to be in a state of flux throughout the world, one can say, however, that it represents an area where China has the opportunity to make important contributions. Those of us who visited the P.R.C. were particularly impressed by their scientists' efforts to correlate research findings with their ancient and distinctively national Chinese concepts (especially those of their non-Western medical traditions) on the one hand, and the contemporary perspective of modern science on the other. A well-known example is the search for electrophysiological correlates of acupuncture points and meridians; less well known (in the West) are the Chinese studies on the possible relationship between EHBF and qigong, an ancient discipline involving movement and deep breathing said to promote health and well being. Through exploring this rich historical tradition scientifically, the Chinese scientists may well contribute fresh ideas to the study of exceptional human functioning.

As those of us attending this conference know, the meeting is being held in England this year in part to commemorate the founding of the Society for Psychical Research 100 years ago, in 1882. To parapsychologists in the West, that date in a certain sense marks the beginning of formal investigation of parapsychological phenomena by the scientific/academic communities. It would also seem fitting that this event mark the beginning of formal exchange between researchers in the People's Republic of China and researchers in the West.

STUDY OF THE EXTRAORDINARY FUNCTION OF THE HUMAN BODY IN CHINA

Chen Hsin† and Mei Lei (Space Medico-Engineering Institute, Beijing, China)

General Background. On March 11, 1979, it was reported for the first time in Sichuan Ribao that a 12-year-old boy, Tang Yu, in Dazu County, Sichuan Province, had been discovered to be able to "recognize the characters (Chinese ideograms) with his ears." This evoked strong repercussions at home and abroad. Consequently, more than ten teenagers who also had this kind of function were discovered one after another in Beijing, Anhui, Hubei, and other places. In September 1979, Nature Journal* (Ziran Zazhi) carried a report on "Nonvisual Pattern Recognition" written by a correspondent of the journal on the basis of his personal observation. This article confirmed that the exceptional function of the human body, or, as it was depicted in the newspapers, "recognizing the characters with ears," actually exists and is worth studying. Other experimental observations by scientists of Beijing University, Anhui Teachers University, and other units, which verified the authenticity of the function, were reported in NJ in 1979 (715, 716, 780, 781).

In February 1980, in Shanghai, the Nature Journal editorial department presided over the "First Science Symposium on the Extraordinary Function of the Human Body," attended by representatives from eight provinces and three municipalities. After this the various exceptional functions of the human body, including "recognizing the characters with ears," became generally known as the "extraordinary function of the human body," which is now the general term being used in the Chinese literature.

With the impetus of the symposium, the research work has developed further in various places, and in May 1981 the "Second Science Symposium on the Extraordinary Function of the Human Body" was held in Chongqing. Some famous scientists submitted their papers and many others read their research reports at the symposium. Diverse thoughts from different schools were incorporated, but no conclusion was drawn at the symposium. Before

---

*All of the references cited in this paper are to Nature Journal and will be indicated by NJ, followed by the year and first page number.

the end of the symposium the Preparatory Committee of the Chinese Human-Body Science Institute was set up after deliberation and consultation. Afterwards, in January 1982, the preparatory committee convened a special discussion in physics.

The China Encyclopedic Almanac of 1981, published by the China Great Encyclopedia Press, uses the term "extraordinary function of the human body" in its column on science and technology, which introduces the development of the study of the extraordinary function of the human body in China, and also points out that "there are still some people holding sceptical attitudes with respect to the authenticity of the extraordinary function of the human body."

Studies of Chinese Scientists. During the past three years, the Chinese scientists have carried out the experimental studies described as follows. Under strictly controlled experimental conditions, the authenticity of the special inductive function of the human body, such as "recognizing the characters with the ears," was verified. To rule out possible artifacts as well as false results, and to insure the level of scientific rigor while continually improving the experimental methods, the experiments have been designed in keeping with the following requirements:

1) A specimen ("target" for recognition and its package) has to possess certain characteristics of "uniqueness" to insure that it not be duplicated and exchanged in designed experimental conditions.

2) The "target" for recognition has to be sealed in "opaque" and "irreversible" forms, so that, under the designed experimental conditions, if the package is opened it will be destroyed and cannot be completely restored; if it is not opened, the "target" in it cannot be recognized with ordinary sight.

3) Both the experimenters and the subject should be unaware of the content of the "target" to insure "double blind" conditions and to avoid hints (cues).

4) Reliable on-the-spot observation must be made by more than one person or by a videorecorder, which can be replayed for examination, or both.

5) The possibility of "guess by chance" should be ruled out statistically from the experimental results; in other words, the results should have "statistical significance."

Under these strict experimental conditions, some subjects whose functions were stronger were tested with dozens of specimens. The rate of absolutely correct identifications was more than 80% (NJ, 1979, 715), which indicated that one of the special inductive functions, the so called "recognizing the characters with the ears," existed objectively.

Scientists in Beijing University further found in experiments that among over 70 children aged about 10, a considerable proportion of subjects had the special inductive function of "recognizing the characters with the ears" (NJ, 1980, 334, 683). They concluded that this kind of function may be a general phenomenon to a certain extent among children in the relevant age group and inferred that this function was probably a potential physiological function of the human body. The "universality" discovered thus far further verified the authenticity of the extraordinary function of the human body and provided more subjects for research work.

Our experimental results also indicated that although the subjects who had the extraordinary function were not rare, there were few who had a stable strong function over the long term. In some conditions, the experimental results could be "reproduced," but they were not as "repeatable" on demand as in ordinary physical and chemical experimentation. They often showed apparent individual differences, and an undulating "instability" in the case of one subject.

As some researchers reported, apart from "recognizing characters with the ear," the human body may possess many other extraordinary functions. The researchers have searched after and observed such functions as psychokinesis, teleportation, and the like. Recording the equivalence-time curve of moving the hands of a watch by the extraordinary function of the human body, and observing the possibility of transferring a specimen out of a container from a hole smaller than the specimen itself are two more examples of extraordinary functions (NJ, 1981, 348, 652).

Some researchers have also carried out experimental investigations to determine the mechanism of the human body's extraordinary functions. The main efforts in this respect are as follows:

> The study of the special properties of the information carrier and human body radiation: To begin with, the "target" was sealed into a container made of different materials and in which there are different-size slits. Then tests were carried out so as to find out the effect of the differences in shielding materials and the size of the slits on the test results, thereby distinguishing some special properties of the information carrier. On the other hand, the corollary human body radiation of a subject in an extraordinary functional state was tested by the use of modern technology. The published papers on this subject include the effect of human body radiation on biodetectors and photo counters and on some phototransistor detectors, as well as the determination of the magnetic field distribution over an individual subject's body surface [NJ, 1981, 114].

Experiments involving irradiation of the ears, hands, and other sites of a person who has extraordinary functions with weak monochromatic light from a spectrometer confirmed that in these sites there existed an ability to perceive and distinguish the color of visible light (NJ, 1980, 336), and that persons who have extraordinary functions could perceive near-infrared light as well (NJ, 1981, 895). Experiments also confirmed that such persons could distinguish the North pole from the South pole of a magnet (NJ, 1981, 114) and could tell North from South by their extraordinary functions (NJ, 1980, 741; 1981, 292). Some researchers have also carried out experiments to investigate the image transfer function under bright-contrast stimulus conditions (NJ, 1981, 897), the perceptibility of an optical image in space (NJ, 1981, 900), and the sensitivity to different light waves (NJ, 1982, 104).

In regard to the study of the property of information processing and display, the published papers (NJ, 1980, 438; 1981, 185; 291; 1982, 274; 276) showed that during the process of recognizing targets by means of the special inductive function of the human body the following characteristics of perception have been experienced by the subjects: unfolding, enlarging, recognizing layer by layer, selecting by contrast, displaying step by step, and adjusting directions automatically.

We consider, however, that experimental research on the extraordinary function mechanism is preliminary, and that it needs further replication and deepening. On the basis of the experimental investigations, some researchers in China have made preliminary inquiries into the extraordinary function mechanism of the human body from a theoretical standpoint.

Information concerning the human body's extraordinary function as recorded in the ancient Chinese literature is now beginning to be collected for evaluation (NJ, 1982, 104). In China, research on the extraordinary function of the human body has already attracted the interest of many scientists who specialize in biology, physics, psychology, and the like. Special attention, active support, and specific direction have also been gained from certain famous scientists. Professor Qian Xue-sen published some special papers (NJ, 1981, 3:483) covering the relationship between the extraordinary function of the human body, qigong, and Chinese traditional medicine, and emphasized the importance of developing the human being's potential capacity and exploring and developing a fundamental discipline of human body science. In his "Inaugurating Fundamental Research on Human Body Science" he pointed out that Chinese traditional medical theory, qigong, and extraordinary function centered around the qigong state are keys to research in the human body sciences, in which the basic principles of extraordinary human body function are included. Based on systems sciences, he also proposed the theory of functional states of the human body. These theoretical viewpoints have been playing an important directive role in launching fundamental research in the human body sciences.

We consider that, in the future study of the extraordinary functions of the human body in China, special attention should be given to the integration of the cream of Chinese traditional culture with the principles of modern science and technology, and the integration of qigong and Chinese traditional medical theory with the research on extraordinary function. This approach will bring the research work on the human body function into the orbit of modern science and technology.

       Conclusion. Research on the extraordinary function of the human body is of great importance, both theoretically and practically. We firmly believe that there is nothing that cannot be understood in the world; there are only things that have not yet been understood. We are full of confidence as to the prospect of the study of the extraordinary function of the human body in China.

Part 5: Invited Addresses

PSYCHICAL RESEARCH AND PARAPSYCHOLOGY: NOTES ON THE
DEVELOPMENT OF TWO DISCIPLINES

Ivor Grattan-Guinness*

> Is there any room for a speculative philosophy distinct
> from Psychology and Ethics, and all particular sciences?
>
> --Cambridge University moral sciences tripos, paper on psychology and metaphysics, April 25, 1882

1. Introduction

The names of the societies which we celebrate at this conference--the Society for Psychical Research (SPR) and the Parapsychological Association (PA)--reflect a change of terms which has occurred over the last 50 years. In this paper I wish to comment on the early days of psychical research 100 years ago and of parapsychology (using the term in its narrower sense, referring to the experimental and technical parts of psychical research) of about 50 years ago, when the Rhines were beginning to publish their results on card tests. While much excellent historical work has been written on both developments, rather less has been undertaken on the more general philosophical milieux within which they occurred. This paper is a tentative exploration--"Notes" only, indeed--of these more general questions. In places I shall draw upon recent work in the history of science, and thus try to draw this discipline to your attention.[1]** But my primary purpose is not historical nostalgia, even though we also celebrate this year the centenary of the Inspectorate of Ancient Monuments; I shall suggest at the end that

---

*I am grateful to the Society for Psychical Research for permission to see the Barrett manuscripts in their possession. The draft of this paper was kindly read by John Beloff, Geoffry Cantor, Anita Gregory, Peter Harman, and Ian Stevenson.
**Notes for this essay begin on page 296.

these events of yore seem still to speak to us today about the current state of psychical research and parapsychology, including their relationship to each other.

2. Psychical Research and the Spirit of Inquiry

> The word spiritual is one of the most difficult and important terms in nineteenth-century thought.
> --Turner, 1974, 3

In 1876 W. F. Barrett submitted a paper to the British Association for the Advancement of Science (BAAS). Entitled "On some phenomena associated with abnormal conditions of mind," it contained a discussion of theoretical and experimental work on hypnotized subjects. There was a row; while he was able to read the paper, only the title was published in the Report of the meeting (Barrett, 1877). The controversy lasted for several weeks in the press (Barrett, 1924b), with distinguished objectors (W. B. Carpenter, W. F. Donkin, R. Lankester) facing equally distinguished supporters (W. Crookes, W. Huggins, A. Pitt-Rivers, 3rd Lord Rayleigh, A. R. Wallace).

I suspect that the refusal of publication was fortunate for the development of psychical research. It was largely on Barrett's initiative that a two-day conference on "Spiritualism and Psychological Research" was held in the London rooms of the British National Association of Spiritualists on January 5 and 6, 1882 (Barrett, 1924a). This event led to the formation of the SPR later in the year as a forum which (among other things) would publish research in this area; indeed, the bulk of Barrett's 1876 paper appeared in the Proceedings (Barrett, 1883).[2] Further, the SPR's immediate decision to organize six committees to investigate particular classes of phenomena, a move which doubtless helped it to succeed where earlier organizations had failed, recalls the BAAS's policy of maintaining standing committees on particular subjects.

The description of these committees, which comprises the opening contribution to the SPR Proceedings, includes an often-quoted statement of policy:

> The aim of the Society will be to approach these various problems without prejudice or prepossession of any kind, and in the same spirit of exact and unimpassioned inquiry which has enabled Science to solve so many problems once not less obscure nor less hotly debated.

The word "spirit" is striking; its use was undoubtedly deliberate, for it would have immediately rung its overtones on the educated minds of the time. There was not only the interest in Spiritualism, shared by Barrett and many others (for some it took the form of membership in Spiritualist churches); there was the general concern with mental processes, and the prominence of psychology, widely conceived, in the philosophical and scientific thought of the time.

An important stimulus at Cambridge for this concern had been the reform of the educational system from the 1820s, led by such men as Adam Sedgwick and William Whewell (Garland, 1980). Their position was informed by a philosophy called "intuitionism" (sometimes "nativism"), according to which man had the capacity to form fundamental ideas transcending experience. It was the task of education to "train the mind" by exercising this capacity. Three subjects came to receive special emphasis: logic (for the forms of thought), mathematics (for the matter of thought), and classics (for contact with the wisdom of the past). The movement was strongly anti-utilitarian, and indeed marked a revolt against Benthamism. It claimed a unity to all knowledge. It showed a strong religious color and attempted a marriage of the truths of science, which were to be attained by inductions from facts, with the revelation of God; for example, "natural theology" was the study of the display of Divine will in the animal kingdom (Brooke, 1977; Yeo, 1979). However, religion itself was conceived of broadly, indeed as the "Broad church," with the universities being disestablished from the Church of England.

The system of education was called "liberal" by its proponents, although liberalism did not extend to the questioning of its own principles. Nevertheless, substantial reforms occurred at Cambridge between 1860 and 1882; Henry Sidgwick was a prominent figure in the new system (Rothblatt, 1968). The new moves included the abolishment (in 1871) of the need to affirm Christian belief to obtain university membership; a strengthening of the standards of teaching, still very low for many undergraduates; the abolition of the requirement of celibacy for Fellows; the furthering of education of women (moves which originally helped to bring Henry and Eleanor Sidgwick together); some reduction in the autonomy of the colleges; increases in the importance and prestige of the University of professorships; and the questioning of the unity of knowledge by emphasis on the variety of disciplines, including the introduction of new triposes. The plurality of disciplines was quite a notable feature of science worldwide, and one manifestation is the creation at that time of many societies, usually national ones, for individual disciplines; thus the creation of the SPR in 1882 is typical in that respect.

Although these changes were quite substantial, several standpoints of the past were maintained, especially the prominent position of psychology and logic. The new moral sciences tripos, for which Sidgwick was sometimes an examiner, included a paper on "Psychology and metaphysics."[3] The journal Mind was created in 1876 as a "quarterly review of psychology and philosophy," and included notices of the SPR's publications fairly regularly.[4] And many intellectuals still affirmed Christian belief in some form or another, including Spiritualism, as we shall shortly see.

Thus psychical research, defined by the SPR in its "Objects" as a study of "that large group of debatable phenomena designated by such terms as mesmeric, psychical, and Spiritualistic," fits into the general ambience of English intellectual thought. For example, logic was often held to be a normative discipline concerned with how we ought to think, while psychology was a descriptive study of how in fact we do think. Thus, given the further link between psychology and psychical research, it is not surprising to find that several major logicians were sympathetic to psychical research: George Boole, with his mathematical psychology of the "laws of thought" (Grattan-Guinness, 1982) and whose wife both propagated his ideas after his death and became a founding Council member of the SPR;[5] Augustus De Morgan, who contributed a long preface to his wife's book, From Matter to Spirit, one of the first extended studies of the test of mediums (De Morgan, 1863); and Lewis Carroll (C. L. Dodgson) and J. Venn, both SPR members. Similarly, the interest of physicists, such as Barrett, Crookes, O. Lodge, Rayleigh, Balfour Stewart, and J. J. Thomson (Wynne, 1979) is not surprising in a climate of thought which granted theological significance to the ether permeating Victorian physics (Cantor, 1981). Further, it is worth noting that a prime research area of these physicists (including much of Rayleigh's joint work with his sister-in-law, Mrs. Sidgwick) was electricity and magnetism.

Two figures of this period are notable for their attempt to weld psychical research into the fabric of their other scientific interests. One was the physicist Sir Oliver Lodge, who throughout his long career both studied the property of the (alleged) ether and saw it as the means of linking the physical and the psychical worlds, including psychical phenomena such as ESP and survival (Wilson, 1971). He claimed

> It is in the interaction of ether and matter that the problems of psychology must find their solution. Matter only serves as an index or pointer, demonstrating the unseen activity all around; and chief among the unseen activities are the etheric agencies guided and controlled by Life and Mind and Spirit (Lodge, 1933, 260-261).

His concern with the means of paranormal communication, over and above any (presumed) powers of the mind and brain, has left him an overly neglected theorist of psychical phenomena.[6]

The other figure was Alfred Russel Wallace. He published his ideas on evolution in the 1850s, and held a view broadly similar to Darwin's on its processes. However, in the late 1860s two connected changes took place: he felt that natural selection was not able to explain many features of human beings (for example, the hairless skin and the power of speech) and he became converted to Spiritualism through witness of psychical phenomena (Kottler, 1974; Smith, 1972). Interested in phrenology from the 1840s, he now posited the existence of a higher consciousness which served as the dynamic cause of both psychical phenomena and of those faculties of humans beyond the ken of natural selection. His enthusiasm for séances contrasts markedly with Darwin's extreme skepticism (recorded in Pearson, 1924, 62-67).

3. Warfare Between Science and Religion?

> It is possible to combine a practically complete trust in the procedure and results of empirical science, with a profound distrust in the procedure and conclusions ... of Empirical Philosophy.
> --H. Sidgwick, 1882, 543

Several of the developments just described involve the relationship between science and religion, especially Christianity. The warfare between these two great regiments of thoughts is one of the best-known features of the intellectual life of the late Victorian period.

Fortunately for our understanding, recent historical research has revealed that the battle reports are largely propaganda, and that a much more complicated situation obtained. J. Moore's The Post-Darwinian Controversies is a particularly valuable source since it includes a history of the propagandizing itself (J. Moore, 1979); and F. M. Turner's Between Science and Religion is especially useful for the history of psychical research, as he studies in detail the positions of F. W. H. Myers, Sidgwick, and Wallace among others (Turner, 1974).

Those men, while not necessarily accepting Christianity, all reacted, in some way or another, to a range of views called "naturalism," which were advocated in the second half of the nineteenth century as a philosophical underpinning for the advancement of science. Briefly, naturalism extolled Nature over God, facts over belief, reason over faith, and matter over spirit. It allowed for the ordering of ideas by the mind and their verification (if correct) by the facts. Thus its underlying psychology was associationist, usually a psychophysical parallelism.

The word "mechanistic" was often used in naturalism: the importance of mechanical principles among the laws of nature (the law of the conservation of energy, for example), natural selection as the mechanism of evolution, the need for a mechanistic theory of the mind, and so on. Since some advocates of naturalism knew little of the science of mechanics, their use of "mechanistic" was not always clear.

Reductionism played some role in the naturalists' framework, on at least two fronts: the desire to reduce the role of metaphysical questions, and the tendency away from Christian dogma. However, there were important differences between naturalists over the extent to which reductionism was to be taken; for example, some advocated positivism while others criticized it, and both atheists and agnostics fell within its scope. It is best understood as a spectrum of positions, with agreement over the basic standpoints described above (Turner, 1974, ch. 2). A brief but illuminating survey of its principles is provided in an article by Sidgwick's former student James Ward (1911) who, like his teacher, rejected naturalism as an adequate philosophy of science.

Prominent figures in naturalism included Alexander Bain, T. H. Huxley, Herbert Spencer, and John Tyndall. A significant background figure was J. S. Mill for his efforts to reduce all knowledge to empirically obtained data and inductions built upon them.[7] Mill held such a view even of logic, in contrast to the logicians mentioned in Section 2 above (Richards, 1980). But to mention Mill's philosophy recalls another important area of controversy of the time, namely, whether science actually did proceed by induction from facts or by the use of hypotheses. Some of the disputes over Darwinism were at this level, which of course is a philosophical matter, not a specifically religious one.

Indeed, the relationship between science and religion was far more complicated during this period than the warfare thesis allows. For example, many theologians accepted Darwinism as an explanation of the processes studied in natural theology (J. Moore, 1979, part 3), while some were willing to see scripture studied by "scientific" principles (the collection of Essays and Reviews in 1859 was an important case). Another significant religious initiative was the encyclical Aeterni Patris, issued by Pope Leo XIII in 1879, which led to a development of relations between science and Thomism.[8]

Conversely, scientists also took initiatives to reconcile their profession with Christian faith. For example, there was the "Scientists' declaration" of 1864-1865, offered as a complement to Essays and Reviews (Brock and Macleod, 1976). Again, while the BAAS barely stomached Barrett's paper on psychical phenomena in 1876, it had been horrified two years earlier when Tyndall, its president for the year (and previously Barrett's chief at the Royal Institution), delivered a long address on religion and science in which he supported the latter much more than the former (Tyndall, 1875). Though he claimed in the ensuing uproar that he had had Catholicism more in mind than religion in general (he was the son of an Orangeman, and the BAAS met in Belfast that year), the anger of the scientists gathered there was barely settled. In particular, in the following year two Scottish physicists, Balfour Stewart and P. G. Tait, published The Unseen Universe: Or Physical Speculations on a Future State, a work which rapidly went through several editions. They sought to refute Tyndall's materialism by claiming a role for theology in (for example) accounting for the origin of the universe (Heimann, 1972). Stewart was cautiously intrigued by psychical phenomena when approached by Barrett about the conference of January 1882;[9] he joined the SPR and indeed became its president for 1885-1887, between the two periods of Sidgwick's presidency.

Thus, while there was a marked decline in the proportion of clergymen in the "professional" science class from the 1860s on (Turner, 1978), elements of reconciliation, or at least coexistence, between science and Christianity were considerable. Journals such as Nature, launched in 1869, originally made great efforts to appeal to professional and lay scientists (Roos, 1981). Organizations included the Metaphysical Society, a discussion club which, during the course of its history from 1869 to 1880, included atheists, agnostics, free-thinkers, Deists, Catholics, Anglicans, positivists, and naturalists, and so had Huxley, Tyndall and Sidgwick among its members (Brown, 1947). Miracles and the supernatural were prominent topics for papers; the quotation from Sidgwick at the head of this section comes from one of his contributions; and Huxley invented the word "agnosticism" with help of discussions there. The Society's chief founder was James Knowles, who later launched the journal, The Nineteenth Century, which published some extracts of SPR reports.[10]

Seen against the alleged background of warfare between science and religion, the disagreements between the SPR and the Spiritualists appear to be a typical battle. However, with the more complex and subtle historical picture now emerging, other possibilities are available (compare Nicol, 1972). One difference, of course, concerned the fact that the SPR had no corporate opinion while the Spiritualists adopted a definite view on survival;[11] another concerned "the great scandal," as Mrs. Sidgwick put it, of "the encouragement [Spiritualism] gives to the immoral trade of fraudulent mediumship" (1911, 708). Thus one criticism is methodological, the other ethical (a professional concern of the Sidgwicks); religious questions are not specifically involved. Indeed, Mrs. Sidgwick, like the Spiritualists, believed in survival (Salter, 1945, 4-5).

In fact, as is well known, many of the SPR's prominent scientific members were Spiritualists--hardly a proper drawing of lines for a battle with science. Indeed, there were probably more Spiritualists among its scientific members than among its humanists (that is, those with a primarily literary training). And this point leads to the remark that the main offices of the SPR were filled during its early decades by humanists--the Sidgwicks, E. Gurney, Myers, and F. Podmore (who was a Spiritualist). In other words, the scientific representation in the SPR was somewhat limited (although, of course, greatly distinguished). This imbalance was a structural weakness of the SPR, given the nature of the subject to which it was addressed; and one consequence which emerged in the early decades of this century is the surely inordinate amount of space devoted to cross-correspondence analysis--over 2,000 pages in the Proceedings, sometimes reading more like extensions of classics tripos than psychical research. "We believe unreservedly in the methods of modern science," Sidgwick had written in one of his presidential addresses (1888, 272); but I imagine, in view of the complications described above and the ones about to follow, that of his circle only his wife was equipped to know what these methods might be.

4. Roads of Reductionism

> What is the world that science reveals to us as the reality of the world we see? A world dark as the grave, silent as a stone, and shaking like a jelly.

> [Is that] the ultimate fact of this glorious world? Why
> you might as well say that the ultimate fact of one
> of Beethoven's violin quartettes [sic] is the scraping
> of the tails of horses on the intestines of cats.
> --James Hinton (Hopkins, 1878, 139)

So far I have sketched out aspects of a picture which shows why psychical research could flourish in late Victorian science. However, there were other philosophical fragrances in the air at the time which found inimical not only psychical research but indeed the whole ambit of "psychology and metaphysics," and wished instead to banish both by reducing them to "acceptable" categories of knowledge or regarding as illegitimate the questions there raised. For convenience I shall call them "positivists," although they include also materialists (who wish to reduce mind to matter) and behaviorists (who reduce alleged psychological notions to patterns or states of behavior). These positions lay at the end of the range of views called "naturalism" in Section 3, which were most enthusiastic for the reductionism, and thus at the opposite end from the critics of naturalism such as Myers, Sidgwick, Wallace, and Ward. These positions gained much ground at the century's turn; I shall briefly outline four movements related, respectively, to popularization, epistemology, psychology, and physiology, for they provide important background to the emergence of parapsychology which is described in Section 5.

(1) Tyndall's 1874 address to the BAAS shocked the theologically orthodox, as mentioned earlier. Both there and in other of his more popular writings on science, he, Huxley, and others promulgated doctrines that though not necessarily atheistic, urged a sovereignty of science over religion, or at least a capture of religious ground by scientific principles. My militaristic metaphor here is deliberate; the "warfare" caricature of the relations between science and religion, mentioned in the last section, was advocated from the 1860s on, especially in some of the "International Scientific Series" of books launched by the American E. L. Youmans, with the help of Huxley, Spencer, Tyndall, and others (J. Moore, 1979, part 1). The History of the Conflict Between Religion and Science (1874) by the positivist scientist and historian J. W. Draper, was an especially influential volume in the series for prosecuting the warfare theory already described. In addition, the series helped to popularize in the U.S. the "Social Darwinism" of Spencer (Sharlin and others, 1976), his attempt to impose on sociology his materialist view of evolution (following the Lamarckian adaptationist tradition), and associationist psychology (Young, 1970, ch. 5).

(2) Professional philosophy in late nineteenth-century England was dominated by various kinds of idealism; it was the pasta of philosophy, psychology, and logic described in Section 2 cooked in the warm vapors of Immanuel Kant and (especially) G. F. Hegel. The young Bertrand Russell drank its exotic juices; but, "It was towards the end of 1898 that Moore and I rebelled against both Kant

and Hegel" (Russell, 1959, 54). From then on Russell adopted an opposite extreme. In 1903 (the year of publication of Myers's Human Personality and Its Survival of Bodily Death) Russell brought out his The Principles of Mathematics, in which he tried to reduce mathematics to logic (a subject now cast in a rather different form from the Boolean and other traditions mentioned earlier). He and Whitehead brought his conceptions to some sort of completion in their Principia Mathematica (1910-1913) (Grattan-Guinness, 1977). The elimination of abstract objects (allegedly) achieved in that system would have earned the approval of Mill (and also of W. K. Clifford, attacker of The Unseen Universe and delight of the teenaged Russell).

Russell then started to apply his reductionist techniques to broader areas of philosophy. By 1918 he came to a philosophy called "logical atomism, " a positivist epistemology based on the idea that propositions are pictures of reality and can be put together like bricks (Russell, 1959, chs. 10-12). His position, and some related thoughts by Wittgenstein, were taken up and generalized in the 1920s by the so-called "Vienna Circle" of philosophers. One of its members, Rudolf Carnap, published in 1928 (as if it were his) an outline of the Circle's ideas on "the logical structure of the world. "

Reductionism was a prime epistemological aim of the Circle, with the logic of relations presented in Principia Mathematica providing much of the machinery (Grattan-Guinness, 1979). Other sciences could be reduced to physics[12] (although Carnap was curiously silent on the details of that subject; for example, he said nothing about either quantum mechanics or relativity, major research areas of the time). Further, each science must come down to its basic principles, to be furnished from "observation statements, " that is, statements verified by direct experience. Metaphysical statements, which were not so verifiable, were thereby rendered "meaningless. " Great emphasis was laid on language; indeed, the Circle was a source of modern language-analysis philosophy (and stood in marked contrast to late nineteenth-century doubts about the power of language to express the full range of possible thoughts). It led to a movement called "logical positivism, " and by the mid-1930s trendy young philosophers were diffusing its ideas elsewhere in Europe. By then, however, because of Hitler, the Circle members themselves had emigrated to the U. S.

(3) The professionalization of psychology owes much to Wilhelm Wundt, who instituted a research laboratory at Leipzig University in the 1870s and drew large numbers of research students, especially from the U. S. (Dolby, 1977).[13] Acknowledging some influence from Mill and Spencer, he taught an associationist brand of psychology (with a Millian inductive logic alongside) with the emphasis laid on experimental studies and the physiological aspects of psychology rather than (for example) the older nativist traditions. However, he also relied on introspection theory rather than comparative techniques.

Wundt wrote a rather skeptical essay on hypnosis (Wundt, 1892) and his approach to psychology was in general unsympathetic to psychical research; no "subliminal self" would have been seen haunting his laboratory. He was not without critics--William James, for one, was quite contemptuous (Perry, 1935, 68)--but his influence was enormous, especially in the U.S., whither his students returned to continue in his style, especially in colleges and universities.

(4) Sidgwick is a good example of a Victorian struggling with uncertainties in his case over religion. Another example, this time concerning psychical phenomena, is the biologist G. J. Romanes. He was very intrigued by psychical phenomena, and attended Barrett's founding conference of January 1882.[14] Later that year he published an important book on animal intelligence in the International Scientific Series (Romanes, 1882), in which he accepted the mind and consciousness in theorizing while treating the subject largely in the evolutionary associationist style of Spencer. He was sympathetic to an evolutionary style of physiology ("myogenesis") then being cultivated at Cambridge by his teacher, Michael Foster (Geison, 1980), a colleague of Sidgwick at Trinity College.[15] He came to reject his earlier interest in psychical research, and, with the violence of the convert, attacked Wallace viciously for advocating the subject (J. Moore, 1979, 187-190). However, he was opposed to naturalism and remained uncertain about the position of Christianity (Turner, 1974, ch. 4).

Romanes' book became well known, passing through several editions over 30 years. Its subject matter was taken up in the U.S. in the early 1900s by a young graduate student who wrote a doctorate on the behavior of rats. Previously impressed by William James's approach to psychology, these studies of animals drove introspection out of his theoretical system and led him to develop behaviorism.[16] His name was J. B. Watson, and he propounded this influential brand of American psychology from the 1920s on (D. Cohen, 1979).

5. On J. B. Rhine and the 1930s

> The work reported in this volume is the first fruit of the policy of naturalization of "psychical research" within the universities.
> --McDougall (foreword to Rhine, 1934, xiii)

One of Wundt's pupils was J. H. Hyslop, who kept the American SPR going in the 1910s; presumably his Spiritualism triumphed over the Leipzig air. During these years, and in the 1920s, the state of psychical research in the U.S. was not encouraging, although Clark University managed to mount a moderately vigorous symposium in 1926 (Murchison, 1928). Divisions over Spiritualism and the mediumship of Mrs. Crandon even led to the formation of the Boston SPR separate from the American SPR (Mauskopf and McVaugh, 1980, ch. 1). Given the tendencies in various related fields described in the preceding section, it is not surprising that the Rhines quickly abandoned mediumship and concentrated on card-guessing experiments in their development of parapsychology, which J. B. Rhine summarized in his book Extra-sensory Perception (Rhine, 1934). On the words "extra-sensory perception" and "parapsychology," which are popularized in that book, see Section 7: Appendix below.

The achievements of the Rhines during this period and the controversies over parapsychology have been described in detail (Mauskopf and McVaugh, 1980; R. L. Moore, 1977, ch. 7). Their work has an interesting prehistory in an attack on behaviorism launched in the early 1920s by William McDougall (see especially Watson and McDougall, 1928), who was soon to be the Rhines' mentor. In a similar vein a leading motivation for the Rhines' research on psychical phenomena was "to discover the whole nature of man and to find out whether something more than just his physical, sensorimotor side exists" (J. B. Rhine and L. E. Rhine, 1980, 309), in marked distinction from the behaviorist norms of their time.

On the other hand, the Rhines' experimental techniques reflect in many ways prevailing views of the time: reductions in the small range of paranormal phenomena investigated, and even in experimental details like using forced-choice rather than free-response tests; and behaviorism in the attempt to detect the phenomena from statistical analysis of (large quantities of) data rather than via direct inspection. There are notable similarities in method between their parapsychology and various aspects of contemporary behaviorist psychology (see, for example, Ellis, 1938 on Gestalt psychology). In particular, laboratory work was valued far above spontaneous evidence, in the hope--felt both by parapsychologists and several kinds of psychologists--of aspiring to the "hard" sciences, where, as we have seen, physics was King. McDougall called the process of aspiration "naturalization" in the quotation at the head of this section, doubtless having in mind the naturalistic philosophies described in Section 3.

Thus I return to the general philosophical atmosphere. As I have described it in Section 4, up to the early 1930s it was basically inimical to the admission of psychical phenomena and also to favorable consideration of psychical research, as emerged later in the decade. By then the Vienna Circle members were placed in various universities in the U.S., and the Philosophy of Science Association was launched in 1934. Its journal, Philosophy of Science, began with an article by Carnap titled "On the Character of Philosophical Problems," an English translation of an orthodox Circle piece on the meaninglessness of metaphysics and the reduction of biology and psychology to physics. Later in the volume, Feigl (1934) gave a "Logic analysis of the psychophysical problem" as "a contribution to the new positivism," in terms of the meanings of "meaning." Not much room for psychical research there, as the publishers of the journal made clear in an advertisement opposite page 387 of volume 2 (1935), where they announced the availability of H. C. McComas' (1935) Ghosts I Have Talked With: "He has investigated the most successful mediums of recent years and has revealed their tricks in every instance. He has duplicated every trick he has seen produced."

This view is hardly new; indeed, Rhine seems to have had a similar opinion of Mrs. Crandon. But it is of special note in a journal besotted with reductionism, the view which underlies the usual forms of criticisms of psychical phenomena now made.[17] Articles in similar vein appeared in the body of the journal (and of course elsewhere) from time to time; a suable, insulting piece (Nabours, 1943), "The masquerade of ESP," possibly marks the extreme.[18]

The same dependence on reductionism, especially reduction to physics, is clear in less polemical writings of the time from elsewhere. For example, Freud, who held a very ambiguous attitude to psychical research,[19] wrote to Immanuel Velikovsky in 1931:

> My own experiences have led me to suppose that telepathy is the real core of the alleged parapsychological phenomena and maybe the only one ... nothing remains to us but to await clarification of this basically physical problem from the hopefully not too distant future (Velikovsky, 1982, 17: my emphasis).

Russell, in his Religion and Science (1935), while allowing as "one line of argument in favour of survival after death ... the phenomena investigated by psychical research" (p. 137), preferred science in general and physics in particular to everything else discussed in the book. He also accepted uncritically the historical caricature of science at war with religion discussed in Section 3 above, and so, in Moore's witty phrase, made himself a "prisoner of war."[20]

6. Some Conclusions

This paper is no more than a collection of notes on a much larger story. That story concerns the development of psychical research, and also of related disciplines over the period (say) 1870-1940, with special attention to general philosophical tendencies and inclinations.

It would be a difficult story to write, but a story well worth the telling; for I am confident that the larger perspective would furnish some new perspectives on the history of psychical research. In particular, it would bring out broader common features where the "local" histories stress differences. For example, the disputes between the SPR and the Spiritualists are rightly held to be important, but they took place in a general atmosphere largely sympathetic to metaphysical issues. Again, the attempt of the Rhines to refute materialism by demonstrating the existence of ESP was doubtless a major clash between contemporary positions; but seen in a wider view, their methods, and the narrowing down of psychical research to parapsychology, seems consistent with prevailing modes of the time against metaphysics (and, to a lesser extent, religion) and for reductionism. Naturalism, described in Section 3, lies in between psychical research and parapsychology.

The difference just noted is a different one from those brought out in the "narrower" histories of psychical research, and it strikes me as one which is more relevant to the current situation. My own correspondence and discussions with people in the field today show me that that difference is still evident in modern views. Some hanker for the phenomena and the general atmosphere of the old days of psychical research; others extol the rigor and the experimental techniques attendant upon parapsychology. While the views are not contradictory, there are, nevertheless, noticeable differences in priority, method, and even object of research. From that point of view, then, and to that extent, we have two different disciplines.

But there are those who recognize this situation, and seek a place between psychical research and parapsychology. Perhaps they stand, therefore, as the new naturalists;[21] in a sense they are successors to Myers and Sidgwick, who 100 years ago searched the ground between science and religion. I send them on their way with a timeless warning from Augustus De Morgan (1863):

> Those who affirm that they have seen faith-staggering occurrences are of course supposed to be imposters or dupes. To this there can be no objection; a pretty world we should live in if the arrangement did not demand moral courage from those who offer evidence of wonders [vii-viii].

7. Appendix: On the History of the Words "Parapsychology" and "Extra-sensory Perception"

It is sometimes thought that Rhine introduced the word "parapsychology" in his Extra-sensory perception. However, its origins go back to a paper by Max Dessoir in 1889. "One indicates by analogy with words like paragenesis, ... paralogism, paranoia...," he wrote "with para-something, which goes beyond or [stands] beside the usual, so perhaps one can call parapsychic the phenomena which emerge out of the normal run of the psyche, parapsychology the science which treats them" (Dessoir, 1889, 342). He came to visualize parapsychology as the border area between psychology and psychopathology; the corresponding objective phenomena were studied in "paraphysics." Richet introduced the term "métapsychique" into French in his SPR presidential address for 1905 (Richet, 1907); covering both parapsychology and paraphysics (in their German senses) and also related physiological concerns, it was more or less a synonym for "psychical research."

Rhine was aware of these terms, but he used Dessoir's in his Extra-sensory perception as a synonym: "Parapsychology, i.e., psychical research." He favored the word for the etymological reasons that Dessoir had also urged, introducing cognates such as "parapsycho-physical" (including levitation and apports) and "parapsychopathological" (psychic healing) (Rhine, 1934, 7). However, these terms did not endure, and "parapsychology" both continued in its traditional role as a synonym and also came to be restricted to the experimental and technical aspects on which the Rhines concentrated. This is an odd, and indeed unsatisfactory, situation; I know of no other discipline of which the name also refers to one of its proper subsets.

Rhine did claim to introduce "extra-sensory perception" in his book, as he later recalled,

> This term was chosen after considerable thought and some discussion with colleagues, but had I realized what a wide usage the expression would receive in the course of years, I would certainly have given it further thought in the hope of arriving at a more convenient and adaptable term (1977, 163).

In fact, this term also has a German prehistory: "Aussersinnliche Wahrnehmung" seems to be due to Gustav Pagenstecher (1924), who used it as the title of his book on psychometry. Presumably Rhine missed this work, although in his book (1934, 19) he cited an earlier work by Pagenstecher on this topic (Pagenstecher, 1922). This ironic touch seems to provide a suitable point on which to close.

NOTES

1. However, this is not the place for sophisticated analysis of the implications and details of the historical record, nor of all the attendant philosophical niceties. A few of these escutcheons are provided in these notes. Specialists in the history and philosophy involved are requested to treat with indulgence the oversimplifications which are inevitably committed.

   Contrary to my usual practice, the bibliography is largely confined to secondary literature; many of the works cited were chosen for their own extensive bibliographies of the primary literature.

2. Barrett tried again with the BAAS in 1883 with a paper on telepathy, which was rejected (SPR Archives, Barrett mss., file A4, letter 11). File A4 contains a large group of letters to Barrett, including 35 from Myers, 15 from Mrs. Sidgwick, and four or more from Gurney, Lang, Richet, Romanes (see note 14 below), and Wallace. File A2 contains 27 letters concerning the conference of January 1882.

3. The examiners for the 1882 paper quoted at the head of this paper were J. Venn, A. T. Lyttleton, J. B. Mayor, and H. S. Foxwell (Cambridge University, 1883, 231). In other

words, Sidgwick happened not to be examining that year. It is amusing to wonder if the quoted question was set by the examiners mindful of Sidgwick's recent activities.

In an interesting detail of history, a first class was awarded on that paper to W. R. Sorley, who was to be Sidgwick's successor in the professorship of moral philosophy at Cambridge in 1900.

4. See against the SPR in the Mind indexes in volume 16 (1891) and n. s. 12 (1903). In addition, Gurney and Myers wrote in the journal on specific topics in psychical research.

An interesting example of the place of "psychology" in the proliferating disciplines is F. Y. Edgeworth's study of welfare economics. Firstly, his book on the subject was entitled Mathematical Psychics (1881). Secondly, it was partly based on Sidgwick's criticism (1879) of Mill's wages-fund theory and also on his theory of ethics. Later he helped the authors of Phantasms of the Living with the discussion of chance in ch. 13.

5. Mrs. Boole resigned at once, as she was the only woman on the Council; the next woman to join the Council, in 1901, was Mrs. Sidgwick (Nicol, 1972, 344-345).

6. On the somewhat similar case of Crookes, see Palfreman, 1976.

Positivists like to assert that Einstein proved that there was no ether. Einstein himself made no such claim. His special theory is a hypothesis about space-time in which the ether is not needed; his general theory is a hypothesis of a broader kind in which the status of the ether is ambiguous, as the work of Lodge and others on the (albeit controversial) topic of ether relativity have shown (Lodge, 1926).

For an excellent survey of the place of the ether(s) in many areas of science, medicine, and theology from 1740 to 1900, see Cantor and Hodge (1981).

7. This is a good example of the complications of the period. Mill and Whewell both believed in grounding science in induction, and thought that truths would be so obtainable. However, they differed over the existence of mental states and the role of cognition (Butts, 1968).

8. On this encyclical see Dauben (1979, 140-142) and Paul (1979, 179-182). It would be interesting to see what influence, if any, this movement had on psychical research in Europe, where Catholicism was a prominent faith. Another movement of that time, which carried most weight in the U.S., was Christian Science.

9. Barrett (see note 2 above), file A2, letter 19. The Unseen Universe was published anonymously; Stewart and Tait admitted authorship in 1876.

It seems slightly surprising that Scottish physicists, and indeed Scots in general, played little role in the early decades of the SPR, since the "common-sense" philosophy that many of them followed gave some prominence both to mental processes and to theorizing by analogy (Olson, 1975). Perhaps Barrett was unlucky in reading his 1876 paper at the BAAS meeting in Glasgow....

10. Gauld (1968, p. 147) lists some early extracts of SPR reports in The Nineteenth Century and The National Review.

11. Another interesting comparison to explore is the question of survival in the context of the late nineteenth-century discussion of "heat death," where according to the current knowledge of geology and thermodynamics the whole universe would eventually slide into one uniform temperature (a situation which the Germans more accurately named "cold death"). This problem sunk deeply into Victorian consciousness, both in science and the arts (Brush 1979). It is not considered in Turner's generally excellent survey of Myers (Turner, 1974, ch. 5).

12. Carnap gave scant attention to biology, starting out from the alleged definition: "The organisms with their essential properties and relations and events which are peculiar to organisms are called biological objects" (Carnap, 1928, art. 137). Psychology was treated in more detail (arts. 19-24, 55-64), and in a manner broadly sympathetic to behavioristic reductions, although he cast doubt on the epistemological claims of behaviorism (art. 59).

13. Study by American students at German universities was a common feature in many disciplines in the period 1880-1914. Doctoral programs were available (unlike the U.S.) for several disciplines; the quality of training was high; the fees were very reasonable; and, as their surnames reveal, the students were often of German or Central European stock.

14. There is an interesting sequence of seven letters of 1881-1882 from Romanes to Barrett, in which he gradually becomes more skeptical about psychical phenomena (Barrett [footnote 2], file A4, letters 104-110). And on July 18, 1881, he doubted that Sidgwick "would be any use" on a committee of "critical" men to investigate the telepathy of the Creery sisters!

15. Physiology was a science which eliminated ethers from its theorizing relatively early, by 1800 (French, 1981). By Romanes' and Foster's time, myogenesis was competing with neurogenesis, according to which muscle tissue needs continuous stimulation from the nervous system (Geison, 1980). Similarly, the "mechanistic" protoplasm theory of life was then being popularized by Huxley (and others) in opposition to vitalism (Geison, 1969).

16. The thesis was published as Animal Education (Watson, 1903). Some interesting historical details arise here concerning pragmatism, a philosophy which (to speak simply) emphasizes meaning, replaces truth by usefulness, and tends to place belief above facts. It is a "soft" form of reductionism, as it can allow a status for mental states and consciousness; it has some kinship with naturalism. Thus its supporters included both believers in psychical phenomena such as William James and F. C. S. Schiller, and skeptics, like John Dewey (on Dewey and James, see Russell, 1946, chs. 29-30). One would expect to see a line of positive influence from Dewey to Watson, who was his pupil; but apparently Watson found Dewey incomprehensible (D. Cohen, 1979, 25).

17. In the old days fraud was seen as an ethical problem (he or she has cheated, it is a disgrace); today it is a reductionist problem (I can duplicate the phenomena by a trick, hence it was produced by a trick). In the same style, credulousness is now regarded only as a property of belief, not of disbelief. Poincaré's remark that "there are two ways of looking at things, to believe everything and to believe nothing, and each is equally stupid" has been forgotten (or made redundant) and replaced by that monument of modern social and political philosophy: double-standardizing.

18. By a touch of (intentional?) editorial humor, Nabours' piece was followed by one entitled "Why Psychologists Tend to Overlook Certain 'Obvious' Facts." On the polemics between Rhine and the psychologists, see Mauskopf and McVaugh (1980, ch. 9).

19. Freud told H. Carrington, in a letter of 1921, that if he had his life to live over again, he might devote himself to psychical research rather than to psychoanalysis. When the news circulated, Freud denied it indignantly; but his biographer Jones found the letter and promised to print it, as evidence, in an appendix (Jones, 1957, 419-420). However, the letter is not reproduced; it should be at p. 473. It appears in Fodor (1971, 84).

Dr. Frank Sulloway tells me that in the American edition of the Jones biography even the promise to print the letter in the appendix is omitted. He puts the situation down to Jones's chaotic filing system while preparing the biography. Freud's behavior may be regarded as a Freudian slip in at least two senses.

20. See J. Moore (1979, 40). This prisonership is more interesting than it appears at first sight. Positivists in science and philosophy tend to be positivist about history also. In this view, history is "the royal road to me," a form of verificationism in which things of the past that I like (such as the conflict thesis for Russell here) are praised and the rest, being mistaken, is deplored or ignored. Among extreme positivists

the notion of history at all is abhorrent. Carnap, for example, regarded himself "as unhistorically minded a person as one could imagine" (I. B. Cohen, 1974, 310).

21. Indeed, some of the newer theories of psi functioning seem to be consonant with pragmatism, whose own kinship with naturalism was noted in note 15 above. From other emphasized points of view, such as feedback and interaction, these theories exhibit the philosophical concerns attending branches of modern science such as systems theory, ecology, and operational research.

REFERENCES

Barrett, W. F. On some phenomena associated with abnormal conditions of mind. Reports of the British Association for the Advancement of Science, 1876, 1877, 164 [title only].

Barrett, W. F. [ibid.]. Proceedings of the Society for Psychical Research, 1883, 1, 238-244.

Barrett, W. F. The early years of psychical research. Light, 1924(a), 44, 395. [Contains the text of Barrett's original invitation to the conference of January 1882.]

Barrett, W. F. Some reminiscences of fifty years' psychical research. Proceedings of the Society for Psychical Research, 1924(b), 34, 275-297.

Brock, W. H., and MacLeod, R. The "Scientists' Declaration": Reflexions on science and belief in the wake of Essays and reviews. British Journal of the History of Science, 1976, 9, 39-66.

Brooke, J. H. Natural theology and the plurality of worlds: Observations on the Brewster-Whewell debate. Annals of Science, 1977, 34, 221-286. [Excellent case study of issues in natural theology.]

Brown, A. W. The Metaphysical Society. New York: Columbia University Press, 1947.

Brush, S. G. The Temperature of History. New York: Franklin, 1979. [Built around his Thermodynamics and history. Graduate Journal, 1967, 7, 477-565.]

Butts, R. E., ed. William Whewell's Theory of Scientific Method. Pittsburgh: Pittsburgh University Press, 1968. [Edition of pertinent texts by Whewell.]

Cambridge University. Cambridge University Calendar. Cambridge: Cambridge University Press, 1883.

Cantor, G. N. The theological significance of ethers. In G. N. Cantor and M. J. S. Hodge (eds.), Conceptions of Ether. Cambridge: Cambridge University Press, 1981.

Cantor, G. N., and Hodge, M. J. S., eds. Conceptions of Ether. Cambridge: Cambridge University Press, 1981.

Carnap, R. Der Logische Aufbau der Welt. Munich: Meiner, 1928. [English trans. by R. George, The Logical Structure of the World. London: Routledge and Kegan Paul, 1967.]

Carnap, R. On the character of philosophical problems. Philosophy of Science, 1934, 1, 5-19.
Cohen, D. J. B. Watson, the Founder of Behaviourism. London: Routledge and Kegan Paul, 1979.
Cohen, I. B. History and the philosopher of science. In F. Suppe, ed. The Structure of Scientific Theories. Urbana: University of Illinois Press, 1974, 308-373.

Dauben, J. W. Georg Cantor: His Mathematics and Philosophy of the Infinite. Cambridge, Mass.: Harvard University Press, 1979.
De Morgan, S. From Matter to Spirit. London: Longman, 1863. [Signed "C. D.," with a preface by "A. B." (Augustus De Morgan).]
Dessoir, M. Die Parapsychologie.... Sphinx, 1889, 7, 341-344.
Dolby, R. G. A. The transmission of two scientific disciplines from Europe to North America in the late nineteenth century. Annals of Science, 1977, 34, 287-310.

Edgeworth, F. Y. Mathematical Psychics. London: Kegan, Paul, 1881. [Interesting philosophical remarks at the beginning.]
Ellis, W. D., ed. A Source Book in Gestalt Psychology. London: Routledge and Kegan Paul, 1938.

Feigl, H. Logical analysis of the psychophysical problem. A contribution to the new positivism. Philosophy of Science, 1934, 1, 420-441.
Fodor, N. Freud, Jung and Occultism. New Hyde Park, N.Y.: University Books, 1971.
French, R. K. Ether and physiology. In G. N. Cantor and M. J. S. Hodge, eds. Conceptions of Ether. Cambridge: Cambridge University Press, 1981, 111-134.

Garland, M. M. Cambridge Before Darwin: The Ideal of a Liberal Education 1800-1860. Cambridge: Cambridge University Press, 1981. [Strongest on the purely educational aspects.]
Gauld, A. The Founders of Psychical Research. London: Routledge and Kegan Paul, 1968.
Geison, G. L. The protoplasmic theory of life and the vitalist-mechanist debate. Isis, 1969, 60, 273-292.
Geison, G. L. Michael Foster and the Cambridge School of Physiology. Cambridge: Cambridge University Press, 1980.
Grattan-Guinness, I. Dear Russell--Dear Jourdain. London: Duckworth, 1977.
Grattan-Guinness, I. On Russell's logicism and its influence, 1910-1930. In Wittgenstein, the Vienna Circle and Critical Rationalism, Vienna: Hölder-Pickler-Tempsky, 1979, 275-280.
Grattan-Guinness, I. Psychology in the foundations of mathematics: The cases of Boole, Cantor and Brouwer. History and Philosophy of Logic, 1982, 3, 33-53.

Heimann, P. M. The unseen universe: Physics and the philosophy of nature in Victorian Britain. British Journal of the History of Science, 1972, 6, 73-79.

Hopkins, E., ed. Life and Letters of James Hinton. London: Kegan, Paul, 1878.

Jones, E. The Life of Sigmund Freud. Vol. 3. London: Hogarth, 1951.

Kottler, M. Alfred Russel Wallace, the origin of man and Spiritualism. Isis, 1974, 65, 145-192.

Lodge, Sir O. Ether. In Encyclopaedia Britannica, 13th ed., supplementary volume 1, 1926, 1026-1029. [Reproduced with additions in 14th ed., volume 8, 1929, 751-755; and Lodge, 1931, 186-204.]

Lodge, Sir O. My Philosophy. London: Benn, 1931.

McComas, H. C. Ghosts I Have Talked With. Baltimore: Williams and Wilkins, 1935.

Mauskopf, S. H., and McVaugh, M. R. The Elusive Science. Baltimore: Johns Hopkins University Press, 1980.

Moore, J. R. The Post-Darwinian Controversies. Cambridge: Cambridge University Press, 1979. [Exceptional bibliography.]

Moore, R. L. In Search of White Crows. New York: Oxford University Press, 1977. [See the critical review by J. G. Pratt in Journal of the American Society for Psychical Research, 1978, 72, 257-266.]

Murchison, C., ed. The Case for and Against Psychical Belief. Worcester, Mass.: Clark University, 1928.

Nabours, R. K. The masquerade of ESP. Philosophy of Science, 1943, 10, 191-203.

Nicol, F. The founders of the S.P.R. Proceedings of the Society for Psychical Research, 1972, 55, 342-369.

Olson, R. Scottish Philosophy and British Physics 1750-1880. Princeton, N.J.: Princeton University Press, 1975.

Pagenstecher, G. Past events seership: A study in psychometry. Proceedings of the American Society for Psychical Research, 1922, 16, 1-136.

Pagenstecher, G. Aussersinnliche Wahrnehmung. Experimentelle Studie über den sogen. [sic] Trancezustand. Halle/Saale: Marhold, 1924.

Palfreman, J. William Crookes: Spiritualism and science. Ethics in Science and Medicine, 1976, 3, 211-227.

Paul, H. W. The Edge of Contingency: French Catholic Reaction to Scientific Change from Darwin to Duhem. Gainesville: University Press of Florida, 1979.

Pearson, K. The Life, Letters and Labours of Francis Galton. Vol. 2. Cambridge: Cambridge University Press, 1924.

Perry, R. B., ed. The Thought and Character of William James. Vol. 2. Boston: Little, Brown, 1935.

Rhine, J. B. Extra-sensory Perception. Boston: Boston Society

for Psychic Research, 1934. [Revised edition, Boston: Branden, 1964, contains an interesting, reminiscing new preface by Rhine.]
Rhine, J. B. Extrasensory perception. In B. B. Wolman, ed. Handbook of Parapsychology. New York: Van Nostrand Reinhold, 1977, 163-174. [Rhine's other article in this volume (pp. 25-47) has valuable information on the history of experimental methods.]
Rhine, J. B., and Rhine, L. E. Afterword. In S. H. Mauskopf and M. R. McVaugh, The Elusive Science. Baltimore: Johns Hopkins University Press, 1980, 307-310.
Richards, J. Boole and Mill: Differing perspectives on logical psychologism. History and Philosophy of Logic, 1980, 1, 19-36.
Richet, C. La Métaphysique Proceedings of the Society for Psychical Research, 1905, 19, 2-49.
Romanes, G. J. Animal Intelligence. London: Kegan Paul, Trench, 1882.
Roos, D. A. The "aims and intentions" of Nature. Annals of the New York Academy of Sciences, 1981, 360, 159-180.
Rothblatt, S. The Revolution of the Dons: Cambridge and Society in Victorian England. London: Faber and Faber, 1968. [Considerable background on Sidgwick.]
Russell, B. A. W. Religion and Science. London: Oxford University Press, 1935.
Russell, B. A. W. History of Western Philosophy. New ed. London: George Allen, 1961.
Russell, B. A. W. My Philosophical Development. London: George Allen, 1959.

Salter, Mrs. W. H. Psychical Research: Where Do We Stand? London: Society for Psychical Research, 1945. [Myers Memorial Lecture.]
Sharlin, H.; Wall, J. F.; and Hollinger, D. A. Spencer, scientism and American constitutional law. Annals of Science, 1976, 33, 457-480.
Sidgwick, Mrs. E. Spiritualism. In Encyclopaedia Britannica, 11th ed., vol. 25, 1911, 705-708.
Sidgwick, H. The wages-fund theory. Fortnightly Review, 1879, n. s. 26, 401-413.
Sidgwick, H. Incoherence of empirical philosophy. Mind, 1882, 7, 533-543. [Lecture delivered to the Metaphysical Society.]
Sidgwick, H. Opening address at the twenty-eighth general meeting. Proceedings of the Society for Psychical Research, 1888, 5, 271-288.
Smith, R. Alfred Russel Wallace: Philosopher of nature and man. British Journal of the History of Science, 1972, 6, 177-199.
Stewart, B., and Tait, P. G. The Unseen Universe: or Physical Speculations on a Future State, London: Macmillan, 1875.

Turner, F. M. Between Science and Religion: The Reaction to Scientific Naturalism in Late Victorian England. New Haven: Yale University Press, 1974.
Turner, F. M. The Victorian conflict between science and religion: A professional dimension. Isis, 1978, 69, 356-374.

Tyndall, J. Presidential address. Report of the British Association for the Advancement of Science 1874, 1875, lxvi-xcvii. [Reprinted in G. Basalla, W. Coleman, and R. H. Nargon, eds. Victorian Science, Garden City, N.Y.: Anchor, 1970, 436-478.]

Velikovsky, I. Mankind in Amnesia. London: Sidgwick and Jackson, 1982.

Ward, J. Naturalism. In Encyclopaedia Britannica, 11th ed., vol. 19, 1911, 274-275.

Watson, J. B. Animal Education. Chicago: University of Chicago Press, 1903.

Watson, J. B., and McDougall, W. The Battle of Behaviourism: An Exposition and an Exposure, London: Kegan Paul, Trench, Trubner, 1928.

Wilson, D. B. The thought of late Victorian physicists: Oliver Lodge's ethereal body. Victorian Studies, 1971, 15, 29-48. [Contains quotations of differing views on psychical research by various physicists.]

Wundt, W. Hypnotismus und Suggestion. Leipzig: Engelsmann, 1892.

Wynne, B. Physics and psychics: Science, symbolic action, and social control in late Victorian England. In B. Barnes and S. Shapin, eds. Natural Order. London: Sage, 1979, 167-186.

Yeo, R. William Whewell, natural theology and the philosophy of science in the mid-nineteenth century Britain. Annals of Science, 1979, 36, 493-516.

Young, R. M. Mind, Brain and Adaptation in the Nineteenth Century. Oxford: Clarendon Press, 1970.

THE SURVIVAL OF DEATH

Robert H. Thouless (Society for Psychical Research)

There are, I think, two questions that can be in our minds when we consider the problem of whether we survive the death of our bodies. The first is as to whether the stream of consciousness, the succession of thoughts, perceptions, and decisions which I call "me" will still go on after my body has died. The second is as to whether the person called "Robert Thouless" will continue to exist as a possible object of social perception to other people after the death and dissolution of his body. These may be called the problems of the "survival of the stream of consciousness" and that of the "survival of personality," respectively. These questions are closely related but are not the same; the answer might be "no" to one of them and "yes" to the other. The second question is the only one that we can hope to answer by empirical methods, so it is the one with which psychical research has been primarily concerned. The answer to the first question can only be directly known to myself. If I survive death I shall know this as directly as I know in the morning that I have survived my night's sleep.

Yet, in a sense, this first question is more important than the other. The importance of the inquiry into the survival of personality may indeed be regarded as that of its answer being an indirect indication of the situation with respect to the survival of the stream of consciousness. If X can be met and recognized after his bodily death, this is a strong indication (though not a coercive proof) that his stream of consciousness is still going on.

I think there is some exaggeration in Professor Zorab's suggestion (p. 125) that survival research ended at about the beginning of the second World War. I think that at about that time it changed its direction but it is still going on and I hope it will continue to do so until its problems are solved or are shown to be insoluble.

The main change of direction seems to have been away from the study of ostensible communications with the departed and the turning towards new lines of research, such as the study of what appear to be memories of past lives, OBEs, and the experiences of the dying. The difficulty in resting evidence for survival on evidence from ostensible communicators from the next world has been that of establishing the identity of these communicators. Reasons for these doubts have increased in recent years. One of the most striking new pieces of evidence against communicators has been the work of the Toronto investigators on the purely fictitious "communicator" Philip. In this case a fictitious character was invented by the sitters and showed many of the characteristics of an autonomous communicator. This obviously raises the possibility of other ostensible communicators being also thought-forms created by the sitters in the séance situation.

One kind of safeguard against this possibility is to base the identification of communicators on the production of information, preselected during the communicator's lifetime. The sealed package tests of Myers and Lodge were of this type. Neither, in fact, succeeded and neither would have proved the identity of the communicator if they had succeeded since success might have been due to the clairvoyant powers of the medium or sitters. I was one of those concerned in the Lodge test; it seemed to me that the basic idea of the "preselected information" test was good but that, in the form used by Myers and Lodge, it was defective, both in the possibility of a spurious result through clairvoyance and in the impossibility of repeated verification; once the packages were opened and their contents known, the test could not be used again.

To overcome these defects I suggested that the identifying information should be the key to a cipher constructed by the intending communicator. Stevenson has suggested a simpler way of achieving the same end by getting his intending communicators to set a combination lock. Both of these tests have the essential feature that there is no written record of the clue and therefore nothing to be the target of clairvoyance. The impossibility of getting the key by clairvoyance can be confirmed by the failure of mediums to obtain the key while the communicator is still alive and not intending to communicate it. If one is to use tests of the identity of communicators, one or other of these tests by unrecorded information is, I suggest, the most rigid way to do it. They have the further advantage that, unlike the sealed package tests, they can be subject to repeated attempts at verification. At present, so far as I know no test of this type has yet succeeded. They must be widely tried out to see whether they can succeed. I am glad to know that our present Chairman (Arthur Berger) is making such an attempt. We must wait and see whether this attempt is successful. If it is, we shall be able to conclude that at least one personality has survived death. If it is not, we must pursue our aim of testing the survival hypothesis by other means, of which there are several promising ones.

There is first the hypothesis of reincarnation (which we may call that of "intermittent revival"), which can be alternative or supplementary to the ordinary spiritist hypothesis of continued survival. I think we can safely say that the work of Ian Stevenson has provided a strong indication that this may sometimes be the case although there is, as yet, no coercive proof of it.

The study of out-of-body experiences is another promising line of research. Some parapsychologists still hold that all OBEs are mere hallucinations. If this proves not to be the case, they provide good supporting evidence for the theories of such neurologists as Penfield and Eccles, who assert the reality of a nonphysical self-conscious self. They suggest that there really is something that might survive death.

Lastly, there is the work of Barrett, Osis, Haraldsson, and Moody on the experiences of the dying. The central question of these researches is whether dying is the end of our stream of consciousness or whether it is a transition to another life. Without undue optimism, I think we may say that it looks as if it may be the latter. If this is the case, it is important that it should be known. Let us go on accumulating evidence on the matter.

A TRIBUTE TO ROBERT H. THOULESS

Arthur S. Berger (Survival Research Foundation)

On this occasion, as we commemorate the founding of the Society for Psychical Research 100 years ago and of the Parapsychological Association 25 years ago, it is proper both to look back and review past years of progress and accomplishment and also to look back and remember all those commanding figures on both sides of the Atlantic who enriched those years with their invaluable contributions, such as Barrett, Broad, Gurney, Hodgson, Hyslop, James, Lodge, Murphy, Myers, Pratt, Prince, Rhine, Richet, and Sidgwick. As Emerson once said: "There is properly no History; only Biography." It is in the lives and exertions of men and women like these that we find our true history.

On the occasion of this joint anniversary, it is my double privilege to add to this honor roll the name of the man you have just seen and heard and to act as his biographer.

Several months ago when I came to England to participate in a conference on survival, my wife and I stayed overnight with Robert and Priscilla Thouless. Till then I had only known and admired Robert Thouless through writings he had published years ago. I found out that his interests are not limited to writing or to psychical research. In earlier years, he was an ardent skier. He went camping, painted, and kept bees. Boating was another hobby. But what impressed me most of all about Thouless was this: As we talked together, and with Ian Stevenson who dropped in, I knew, as I think we all know from just having heard him, that he has lost none of the acuity, criticalness, and flexibility of mind that he demonstrated in his publications of twenty and thirty years ago. I consider myself lucky that we had time only for talk and dinner and did not get around to playing chess, which he still plays and plays, I suspect, with equal acuity.

Nor has he lost his sense of humor. Since I am conducting a survival research project to carry out large-scale and multiple replications of the cipher and combination lock tests for survival, I invited Thouless to participate in the project. He replied: "I should be happy to be your first registrant [but] I shall not feel any obligation to die any sooner because registered."

Nor has he lost his taste for travel. His lovely and devoted wife, Priscilla, whom he married in 1924, keeps him young and on the move from their home here in Cambridge to interesting places. A few months ago, when Britain was in the grip of one of the worst blizzards in 300 years, Robert Thouless wrote to me that he and Priscilla were thinking about the week they spent during another winter with the alligators at the Everglades near my home in Florida. They have also spent time in Melbourne, Australia, where Thouless lectured at the university in 1962. They still visit their daughter, Susan, who is married to a geneticist and lives in Canberra, and they recently went to see their son, David, who is a professor of physics at the University of Washington in Seattle. It is quite difficult to remain stationary when one has nine grandchildren and six great-grandchildren in various parts of the world as do Robert and Priscilla Thouless.

On this occasion, as we review past years of significance for psychical research, we should linger especially over 1934, for in that year Rhine's Extra-sensory Perception was published. Rhine's work contributed directly to at least four things of great consequence: It provoked widespread public and scientific attention. It made parapsychology into an experimental discipline. It placed parapsychology in the climate of a university laboratory and produced other university centers of parapsychology. And, finally, it was responsible for starting Thouless' interest in parapsychology and for allowing the gateway to psychical research to swing open for him in 1934.

Had he entered parapsychology earlier, the benefit to us would have been greater. As it was, the fields of education and psychology gained. Born on July 15, 1894, at Norwich and educated at Norwich Middle School and later Corpus Christi College, Cambridge, from which Thouless took his B.A. degree in Natural Science with honors, he served during the Great War as a signal officer from 1915 to 1919. Thouless thereafter received his Ph.D. from Cambridge and, starting in 1921, taught psychology at Manchester and Glasgow Universities. In 1923, he published An Introduction to the Psychology of Religion. The revised edition of this book, published in 1971, is still in print. In 1925, General and Social Psychology was published, and, in 1932, perhaps his best known work, a book on psychological logic, was published. In England it was entitled Straight and Crooked Thinking and, in America, How to Think Straight, a title Thouless doesn't think is as good as the original. This very successful book has been revised several times and is still in print. In addition to these books, Thouless also published articles in the British Journal of Psychology. Then, in 1938, he began and continued teaching psychology at Cambridge until his retirement in 1961.

But we need not be jealous of education and psychology. If they profited from his intellectual activity, so have we. Thouless, who was once described by Rhine as "one of parapsychology's most constructively critical thinkers" (JP, 1972, 242), has published about 90 articles and numerous book reviews in the Proceedings and Journal of the SPR and the ASPR and the Journal of Parapsychology. He has also written two books on experimental psychical research which I shall mention.

He served as a Council Member of the SPR, as its President from 1942 to 1944, and is today one of its Vice-Presidents. Like the leading figures of the past who made contributions of distinction to psychical research and are cited frequently in the parapsychological and scholarly literature, authors and researchers find in Thouless an unending source of ideas and enlightenment. In what has become one of the important books dealing with psychical phenomena and psychical research, Benjamin Wolman's Handbook of Parapsychology (Van Nostrand Reinhold, 1977), there are 29 references to Thouless. In the Journal and Proceedings of the SPR and of the ASPR there are over 250 references to him and in the Journal of Parapsychology 140 references. These, however, are the publications of co-workers in and friends of psychical research. But when we find him cited in works hostile to psychical research, such as that of archcritic Professor C. E. M. Hansel, we have some truer measure of his influence. In Hansel's book ESP: A Scientific Evaluation (1966), there are more references to Thouless than to any of the Olympians I mentioned except Rhine and Pratt.

One of Thouless' distinctive contributions involved the terms "extrasensory perception" and "psychokinesis" and vastly simplified the issue of what was really taking place in these processes. The term "ESP" used to designate telepathy and clairvoyance, committed us to the theory that what was occurring in this process was some kind of "perception" like seeing, hearing, tasting. Perhaps a person guessing the symbol on a target is "perceiving" and gaining knowledge in some extrasensory way, perhaps not. Similarly, the term "psychokinesis" committed us to the theory that an immaterial mind was directly influencing a material object which might not be the case at all. It was Thouless' view, and that of his colleague, B. P. Wiesner, that it would be simpler and better to discard these terms and to use instead a term that suggested no theory about what was really taking place. So he proposed a neutral term to include both ESP and PK and which is today used by everyone everywhere, not only in the press and popular literature, but in parapsychological writings and vocabulary as well. We call these phenomena "psi," the twenty-third letter of the Greek alphabet and the first letter in the Greek word "psyche" meaning "mind" or "soul."

Thouless also suggested that the term "psi gamma" be used for cognitive phenomena, such as telepathy, clairvoyance and precognition, and the term "psi kappa" for the kinetic phenomena in which material objects are influenced without the use of physical energy. Although not as well established as "psi," these theory-free classifications are preferred by many parapsychologists.

As we glance through Thouless' writings, we see reflected there a very important concern: the lagging development of psychical research, one main reason for which is illustrated by the story Ducasse (JASPR, 1954, 1-20) liked to tell of the student who found a sea shell and took it to his professor. The professor, not finding any scientific classification into which the shell fit, threw it on the floor, crushed it with his shoe and told the student, "There is no such shell." I also like the way Thouless describes the attitude not only of professors but of most people of ignoring the facts of psychical research:

> It is as if they believed that God created a universe which was orderly on the whole, and that the ordinary facts of science fitted into this orderly universe: facts like the movements of material bodies, radiations, electric currents, material brains, and nerve processes. Then, having created a 99 per cent orderly universe, He created a few disorderly odds and ends like telepathy, psycho-kinesis, precognitions, hauntings and materialisations, which do not fit anywhere [JASPR, 1947, 162-163].

He puts his finger on the continuing problem of the ostrich-like skeptics who either pretend the odds and ends are not there or would leave them to the eccentric psychical researcher to study. Thouless disagrees with those who say psi phenomena have not been proved. He believes the reality of psi phenomena has been established, and yet we continue to propose and carry out more experiments to establish this reality in order to accumulate more evidence to convince the skeptics. They remain skeptical, Thouless says, not because evidence is absent but because psychical research is not developing. If it is to develop, we must go on to new experiments and new understanding until the seemingly disorderly odds and ends fit. To this end Thouless sought to find a way of viewing the problem so that psi gamma and psi kappa would seem no odder than ordinary perception and motor behavior.

In working toward this goal he succeeded in making another contribution of distinction to psychical research. Together with B. P. Wiesner in 1947 he published a paper entitled, "The Psi Processes in Normal and 'Paranormal' Psychology" (PSPR, 1947, 177-196), which presented a concise and careful hypothesis to account for ESP and PK and which Pratt wrote "should be required reading for all students of parapsychology" (JASPR, 1948, 142-145). This paper presented the theory of the Shin, an immaterial psychical component in the human being which operates in all our behavior and in all functions, both normal and paranormal, which take place in us all the time. This component not only interacts with outside objects and outside brains and nervous systems but also with the brain and nervous system of the individual in whom it is found. The Shin is similar to what philosophy and religion have called the "soul" or "spirit" but to avoid the connotation of something supernatural a neutral term, the twenty-first letter of the Hebrew alphabet, is used instead to describe it. Presumably students of parapsychology have followed Pratt's admonition and have made themselves familiar with the Thouless-Wiesner theory so that no detailed description of it is necessary. It suffices to say that it converts disorderly odds and ends like psi gamma and psi kappa into extensions of normal functions, psi gamma's counterpart being ordinary perception and psi kappa's ordinary motor behavior. The Shin hypothesis stands as an ingenious attempt not only to accommodate paranormal and normal events but it can also be used as the source of ideas for future research. It was so recognized by Schmeidler and McConnell (ESP and Personality Patterns, Yale University Press, 1958, 108).

The hypothesis has an additional profound implication for parapsychology because, of all disciplines, it is the only one trying to part the curtain of mystery drawn over human nature. Mind-body dualism was one of the oldest views of this nature, a view rudely pushed aside by modern science to make room for a monistic conception of the human being. Before the Shin theory, Rhine maintained that psi is nonphysical, but dualism was restored to the attention of thinkers and parapsychologists only with the advent of Thouless' theory of an immaterial component existing and operating in the human being, for now dualism was based not on religious or philosophical arguments, but on a careful construct hinged to facts from parapsychology and psychology. For many parapsychologists who see parapsychology as the study of the vital question of what the human being is and for many who see human nature as dualistic, the Thouless-Wiesner theory is a tool of major importance.

Like a cut diamond, psychical research has many facets. It appeals to some because it probes the mystery of human nature. Other researchers find its appeal in the practical application of psi abilities in many areas ranging from archaeology and healing and crime detection to winning at horse races and avoiding precognized disasters. Psychical research provided F. W. H. Myers with material that could be used as a foundation for his theory of a Subliminal Self and a cosmic philosophy. For Curt J. Ducasse psychical research offered a basis for philosophizing about nature, mind and death (these three, by the way, comprising the title of a book he published in 1951). For G. N. M. Tyrrell the phenomena of psychical research were important because they all "point toward the existence of a region of the human personality lying behind consciousness, hidden from view" (The Personality of Man, Penguin, 1947, 253).

Now Robert Thouless does not suggest that the evidence of psychical research is devoid of practical, psychological, and philosophical importance and that it may not lead to a greater understanding of cosmic problems and the mystery of human nature and destiny. But his approach toward it has always been quite different from the others and different in a very important way. He saw parapsychology as an unsolved puzzle. He approached it as an experimenter who could not resist trying to solve it.

As I said before, Rhine's experiments at Duke sparked Thouless' interest in this puzzle. The experimental approach appealed to him because he was, in the first place, an experimental psychologist whose main interest was in the experimental study of visual perception. Second, he agreed with Rhine that the observation of spontaneous cases could not provide convincing evidence of psi phenomena and that there must be an insistence on experiments and on the use of statistical methods. In Thouless' view, the main benefit to be gained from experiment in psychical research was that the experimental method allows us to get "definite answers to a wide range of questions that can be answered only vaguely or not at all" by the spontaneous cases.

He thereafter published two excellent books dealing with the experimental facet of psychical research: Experimental Psychical Research (Penguin, 1963) and From Anecdote to Experiment in Psychical Research (Routledge & Kegan Paul, 1972). The first book was written "to give a general picture of experimental psychical research" and was intended for the general reader. The second was written not only for the general reader but for those doing scientific research in other fields as well. This book is, without a doubt, Thouless' major work in the field of psychical research and a fitting companion to Straight and Crooked Thinking, his major work in the field of psychology. Rhea White, in reviewing it said that it was as essential as a bathing suit for anyone wanting to get into the experimental swim (JASPR, 1973, 304-309), and in his review of the book D. J. West spoke of Thouless' "characteristically lucid style and urbane logic that puts to shame most writing on the subject" (JSPR, 1972, 164-167). Thouless himself calls this book "my main contribution to parapsychology." Like the paper he co-authored in 1947 this book should also be required reading for all students of parapsychology. Regrettably, From Anecdote to Experiment in Psychical Research is going out of print.

In both books he takes up the problems associated with the study of spontaneous cases which he considers of limited value, a conclusion shared by other researchers, including that great collector of spontaneous cases, Louisa E. Rhine. He deals with experiments in reproducing drawings, with card-guessing experiments and with various other kinds of experiments in both ESP and PK. There are interesting treatments of trick performances of telepathy and clairvoyance on the stage and of how far chance coincidence can be excluded in experimental work and a discussion of the experimental evidence for psi and what the critics say.

In neither book does Thouless attempt to propagandize for the reality of paranormal phenomena. If his books are propaganda, they are propaganda in favor of the experimental method because, as he wrote, "I do not believe that psychical research at this stage can profitably advance by any other road" (Experimental Psychical Research, 16).

Thouless is no armchair experimentalist. He tried himself to create situations in which paranormal phenomena would happen at times and places of his choosing; he conducted extensive experiments in card-guessing and with dice and coin-spinning which have considerably advanced our technique and understanding of ESP and PK.

Just as Thouless has travelled to many places of interest in Australia and America, so his inquiring mind has gone from one interesting subject to another and in each case has added to our knowledge. Besides studying the effect on psi of the feedback of information to a subject, decline and salience effects, and statistical evaluation, he has dealt with problems of precognition, with theories of hypnosis, with experimental design and with Whately Carington's lengthy investigation into the autonomy of spirit communicators which Thouless found to be replete with errors so clear that Carington was forced to acknowledge that he saw no way of reversing Thouless' conclusions (Fodor, JASPR, 1937, 365-366). In conjunction with Brier, Thouless developed the majority vote technique.
He also examined the homing capacities of and orientations toward home ground of birds. What struck him also was the area of unconventional or "psychic" healing whose value is sharply disputed by practitioners of conventional medicine. Healing seemed to him espe-

cially ripe for experimental investigation of whether there was anything paranormal in the cures allegedly effected by prayer, by anointing with oil, or by "spirit doctors" such as "Dr. Fritz," whom the Brazilian healer Arigo claimed helped him treat 300 patients daily. Moreover, the area presents a challenge to researchers; it has always been extremely difficult to obtain any verifiable factual foundation for the claims that human patients have been cured by healers. Experiments have been limited to laboratory mice, yeast growth, enzyme solutions. Described in Thouless' books dealing with the experimental method is a neatly designed absent healing experiment to test the question of paranormality. Although hospital policy has not permitted this experiment to be carried out, it beautifully illustrates how Thouless proposed to avoid dogmatic assertions and denials in an important area of parapsychological concern. As with the Shin hypothesis, his experimental design offers us another starting point for research ideas and for expanding our knowledge.

Unlike Rhine, Murphy, Ducasse, and others who made their way into psychical research because of an interest in the survival question, Thouless was attracted to the field only because of the experimental work that could and should be done. His interest in survival arose later. You have just heard him say that, as we grow older and the event of bodily death and dissolution becomes more imminent, we are bound to get interested in whether bodily death entails the end of our stream of consciousness. But I think he was also attracted to the question of survival because, as an experimenter, he is fascinated by puzzles. It was also clear to him as an experimenter that the survival question needs experimental study because of the irrational credulity of some people and the equally irrational incredulity of others toward this question. But what kind of experimental investigation could be made?

In support of the survival hypothesis heavy reliance has always been placed on mediumistic communications purporting to come from the dead. The pioneers of psychical research, however, were in many cases not overly impressed with mediumistic communications. They were acutely aware of the problems associated with this kind of evidence. If the facts related by a medium were known only to the dead person and to no one alive, they could not be verified and were valueless as evidence. If they were known to the sitters or even to any living person other than the sitter no matter where he or she might be in the world, the early researchers recognized the possibility that the living person might be the source of the medium's knowledge; that is, they admitted the existence of what today is known as "super ESP" or "extended telepathy." For this reason, early in the history of psychical research the first serious investigators cast about for some test under which facts might be verified which were not known to any living mind. As we know, Myers devised such a test. In January 1891 he sent his close friend, Oliver Lodge, a sealed envelope with the intention of communicating its contents posthumously through a medium. Three years after his death when a script of the automatist Mrs. Verrall seemed to come from the Myers personality and to contain allusions to the envelope and a description of its contents, the envelope was opened. The result has been doubt and debate over whether what was received by the medium corresponded to what Myers had sealed in his envelope. Lodge and others saw that they did not match, but, since then, Salter has argued that if the Verrall script is interpreted correctly, it will be seen to have a clear relation to Myers' message.

From Thouless' point of view as an experimenter, the Myers test for survival was faulty on several counts. A test for survival should give a result that is clearly either right or wrong. Additionally, as soon as the Myers envelope was opened and its contents disclosed, its value as a test ceased permanently. And even if the ostensible Myers communication had been declared a clear success, the test would still be open to the objection that the medium could have obtained the message by having read clairvoyantly the paper inside the envelope. Thouless therefore set about to design a scheme that could be tested any number of times and which would involve the posthumous communication of data that were neither known to any living person nor left in writing. Moreover, the scheme would yield a clear-cut result that would not be subject to doubt or interpretation. His efforts have resulted in a test for survival which consists of a test message prepared in cipher by the use of a standard method of encipherment with a key passage or key words which are not told to anyone or left in written form. They are to be remembered during life and, if possible, to be communicated after death. (PSPR, 1948, 253-263).

Thouless' test greatly reduces the possibility of telepathic leakage from the living because no living person possesses knowledge of the key and because, as part of the test, during the preparer's life sensitives try over and over again to learn this key. This test also overcomes the problems of the sealed envelope test. Since a key is not left in writing it cannot be read by clairvoyance. Whereas the sealed envelope lost its value once it was opened and its contents revealed, the test message left can be examined any number of times and tested by wrong passages or words without being compromised. Nor can there ever be any doubt or room for interpretation about a passage or word. A key either breaks or does not break a test message. Only the secret key will break it and allow it to be read. The communicating of the key after death and the decipherment of the message would be strong evidence of the posthumous identity and survival of the person who prepared the test and who alone knew the key.

Thouless' cipher test for survival is an ingenious postmortem experiment which, like his other work, has provided a reservoir of research ideas for other researchers, such as Ian Stevenson with his combination padlock test for survival, Frank Tribbe with his cipher test for survival, and my own large-scale program to marshall the results of experiments based on multiple replications of these tests. As the father of these tests, Thouless has given survival researchers the opportunity to make a major advance in the experimental investigation of the survival question. I consider it a contribution of great distinction to parapsychology. Thouless himself wrote in his most recent letter to me, "I think that was my most significant contribution to parapsychology. In fact, it is the only one I could claim as having any significance." Of course, he is too modest.

In addition to his significant contributions elsewhere in psychical research, Thouless made another to survival research three years ago in which the first serious attempt was made to describe the kinds of theories that might be held about survival (JSPR, 1979, 1-8). Clarifying the problem of survival is surely as vital as experimenting with it.

Frequently we hear and read references to "a future Einstein of parapsychology," a phrase sometimes interpreted to mean that parapsychology is destined to become a branch of physics. This oft-quoted phrase comes from a significant paper Thouless published in the Journal of Parapsychology (JP, 1969, 283-299), which not only defines the phrase and the part this future Einstein is to play in the drama of parapsychology, but also how Thouless visualized his and our roles in that drama. The pith of the paper is that ESP and PK are anomalies we must expect to be rejected until a new explanatory system is put forward to accommodate them. We are not and are not to think of ourselves as Einsteins, however, and it is not our task to think out a new paradigm. Our job now is to do more detailed and careful research and to expand and make more exact our knowledge about psi and, in these ways, to lay the groundwork for an Einstein of some distant day to put forward a new explanatory system.

No one, and certainly not Thouless' Boswell, at this stage, can assess with any degree of precision the tangible and intangible benefits with which Thouless has enriched the history of psychical research. They cannot be listed in detail as assets are listed in an accounting ledger. But we can be sure that Thouless, now 88, in terms of both age and length of time dedicated to the work of the SPR and PA is one of the oldest members of both these organizations and has performed his task long and magnificently.

We are today fortunate that Robert H. Thouless, the man, the educator, the psychologist, the psychical researcher, the theoretician, the experimentalist, a giant figure who has influenced our lives and our field of interest and endeavor, is here with us so that we are able to express our feelings and esteem for him. Today he joins a distinguished company on the honor roll of those Olympians who have given so much and so well to psychical research. Whether they know that we remember them now depends on whether there is survival after death and communication between this and another world. But, happily, in the case of my biographee, we need be troubled by no doubts about spirit survival and communication. So today let us pay tribute to Robert H. Thouless for having devoted his first-rate abilities to making possible not only many accomplishments of past years but for helping to pave the way for the parapsychological Einstein of the future.

PARAPSYCHOLOGY, THE WILD CARD IN A STACKED DECK: A LOOK AT THE NEAR FUTURE OF MANKIND (Abstract of Invited Address)

Robert A. McConnell (University of Pittsburgh)

This invited lecture appears in documented and slightly expanded form as Chapter 7 in Parapsychology and Self-Deception in Science (R. A. McConnell, editor and publisher). Because of its length, it is presented here in abstract form.

In that chapter, I analyze the probable course of world events between now and A.D. 2000 on the basis of the first and second laws of thermodynamics and the present state and rates of change (and possible, higher-order rates of change) of the following global factors: energy production, arable land, food production, available fresh water, acid rain, atmospheric carbon dioxide, forest area, metallic ore reserves, population growth, Third World debt, genetic deterioration, and moral degradation in the industrialized countries.

In my view, the end of the Age of Heroic Materialism marks the beginning of an Age of World Poverty. I conclude on the basis of U.S. Government-published projections that there will be half a billion deaths caused directly or indirectly by starvation before A.D. 2000.

I offer specific, speculative, political, military, and parapsychological predictions and suggest two broad areas, namely military and philosophical, where parapsychology might alter the course of history.

I also speculate that with the major powers now reduced to nuclear stalemate, parapsychology may provide the future weapons of choice. On the other hand, by leading toward a scientific understanding of the spiritual nature of humanity, parapsychology might generate the kind of popular enthusiasm that could trigger a moral revival such has not been seen in several centuries.

I believe that Cartesian dualism and its philosophic offspring, upon which our present civilization was built, are incompatible with present knowledge of psi phenomena and that, in time, it will be shown that people have psychic relations that imply new concepts of moral responsibility.

Part 6: Presidential Address

THREE OPEN QUESTIONS

John Beloff

I must apologize if the somewhat cryptic nature of my title has kept you guessing but I can assure you that there is nothing cryptic about the questions themselves. They are the most obvious, but also, I believe, the most important questions that concern us and that our founders bequeathed us. First, then, does psi exist? Are there any genuinely paranormal phenomena or are all the phenomena that we have been studying over the past hundred years no more than ostensibly paranormal? My second question concerns the nature, as opposed to the existence, of psi. In particular, are psi phenomena just a peculiar feature of the physical world which physicists have somehow overlooked but which will eventually be brought within the purview of an extended physics? Or, are they, on the contrary, manifestations of quite another order of being, of a mental, spiritual, transcendental, numinous world that has its own nature and its own laws? My third question is the perennial question of survival. And, by "survival," let me hasten to add, I mean personal survival, survival as Myers would have understood the term. I shall not here be concerned with survival in some esoteric sense as it may figure in the speculations of certain current theorists such as W. G. Roll. Nor shall I be discussing reincarnation, despite the many remarkable cases which Ian Stevenson has brought to the attention of the learned world, since that raises questions of a different kind, not the least of which is what we mean by saying that distinct personalities separated in time are episodes in the existence of one and the same metaphysical self, whereas the question to which I shall address myself is whether we, as individuals, continue to have experiences and to engage in mental activity after our brain and body have ceased to function.

That these three questions are both fundamental and contentious has surely been abundantly demonstrated by the deliberations of this conference. In calling them "open questions" I wish to imply that, in present circumstances, a perfectly rational case can be made for answering them in the one way as in the other. This does not mean that we are not entitled to hold an opinion as to which answer we think is correct; like the rest of you I have my

opinions, but we should never forget that these are no more than
opinions. My quarrel, as always, is with the dogmatists on both
sides. The people we have to beware are those who assure us that
the questions are already settled or, even more insidiously, perhaps, that the questions are meaningless or irrelevant. In this paper it is the questions as such that I want to focus on, not the answers. What precisely is at issue when we raise such questions?
What hope is there of ever reaching a definitive answer or at least
a consensus of informed opinion?

There is, at the present time, one vociferous school of
thought--sociologists of knowledge is how they usually style themselves--who maintain that it is not only in questions of ethics or
religion or politics that there can be no uniquely correct answer;
even in the so-called hard sciences the answer that one arrives at
will depend on the assumptions with which one began or, to use their
favorite expression, on the particular paradigm that one adopts. (A
lively example of this approach as applied to the problems of the
paranormal in general and metal-bending in particular is to be found
in Collins and Pinch [1982].) I mention this in order to dissociate
myself from this point of view. As I see it, if a question is scientific then it has a definite answer even if we may never be in a
position to know for certain what that answer is. An example of
an open question in my sense is whether there is intelligent life
elsewhere in the universe. This question has been debated since
antiquity and rational arguments have been adduced both for a positive and a negative answer even though no final confirmation may
ever be forthcoming.

Having now explained what I mean by an "open" question, let
us turn to the first of our three questions, that of the existence of
psi, surely for all of us the basic question in the sense that if the
answer is negative our other two questions do not arise. It is a
question that has tormented me all my life. Henry Sidgwick, in his
first presidential address to the newly founded SPR, remarked on
what a scandal it was that there should still be controversy over
the very existence of these age-old phenomena and it is, I fear, a
measure of our failure that a hundred years on the controversy still
persists. It is no use our pretending that only those who are ignorant or prejudiced still doubt the existence of psi. In the first place
it is untrue--we can all think of plenty of counter-examples--but,
even if it were true, it is still our business to overcome such ignorance and prejudice as there may be, for, until we do, the prospects for doing serious work in our field will remain pitifully limited. It is, of course, understandable that those who are active in
research resent having their morale undermined by total disbelievers;
psi research, after all, demands such a degree of dedication in the
face of all the frustrations to which it is exposed that doubt becomes
a luxury but, in the parapsychological community as a whole, there
is, it seems to me, still far too much complacency on this score.

The case for skepticism has already been debated at length
at this gathering but, if I might try to put it in a nutshell, it comes

to this. Paranormal claims must, by definition, challenge what we
now consider to be a well-founded knowledge about the world. Now
it is a rule that the more extraordinary the claim the stronger must
be the evidence to support it. But even the strongest parapsychological evidence is, by common consent, unsatisfactory and defective
in one or more respects. Hence, until such a time as the evidence
for psi becomes overwhelming, it will always be more rational to
doubt than to believe. This argument, as far as I can see, is sound
and I shall not try to fault it. Instead I will point out that when we
move from the general plane to the concrete case the argument begins to look very different. Before I do so, however, allow me at
this point to introduce a personal note. I am, I consider, particularly well equipped to appreciate the skeptical viewpoint. I have
always tried to cultivate a critical attitude towards most things; I
am entirely lacking in religious faith and think of myself in this
connection as a rationalist or agnostic. I regard the dangers from
excessive credulity as far more serious than the dangers from excessive conservatism; indeed I sometimes think that if paranormal
phenomena were more common and more widely credited our entire
civilization might be swept away on a tide of irrationalism. Psi,
moreover, has never intruded into my private life as, to judge by
many recent surveys, it has with perhaps a majority of the population. Much of my professional life has been devoted to the search
for some incontrovertible piece of evidence for the paranormal but
this has somehow always eluded me. Why, then, as I am so often
asked, do I remain an incorrigible sheep? My answer is as follows.
When I contemplate some of the strongest evidence in the literature
I find the so-called normal explanations far more implausible and
far-fetched than a frank acceptance of the reality of psi.

   To illustrate my point let us now consider a particular case
which, though highly untypical of our field, is widely known and
brings out the dilemma I am discussing in its acutest form. It is
the case of the medium D. D. Home whose career was, without
doubt, the most remarkable in the entire history of psychical research. Now the first point I want you to note about Home is that
he never lacked enemies during his lifetime nor detractors after his
death. Indeed the hatred he inspired in some was so virulent that
otherwise honorable men did not scruple to invent the most outrageous lies about him, while his posthumous reputation has been under
almost continuous assault from Podmore and Solovovo in the early
days to Trevor Hall and G. W. Lambert in our own time. I mention these facts so as to emphasize that the motivation to expose and
discredit Home was at all times extremely high. Now the astonishing fact--and it is a fact we should never allow ourselves to forget--
is that from that day to this no one has ever come forward with a
normal explanation for the principal phenomena--notably the levitation of large tables--that is even remotely plausible! Since mechanical contrivances can be ruled out in this instance the only suggestion that is even worth discussing--and it was already widely
current at the time--is that everyone who sat with Home was hallucinated to see what he wanted them to see. Now, if there was on
record a case of even one sitter who failed to see what everyone

else said they saw, this hallucinatory hypothesis would have to be taken very seriously. But, in the absence of any such case it means that we are attributing to Home a power that is only a degree or so less paranormal than the power it purports to explain! It is, moreover, a power that has no known precedent or parallel. Not even the most successful stage hypnotist has ever dared claim such omnipotence and Home never used any known hypnotic procedure, whereas there have been numerous instances down to the present time of alleged table-levitations. The only option that I can see that remains to the skeptic is to suppose that all the witnesses --and there were a great many--uniformly and consistently lied in Home's favor. But what conceivable inducement could they have had to do so? It begins to look, at this point, as if we have here reached the condition which the philosopher, David Hume, thought could alone justify belief in a miracle--though he never expected it to be fulfilled--where the falsehood of the testimony would be even more miraculous than the miracle to which it testified!

What, then, can we conclude from this case? Must skeptics concede defeat on pain of condemning themselves as irrational? That would be ironical indeed, seeing that Home flourished before the SPR had yet been founded. But I do not think that is necessary. As long as the skeptic does not pretend to have an explanation when he or she blatantly has nothing of the sort, he or she is still entitled to declare: "Rather than accept these facts at face value, with all that that implies about the sort of universe we inhabit, I prefer to believe that the evidence is flawed even if I cannot specify or even conceive what that flaw might be." Historically, as we know, Home failed miserably in his attempts to convince his contemporaries. Not only was he dismissed out of hand as a vulgar charlatan by intellectuals, such as George Eliot, who had never attended a séance; but even a scientist, such as Francis Galton, who had done so and had expressed himself in writing (in a letter to his cousin, Charles Darwin) as entirely satisfied with the conditions in which he was able to observe the table levitations, eventually succumbed to what Brian Inglis has so aptly called "retrocognitive dissonance" and lost interest. We have heard Piet Hein Hoebens argue that, since we have no time machine that could enable us to go back and witness Home in action, the rational thing to do is to focus on the present. But, while I would agree with him that historical cases can never amount to a proof, neither can present evidence dispose of historical cases. Thus the fact that there is no one today who can do what Home claims to have done does not imply that Home was a fake. Home, after all, was a unique individual and the product of unique historical circumstances. Hence we can no more expect to find a contemporary Home than we can hope to find a contemporary Shakespeare. Every generation, no doubt, will produce its quota of gifted poets and dramatists and, if I am right, there will be people in every generation with paranormal powers but no second Shakespeare and no second Home. Before I finally leave the case of Home I would like to mention that, at long last, we are to have a biography in English that is worthy of the man. Its author is the well-known English writer Elizabeth Jenkins, and it is to appear in late 1982

(Jenkins, 1982). I may add that the author has acknowledged her debt to the research work of George Zorab, whose own biography of Home has not so far been published in English.

Physicalism is the doctrine stating that every event that occurs can in principle be explained in terms of the laws of physics. When applied to the human organism physicalism becomes the doctrine that the brain, qua physical system, is directly responsible for everything that we actually do, or say, or think, and that mind or consciousness has no explanatory value. This doctrine may strike some of you as perverse but I can assure you that it is currently the prevailing orthodoxy among philosophers, experimental psychologists, and neurophysiologists. It is, of course, hard to reconcile with the existence of psi since nothing that we know about the brain suggests that it should possess paranormal powers but, since orthodox philosophers and scientists take no account of parapsychology, this does not disturb them.

It would be no exaggeration to say that a large part of the motivation for the founding of the SPR was precisely the challenge it represented to the dominant scientific materialism of late Victorian England, the materialism of Huxley, of Tyndall, of Spencer, and of the rest. Similarly, the founding of the first university laboratory of parapsychology by McDougall and Rhine in the late 1920s was likewise inspired by the urge to refute behaviorism that was then the dominant school of American psychology. Yet, at the same time, there has been from the start a different current of thought which regarded psi not as the exception to the universality of physical law, but rather as a pointer to the incompleteness of physical theory. It was no accident that membership of the SPR in its early years included no fewer than eight members of the Royal Society. The lure of physical mediumship was to some scientists of that time irresistible. During the past decade we have witnessed once again an influx of physicists into our ranks and, again, for much the same reason. This time the advent of Geller and the resurgence of physical phenomena in the shape of paranormal metal-bending was the principal bait.

But now we come to a curious twist in our story. It had become clear by this time that psi phenomena could never be reconciled with classical physics. But modern physics, as we are constantly reminded, is very different. It has its own budget of paradoxes and seems more promising as a possible means of explaining the paranormal. The result has been a new movement which I shall call, for convenience, "paraphysics." It is essentially an attempt to build bridges between quantum theory and parapsychology. So far it has proved no more acceptable to the scientific establishment than traditional parapsychology, but meanwhile, it has revitalized parapsychology in various interesting ways. The most important outcome of this new development is, undoubtedly, what is called "observational theory," that is, briefly, the idea that the critical event in any psi process lies in the reception of the feedback. It has already had a considerable influence on the design of parapsychological experiments, especially in alerting us to the importance of the potential psi experimenter effect. But the prime question that here concerns us is whether paraphysics can achieve that integration of physics and parapsychology that would vindicate the doctrine of physicalism?

A layman like myself must naturally tread very cautiously when discussing such a question; I can only plead that, while the equations and formalisms of quantum theory are not in dispute, the physicists themselves are still very much divided as to their legitimate interpretation or extrapolation. The diverse views of different physicists on this issue are discussed in Chapter 4 of Collins and Pinch (1982). Now there are various features of observational theory that give cause for disquiet and to which logical objections have been raised (see Braude, 1979, 100-124) but, to me at least, its fatal weakness is that it is rooted in the metaphysics of idealism. Its point of departure appears to be the assumption that the physical world remains in an indeterminate state until the instant when an observation is made, whereupon there occurs what is called the collapse of the state vector. I am afraid that, to me, this assumption makes no better sense now, when it is put forward on scientific grounds, than does the similar proposition that was propounded by Berkeley on purely philosophical grounds in the early nineteenth century. I do not believe that our universe is mind-dependent in this way. On the contrary, I believe that no more than an infinitesimal proportion of all the physical events which take place throughout space and time ever come under observation and yet the observations themselves would make no sense but for the assumption that these events occur in a determinate fashion. I further believe, incidentally, that everyone else agrees with me on this point unless, that is, the person in question happens to be engaged in defending some sophisticated philosophical position.

Thus, far from vindicating physicalism, observational theory turns physicalism on its head by assigning consciousness, now regarded as the "hidden variable" of the quantum equations, a cardinal role in the determination of reality. Matter, on this showing, becomes, as it were, a product of mental experiences rather than its cause. Now, this may, indeed, spell a victory over traditional mind-matter dualism but it is about as far removed as one could get from the physicalism which I earlier described as the current orthodoxy of philosophers and scientists. Nevertheless, the development of paraphysics has certainly made it much harder to give a straightforward answer to our second question, whether psi is physical or nonphysical.

Having criticized observational theory I would like finally to pay a tribute to one feature of it which is, I believe, entirely salutary, namely its insistence on the teleological or goal-oriented aspect of psi. Once you start searching for an underlying mechanism that would explain how the psi process works you are irretrievably sunk. There can be no such mechanism, no hidden energies, no mysterious radiations, no invisible wires or levers. In this respect the operations of our sensory and motor systems provide a misleading analogy however tempting at first glance. If psi occurs at all its functions teleologically: we will the ends but the means follow automatically. My friend Michael Thalbourne (1982), never at a loss for a neologism, calls this "psychopraxia."

Before we turn to our third and final question allow me to digress for a moment in order to mention, with a heavy heart, that one of the outstanding exponents of paraphysics, Richard Mattuck, is with us no more. He died unexpectedly in May from a heart attack. He had already submitted a paper for this conference that we were proud to accept but, alas, he did not live to present it. I have no doubt, however, that there are others who will be able to carry on from where he left off so that his labors will not be in vain.

One of the traditional attractions of dualism was that it held out the possibility, at least, that the mind might continue to exist and to function even when there was no longer a brain or body for it to animate. As an avowed dualist myself, I ought to be able to take survival in my stride. In fact, however, when I contemplate my own impending death I find it exceedingly hard to suppose that I shall survive in any shape or form. This may just be due to my earth-bound imagination; perhaps if I were to undergo an out-of-body or a near-death experience I should then feel differently, but there it is. Unlike the late C. D. Broad (1962), who said that he would be rather more annoyed than surprised should he find himself outliving his body, I would be very surprised but, at the same time, happy to find my dualism confirmed in this dramatic way. I mention these few personal details not because I wish to add yet another jarring voice to the many we have heard already on this contentious topic but so that you should know where my own bias lies. Thus, on the one hand it would suit me philosophically if survival were to be validated yet, on the other, the evidence I am offered taxes my credulity. This ambivalence may be an advantage in this instance since it enables me to feel some sympathy with both opposing parties. And, in what follows, I shall try to show that, on current reckoning, a rational case can be made for either a positive or negative answer to the question of survival.

Certain philosophers in recent years, notably Antony Flew, made a concerted attempt to show that the very notion of personal survival was based on a philosophical mistake. Very briefly, their argument was that the concept of a person implies a reference to an individual body so that the idea of a disembodied self is incoherent (see Flew [1972] and Penelhum [1970]). There are still philosophers who agree with Flew that the possibility of disembodied survival can be ruled out on a priori grounds of a logical or semantic kind. However, if you are impressed by this line of argument I would urge you to read a new book by Geoffrey Madell (1981) entitled The Identity of the Self. Madell, a philosophical colleague of mine at Edinburgh, is all the more telling in this context, inasmuch as he is not concerned with the problem of survival but rather with the question of what we mean by saying of two disparate experiences that they are experiences of one and the same self and he comes to the conclusion--unanswerable, as far as I can judge--that self identity is strictly unanalyzable; in particular he demolishes the claim that it could be made to depend on any sort of physical criteria.

Most people, however, appeal to science rather than to the subtleties of philosophy as a reason for rejecting the belief in survival. Certainly it has never been easy to fit survival into an evolutionary view of man as Tennyson must have been among the first to realize. What benefit could it confer on the species? Nature, we know, in its perpetual self-renewal is prodigal with the individual life; why should man expect immortality? However, the very existence of psi raises doubts about the comprehensiveness of the scientific world view so we cannot obviously stop there. More worrisome, I think, is the sheer disparity between the number of people who have died and the number of those who are even alleged to have communicated with the living. This might, of course, be put down to the sheer technical difficulties of postmortem communication--from the fact that we have received no communications from advanced civilizations elsewhere in space it does not follow that none exist--but it does make us want to scrutinize with special care such communications as we do receive. And here it disturbs me that so few communications have anything, or at least anything intelligible, to tell us about postmortem existence; nearly always the communicator is intent on establishing his identity and perhaps adding a comforting word or so for the bereaved. Of course it might be that only very few people are able to survive death, just as only very few people are able to levitate tables. George Pellew might have lingered on for a while to greet his friends when they sat with Mrs. Piper without this implying that death is anything other than a terminus for the likes of you and me. When we are all so much in the dark every possibility should be kept in view.

But when all the arguments against survival have been registered, the fact remains that there is, in the mediumistic literature, a large number of very striking cases where the most straightforward explanation would be that someone on the other side is striving to make his or her presence known. No one, for example, who reads Alan Gauld's forthcoming book Mediumship and Survival can be left in any doubt about this (Gauld, 1982). True enough, most of Gauld's cases derive from the earlier literature, but this may merely reflect the fact that mediumship has declined since the heyday of spiritualism. There is no one today who can compare with the great Gladys Osborne Leonard who was, I may add, born in the very year that the SPR was founded. It is not, therefore, lack of evidence that makes us doubt survival but rather the fact that the evidence admits of more than one interpretation. And this brings me to the crux of the question, the controversy between the survivalists and the proponents of the so-called "super-ESP hypothesis." According to the latter, of whom George Zorab has been the spokesman at this conference (see p. 125) since we know of no limitations on the operation of psi, it is always preferable to attribute all manifestations, no matter how suggestive of postmortem activity, to the paranormal powers of the medium who, after all, exists in the flesh, than to discarnate communicators who are purely hypothetical entities.

The super-ESP hypothesis has much to be said in its favor. I would add, moreover, that recent developments have enhanced its credibility if only because current conceptions of psi make it all but impossible to draw any valid distinction between simple ESP and super-ESP. One has only to think of what is involved in, say, the psi-experimenter effect or the group-PK effect to appreciate this point. Nevertheless, a supporter of the super-ESP hypothesis would be going too far in wanting to claim that the living medium must always take precedence over the deceased person as the source of the message. Nothing beyond positivistic dogma, after all, need prevent a scientist from positing whatever hypothetical entities his theory may demand. Hence, if survivalists could show sufficient evidence of purpose and initiative in the putative communicators, as they appear to have done in some of the more striking drop-in cases, the balance of plausibility could well tilt in favor of the survival hypothesis. An example may serve to bring out my point. Soon after the death of Conan Doyle in the summer of 1930, Harry Price organized a séance, with Eileen Garrett as medium, to see whether contact might be established. Had Conan Doyle come through on that occasion I think we would all be tempted to say that Mrs. Garrett's unconscious had obliged with an act of appropriate personification. But what came through, to everyone's surprise, was the voice of Capt. Irwin of the ill-fated R-101 airship that had crashed so tragically a few days before and this voice proceeded to pour out a stream of technical information concerning the causes of the disaster. Now, assuming the facts are as reported (Fuller, 1979, Ch. 11), a survivalist interpretation would seem to make better sense than crediting Mrs. Garrett either with super-ESP or a fantastic imagination although, curiously enough, Eileen Garrett herself came to reject belief in survival.

We have now considered each of our three open questions and it remains only for me to say something about the prospect of our ever reaching an agreed answer. I propose to take them in the reverse order to that in which I presented them. The survival question, for reasons which by now must be obvious, strikes me as the least amenable to a solution within the foreseeable future. I happen to be one of those who have dutifully set a combination lock for Ian Stevenson, but I realize, as he does too, that even if I were to succeed in communicating my code number after my death, that would not settle the matter. It could always be said that, if telepathy is truly time-independent, my medium might have reached back in time and plucked the information from my living memory and the fact that no medium had done this while I was alive could be put down to the fact that mediums in general are more motivated to produce evidence for survival than to demonstrate telepathy with the living. In the nature of the case, therefore, there could be no decisive proof of survival so long as there exist no known constraints on the use of psi by the living. The most we can expect to see is one of the alternative explanations gaining at the expense of its rival.

As regards the dispute between physicalist and transcendentalist, a resolution seems equally remote at the present time if only because of the extraordinary difficulty in agreeing as to what should count as a physical explanation. One development that could possibly clinch the matter in favor of the physicalist would be the construction of a machine that exhibited psi abilities. It seems likely, however, that this possibility will remain indefinitely in the realm of science fiction. Failing that, the next best thing from the standpoint of the physicalist would be to show that psi was a property of plants or microorganisms or tissue culture or other such living but mindless systems, although even here some might prefer to treat such evidence as support for vitalism. Otherwise, much will depend on the continued success of the paraphysicists in generating testable hypotheses. Meanwhile, for my part, I see no reason to abandon my own longstanding conviction that psi represents essentially the influence of mind on the physical order and, hence, that parapsychology affords the ultimate testing-ground for the mind-body problem.

We return, finally, to the basic question with which we began. Is the state of affairs that once scandalized Henry Sidgwick to be allowed to continue indefinitely or can we look forward to a new era when the reality of the phenomena, at any rate, is no longer in dispute? At last year's PA Convention, I ventured to suggest that what was needed now was for the representatives of official science to set up a commission of inquiry to examine our claims. The snag here is how we are to convince those in authority that it would be worth their while to undertake such an inquiry. On reflection, I think the only way we could get things moving would be to use financial inducement. Given adequate funds--a few million pounds would probably suffice--I believe the existential question could be decisively settled within a very short time. I envisage a three-stage program. The first stage would consist of a massive screening operation, worldwide if need be, to discover promising subjects. The second stage would involve training those subjects to perform under stringent laboratory conditions and in front of critical observers and cameras. Then, at the third stage, the bigwigs of science, suitably remunerated, would be called upon to witness the conditions and vouch for the results. In addition, a complete recording and documentation of these sessions would be made for the benefit of the world at large. In this way posterity would not need Hoebens' time-machine to find out what actually went on during these critical tests. (In fact, if we are very fortunate the problem of authentication could be short-circuited by the production of a paranormal object that could be placed in permanent exhibition.)

All this, of course, is predicated on the assumption that psi exists. If this assumption is false, the situation becomes rather more complex. Since one can never prove a negative, parapsychology could never be felled at a single blow. The only way, then, that the present stalemate could be broken would be by the gradual abandonment of all serious research when one attempt after another failed to obtain positive results where proper safeguards were observed. The critics would step up their campaign of attrition; there would be a crisis of confidence; and, eventually, the great adventure which began officially a hundred years ago would grind to a halt. However, let me hasten to add, in conclusion, that this is not the scenario that I foresee. On the contrary, I am hopeful that when we come to celebrate our bicentenary--perhaps, even, in the lifetime of many of you who are here today--the reality of the phenomena will no longer be in question. But, as always, time alone will tell.

REFERENCES

Braude, S. E. ESP and Psychokinesis: A Philosophical Examination. Philadelphia: Temple University Press, 1979.

Broad, C. D. Human personality and the question of the possibility of its survival of bodily death. In Lectures on Psychical Research. London: Routledge and Kegan Paul, 1962.

Collins, H. M., and Pinch, T. J. Frames of Meaning: The Social Construction of Extraordinary Science. London: Routledge and Kegan Paul, 1982.

Flew, A. Is there a case for disembodied survival? Journal of the American Society for Psychical Research, 1972, 66, 129-144.

Fuller, J. G. The Airmen Who Would Not Die. New York: Putnam's, 1979.

Gauld, A. Mediumship and Survival: A Century of Investigations. London: Heinemann, 1982.

Jenkins, E. The Shadow and the Light: A Defence of Daniel Dunglas Home. London: Hamish Hamilton, 1982.

Madell, G. The Identity of the Self. Edinburgh: Edinburgh University Press, 1981.

Thalbourne, M. A. A Glossary of Terms Used in Parapsychology. London: Heinemann, 1982.

Part 7: The J. B. Rhine Lecture

PARAPSYCHOLOGY: STATUS AND PROSPECTS*

Hans J. Eysenck

It is an honor and a pleasure to have been invited to give the J. B. Rhine Lecture, as Rhine was a good friend of mine and a man I admired for both his integrity and his originality. By a felicitous coincidence this is the centenary of the Society for Psychical Research, and the 25th Anniversary of the Parapsychological Association. By an equally felicitous coincidence this meeting is held at Trinity College, and of course most of the founders of the Society for Psychical Research were Trinity men. The impressive surroundings of this hall, with a picture of Newton gazing down upon us, tempt us to consider the status and prospects of parapsychology: how far have we come, what have we achieved, and where are we going.

What scientists and society think of a given discipline depends on both scientific and social factors. In the short term these are unfortunately largely uncorrelated, even though in the long term scientific achievement may alter and mold social acceptance. But in the short run the Zeitgeist and other similar factors are more likely to be influential than scientific achievement, particularly as the latter is largely unknown to lay commentators and is equally unlikely to be appreciated by scientists in other disciplines who normally cannot be bothered to read parapsychological literature. Most people class parapsychology with astrology, and I think it is interesting to consider some similarities and some differences between the two. Having just written one book on parapsychology and another on astrology, surveying the available evidence and trying to come to a reasoned conclusion about the claims made for both, I feel that such a comparison may be of interest (Eysenck and Nias, 1982; Eysenck and Sargent, 1982).

Going carefully through the literature on experiments usually quoted as the strongest supports for parapsychology and astrology, we attempted to assess these studies for rigor, experimental design,

*Delivered August 20, 1982

statistical treatment, and accuracy of interpretation of results. The outcome was quite interesting. In the astrological field, where the great majority of studies have been done by astrologers and people who were not trained in psychological methods, the best one could conclude was that while the results seemed positive and interesting, they were not conclusive, leaving the verdict as "nonproven," to use the old Scottish formula. When we followed up what looked like promising results we usually found that alternative hypotheses could explain the results equally well, and when we conducted experiments to test these alternative hypotheses, they emerged victorious. The only exception was the work of Michel and Françoise Gauquelin, who found what we considered incontrovertible evidence for a relationship between the position of certain planets at birth, and professional and personality characteristics of famous sportsmen, soldiers, actors, scientists, doctors, etc. Again we carried out analyses of a novel kind on their data, and these, too, came out with very positive results (Gauquelin, Gauquelin, and Eysenck, 1979, 1981). The interesting point to note here is that the Gauquelins are trained psychologists and statisticians, and hence are aware of all the artifacts and difficulties that bedevil work in this field.

In astrology there seems to have been no improvement over the years as far as methodology is concerned, but the story is quite different in parapsychology. Possibly due to the fact that most of the investigators have been trained as experimental psychologists, with a good background in statistics, parapsychological research has improved almost beyond recognition during the past 40 years in which I have been associated with it. Sources of error have been eliminated, psychological complexities have become recognized, including those of motivation, fatigue, inhibition, etc., and statistical methods have been improved to a marked extent. I think it would be true to say that experiments in parapsychology are at least as rigorous as most of those published in psychological journals in more "reputable" fields, and probably more so. As far as its present status is concerned, taking a purely scientific point of view, it may be said that parapsychology has reached the same level of integrity and control as has psychology as a whole. This is a very important conclusion, and it brings with it the corollary that to deny the reality of parapsychological phenomena at this point of time would be to deny the efficacy of well-attested methods of research design and statistical analysis in bringing us nearer to the truth. If these methods are appropriate to psychology as a whole, they are appropriate to parapsychology, and those who deny the reality of some, at least, of its findings are unlikely to have read the large experimental literature, and to have considered in detail the controls imposed, or the statistical analyses made. This great advance over the years bodes well for the prospects of parapsychology as a scientific discipline.

There are, of course, considerable difficulties which parapsychology faces, and which are not shared by all other psychological disciplines. One of the most important of these is the fact that parapsychological phenomena are difficult to replicate, and that only some people seem to have parapsychological ability. Critics often point to these facts as being fatal, but a simple consideration of the situation in the "hard" sciences suggests that this condemnation is inappropriate. At the turn of the century, for instance, physicists discovered the existence of super-conductivity, i e., a property of certain metals and alloys to lose all resistance to the passage of electric current at temperatures near to absolute zero, i.e., around 5°K. It is well known that only some metals and alloys show this effect; others do not. This has not bothered physicists in investigating the phenomenon, or in making it part of their science. The problem of why certain metals and alloys show super-conductivity, while others do not, remains of course; but this is a legitimate part of "ordinary science," as Kuhn would say. Similarly regarding "super-fluidity," another surprising phenomenon that occurs at very low temperatures, the fact that it is only certain elements or combinations of elements that show an effect does not mean that these phenomena should not be investigated; and we may say the same about psychological phenomena, such as those involved in parapsychology, hypnosis, etc.

When we come to the replication of parapsychological phenomena, we may remember also that many psychological experiments are difficult to replicate, and the phrase "failure to replicate" is perhaps the most frequent combination of words to be found in the titles of articles in psychological journals! There are of course ways and means of reducing this failure, so fatal to hopes of building an organized science, and it may be worthwhile to look at the reasons for such failures. In my view, they are linked very closely with the fact that parapsychological phenomena (and many other psychological phenomena as well!) are inextricably linked with the existence of individual differences, personality differences, etc. It may be worthwhile to go into this particular question in some detail.

Perhaps the best known source of differences in performance on parapsychological tasks was originally suggested by Schmeidler, in her proposition that "goats" and "sheep" would differ significantly in their reactions to experimental situations involving parapsychology, with sheep giving positive results and goats giving either insignificant or negative results. Much work has since verified these predictions, and it may be that investigators who simply average the results obtained over a random group of subjects may obtain insignificant results because the positive efforts of the "sheep" are offset by the negative efforts of the "goats."

In 1967 I suggested that it was likely, on the basis of some fundamental theoretical considerations of the nature of psi phenomena, that extraverts would be more likely to show such phenomena than introverts, and many investigations have since shown that this hypothesis does indeed give rise to replicable and verifiable differences between these personality types (Sargent, 1981). There appears to be some relationship between being introverted and being a "goat" and being extraverted and being a "sheep," but the relationship is not close enough to identify these two sources of individual variation (Thalbourne and Haraldsson, 1980). It would seem to be that if we are searching for research designs giving replicable results, we should begin by a proper process of subject selection, in the sense that if we want positive results, we should select extraverted subjects who are also "sheep," while if we want to have negative results, we should select "goats" who are also introverted. Hypnotists routinely select their subjects on the basis of tests of "primary suggestibility," as Eysenck and Furneaux (1945) have termed this particular trait, just as physicists select for work on superconductivity certain metals and alloys; there is no obvious reason why psychologists and parapsychologists should not be equally selective.

Suitable selection of subjects is one step towards the elusive goal of having a properly reproducible paradigm in parapsychology. Another step involves the selection of suitable test procedures. Recent work employing the Ganzfeld technique suggests that this may be considerably superior to older methods, such as the use of Zener cards, and it seems that there is a wide spectrum of testing procedures, greatly differing in the likelihood of producing parapsychological phenomena. Future work should concentrate on the best of these, and relegate the others to the historical museum of outdated procedures.

A third and equally vital step is the use of what I have called "indirect techniques." It was noted early in the history of parapsychology that there was a distinct tendency in long runs for fatigue or inhibition phenomena to occur, very much as one would expect from even the most elementary knowledge of psychological testing. Such effects could be predicted from psychological theory, and they were detected in runs that had been recorded several years previously, so that clearly the effect was not due to preconceived notions, biases, and errors, and the results showed even in data which on the whole did not give significant results in favor of psi. It is such secondary effects which link psychological factors of a well-known kind with parapsychological experimentation, and which are to some degree incidental to the run of the experiments, which can provide the strongest evidence in favor of parapsychology.

Fatigue effects are one example; learning effects using reinforcement, perhaps by means of KR (knowledge of results), as advocated by Tart, are another obvious candidate. Here, too, we have ample evidence in laboratory psychological studies to make us expect such an effect, and the evidence suggests that the learning effect can actually be demonstrated.

What I would suggest is that we are within sight of the reproducible parapsychological experiment. What we need to do is to select subjects in a suitable manner, select methods of testing to the best of our available knowledge, and to minimize fatigue effects and maximize learning effects. Combining all these should result in experiments which are at least as replicable as the better established phenomena in ordinary psychology. I do not think that such experiments are particularly important for the internal development of parapsychological principles, but they would be of the utmost importance in connection with what we might perhaps call our "public relations"; replicable results might convince even the most biased and bigoted of the reality of parapsychological phenomena.

I mentioned at the beginning of my talk that for the acceptance of any scientific data, we must bear in mind both scientific and social factors, and in dealing with the concept of public relations I have already begun to turn from the former to the latter. Parapsychologists often feel that it is only in the so-called "crypto sciences" that the hostile Zeitgeist manifests itself, that similar phenomena are not to be found in experimental psychology, or the hard sciences. This is clearly not true. Boring (1950), in his History of Experimental Psychology, invokes the Zeitgeist quite frequently, and any student of the history of the exact sciences will be able to adduce many examples of its importance. Thomas Young, for instance, one of the pioneers who first contradicted Newton's view that light was propagated by means of small corpuscles, and who instead favored a wave theory, wrote his papers under an assumed name because he was afraid that as a medical doctor he would encounter great hostility and prejudice among his patients because he dared to contradict the divine Newton. When his identity became known, this is what actually happened--he lost large numbers of his patients! The same was true of Harvey, who discovered the circulation of the blood. Although he was the King's Physician, he encountered much hostility and lost many patients. Many other cases could be quoted from the history of science.

In psychology, one might cite the unreasoning hostility to all references to genetic influences on intelligence, personality, abnormal behavior, etc. which is so apparent in the literature, and even more so in the classroom. There are, of course, scientific criticisms to be made of some of the methods used by behavioral geneticists, and the types of analyses carried out, but much of the criticism that is found, even in scientific publications, in textbooks of psychology, etc. is entirely a child of the Zeitgeist, and is evidence of nothing more than the ignorance of the critics. Thus a well-known criticism, originally voiced by a former President of the American Psychological Association, and now repeated in many textbooks, states that to try and assign differential importance for the development of the phenotype to genetic and environmental factors is like trying to decide whether the length or the width is more important in determining the size of a field. Now all the methods of dealing quantitatively with polygenetic phenomena employ analysis of variance; what is attempted is to decide what proportion of the total variance is due to various factors, such as additive genetic factors, dominance, epistasis, assortative mating, within family and between family environmental differences, etc. Clearly a single field has no variance, and hence is completely irrelevant to any discussion of the methods of behavioral genetics. If we had a thousand fields varying in length and width, we could easily determine the relative importance of length and width in determining the total size of the particular population of fields we are dealing with.

Next, just as we have many myths in parapsychology, so we have similar myths in psychology, again deriving from the Zeitgeist. My first experience of such myths in parapsychology occurred early in my life, when as a student I attended lectures by a Dr. Hadfield at the University of London. He was a psychoanalyst and lectured on abnormal psychology. He devoted a whole hour to a discussion of (or rather a diatribe against) ESP in general, and Rhine in particular. Among the things he told us was that the Zener cards were so thin that one could see the symbols through the back of the cards, and hence people succeeded by this hardly extrasensory means in getting better than chance results. I immediately went away, bought some Zener cards, and read Rhine's publications and other material. Nobody I showed the cards to managed to see through the backs of them, and reading Rhine's account of his experiments convinced me that Hadfield had either not read the original material or, whether on purpose or not, had given us a completely erroneous account. When I challenged him on the point he became abusive, rather than trying to defend his view, a reaction which no doubt has good psychological explanations, and often occurs in similar circumstances, but which is not in the best interests of scientific advancement!

Consider the existence of a myth of equal proportion in behavioral genetics. It is often suggested that because there is a strong genetic component in criminality, therefore, critics suggest, the geneticist must hold the view that such criminality is predestined, and there is nothing that can be done about it. But this, of course, is nonsensical. Heritability estimates are population parameters, and may differ from one population to another, from one country to another, and from one time to another. If we found better ways of dealing with criminality, we might very well reduce the heritability of the phenotypic behavior, and increase the amount of environmental determination. To take a fanciful example, consider the female bosom. At the moment its size, shape, and consistency are largely determined by genetic factors, if we leave out of account such unusual circumstances as starvation. Yet it is not fanciful to imagine that the recent advances in silicone injection, plastic surgery, etc. will make it possible in 50 years' time to contemplate a population, perhaps made up of Californian women, where genetics plays only a very small part, and environmental circumstances are much more influential! The myth of the complete determination of behavior by genetic factors, so arduously propagated by ideological opponents of genetic determinants, is nothing but scientific nonsense, but it certainly has exerted a very powerful influence. Similarly, myths regarding parapsychology are very important, and determine the attitude not only of laypersons, but also of many scientists.

One reason why psychologists and other scientists tend to berate parapsychology and accuse it of not being a science is the absence of any theory which might account for the facts uncovered. However, such criticisms are clearly not very meaningful. Do we

have agreed theories of intelligence, of personality, or of learning
and conditioning, let alone memory, in psychology? To raise this
question is to know what the answer is. Typically textbooks of personality or of learning contain a large number of chapters, each
outlining one particular person's theory and contributions, but no
discussion of ways in which these can be combined to give a single
paradigm acceptable to all psychologists working in that field. Why
should we expect parapsychology to do what has not been achieved in
psychology as a whole? To do so is unreasonable, and the lack of
theory, while true, is certainly not a reason for abandoning parapsychology as nonscientific.

But, as many hard scientists say, perhaps psychology is not
a science at all, so that parapsychology is simply in bad company
by associating with psychology. This may of course be true; James
long ago pointed out that psychology was not a science, but rather
the hope of a science, and perhaps the situation has not changed all
that much. But it is not the absence of a universally agreed theory
which must be held responsible for this. If you look at physics,
for instance, we find that there is no agreed theory of gravitation.
Newton advanced the hypothesis of propagation through empty space
("action at a distance") of attractive forces, but of course realized
himself that this was quite unacceptable as a theory. In modern
times we have two such very different and even contradictory hypotheses as Einstein's relativity theory, which attributes gravitational phenomena to distortions of the geometry of space, and quantum
theory, which invokes the graviton and particle interchange. No
physicists would claim to know the causes of gravitation, or to have
a unified theory of gravitation; why should we expect psychology in
general, and parapsychology in particular, to do better than that?
Similarly, there is no agreed theory of heat, and many other examples could be given.

What is true, of course, is that there are what Kuhn calls
"paradigms" in these sciences, and psychology is certainly to be
faulted for lacking for the most part such paradigms, just as parapsychology does. It is for this reason that I was suggesting con-
centrating on a single replicable type of experimental design which
could be regarded as a paradigm, and on which all parapsychologists
could agree, and from which they might branch out to study various
parameters related to that paradigm. I feel very strongly that only
in this way will we make parapsychology scientifically acceptable.

I have been concerned in this talk mainly with the present
status of parapsychology, but I have incidentally suggested certain
ways of advance which might improve our prospects for the future.
Even so, many critics ask the simple question: "What is the good
of it all?" Even if we could demonstrate the existence of parapsychological phenomena, they would appear to have little practical importance, and theoretically to go counter to much of what is thought
in physics. I think the most obvious answer is the one given by
Faraday many years ago, when he introduced at a public gathering
a very small model of his recently invented dynamo. An old lady

approached him and said: "Mr. Faraday, what is the good of this dynamo?" Faraday replied: "Madam, what is the good of a baby?" The answer is that it is impossible to foretell future developments, and that to believe that one can do so is a sign of simple-mindedness. Only a dozen years or so before the explosion of the first atomic bomb, both Einstein, the leading theoretical physicist of his time, and Rutherford, the leading experimental physicist, put forward statements which said that the disintegration of the atom would never lead to any practical consequences! If such great scientists can be wrong, and shown to be wrong after such a short period of time, on matters on which they were the greatest living experts, how would anyone dare to predict what might or might not be the importance of parapsychology in the future? I think if parapsychology sticks to its chosen route, namely that of proper experimental investigations, rigorously controlled, analyzed by approved statistical methods, and interpreted with conservative caution, then we will undoubtedly improve our understanding of nature, and may contribute a very novel and important element to our knowledge of the universe. In contemplating such a moderately satisfactory present, and such an exciting and promising future, let us not forget the man who started this whole line of research. J. B. Rhine, a good man and a great scientist, would, I think, be pleased with the present, and excited about the future! The main guidelines of our work nowadays stem from his understanding of the needs of the discipline, and we can not do better than to follow his advice and example.

REFERENCES

Boring, E. G. History of Experimental Psychology. New York: Appleton-Century-Crofts, 1950.

Eysenck, H. J. Personality and extra-sensory perception. Journal of the Society for Psychical Research, 1967, 44, 55-71.

Eysenck, H. J., and Furneaux, W. D. Primary and secondary suggestibility: An experimental and statistical study. Journal of Experimental Psychology, 1945, 35, 485-503.

Eysenck, H. J., and Nias, D. Astrology: Science or Superstition? London: Maurice Temple Smith, 1982.

Eysenck, H. J., and Sargent, C. Explaining the Unexplained. London: Weidenfeld & Nicolson, 1982.

Gauquelin, M.; Gauquelin, F.; and Eysenck, S. B. G. Personality and positions of the planets at birth: An empirical study. British Journal of Social and Clinical Psychology, 1979, 18, 71-75.

Gauquelin, M.; Gauquelin, F.; and Eysenck, S. B. G. Eysenck's personality analysis and position of the planets at birth: A replication on American subjects. Personality and Individual Differences, 1981, 2, 346-350.

Sargent, C. L. Extraversion and performance in "extra-sensory perception" tasks. Personality and Individual Differences, 1981, 2, 137-143.

Thalbourne, M., and Haraldsson, E. Personality characteristics of sheep and goats. Personality and Individual Differences, 1980, 1, 180-185.

ERRATA

W. G. Roll

Ian Stevenson has drawn my attention to two errors in my abstract "Memory, Mediumship and Reincarnation" (RIP 1981, 182-184). The facts are important in evaluating the theory that rebirth memories, like postmortem apparitions and mediumistic communications, may be due to "psi memories." Such "memories," according to my theory, are associated with the physical locations where the deceased live and with people with whom he or she was associated when living (whether or not these individuals figured in the events and whether or not they can recall them).

I suggested that the link between the rebirth memories of Kumkum Verma and the life of Sundari, the first personality, might have been Dr. Verma, Kumkum's father, since he had friends in the village where Sundari had lived and often visited there. As Stevenson reminds me, Darbhanga is no village but a city. Sundari died around the age of 50 about 1950 when Darbhanga had a population of more than 100,000 (Webster's New Geographical Dictionary lists a population of 132,059 in the 1978 edition).

In the case of Indika Guneratne, it was a friend of Indika's father, not her father, who had attended the previous personality when he was ill and who might have supplied the link between that person and Indika's family.

In my abstract I stated that in five cases (of the seven I was considering) "the personal connections between the families contributed to the verification of the cases." Stevenson tells me he is convinced that the personal connections between the child and the family or friends of the first personality did not play an essential role in the verification of the five cases in question.

NAME INDEX

Adamenko, V. 110
Andrade, H. 111
Angelini, R. 179, 185-87
Ankenbrandt, K. W. 242
Arathoon, P. 39-42
Arigo, J. 202-03, 226, 231-34
Aristotle 81
Atkinson, G. 185

Bailly, J.-P. 148-49
Bain, A. 288
Balfour, G. W. 78
Ballard, J. A. 195-96
Barker, P. 152-54, 157-59, 269
Barrett, W. F. 126-27, 270, 284, 286, 288, 292, 296-98, 300, 306-07
Barrington, M. R. 72-75, 93
Basalla, G. 304
Batcheldor, K. xii, 35, 37-38, 45-56, 193, 249, 260
Beattie, J. 242
Beauchamp, Miss S. 206
Beethoven, L. van 290
Beloff, J. xi-xiii, 13, 122, 140, 199-200, 224, 228-30, 283, 317-27
Bender, H. 17, 143-44, 270
Bennett, E. 78
Benor, D. xii
"Benson, Miss" 80
Beraud, M. 70-72
Berendt, H. C. 43-44
Berger, A. xii, 123-25, 306-16
Bergin, A. E. 211
Bergson, H. 143
Berkeley, G. 322
Bernheim, H. 3

Bierman, D. xii, 57, 97
Birnholz, J. 230
Bisson, Mme. 70-71
Björkhem, J. 117
Blackmore, S. J. 17-21, 24, 202-3, 226, 231-34
Blondot 30
Blundell, G. 105
Boatman, B. 98
Bogart, D. N. 269
Bohm, D. 119
Boole, G. 286, 291
Boole, Mrs. G. 286, 297
Boring, E. G. 5, 332, 335
Bose, J. C. 110
Bramwell, M. 3
Braud, W. 46, 55, 67, 163-65, 182-85, 187-89
Braude, S. 322, 327
Brier, R. 312
Britten, B. 29
Broad, C. D. 307, 323, 327
Brock, W. H. 288, 300
Brooke, J. H. 285, 300
Brookes-Smith, C. 50, 53, 249
Broughton, R. 99, 115-16
Brown, A. W. 289, 300
Brown, R. 28
Brush, S. G. 300
Burdick, D. S. 273
Burt, C. 30
Butts, R. E. 297, 300

Cantor, G. N. 283, 286, 297, 300
Carington, W. 117, 118, 128, 312
Carlyle, T. 123
Carnap, R. 291, 293, 298, 300,

301
Carpenter, J. 268
Carpenter, W. B. 284
Carr, B. xiii, 224
Carrington, H. 76, 299
Carroll, L. 286
Cassirer, M. 75-77
Chattopadhya, A. 110
Chen Hsin 278-82
Choudhury, J. K. 110
Claudewitz, K. 145-47
Clifford, W. K. 291
Cohee, J. C. 195-96
Cohen, D. 292, 299, 301
Cohen, I. B. 300, 301
Coleman, W. 304
Collins, B. A. 79
Collins, H. M. 137, 318, 322, 327
Coly, L. 164, 182, 187, 268
Cook, E. W. 214-17
Cook, I. A. 159-63
Cornell, A. D. xiii, 135, 224
Cousins, N. 212
Coutinho, T. xii
Cox, W. E. xii, 113-14, 116
Crandon, M. 292, 294
Cranston, S. L. 123
Creery sisters 298
Croiset, G. 16, 17, 143-45
Crookes, W. 284, 286, 297
Curtis, T. A. 159-63

Darwin, C. 286, 320
Dauber, J. W. 297, 301
Davey, S. J. 27
David-Neel, A. 205
Davitashvili, J. 258
Dean, D. 100-01, 103
Delanoy, D. 199-200
De Mattei, R. J. 103-05
De Montesquiou, R. 78
De Morgan, A. 286, 295, 301
De Morgan, S. 286, 301
Dennis, M. 129
De Noailles, A. 72-73
Despard family 78-79
Dessoir, M. 295, 296, 301
Dewey, J. 299
Dilley, F. 122
Dingwall, E. J. 75
Dodgson, C. L. 286

Dolby, R. G. A. 291, 301
Donkin, W. F. 284
Doyle, A. C. 325
Drake 199
Draper, J. W. 290
Driesch, H. 119
Drucker, S. A. 269
Ducasse, C. J. 309, 311, 313
DuNann, D. 105
Dunne, B. J. 154-57, 159-63
Dunseath, W. J. R. 8
DuPlessis, Y. 147-49
Dupre, F. 202

Eccles, J. C. 306
Edgeworth, F. Y. 297, 301
Edwards, M. 62-64, 66, 68
Ehrenwald, J. 52
Einstein, A. 297, 334-35
Eisenbud, J. 122
Eldridge, T. M. 195-96
Eliot, G. 320
Eliot, T. S. 43
Ellis, W. D. 293, 301
Emerson, R. W. 307
Eva C. 70-72
Evans 212
Evans, C. 10
Evans, H. 204-207
Evans, J. 78
Eysenck, H. xii, 328-35
Eysenck, S. B. G. 329, 335

Faraday, M. 334-35
Feigl, H. 293, 301
Festinger, L. 69, 90
Feyerabend, P. 140
Field, G. 208
Flew, A. 323, 327
Fodor, N. 299, 301, 312
Foster, M. 292, 298
Foxwell, H. S. 296
Frank, J. D. 213
French, R. K. 298, 301
Freud, S. 3, 294, 299
Fuller, J. G. 325, 327
Furneaux, W. D. 331, 335

Galton, F. 320
Garbutt, J. T. 104

Name Index

Garfield, S. L. 211
Garland, M. M. 285, 301
Garrett, E. 325
Gauld, A. 1-3, 77, 129, 135, 274, 298, 301, 324, 327
Gauquelin, F. 329, 335
Gauquelin, M. 329, 335
Geertz, C. 256
Geison, G. L. 292, 298, 301
Geley, G. 70-74
Geller, U. 142, 321
George, L. 188
Giesler, P. 46, 193, 241-44, 248-50, 254-56
Girard, J.-P. 113
Gladden, P. 100
Gladden, R. 100-01
Godman, C. 143-44
Goldney, K. M. 29
Gooding, G. 79
Grad, B. 66, 100, 212
Grattan-Guinness, I. xii, xiii, 283-304
Gregory, A. xiii, 204, 283
Greville, T. N. E. 120-23, 146
Grosse, M. 106
Grosso, M. 122
Guarcello, R. 179
Gurney, E. xi, 129, 296, 297, 307

Hadfield, Dr. 333
Haight, J. M. 93
Hall, T. 319
Hansel, C. E. M. 145-47, 309
Hansen, G. P. 115-16, 268-69
Haraldsson, E. 122, 129, 147, 195, 197-98, 306, 331, 335
Harary, K. 163, 251-54
Harman, P. 283
Harner, M. J. 206
Harris, J. 232-34
Harvey, W. 332
Hasted, J. 37-42, 105-06, 112
Haynes, R. 69
Head, J. 123
Hearne, K. M. T. 221-23
Hearnshaw, L. S. 30

He Chongying 277
Hegel, G. F. 290-91
Heimann, P. M. 288, 301
Heloise Gr. 39, 41
Hess, D. 46, 193-94, 256
Hibbard, W. S. 268
Hickman, J. L. 261-62
Higginson, P. 100
Hinton, J. 290
Hitching, F. 14
Hitler, A. 291
Hodge, M. J. 297, 300
Hodgson, R. 27, 76-77, 307
Hoebens, P. H. 15-17, 143, 320, 326
Hollinger, D. A. 303
Holst, I. 29
Home, D. D. 15, 69, 319-21
Honegger, B. 230-31, 255
Honigfeld 212
Honorton, C. xi, 9, 21-26, 31, 112, 147, 157-59, 163, 224, 268
Hopkins, E. 290, 302
Houdini, H. 70
Hövelmann, G. 137-40
Hubbard, G. S. 101
Huggins, W. 284
Hume, D. 15, 320
Humphrey, B. S. 101
Hurst, L. A. 234
Hurter, J. 144
Huxley, T. H. 288-90, 298, 321
Hyman, R. xi, 10, 21-26
Hyslop, J. H. 292, 307

Inglis, B. 69-72, 320
Inyushin, V. M. 111
Irwin, Lt. 325
Irwin, H. J. 119, 231
Isaacs, J. xii, xiii, 31-35, 37-38, 45-46, 52-55

Jacquay, S. 144
Jahn, R. G. 152, 154-57, 159-63
James, W. 3, 117, 292, 299, 307, 334
Janet, P. 3
Jenkins, E. 320-21, 327

Johnson, M. xiii, 7, 59, 81, 93, 99, 118, 140, 218
Johnson, R. 119
Joines, W. T. 273
Jones, E. 299, 302
Josephson, B. xii
Jourdain, E. F. 78
Jung, C. J. 85, 145, 206, 255, 270
Jungkuntz, J. 199-200

Kammerer, P. 30
Kampman, R. 29
Kant, I. 290
Kanthamani, H. 190-91
Kappers, J. 150-51
Karolyi, G. 107
Katz, J. O. 218-21
Keil, H. H. J. 35-38
Kejariwal, P. C. 110
Kelly, E. 14
Kennedy, J. 8, 269
Kirby, B. C. 118
Knapp, R. H. 104
Knowles, F. W. 210-14
Knowles, J. 289
Koestler, A. 30
Kornwachs, K. 85
Kottler, M. 286, 302
Kragh, U. 197
Kreiman, N. 93-94, 96
Krippner, S. xii, 120, 258-59, 261, 276
Kuhn, T. S. 90, 330, 334
Kusche, L. 27

LaBerge, S. 230
Lakatos, I. 18
Lambert, G. W. 319
Lambert, R. 70
Lang, A. 241, 296
Lankester, R. 284
Lashley, K. S. 84
Leo XIII, Pope 288
Leonard, G. O. 127-28, 324
LeShan, L. xii
Locke, R. G. 238-40
Lodge, O. 76, 286, 297, 302, 305, 307, 313, 314
Luthman, M. 163
Lyttleton, A. T. 296

McAdam, P. 143-45
McBeath, M. K. 66-68, 113-15
McCain, D. L. 269
McClenon, J. 48-52
McComas, H. C. 293, 302
McConnell, R. xiii, 310, 316
McDougall, W. 292-93, 304, 321
McHarg, J. F. 207-210
MacKenzie, A. 77-80
Macleod, R. 288, 300
McVaugh, M. R. 292-93, 299, 302
Madell, G. 323, 327
Maisey, Mrs. 79
Margaret D. 209
Marie Antoinette 79
Marks, D. 14
Markwick, B. 29, 63, 228-30
Marsh, M. 118
Mattuck, R. 323
Maudsley, H. 3
Mauskopf, S. H. 292-93, 299, 302
May, E. C. 98, 101, 104
Mayor, J. B. 296
Meheust, B. 205
Mei Lei 278-82
Messer, E. 269
Mill, J. S. 288, 291, 297
Millar, B. 59, 85, 99
Mischo, J. 165-69
Mishlove, J. 10
Mitchell, J. L. 259-61
Mitchelmore, C. 208
Moberly, C. A. E. 78
Montagno, E. xii, 270-73
Moody, R. 122, 306
Moore, G. E. 290
Moore, J. R. 287-88, 290, 292, 294, 299, 302
Moore, R. L. 293, 302
Morton, R. C. (pseud.) 77
Moses, W. S. 127
Muhl, A. 29
Mulgrew, J. 182-85
Murchison, C. 292, 302
Murphy, G. 117-18, 307, 313
Murphy, M. 261
Murray, D. M. 245-48
Myers, F. W. H. xi, 29, 76-77, 126-27, 129, 287, 290-

Name Index

91, 295-98, 305, 307, 311, 313-14, 317

Nabours, R. K. 294, 299, 302
Nandagopal, D. 107
Nargon, R. H. 304
Nash, C. B. 137
Nashold, B. 272
Neihardt, J. G. 49, 51
Nelson, R. D. 154-57, 159-63
Neppe, V. M. 226-28, 234-37
Newton, I. 328, 332, 334
Nias, D. 328, 335
Nicol, J. F. 29, 289, 302
North, S. 39, 41-42
Norwood, B. 200-201

Oesterreich, T. K. 70
Olson, R. 298, 302
Osborn, E. 79
Osis, K. 118, 122, 128-32, 306
Ossowiecki, S. 72-75
Ostrander, S. 110
Osty, E. 70, 117
Owen, I. 121

Pagenstecher, G. 117, 296, 302
Palfreman, J. 297, 302
Palladino, E. 69, 75-77
Palmer, J. xiii, 15, 28, 46, 52, 55-61, 90, 129, 178, 195, 231, 233, 269
Parker, A. 6-10, 24
Parsons, D. 112
Pasricha, S. 214-17
Paul, H. W. 297, 302
Pauli, W. 145
Pearson, K. 286, 302
Pellew, G. 324
Penelhum, T. 323, 327
Penfield, W. 272-73, 306
Perovsky-Petrovo-Solovovo, M. 69-70, 319
Perry, R. B. 292, 302
Philipson, O. 232

Phillips, P. 62, 66-68, 113-15
Piddington, J. G. 78, 206
Pinch, T. J. 137, 318, 322, 327
Piper, L. 2, 127, 324
Pitches, L. 112
Pitt-Rivers, A. 284
Podmore, F. 69, 319
Poincaré, J. H. 299
Pratt, J. G. 118, 123, 146, 302, 307, 309-10
Pribram, K. 119
Price, H. 325
Prince, M. 3, 206
Prince, W. F. 307
Puri, I. 189
Puthoff, H. xiii, 14, 244, 249, 275-78

Qian Xue-sen 281

Randi, J. 112-13
Rao, K. R. 121, 140, 178, 189-93, 200-01, 255, 263-64, 267
Rao, P. V. K. 189-90
Rayleigh, Lord 284, 286
Rees, D. 28
Reynolds 103
Rhine, J. B. xv, 3-4, 103, 146, 263, 283, 292-96, 299, 302-303, 307-11, 313, 321-328, 333, 335
Rhine, L. E. 201, 283, 293-94, 303, 312
Richards, J. 288, 303
Richards, J. T. 49, 114-16
Richet, C. 69-70, 72-73, 76, 295-96, 303, 307
Ring, K. 122
Robert G. 207-09
Robertson, D. 39-42, 105-06
Rogo, D. S. 79
Roll, W. G. xii, xv-xvi, 117-22, 132-36, 270-73, 317, 336
Romains, J. 275
Romanes, G. J. 292, 296, 298, 303
Rony M. 43-44
Roos, D. A. 288, 303

Rosenthal, R. 213
Rostand, E. 72
Rostand, J. 30
Rothblatt, S. 285, 303
Rothschild, F. S. 43-44
Rubin, D. B. 213
Rudolph, L. 268
Russell, B. A. W. 290-91, 294, 299, 303
"Ruth" 205
Rutherford, E. 335
Ryan, F. 143
Ryzl, M. 118, 268

Sabom, M. 122
Sai Baba, S. 142
Saintyves, P. 263
Salley, R. D. 230
Salter, Mrs. W. H. 289, 303
Salter, W. H. 29, 313
Samararatne, G. 214-17
Sargent, C. xiii, 21, 190-93, 328, 330, 335
Schatzman, M. 205
Schechter, E. I. 152-54
Schiller, F. C. S. 263, 299
Schlitz, M. J. 190-93, 238-40, 266-68
Schmeidler, G. R. 1, 3-6, 93-96, 103, 117, 124, 130, 310, 330
Schmidt, H. 13, 64, 86, 145-47, 166-68, 191, 218
Schopenhauer, A. 123
Schossberger, J. 43
Schouten, S. 14, 224
Schrenck-Notzing, A. von 70-71
Schroeder, L. 110
Schroeter, W. 163-65
Schwartz, S. A. 103-05, 256-57, 268
Schweitzer, A. 212
Scott, C. xi, 11-15, 268
Sedgwick, A. 285
Shafer, D. 182-85
Shafer, M. G. 62-68
Shakespeare, W. 320
Shannon, C. E. 85-86
Shapin, B. 164, 182, 187, 268
Shapiro, A. 211, 213

Sharlin, H. 290, 303
Shaw, S. 62-64, 66, 68
Sheldrake, R. 81-85
Sidgwick, E. 76-77, 285-86, 289, 296-97, 303
Sidgwick, H. xi, 28, 76, 126-27, 285, 287, 289-90, 292, 295, 297, 303, 307, 317, 326
Singer, P. 242
Smith, R. 286, 303
Soal, S. G. 13, 29
Solfvin, J. xii, 59, 210-14, 229
Sondow, N. 157-59
Sorley, W. R. 297
Sparrow, M. 121
Spencer, H. 288, 290-92, 321
Spiegelberg 240
Spinelli, E. 105
Spirkin, A. 262
Stanford, B. 179-80
Stanford, R. 98, 178-82, 185-87
Stepanek, P. 118, 268
Stevenson, I. xi, xiii, 1, 3, 5-6, 122-24, 129, 214-17, 272, 283, 305-307, 314, 317, 325, 336
Stewart, B. 286, 288, 297, 303
Stratton, F. J. M. 77
Sulloway, F. 299
Swann, I. 102
Swets, J. A. 186
Szmurlo, Prof. 74

Taetzsch, R. 268
Tait, P. G. 288, 297, 303
Tang Yu 275, 278
Targ, R. 14, 244, 249, 251-52, 264-66
Tart, C. 7, 10, 52, 97-99, 101-02, 147, 170-77, 221-23, 269, 331
Taylor, J. 112-13
Tellegen, A. 185
Tenhaeff, W. H. C. 16
Tennyson, A. 324
Thalbourne, M. A. 62-64, 66-68, 89-92, 199-200, 323, 327, 331, 335

Name Index

Thomson, J. J.   286
Thouless, P.   307
Thouless, R. H.   xii, 124, 268, 304-16
Timm, U.   98, 102, 141-43
Torrance, P.   103
Tremmel, L.   163
Tribbe, F.   314
Tringale, S.   132-36
Troscianko, T.   19, 202-03
Turner, F. M.   284, 287-88, 292, 298, 303
Turner, V. W.   256
Tyler, L.   10
Tyndall, J.   288-90, 304, 321
Tyrrell, G. N. M.   311

Uhlenhuth   212

"V.," Mr.   29
Van de Castle, R. L.   241
van der Velden, I.   57-61
Varvoglis, M.   152-54
Veley, M.   29
Velikovsky, I.   294, 304
Venn, J.   286, 296
Verrall, H. (Mrs. W. H. Salter)   289, 303
Verrall, M. (Mrs. A. W.)   313-14
Vilenskaya, L.   110
von Lucadou, W.   85-89, 165-69
von Weizsäcker, E.   86

Walker, E. H.   xii, 86-88
Wall, J. F.   303
Wallace, A. R.   284, 286-87, 290, 292, 296
Ward, J.   287, 290, 304
Watkins, A. M.   212
Watkins, G. K.   212
Watson, J. B.   292-93, 299, 304
Weiner, D. H.   93, 116, 190-91, 269
Weiner, J. S.   30
West, D. J.   xiii, 11, 27-30, 79, 234, 242, 312
West, R.   105

Whewell, W.   285, 297
White, R. A.   xv, 45, 48-52, 251-52, 312
Whitehead, A. N.   291
Whitson, R.   269
Wiesner, B. P.   309-11
Wigg, H. H.   107
Wiklund, N.   9, 24
Wilde, O.   29
Wilkins, M.   112
Willie G.   39, 41
Wilson, D. B.   304
Wilson, I.   28-29
Wittgenstein, L.   291
Wittman, W.   169
Winkelman, M.   245, 248
Win Maung, U   214-17
Wolf   212
Wolkowski, Z. W.   113
Wollman, M.   95
Wolman, B. B.   8, 98, 129, 224, 268, 308
Worrall, O.   100
Worring   268
Worth, P.   28
Wundt, W.   291-92, 304
Wynne, B.   286, 304

Yeo, R.   285, 304
Youmans, E. L.   290
Young, R. M.   290, 304
Young, T.   332

Zorab, G.   125-28, 305, 321, 324

SUBJECT INDEX

Abbey House haunting case 77
Acta Universitatis Ouluensis 29
acupuncture 277
addresses, invited xii
Advances in Neurology 212
Advances in Parapsychological Research 120
Adventure, An 78
Aeterni Patris 288
age
    at first speaking about previous life 215
    at stopping speaking about previous life 215-16
    differences 105, 232-33, 247-48
    of subjects 32, 43, 62, 97, 245, 271
agents; see also subjects
    active 89, 91-92, 207
    deceased vs. living 49-51, 53
    of poltergeist cases 134, 136
    relationship of, to percipients 89, 130, 213-14, 224
ALGERNON 163-65
ALICE 163
altered states of consciousness xii, 3, 58, 118, 134-35, 207, 226-40, 242, 248-50, 271; see also consciousness; dissociation; dreams; Ganzfeld; hallucinations; hypnosis; out-of-body experiences; possession
American Association for the Advancement of Science (AAAS) 9, 140
American Psychological Association 332
American Seances with Eusapia Palladino, The 76
American Society for Psychical Research (ASPR) 128, 292
amnesia 3
Anatomy of an Illness 212
Andhra University 189
Anhui Teachers University 278
animal
    behavior 83, 292
    intelligence 292
    psi 267
Animal Education 299
Annual Review of Psychology 10
anpsi 267
anthropology 241-50, 256-57, 260; see also field studies
apparatus xii, 5, 8, 32-33, 39-41, 53, 57, 100, 104-05, 107-08,

110, 114, 152-77, 219, 222, 277; see also random event generators
apparitions 8, 19-20, 27-28, 77-80, 117, 121, 126, 128-36, 204, 237, 274, 309; see also hallucinations
   "Chopper" 142
   collective 129-30
   location and 130, 135
   physical phenomena and 130, 133, 135-36
   theories of 129, 131-32, 136
archaeology, psychic 6, 311
archetypes 206, 270
Arizona State University 27
artifact 46-47, 49-50, 53-57
   vs. psi 31-32
arts 298
Association for Humanistic Psychology 259
association, laws of 117-19
astrology 328-29
attitudes 90, 328, 332-33; see also belief; critics; doubt; fear of psi; resistance; sheep-goat effect; skepticism
   toward experimental situation 8, 93-94, 157, 193
   toward Ganzfeld 186
   toward healing 211-13
   toward out-of-body experiences 131, 234
   of parapsychologists 4, 35-37, 139-40, 222, 229, 259-61
   toward psychical research 2-6, 9-10, 131, 292, 294, 298-99, 309, 318-19
   toward psychokinesis 35-37, 69-70
   toward reincarnation 122-23
   toward survival 289
Audience Selection Poll 129
aura 107-110, 135, 235
Australia 243, 307
Automatic Writing 29
automatism 3, 28-29, 226

BBC-TV 208-209
Batcheldor approach xii, 38, 45-61, 249-50
Behavior and Brain Sciences 213
behavior of subjects of reincarnation-type cases 217
behaviorism 290, 292-93, 298, 321
Beijing (Peking) 276
   Medical College 276
   Teachers' College 276
   University 276, 278, 280
belief 17, 46-50, 53-57, 90-91, 131, 193-94, 237, 242, 299; see also attitudes; bias; expectation; sheep-goat effect
   in healing 211-12, 214
   in psi 15, 19-20, 27, 197-98, 202-203, 317-19
   instant vs. long-term 46
   in survival 323-35
Benthamism 285

Bermuda Triangle 27
Bermuda Triangle Mystery Solved 27
Between Science and Religion 287
Beyond the Body 231
Bhagavad Gita 256
bias 14, 130-32, 242, 331
 in data collection 129-32, 240
 in reporting 22, 24, 27
 judging 194
 REG 180
 response 269
Bible 125, 256
biochemistry 30
biology 81-82, 293, 298
Birkbeck College 39, 41, 105, 112
birthmarks 217
"blended" state 47-48, 53
blood pressure 222
body
 image 233
 weight, changes in 105-06
book tests 128
Borley Rectory 27
Boston Society for Psychic Research 292
brain 119
Brain 234
Brain and Perception Laboratory 17, 202, 231-32
British Association for the Advancement of Science 126, 284, 288, 290, 296, 298
British Journal of Psychology 308
British Medical Journal 28
British National Association of Spiritualists 284
Brugmans experiment 13-14
Buddhists 205
Bulletin of the British Psychological Society 276
Burma 215

Cambridge Research Laboratories (U.S. Air Force) 147
Cambridge University xi, 10-11, 27, 75-77, 126, 190, 224, 285, 292, 296-97, 300, 308
 Society for Psychical Research (CUSPR) 224-25
Case of the Midwife Toad, The 30
Catholicism 2, 288, 297
causality 86
Census of Hallucinations 28
chair experiments 17, 143
chance 297, 312; see also coincidence
change-in-state hypothesis 8
Chantecler 72
Charlottesville survey 28
Cheltenham case 77-80
Cheltenham Ghost, The 79

chemistry 82-83
Child and Youth Psychiatry Clinic 6
childbirth 230-31
China, People's Republic of xiii, 275-82
China Encyclopedic Almanac 279
Chinese Academy of Sciences 276
Chinese Human Body Science Institute 279
Chongqing 276, 278
Christian Science 297
Christianity 126, 287-88, 292
Church of England 285
cipher test 305-307, 314
circadian cycle 272-73
City College, CUNY 1, 3, 93, 117
Civil War (American) 207-209
clairvoyance 19, 72-75, 94, 118, 126-28, 185, 245, 248, 274, 305-06, 309, 312, 314; see also remote viewing; tests (GESP)
    mistakes in 143-45
Clark University 292
classics, study of 285
cognitive dissonance 50, 90
cognitive variables 103, 271; see also attitude; belief; consciousness; imagery; intelligence; memory; psychological factors
    absorption 185
    abstract abilities 245
    attention 147, 152-53
    cognition 118-19, 297
    cognitive lability 182-85
    concentration 34, 187, 212-213, 222
coincidence 19-20, 144-45, 255, 312; see also chance; synchronicity
collective experiences 129-30, 235-36
College of Psychic Studies 79
combination lock test 305-07, 325
Commission for the Development of Human Potential 259
Committee for the Scientific Investigation of Claims of the Paranormal 9, 112
communication 256; see also language; mediums and mediumship
    between USSR and USA 258-59, 261-62
    drop-in 325
    mind/machine 179-80
    with deceased 121, 123-28, 305-06, 312-13, 324-25
Communication and Parapsychology 268
Concepts and Theories in Parapsychology 164, 182, 187
conditioning 99, 334; see also learning; training
Conjuring Up Philip 121
consciousness 9, 50-51, 53-54, 87, 119, 129, 135, 189-90, 240, 286, 292, 299, 321-22; see also altered states of consciousness
control, illusion of 202-03
Cornell University 30, 193
Corpus Christi College 308
criminality 333
critics xi, 5, 9-18, 21, 23-26, 35-38, 47, 77, 91, 112, 115, 140, 143, 145-47, 221-23, 230, 242, 256, 259, 276, 294, 308-09,

312, 319, 326-27, 332-34; see also skepticism
cross-correspondences 2, 289
cryptomnesia 29, 207-09, 217
crystallization 82-83
cultural factors 123, 131, 206-07, 237, 241, 243, 260; see also anthropology
Cyril Burt, Psychologist 30

Danish Society for Psychical Research 145
Darwinism 2, 288; see also evolution
  Social 290
data collection 129-32
death, mode of 215-17
deathbed visions 305-06
deception 46; see also trickery
decline effect 23, 30, 89, 97-99, 119, 121, 150, 158-59, 312, 331
déjà vu 226-28
dermo-optic perception 147-49, 275
dietary effects 219
differential effect 189
Diseases of the Nervous System 212
displacement 55, 89, 103, 192, 230
dissociation 3, 28-29, 57, 206, 232; see also altered states of consciousness; multiple personality; possession
Dissociation of a Personality 206
distortions 71
  perceptual 27-28, 232-34
diurnal cycle 219
divergence problem 85, 88
"divided" state 47-48, 54
divination 248-50, 263
Division of Parapsychology 7
"Dr. Fritz" 313
doctrinal compliance 52; see also experimenter effect
doubt 54, 69; see also attitude; belief; skepticism
dowsing 127
dreams xii, 51, 84, 227-30
  lucid 229-30
  psychic 6
  veridical 235
drugs 150, 205-06, 211, 233
dualism 310-11, 316, 322-33
Duke University 311

EEGs 5, 8, 218-20, 222-23
ESP 309; see also clairvoyance, forced choice, free response, psi, remote viewing, spontaneous cases, telepathy, tests (GESP), theories
  memory and 17, 93-96, 117, 119
  super- 121, 313, 324-25
ESP and Parapsychology: A Critical Re-evaluation 145, 309

ESP and Personality Patterns   310
economics   297
ectoplasm   71
education   285, 298, 308; see also schooling
egrigor   205
electricity   286
Encyclopaedia Britannica   8
Enfield poltergeist subject   106
engrams   84
environment   56-57, 118-19, 130, 154, 262, 272, 332-33
    awareness of   228
    clinic vs. laboratory   211
epilepsy   135, 226-27, 236, 271-73
epistemology   290-91, 298
Error and Deception in Science   30
Esalen Institute   259, 261
Essays and Reviews   288
ether   286, 297-98
ethical issues   258-62, 264, 289, 299
Europe   297
    parapsychology in   7, 38, 297
European Journal of Parapsychology   38, 85, 99, 197, 213, 224, 271
evoked potentials   218-21
evolution   125, 286-87, 290, 292, 324; see also Darwinism
exceptional human body function   275-82
Executive ESP   103
expectation   77-78, 96, 129, 141, 212-14; see also belief
Experiential Learning Laboratory   238
Experimental Psychical Research   311-12
experimenter effect   6, 9-10, 12, 17, 30, 50, 52, 89, 91, 93, 96, 193-94, 211, 213-14, 240, 267, 322, 325; see also bias
experimenters; see also experimenter effect
    credentials of   277
    incompetence of   11-12
    inexperienced   147
    psi-inhibitory vs. successful   10, 17-20, 222
    second   146
    students as   7, 21, 179
"explicate" world   119
extraordinary human body function   175-82
extrasensory perception   see ESP
Extra-sensory Perception   3, 293, 295, 308
extraterrestrial beings   204-05
extraversion   8, 153, 169, 199-200, 330-31
Eyeless Sight   275

FRNM   see Institute for Parapsychology
fantasy   80, 129, 204-05, 215-17
FATE   36, 208
fatigue effects   331
fear of psi   35, 37; see also resistance

feedback 9, 31, 33, 47, 57-59, 63, 97-99, 101, 104, 147, 152, 157-59, 163, 168, 170-71, 178, 181, 186-88, 191, 198, 218-20, 228, 312, 321, 331
field studies 241-43, 248-50, 264; see also anthropology; spontaneous cases
fields 82
   interpersonal 118
   magnetic 82, 111, 280
   morphogenetic 82
forced choice 90, 98, 103, 228, 293
formative causation, hypothesis of 81-85
fraud 13, 29-31, 35-36, 44, 50, 53, 62, 64, 70-71, 76, 80, 112-14, 116, 123, 141, 236-37, 270, 289, 299; see also criticisms; trickery
Fraunhofer Institut für Arbeitswirtschaft und Organisation 85
free response 57-61, 89-91, 159-60, 163, 228, 230, 244, 249-50, 269, 293
From Anecdote to Experiment in Psychical Research 311-12
From Matter to Spirit 286

Gallup Poll 129
galvanic skin response 222-25
Ganzfeld xi, 5, 8, 9, 18, 21-26, 56, 58, 183-86, 331
General and Social Psychology 308
genetics 332-33
geology 298
Georgia, Republic of 258
Germany 298
ghosts see apparitions
Ghosts I Have Talked With 293
Givat Sha'ul Mental Hospital 43
goal-oriented processes 48, 53-54, 65, 86, 322-23
Grace Cathedral 253
Grandfather Bull case 78
gravitation 334

hallucinations 3, 28, 129-30, 135, 204-07, 227, 231-32, 234, 270-71, 306, 319-20
   auditory 229, 233, 237
   olfactory 234-37
hallucinogens see drugs
Hammid experiments 14
Handbook of Parapsychology 8, 98, 129, 224, 268, 308
Handbook of Psychotherapy and Behavior Change 211
handedness 103, 105
Harvard Medical School 230
hauntings see apparitions
Hauntings and Apparitions 77-78
head injury 207-08
healing, paranormal xii, 2, 6, 100-01, 142, 210-14, 262-63, 266-68, 296, 311-13

Subject Index 351

health 261-62
heart rate 222-23
heat 334
"heat death" 298
Hebrew University of Jerusalem 43
hemispheric differences 9, 103-05
Heymans experiment see Brugmans experiment
hidden variables 9, 87, 322
history 299-300
   in Chinese traditional literature 277, 281-82
   of psychical research xi, 1-6, 69-80, 120, 122, 125-28, 283-304, 307-08, 320
   of science 283-90, 297, 300, 328, 332
History of Experimental Psychology 332
History of the Conflict Between Science and Religion, The 290
holography 81, 84, 119
homing 312
How to Think Straight 308
Human Personality and Its Survival of Bodily Death 29, 129, 291
humor 55
hypnosis 1, 3, 6, 29, 48, 52, 55-61, 126, 144, 204-05, 224-25, 284, 292, 312, 320, 330-31
   age regression 208
hysteria 29, 271, 273

Iceland 197
idealism 290, 322
Identity of the Self, The 323
ideoplasty 71-72
imagery 9, 84, 130, 228-32; see also visualization
   control of 231
   training 187-89
implicate order 119
Imprisoned Splendour, The 119
incline effect 34-35, 98-99
India 215-16
induction 285, 288, 291, 297
information 85-89, 92
Institut de Paraphysique 113
Institut für Grenzgebiete und Psychohygiene 143
Institut Métapsychique International 72, 147
Institute for Parapsychology 115-16, 178, 188-90, 200, 238, 263, 268
intelligence 103, 332, 334
International Crops Research Institute for Semiarid Tropics 81
International Journal of Parapsychology 29, 221, 268
International Physicians for the Prevention of Nuclear War 261
International Scientific Series 290, 292
Introduction to the Psychology of Religion, An 308
intuitionism 285

J. B. Rhine Address xii, 328-35
Jadavpur University 110
John E. Fetzer Foundation 154, 159
John F. Kennedy University 241, 245, 248, 254
Journal of Abnormal Psychology 185
Journal of Clinical Investigation 212
Journal of Indian Psychology 119
Journal of Nervous and Mental Disease 123
Journal of Parapsychology 4, 24-26, 93, 101, 103, 115, 118-19, 159, 166, 200, 212, 268-69, 308, 315
Journal of the American Society for Psychical Research (JASPR) 8, 28, 46, 56, 58, 60, 97-98, 101-02, 118, 122-23, 130, 195, 210, 212, 218, 229-30, 232-33, 236, 272-73, 308-10, 312
Journal of the History of the Behavioral Sciences 52
Journal of the Institution of Engineers 110
Journal of the Society for Psychical Research 2, 9, 27-28, 35, 39-41, 52-53, 77-79, 122, 221, 224, 249, 308, 312, 315
judging 19, 26, 57, 60, 159-64, 194

K. I. B. Foundation 105
Kings College 100, 112-13
Kirlian photography 8, 110
Koran 256
Korsakoff state 208

lability 46, 54-55, 164, 187
 cognitive 182-85
Lamarckianism 290
language 239-40, 256, 286, 291
Lawyers for Social Responsibility 261
learning 94, 97-99, 101-03, 331, 334; see also conditioning; schooling; training
Lebanon 215-16
Leipzig University 291-92
levitation 15, 45-47, 76, 106, 296, 319-20, 324
liberalism 285
life force 111
life, other, in universe 318, 324
light 332
 infrared 100-01
 perception of 281
Light 79
location effects 130
logic 285-86, 288, 290-91, 308
lucidity 73, 230
luck 94-96

McDonnell Foundation 154, 159, 170, 173
McDonnell Laboratory for Psychical Research 62-68, 89, 113-14,

199
magic 205, 241, 263
Magic and Mystery in Tibet 205
magnetism 286
Maimonides 163
majority vote technique 268-69, 312
Malanesians 263
mana 263
Manitoba 243
materialism 122, 288, 290, 294, 321; see also mechanism; mind-matter relationship; physicalism
materializations 27, 70-71, 76-77, 296, 309
Mathematical Psychics 297
mathematics 285, 291
Matin, Le 71
meaning 254-56, 293, 299
mechanism 81-82, 84-85, 287, 298; see also materialism; physicalism
medicine 297, 312
    traditional Chinese 277, 281-82
meditation 51, 187, 237
    transcendental 189-90
mediums and mediumship xii, 3, 8, 28-30, 50, 53, 69-77, 85, 117, 120-21, 124, 127-28, 142, 235, 258-59, 274, 286, 289, 292-94, 305-06, 313, 319-21, 324-25
Mediumship and Survival 324
memory 81, 83-85, 129, 334
    in reincarnation cases 216-17
    morphic resonance theory of 83
    of "psychic" events 20
    pseudo- 208
    theory of ESP 17, 81, 83-84, 93-96, 117, 119
    traces 81, 83-84, 117
mental processes see mind; strategy, mental
metal-bending see PKMB
Metaphysical Society 288
metaphysics 121-22, 126, 131, 290-91, 293-95; see also philosophy
metempsychosis see reincarnation
methodology 6, 8-10, 96, 137, 139-40, 159, 193, 238-44, 256, 264, 289, 293, 311, 329, 331; see also Batcheldor approach; feedback; forced choice; free response; learning; relaxation; repeated guessing technique; training
    criticisms of 13-14, 22-23, 25-26, 53, 99, 112-13, 145-47, 222-23
    in apparitions research 129-31
    in Chinese studies 279
    in healing studies 267-68
    in survival research 124
mind 2-3, 117-18, 273, 284, 287, 292, 297-99, 321; see also mind-matter relationship
Mind 285, 297
mind-matter relationship 10, 44, 118-19, 122, 126-27, 286-87, 290, 304, 309-10, 317, 321-24, 326

Mind Out of Time? 28
Mind Science Foundation 67, 163, 182, 187, 190, 238, 266
"minilab" 113-15
miracles 2, 15, 289, 320
Miroir, Le 70-71
Mobius Group, The 103, 256
moral sciences 285
morphic resonance 81-85
morphogenetic fields 82
Morton case 77-79
Moscow 262
multiple personality 3, 28-29, 136; see also dissociation; possession
myogenesis 292, 298

names mentioned by subjects
 of object reading experiments 151
 of reincarnation cases 216-17
National Review, The 298
National Society of Human Body Science (China) 276
nativism 285, 291
natural selection 286-87
natural theology 285, 288
naturalism 287-88, 290, 292-93, 295, 299-300
Nature 14, 288
Nature Journal (Ziran Zazhi) 275-81
near-death experiences 6, 20, 122, 305-06, 323
Necker cube 183-84, 188
neurogenesis 298
New Guinea 243
New Science of Life, A 81
New Scientist 10, 30
Newsletter of the National Schizophrenia Fellowship 232
newspaper tests 128
Nineteenth Century, The 289, 298
Norwich Middle School 308
N-rays 30
North America, parapsychology in 7
North London Polytechnic Institute 204
nuclear warfare 253
Nyoro 242

object reading see psychometry
observational theory see theories
observers of apparitions 129-30
occultism 9-10, 140
occupation 103, 105
Ockulta Problemet, Det 117
Offene System I. 86
Ogonyok 262
Omni 103, 268

Subject Index 355

Organizing Committee xiii
out-of-body experiences 6, 8, 18, 20, 28, 130-31, 205, 229-34,
    305-06, 323
  fetal 230

PK 71-72, 89, 185, 187, 189, 218, 280, 309; see also Batcheldor
    approach; materializations; PKMB; poltergeists; spontaneous
    cases; tests (PK); theories
  control of 47-48
  directly observable 37
  distribution of 45
  goal-oriented 48, 53-54
  limitations of 102
  macro- 35-37, 45-55, 57, 102, 113-16, 260
  micro- 31-37, 52, 57, 255
  pseudo- 35-36
PKMB xii, 8, 30-44, 55, 62, 112, 318, 321
  distribution of 34, 38
  filming of 43-44
  micro- 31-37, 52
  spontaneous 32, 38, 55
pain 210
Paranormal Foreknowledge 122
paraphysics 295, 321-23, 326
Parapsychological Association xi, 3-4, 7, 9, 13, 21, 140, 259,
    261-62, 276, 283, 306, 315, 328
  conventions 35-37, 113, 192, 199, 253, 326
  proceedings of   see   Research in Parapsychology
Parapsychological Journal of South Africa 234
parapsychology; see also history; methodology; psychical research
  course in 4
  doctorates in 7, 9
  funding in 4-7, 9, 140, 253-54, 256, 326
  future of xii, 251-57, 315-16, 334-35
  recommendations for 137-40, 252-57, 310
  research institutions in 7
  spontaneous case studies vs. experimental 8, 16, 18, 27, 243-
    44, 255-56, 293, 295, 311-12
  student research and 7
  vs. other science 10-15, 30, 137, 140, 286, 295, 321, 329-30
Parapsychology and Self-Deception in Science xiii, 316
Parapsychology Foundation 148, 170, 173, 195, 245
Parapsychology Review 140, 230-31, 248
Parapsychology Sources of Information Center 45, 48, 251
Parapsykologi 7
Peking see Beijing
People's Daily, The 275
perception 129, 221, 239-40, 311
  dermo-optic 147-49, 275
  ESP and 9, 145, 309-10
  faulty 27-28, 35, 232-34
  of light 281

subliminal 189-90
   time 103-04, 186, 225, 228
percipients; see also subjects
   relationship of, to agents 89, 130, 213-14, 224
   relationship of, to targets 118-19
personalities 317
   fantasy-prone 134
   merging of 121
   multiple 3, 28-29, 136
Personality of Man, The 311
personality tests; see also psychological tests
   Barber and Wilson Inventory of Childhood Memories and Imaginings 134
   Bett's Imagery Scale 8
   Cattell's Sixteen Personality Factor Questionnaire 199
   Creative Imagination Scale 57, 59
   Defense Mechanism Test 197-98
   EWL Scale 169
   Eysenck's Personality Inventory 199
   FPI Scale 168-69
   Gordon's Test of Visual Imagery Control 188-89
   Holland Occupational Scale 103
   IPC Scale 168-69
   Marks' Vividness of Imagery Questionnaire 188
   MMPI 199
   Myers-Briggs Personality Indicator 153
   Paivio's Individual Differences Questionnaire 188
   Social Introversion Scale 199
   Speilberger's State-Trait Anxiety Inventory 195
   Tellegen Absorption Scale 57, 59, 153, 185, 187
   Word Association 128
personality variables xii, 8, 117-19, 169, 237, 311, 330, 332, 334; see also cognitive variables, psychological variables
   aggression 169
   astrology and 329
   creativity 103
   defensiveness 197
   extraversion 8, 153, 169, 199-200, 330-31
   hypnotic susceptibility 211, 225
   internality/externality 169
   neuroticism 169
   suggestibility 237, 331
personation 207-210
Persuasion and Healing 213
phantasmogenetic center 129
Phantasms of the Living 297
phantom leaf effect 110-11
"Philip" 121, 305
Philippines 245
Phillips University 137
philosophy 283-93, 296-300, 310-11, 316, 321-24
Philosophy of Science 293
Philosophy of Science Association 293

Subject Index

phobias 216
Phoenix 242
photography
  Kirlian 8, 110
  of alleged PK events 43-44, 71, 113-14
phrenology 286
physical factors 206-07, 210
physicalism 321-22, 326; see also materialism
physics 82, 86-88, 286, 291, 293-94, 315, 317, 321-22, 330-31, 334
physiological aspects 8, 99, 134-36, 147, 218-25, 230, 234, 236, 262, 271-72, 291; see also blood pressure; EEGs; epilepsy; galvanic skin response; heart rate; hemispheric differences; temperature
physiology 290, 292, 298
piezoelectric sensors 39-42
Piltdown Forgery, The 30
Piltdown skull 30
placebo 211-13, 266
plant telepathy 8
police cases 16, 143-45
poltergeists xii, 8, 18, 78-79, 88, 125, 132-36, 142, 256, 270-74
  agents of 134, 136
  Berini case 132-36
  CNS disturbances and 135
  "crude" vs. "smart" 272
  medical factors and 134-36
  rotating beam theory of 273
Poltergeists 135
positivism 287, 290-91, 293, 297, 299-300
possession 248; see also multiple personality
Post-Darwinian Controversies, The 287
pragmatism 299-300
prayer 313
precognition 44, 89, 94, 102-05, 128, 132, 160, 162, 199, 223, 309, 311-12
Presidential address, PA xii, 121, 317-27
Price (Pat) experiments 14
Princeton 10, 152, 154, 159
Principia Mathematica 291
Principles of Mathematics 291
Proceedings of IEEE 154, 269
Proceedings of the American Society for Psychical Research 117, 308
Proceedings of the Parapsychological Association 118; see also Research in Parapsychology
Proceedings of the Society for Psychical Research 2, 12, 27-29, 37, 77-78, 117, 119, 143, 206, 242, 270, 284, 289, 308, 310, 314
process-oriented research 8, 18
Program Committee xiii
"protocolitis" 69
psi; see also ESP, PK, spontaneous cases, theories

contiguity 119-20
definition of 10-11, 18, 255, 309
distribution of 38
elusiveness of 85-86, 88, 141, 170, 263
existence of 18-20, 310, 317-21, 326-27
falsification and 11, 15, 18, 141
high-scoring performances of 141-42
nature of 12, 37, 85-89, 102, 139, 317, 321-26
psi-hitting 89-90, 93-94, 97-98, 162, 184
psi-in-process approach 193, 243-44
psi-mediated instrumental response 257
psi-missing 21, 58, 66-68, 89-91, 93, 97, 103, 162, 165, 264, 266, 268
psi structure 117-20, 136
Psi: What Is It? 201
Psychic Criminology 268
Psychic Discoveries Behind the Iron Curtain 110
psychical research 85, 283-86; see also history; parapsychology
attitudes toward 2-6, 9-10, 131, 292, 294, 298-99, 309, 318-19
definition of 10, 283, 295-96
founders of xi, 2-3, 260, 263, 286
personnel of 2-4, 7
philosophical background of 283-96
subject matter of 1-2, 6-8, 37-38, 285, 305, 311
vs. parapsychology xii, 283-84, 294-95
Psychical Research Foundation 117, 120, 123, 132, 270-71
Psychical Research Today 79, 234
Psychoenergetic Systems 32, 35, 45, 53, 55
psychological factors 8, 12, 24, 34, 38, 79, 86-87, 103, 118, 130, 169, 193, 205-07, 211, 213, 223, 230, 260, 329-31; see also attitudes; Batcheldor approach; belief; cognitive variables; expectation; fear of psi; personality tests; personality variables; psychological tests; relaxation; resistance; sheep-goat effect
anxiety 99, 195-96, 226, 239-40
as alternate explanation to psi 19-20, 44, 79
competition 190-93, 198, 200-01
control 19, 202-03
effort 34, 48, 54-55
emotion 89, 117, 224-25, 271-72
enthusiasm 93-94, 157
fatigue 329, 331
hypnotic imagination 56-61
in poltergeist cases 135, 271, 274
incentive 178, 181, 192, 198
inhibition 329, 331
intention 44, 154, 156, 187, 211-12, 214, 263
interpersonal relationship 89, 120, 135
mood 94, 96, 227, 268
motivation 34, 97-99, 163, 165, 187, 206, 329
need 9, 27-28, 90, 237
passivity 224
purpose 325
stress 230-31, 261

volition 44, 190-93, 200-01
psychological tests; see also personality tests; word association tests
  Differential Aptitude Test 232
  Space Relations 231-32
  Stroop Test 188
  Time Metaphor Test 103-04
psychology 1-3, 9-10, 243, 257, 284-87, 290-93, 295, 297-98, 308, 311, 321, 329-34
  associationist 287, 290-91
  gestalt 293
  humanistic 8
  social 8
Psychology Today 36
psychometry 74-75, 117, 119, 121, 150-51, 296
psychon theory 117-18
Psychopharmacologia 212
Psychophysical Research Laboratories 23, 31, 112, 152, 157, 163
psychophysiology 8
psychopraxia 323
psychosomatic effects 3
psychotherapy 2
publication 53, 70, 75, 210, 262, 284
  delay of 77
  of null data 6, 22, 24-25
publicity 35-37
Purdue University 195-96
pyramid effects 8

Qigong 277, 281-82
quantum theory 9, 187, 291, 321-22, 334
Questions of Philosophy 258

RSPK see poltergeists
radiation 108-10, 147, 280
random event generators (REGs) xii, 5, 31, 52-53, 55, 57-58, 64-65, 67, 97-99, 101, 145-47, 152-59, 164, 166, 168-69, 178-81, 187-88, 191, 218-19
randomness 9, 23, 26, 29, 59, 65-66, 164, 166-67, 170-71, 173-77, 255
  and illusion of control 202-203
RAND table 179-81, 186
raps see sounds
reaction formation 90
REGs see random event generators
Red Badge of Courage, The 209
reductionism 287, 289-92, 294-95, 299
redundancy techniques 268-69
refereeing 131
reincarnation 2, 6, 8, 28-29, 85, 117, 121-23, 209, 214-17, 305-06, 317

Reincarnation in World Thought   123
relativity   291, 334
relaxation   5, 9, 51, 55-56, 103, 186, 188, 195-96, 225, 229, 238
religion   125, 262, 285, 292, 295, 310-11
   and science   285-90, 294, 296, 317
Religion and Science   294
REM state (rapid eye movement)   230
remote viewing   5, 8, 159-63, 238, 244, 249-50, 264-66, 277; see also clairvoyance
   "associational"   265-66
   physical effects in   277
repeated guessing technique   268-69, 312
replication   9, 11-12, 21-24, 30, 38, 89, 91-93, 96, 137-38, 147, 197, 245, 248, 252, 255, 263-64, 329-32, 334
   conceptual vs. strict   193-94
Research in Parapsychology (RIP)   xi, 7-8, 38, 55, 60, 62, 66, 93, 102, 121, 128-29, 131, 154, 189, 197, 255-56, 268-69, 273
Research Institute for Psi Phenomena and Physics   97
Research Letter   122
resistance   45-51, 54, 58, 91, 193-94, 249-59, 262; see also fear of psi
retrocognition   74-75
"retrocognitive dissonance"   69-72, 320
Revue Métapsychique   72
Richmond College   105
rotating beam theory   273
Royal Society   321
Russians   205; see also Soviet Union

SRI International   98, 251, 264, 275
St. John's University   178-79, 182, 185
St. Joseph's University   137
salience effects   312
San Blas Islands   243
Saybrook Institute   100, 258
schizophrenia   227, 232-34
schooling   245, 248; see also education; training
science   309, 317, 321, 324
   history of   283-90, 297-300, 328, 332
   plurality of   285
   religion and   285-90, 294, 296, 317
Science   186, 230
science fiction   205, 326
Scientific American   111
Scots   298
screening, of subjects   see subjects, selection of
séances   27-28, 45, 125, 205, 286, 320, 325; see also sitter groups
Secret of the Golden Flower   256
sensory cues   23, 26, 64, 228
sensory input   9, 135, 147, 232
sex
   change in reincarnation cases   217

Subject Index

differences 105, 196, 232-33, 248
 of subjects 31, 59, 62, 197, 200-01, 271
Shackleton experiments 13, 29
shamans 58, 142, 244, 248-50
Shanghai 275-76
sheep-goat effect 8, 19, 56, 60-61, 89-92, 94-96, 168-69, 195-200, 202-03, 330-31
 scale, Australian 199
 scale, Icelandic 197
Shin 310, 313
Sichuan Daily 275, 278
SIEMANS Co. 165
Sitaram Bhartia Institute of Scientific Research 110
sitter groups 45-56, 106, 305; see also seances
Skeptical Enquirer, The 10
"skepticemia" 69
skepticism 11-30, 49-51, 56, 69-72, 91, 113, 279, 286, 292, 298, 309, 318-20; see also critics
skills, unusual 217
slate-writing 27
Soal-Goldney experiments 142
Soal-Shackleton experiments see Shackleton experiments
Soal-Stewart experiments see Stewart experiments
social factors 256; see also cultural factors
social issues 258-62
socialization 245
Society for Psychical Research xi, xiii, 1-3, 12, 28, 69, 72, 75-77, 79, 93, 127-29, 204, 206, 242, 270, 276-77, 283-86, 288-89, 294, 297-98, 304, 306, 308, 315, 317, 320-21, 324, 335
 committees of 284
 conference (1981) of 89, 202
 Council of 286, 297, 308
 founders of xi, 127, 270, 284, 288, 335
 membership of 127, 289, 298, 321
 publications of 2-3, 27, 284, 289
sociolinguistics 256
sociology 290, 318
SOLAT questionnaire 103-04
SORRAT xii, 48-52, 115
SORRAT 49, 115
sounds 45, 76, 130, 135, 271, 274
South Africa 228
South African Society for Psychical Research 226
Soviet Academy of Sciences 259, 262
Soviet Institute for Psychiatry and Foreign Affairs 259
Soviet Ministry of Health 262
Soviety Psychology and Psychiatry 275
Soviet Union xiii, 258-59, 261-62, 275
space 82, 86, 118, 297, 322
Space Medico-Engineering Institute (China) 278
Spiritualism 1, 32, 45, 53, 125-27, 130, 235, 237, 284-86, 289, 292, 294, 324
spontaneous cases 18, 27, 32, 55, 62, 113-15, 204-17, 224, 235,

242, 255, 293, 311-12; see also field studies
   collective   129-30, 235-36
Sports Illustrated   195
Sri Lanka   215
State Science Commission (China)   276
Statistical Package for the Social Sciences   247
statistical procedures   6, 8, 22-26, 30, 247, 312
Stewart experiments   29
Story of Ruth, The   205
Straight and Crooked Thinking   308, 312
strain gauges   30, 39, 40, 42
strategy, mental   34, 65, 67, 101, 154, 157; see also visualization
subjects; see also agents; percipients
   animals as   212-13
   authors as   107, 218-19, 228-30
   babies as   97
   blind   149
   children as   xiii, 18-19, 112, 245, 275-76, 278, 280
   entertainers as   36
   meditators as   105
   mediums as   235
   naive   90-91, 199-200, 211-12
   psychokinetes, ostensible, as   62-64
   schizophrenics as   232
   selection of   32, 34, 38, 55-58, 93-94, 147-48, 150-51, 157-58, 326, 331
   students as   19, 56, 179, 185, 189, 195, 199, 200-02, 231-32
   in survival tests   124-25
   talented   8, 97-99, 170, 222
   temporal lobe patients as   235-36
subliminal perception   189-90
subliminal self   311
suggestion   46, 48-56, 130, 236, 266; see also hypnosis
Supernormal Faculties in Man   117
surveys   7, 10, 14, 21, 28, 38, 129, 319
survival   50, 85, 118, 137-38, 286, 289, 294, 298, 304-06, 313-15, 317, 323-25
   assumptions about   123-25
   classes of   124-25
   personal   120-22
   psi structure theory of   117-22
   research   xii, 8, 117-36, 138
   tests of   124-25, 305-07, 313-15, 325
Survival Research Foundation   xii, 123
Symposia of the Society of Experimental Biology   84
synchronicity   145, 207, 255; see also chance; coincidence

targets   26, 118-19
   affect of   195-96
   aluminum rods as   112
   associational   265-66
   auditory   182-83

Subject Index

candy as 246-47
cards as 115
carp scales as 72
circles as 103
distilled water as 100-01
electrical fuses as 67-68
emotion as 224-25
encodability of 185-87
invisible ink as 74
perception of 46, 55, 178-81
photographic plate, undeveloped, as 74
photographs as 59
plants as 67
saline as 67, 100
sequences 190-91
temporal definition of 221-22
touching of 31, 39, 42, 44
words as 73, 94-95, 268
Tarot 18
Technika Molodezhi 110
telepathy 19, 30, 72-75, 84, 126-28, 184, 209-10, 212, 214, 294, 296, 298, 309, 312, 314, 325
 plant 8
teleportation 280; see also levitation
temperature
 body 219
 changes 130
terminology 37, 120-21, 138-39, 195-96, 228-29, 283, 289, 293, 295-96, 309
testimony 27-30, 274, 320
tests (dermo-optic perception) 147-49
tests (GESP) 30, 102, 118-19, 202-03; see also book tests; chair experiments; forced choice; free response; remote viewing
 apparatus for 163, 170
 DMT and 197-98
 high-scoring 142
 in China 277, 279, 280-81
 in dream state 228-30
 learning theory and 93-96
 mistakes in 143-45
 of Barrett 126-27
 schooling and 245-48
 subliminal perception and 189-90
 with affective targets 195-96
 with ALGERNON 163-65
 with auditory targets 182-83
 with competition and volition 190-93, 198, 200-01
 with drawing 62-64
 with electrical shock 222-23
 with Ganzfeld 21-26, 183-86
 with hypnosis 56-61, 126, 144, 224-25
 with Necker cube 183-84, 188
 with Ossowiecki 72

with shamans 244, 248-50
with Transcendental Meditation 189-90
word association 185-87
tests (healing) 100-01, 210-14, 267-68, 313
tests (PK) 63, 98-99, 101-02
   effect of distance in 67-68
   sample size in 154-57
   suggestions for 112-13
   with ALGERNON 163-65
   with electrical fuse 67-68
   with living systems 267-68
   with perceptually similar targets and non-targets 178-81
   with PKMB sensor 33-34, 41-42
   with REGs 31, 52-53, 55, 57, 64-68, 97-99, 101, 152-59, 164-69, 178-81, 187-88, 218-21
   with saline solution 66-67
tests (precognition) 102-05, 197-200
   criticisms of 145-47
tests (survival) 124-25, 305-07, 313-15, 325
Thailand 215-16
theology 288, 297
theories 5, 9, 37, 48-49, 51, 56, 85-92, 117-19, 281, 286, 300, 309, 315, 333-34; see also Batcheldor approach, formative causation, learning
   biosemiotic 44
   conformance 9
   field 9, 117-22, 136
   holistic 82, 86
   memory 17, 93
   "mental entity" 120-21
   observational 8-9, 58, 85-88, 91, 97, 257, 321-22
   of apparitions 129, 131-32, 136
   of phantom leaf effect 111
   of PKMB 44
   psi structure 117-22, 136
   psychon 117-18
   Shin 310-11, 313
   systems 9, 85-89, 300
   teleological 9, 86, 92
thermodynamics 298
Thomism 288
time 82, 86, 118, 130, 169, 297, 322, 325
   of poltergeist occurrences 272-73
   perception 103-04, 186, 225, 228
Time 195
"Tonight" 208
traces, psychic 117-19
training 31-35, 52, 142, 147-48, 170, 326; see also conditioning; learning
   imagery 187-89
transcendence 251
trials, number of 22, 24-25, 145-46
trickery 27-28, 35-36, 46, 142; see also fraud

Trinity College xi, 292, 335
tulpa 205

UFOs 204-05
Umbanda 248-50
unconscious 47-48, 205-07
   collective 85
United Kingdom 7, 258
United States 215, 258, 290-93, 297
universities 285, 292, 298
University of
   Adelaide 107
   Aston 31, 45, 52
   Bristol 17, 202, 226, 230-31
   California, Davis 97, 101, 170, 173, 221
   Copenhagen 145
   Dundee 207
   Edinburgh 199, 228, 323
   Freiburg 85, 141, 165, 168, 270
   Glasgow 308
   Iceland 195, 197
   Lancaster 218
   London 39, 100, 105, 333
   Manchester 308
   Maryland 48
   Nottingham 1, 274
   Oregon 21
   Pittsburgh 316
   Tasmania 35
   Upper Alsace 144
   Utrecht 10, 55-56, 58, 81, 93, 178, 210, 218
   Virginia 1, 7, 214, 241
   Witwatersrand 226
Unseen Universe: Or Physical Speculations on a Future State, The 288, 291, 297

Versailles case 27, 78-79
Very Peculiar People 75
"Vienna Circle" 291, 293
visions 204, 233-34
visualization 34, 65, 103-04, 187-89, 238-39; see also imagery
vitalism 298, 326
voice phenomena 142

Wales 28
Washington Research Center 230, 251-52
Washington University 199
Weekend 208-09
weight
   body, changes in 105-06

loss and life force 111
Wholeness and the Implicate Order 119
wish fulfillment 236
Witchcraft and Sorcery in East Africa 242
"woman in brown" case 79-80
women 285, 297
word association tests 128, 185-87
workshops xii
writing
   automatic 3, 28-29
   direct 116
   posture 103, 105

Xian 276

Zeitschrift für Parapsychologie 38-39, 137, 169
Zener cards 243, 331, 333
Zetetic Scholar, The 10, 13
Ziran Zazhi see Nature Journal